Contents

Introduction

Many things have changed since factory outlets first came on the scene. Today the new centers offer a variety of shopping, dining, and entertainment options. They are also attractive and inviting, which adds to the pleasure of shopping for bargains. Most centers are easily accessible from Interstate or major highways. Some are near large cities while others are situated in scenic surroundings. *Factory Outlet Shopping* is your guide to 301 of the best bargain shopping destinations in the U.S. where you'll find savings of 40 to 70 percent everyday!

Factory Outlet Shopping is organized by state with a map that shows the location of outlet centers. A reference number is assigned to cities and towns that have one or more factory outlet centers. This number will help you easily locate them on the map and the descriptive information. All descriptions are alphabetical, first by city and then by center. Descriptions include an address, phone number, hours, and driving directions. Most factory outlet centers also have a web site where you can obtain coupons, sale information, or order products online.

Following each description is a list of stores in alphabetical order. The list is divided into two categories: *Stores* and *Eats & Treats*. Additionally, each store is assigned a number to help identify the type of merchandise available. See below for a list of product categories and type numbers.

Stores

Description	Type #
Family Apparel & Footwear	1
Luggage, Leather & Accessories	2
Jewelry, Eyewear & Accessories	3
Home & Electronics	4
Gifts, Books & Music	5
Hobbies, Toys & Sports	6
Computers, Cameras & Phones	7
Health & Beauty	8
Specialty	9

Eats & Treats

Description	Type #
Snacks, Sweets & Treats	10
Restaurant & Quick Bites	11

Additional Notes

VF Factory Outlets contain the following stores: Brittania, Healthtex, JanSport, Jantzen, Lee, Red Kap, Riders, Vanity Fair, Vassarette, and Wrangler. These stores-within-a-store are not listed individually on the charts but are simply listed as VF Factory Outlet.

The word "the" has been omitted from store listings. For example, if a store's name is "The Grill," it is listed as "Grill."

Factory Outlet Shopping

Traveler's Guide to Bargain Shopping the USA

Published by:
Roundabout Publications
PO Box 19235
Lenexa, KS 66285

800-455-2207

www.TravelBooksUSA.com

Please Note

Every effort has been made to make this book as complete and as accurate as possible. However, there may be mistakes both typographical and in content. Therefore, this text should be used as a general guide to the factory outlets presented. Although we regret any inconvenience caused by inaccurate information, the author and Roundabout Publications shall have neither liability nor responsibility to any person or entity with respect to any loss or damage caused, or alleged to be caused, directly or indirectly by the information contained in this book.

Factory Outlet Shopping Copyright © 2002 by Roundabout Publications. Printed and bound in the United States of America. All rights reserved. No part of this book may be reproduced in any form or by any electronic or mechanical means including information storage and retrieval systems without permission in writing from the publisher, except by a reviewer, who may quote passages in a review. Published by: Roundabout Publications, P.O. Box 19235, Lenexa, Kansas 66285. Phone: 800-455-2207. Internet: www.travelbooksusa.com

Library of Congress Catalog Control Number: 2001119966
ISBN: 1-885464-04-5

1 0 1 9 7 7

Publisher's Cataloging-in-Publication

Herow, William C.
    Factory outlet shopping : traveler's guide to bargain shopping the USA / William C. Herow. -- 1st ed.
    p. cm.
    LCCN: 2001119966
    ISBN: 1-885464-04-5

    1. Outlet stores--United States--Guidebooks.
    2. Shopping--United States--Guidebooks.   I. Title.

TX336.H47 2002   381'.15'02573
                                  QBI02-200001

Alabama

1 • Bessemer
2 • Boaz
3 • Foley
4 • Opelika

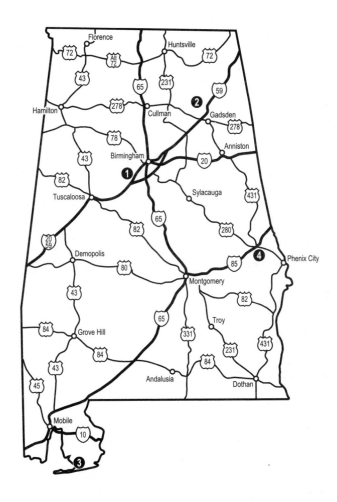

1 BESSEMER

1A • WaterMark Place

www.watermarkoutlets.com
Address 4500 Katie's Way ***Phone***
866-2Watermark or 205-425-
4554 ***Hours*** Mon-Sat 10-9, Sun
12-6 ***Location*** Twenty minutes
west of Birmingham off I-59/20,
exit 108 (Academy Drive), turn
right. At the first traffic light turn
right and follow the signs.

STORES

- Banana Republic (1)
- Bass (1)
- Big Dog Sportswear (1)
- Book Warehouse (5)
- Carter's Childrenswear (1)
- Claire's Accessories (3)
- Croscill (4)
- Dress Barn (1)
- Duck Head (1)
- Etienne Aigner (1)
- Famous Brand Footwear (1)
- Gap Outlet (1)
- Harry & David (5)
- KB Toys (6)
- Koret (1)
- L'eggs Hanes Bali Playtex (1)
- Levi's / Dockers (1)
- Liz Claiborne (1)
- Mikasa (4)
- OshKosh B'Gosh (1)
- Pacific Sunwear (1)
- Polo Ralph Lauren (1)
- Reebok (1)
- Rue 21 (1)
- Samsonite (2)
- Strasburg Children (1)
- Tommy Hilfiger (1)
- Totes / Isotoner (3)
- Van Heusen (1)
- Vitamin World (8)
- WestPoint Stevens (4)
- Wilson's Leather (1)
- Zales The Diamond Store (3)

EATS & TREATS

- Daniel's Pizza (11)
- Harvester's Bread Company (11)
- Kim's Chinese (11)
- Marvel City Burgers (11)
- Steel Works Bar-b-que (11)

2 BOAZ

Boaz is a small town nestled in the
foothills of the Appalachians, 50
miles southeast of Huntsville. Boaz
is one of the largest outlet shopping
areas in the South. Here you will
find several outlet malls, most
within walking distance of each
other. To reach Boaz from
Huntsville follow US 431 south to
intersection of Billy B Dyar Blvd,
then west to outlets. From
Birmingham take I-59 north to exit
183, follow US 431 north to Billy
B Dyar Blvd, then west to outlets.

2A • Boaz Fashion Outlets

www.boazfashionoutlets.com
Address 501 Elizabeth St ***Phone***
256-593-1199 ***Hours*** Mon-Sat 9-
9, Sun 12-6 ***Location*** See above
introduction to Boaz.

STORES

- Bible Outlet (5)
- Black & Decker (4)
- Carter's Childrenswear (1)
- Casual Corner (1)
- Casual Corner Woman (1)
- Claire's Accessories (3)
- Corning Revere (4)
- Dalton Rug (4)
- Dress Barn (1)
- Dress Barn Woman (1)
- Duck Head (1)
- Factory Brand Shoes (1)
- Fossil (2)
- Interior Alternative (4)
- Izod (1)
- Levi's (1)
- Motherhood Maternity (1)

- Music 4 Less (5)
- Oneida (4)
- Petite Sophisticate (1)
- Polo Ralph Lauren (1)
- S & K Menswear (1)
- Samsonite (2)
- Springmaid Wamsutta (4)
- Stone Mountain (2)
- Tommy Hilfiger (1)
- Vitamin World (8)
- Zales The Diamond Store (3)

EATS & TREATS
- Rocky Mountain Chocolate (10)

2B • Boaz Outlet Center
www.marshallcountycvb.com
Address 423 S McCleskey St **Phone** 256-593-9306 **Hours** Mon-Sat 9-9, Sun 12-6 **Location** See above introduction to Boaz.

STORES
- $9.99 Stockroom (1)
- Athlete's Foot (1)
- Bon Worth (1)
- Euro Collections (1)
- Interiors For Less (1)
- KB Toy Liquidators (6)
- Minerals & More (9)
- Nova 9 Cinema (9)
- Nova Entertainment / Bowling (9)
- Paragon Factory Store (4)
- Rack Room Shoes (1)
- Variety House (9)
- WestPoint Stevens (4)
- Zales The Diamond Store (3)

2C • Factory Stores of America
www.chelseafactoryoutlets.com
Address 200 Lackey St **Phone** 256-593-2930 **Hours** Mon-Thu 9-6 (Apr 1 - Dec 31, 9-8), Fri-Sat 9-9, Sun 12-6. **Location** See above introduction to Boaz.

STORES
- Banister / Easy Spirit (1)

- Bon Worth (1)
- Capacity (1)
- Kat's This & That (9)
- Kitchen Collection (4)
- Paper Factory (9)
- Rue 21 (1)
- VF Factory Outlet (1)

EATS & TREATS
- Cake Shop Bakery & Eatery (10)

2D • Tanger Outlet Center
www.tangeroutlets.com
Address 290 Billy B Dyar Blvd **Phone** 800-405-2193 or 256-593-9255 **Hours** Mon-Sat 9-9, Sun 12-6 **Location** See introduction to Boaz.

STORES
- Allen Edmonds (1)
- Bass (1)
- Easy Spirit (1)
- Eddie Bauer (1)
- Gap Outlet (1)
- Geoffrey Beene (1)
- L'eggs Hanes Bali Playtex (1)
- Lenox (4)
- Liz Claiborne (1)
- Mikasa (4)
- Nautica (1)
- OshKosh B'Gosh (1)
- Reebok (1)
- Van Heusen (1)
- Welcome Home (4)

EATS & TREATS
- Burger King (11)

3 FOLEY

3A • Riviera Centre Factory Stores
www.shoprivieracenter.com
Address 2601 S McKenzie St **Phone** 888-Shop333 or 251-943-8888 **Hours** Mon-Sat 10-9 (Jan 1 - Feb 28, 10-7), Sun 11-6 **Location**

Southeast of Mobile, just 8 miles from the Gulf Coast. Take exit 44 off I-10 onto Hwy 59 south. The center is 22 miles on the left.

STORES

- American Outpost (1)
- Banana Republic (1)
- Banister / Easy Spirit (1)
- Bass (1)
- Bible Factory Outlet (5)
- Big & Tall Factory Store (1)
- Big Dog Sportswear (1)
- Black & Decker (4)
- Bombay Outlet (4)
- Bon Worth (1)
- Book Factory (5)
- Bose Factory Store (4)
- Bostonian Clarks (1)
- Brooks Brothers (1)
- Bruce Alan Bags (2)
- Bugle Boy (1)
- Burlington Brands (1)
- Calvin Klein (1)
- Camp Coleman (6)
- Carter's Childrenswear (1)
- Casual Corner (1)
- Casual Corner Woman (1)
- Chico's (1)
- Children's Place Outlet (1)
- Claiborne Menswear (1)
- Claire's Accessories (3)
- Coach (2)
- Coastal Cotton (1)
- Corning Revere (4)
- Cosmetics Company Store (8)
- Cost Cutters Salon (8)
- Country Clutter (4)
- Craftworks (4)
- Dalton Rug (4)
- Dansk (4)
- Danskin (1)
- Dexter Shoe (1)
- Disney Catalog Outlet (5)
- Dress Barn (1)
- Duck Head (1)
- Eddie Bauer (1)
- Elisabeth (1)
- Ellen Tracy (1)
- Etienne Aigner (1)
- Factory Brand Shoes (1)
- Famous Brands Housewares (4)
- Fila (1)
- Florsheim (1)
- Fossil (2)
- Fragrance Outlet (8)
- Fresh Produce (1)
- Gap Outlet (1)
- Geoffrey Beene (1)
- Haggar (1)
- Harry & David (5)
- Hartstrings (1)
- Hoover Outlet (4)
- Hush Puppies & Family (1)
- Izod (1)
- J Crew (1)
- Jockey (1)
- Johnston & Murphy (1)
- Kasper ASL (1)
- Kitchen Collection (4)
- Koret (1)
- Las Vegas Discount Golf/Tennis (6)
- Le Creuset (4)
- L'eggs Hanes Bali Playtex (1)
- Levi's Outlet by Designs (1)
- Liz Claiborne (1)
- Liz Claiborne Shoes (1)
- Maidenform (1)
- Mikasa (4)
- Mossy Oak Outdoor Outlet (1)
- Motherhood Maternity (1)
- Music For A Song (5)
- Naturalizer (1)
- Nautica (1)
- Nike (1)
- Nine West (1)
- Noritake (4)
- Olga Warner (1)
- Oneida (4)
- OshKosh B'Gosh (1)
- Pacific Sunwear (1)
- Paper Factory (9)
- Perfumania (8)
- Perry Ellis (1)
- Petite Sophisticate (1)
- Pfaltzgraff (4)
- Polo Ralph Lauren (1)
- Rack Room Shoes (1)
- Reebok (1)
- Remington (4)
- Robert Scott & David Brooks (1)
- Rockport (1)
- Rue 21 (1)
- S & K Menswear (1)
- Samsonite (2)
- SAS Factory Shoes (1)
- Seiko (3)
- Shadowline (1)

- Sider / Keds (1)
- So Fun! Kids (1)
- Socks Galore (1)
- Stifflers Santa's Nook (9)
- Strasburg Children (1)
- Stride Rite Keds Sperry (1)
- Sunglass Hut (3)
- Timberland (1)
- Tommy Hilfiger (1)
- Tommy Hilfiger Jeans (1)
- Totes / Sunglass World (3)
- Toys Unlimited (6)
- Van Heusen (1)
- Vans Shoes (1)
- VF Factory Outlet (1)
- Vitamin World (8)
- Wallet Works (2)
- Waterford Wedgwood (4)
- Welcome Home (4)
- WestPoint Stevens (4)
- Zales The Diamond Store (3)

EATS & TREATS
- CinnaMonster (10)
- DiBella's Pizza (11)
- Franks & Co (11)
- Mr Wok (11)
- Pasta Factory (11)
- Quick-Chick (11)
- Southern Swirls (10)
- Texas Mesquite Grill (11)

- Capacity (1)
- Carolina Clock & Rug (4)
- Carter's Childrenswear (1)
- Corning Revere (4)
- Dress Barn (1)
- Dress Barn Woman (1)
- Duck Head (1)
- GNC (8)
- Kitchen Collection (4)
- L'eggs Hanes Bali Playtex (1)
- Paper Factory (9)
- Rack Room Shoes (1)
- Rue 21 (1)
- Springmaid Wamsutta (4)
- Van Heusen (1)
- Welcome Home (4)

EATS & TREATS
- Food Court (11)

4 OPELIKA

4A • USA Factory Stores
Address 1220 Fox Run Ave *Phone* 334-749-0561 *Hours* Mon-Sat 9-9, Sun 12-6 *Location* A few miles east of Auburn in eastern Georgia. The center faces I-85 and is just off US 431. Take exit 62 off I-85, travel west to Fox Run Parkway and follow the signs.

STORES
- Bass (1)
- Bible Factory Outlet (5)
- Bon Worth (1)
- Bugle Boy (1)

Arizona

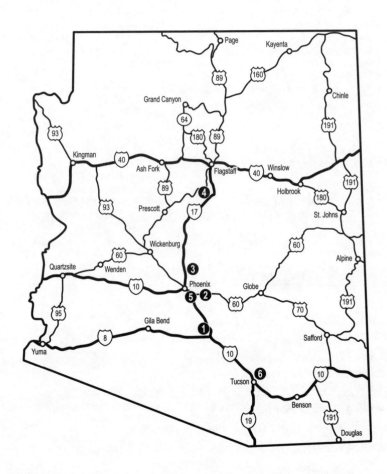

1 CASA GRANDE

1A • Tanger Outlet Center
www.tangeroutlets.com
Address 2300 E Tanger Dr **Phone** 520-836-9663 or 800-405-5016 **Hours** Mon-Sat 9-8, Sun 10-6 **Location** Traveling south from Phoenix take exit 198 off I-10. Turn right, follow to traffic light, then right onto Tanger Drive.

STORES
- 50% Off Card Store (5)
- Bass (1)
- Big Dog Sportswear (1)
- Bon Worth (1)
- Cactus Carlos (9)
- Corning Revere (4)
- Dexter Shoe (1)
- Dress Barn (1)
- Dress Barn Woman (1)
- Elisabeth (1)
- Factory Brand Shoes (1)
- Florsheim (1)
- Gap Outlet (1)
- GNC (8)
- Guess? (1)
- Izod (1)
- Kitchen Collection (4)
- Koret (1)
- L'eggs Hanes Bali Playtex (1)
- Levi's Outlet by Most (1)
- Liz Claiborne (1)
- Mikasa (4)
- Naturalizer (1)
- OshKosh B'Gosh (1)
- Paper Factory (9)
- Perfumania (8)
- Pfaltzgraff (4)
- Publishers Warehouse (5)
- Reebok (1)
- Rue 21 (1)
- Samsonite (2)
- Van Heusen (1)
- WestPoint Stevens (4)

EATS & TREATS
- Cinnamon Stop (10)
- Dreyer's Grand Ice Cream (10)
- Sub King (11)
- Wendy's (11)

2 MESA

2A • Factory Stores of America
www.chelseafactoryoutlets.com
Address 2050 S Roslyn **Phone** 480-984-0697 **Hours** Mon-Sat 10-8, Sun 11-5 **Location** From US 60 (Superstition Freeway) take exit 187 (Power Rd), go south to Baseline Rd. Located on the southeast corner of Power and Baseline Roads.

STORES
- All Star Music (5)
- American Southwest & Mexican Furniture (4)
- Banister Shoes (1)
- Bass (1)
- Bon Worth (1)
- Book Warehouse (5)
- Casual Corner (1)
- Changes (1)
- Corning Revere (4)
- Creative Impressions (9)
- Dress Barn/Dress Barn Woman (1)
- Factory Brand Shoes (1)
- Fieldcrest Cannon (4)
- Izod (1)
- KB Toy Liquidators (6)
- Ken Messore Organs & Music (5)
- Kitchen Collection (4)
- Model Home Center (9)
- Paper Factory (9)
- Payless Outlet (9)
- Rue 21 (1)
- Samsonite (2)
- Styles For Less (1)
- Swordcreek Gifts (5)
- Van Heusen (1)
- VF Factory Outlet (1)
- Vitamin World (8)
- Wallet Works (2)

EATS & TREATS
- Creative Ice Cream (10)

3 NEW RIVER

3A • Outlets at Anthem
www.anthemoutlets.com

Address 4250 W Anthem Way *Phone* 888-482-5834 *Hours* Mon-Sat 10-8, Sun 11-6 *Location* Just 25 miles north of downtown Phoenix on I-17, exit 229.

STORES

- AJ Fashions (2)
- All Star Board Shop (6)
- American Southwest & Mexican Furniture (4)
- Ann Taylor (1)
- Ashworth (1)
- Bass (1)
- Bath & Body Works (8)
- Big Dog Sportswear (1)
- Black & Decker (4)
- Bon Worth (1)
- Bose Factory Store (4)
- Bullseye Wireless.com (7)
- Cactus Carlos (9)
- California Luggage (2)
- Candels & More (5)
- Carter's Childrenswear (1)
- Casual Corner (1)
- Casual Corner Woman (1)
- Claire's Accessories (3)
- Country Clutter (4)
- D & J Jewelry & Gifts (3)
- Designer Brands Accessories (2)
- Dexter Shoe (1)
- Dockers Outlet (1)
- Dress Barn/Dress Barn Woman (1)
- Easy Spirit (1)
- Factory Brand Shoes (1)
- Famous Brands Housewares (4)
- Gap Outlet (1)
- Geoffrey Beene (1)
- Gold Mountain Mining Co (9)
- Harman Audio (4)
- Harold's (1)
- Hartstrings (1)
- Izod (1)
- Jockey (1)
- KB Toys (6)
- Kitchen Collection (4)
- Le Creuset (4)
- Leather Loft (2)
- L'eggs Hanes Bali Playtex (1)
- Levi's (1)
- Mikasa (4)
- Motherhood Maternity (1)
- Music 4 Less (5)
- Naturalizer (1)

- Nautica (1)
- Nike (1)
- Nine West (1)
- OshKosh B'Gosh (1)
- Paper Factory (9)
- Payless Shoe Source (1)
- Perfect Look Outlet Salon (8)
- Perfumania (8)
- Petite Sophisticate (1)
- Polo Ralph Lauren (1)
- Quiksilver (1)
- Quilted Kottage (9)
- Rack Room Shoes (1)
- Radio Shack (7)
- Reebok (1)
- Rue 21 (1)
- Rug Decor (4)
- Springmaid Wamsutta (4)
- Stride Rite Family Footwear (1)
- Sunglass Hut / Watch Station (3)
- Sunglass Outlet (3)
- Tribal Treasures (5)
- Ultra Diamond & Gold (3)
- Van Heusen (1)
- Vitamin World (8)
- Welcome Home (4)
- Western / E-Z-Go Golf Cars/E-Bike (9)

EATS & TREATS

- Auntie Anne's Pretzals (10)
- Burger King (11)
- CinnaMonster (10)
- Fuzziwig's Candy Factory (10)
- Great Steak & Potato (11)
- Rocky Mountain Chocolate (10)
- Subway (11)
- Taco Bell (11)
- Villa Pizza (11)
- Wok King (11)

4   SEDONA

4A • Prime Outlets Sedona

www.primeoutlets.com

Address 6601 S Hwy 179 *Phone* 520-284-2150 *Hours* Mon-Sat 9-7, Sun 10-6 *Location* South of Flagstaff in central Arizona. From I-17 take exit 298 (Sedona/Hwy 179) north 7 miles to the Village of Oak Creek, Sedona.

STORES

- Anne Klein (1)
- Banister / Easy Spirit (1)
- Bass (1)
- Big Dog Sportswear (1)
- Book Warehouse (5)
- Bruce Alan Bags (2)
- Cactus Carlos (9)
- Casa de Sedona (9)
- Dansk (4)
- Dress Barn (1)
- Factory Brand Shoes (1)
- Gap Outlet (1)
- Geoffrey Beene (1)
- Izod (1)
- J & J Fine Diamonds (3)
- Jones New York Sport (1)
- Kidz Outlet (1)
- Maidenform (1)
- Oak Creek Indian Traders (2)
- Oneida (4)
- Sedona SuperVue Theater (9)
- Tommy Hilfiger (1)
- Totes / Sunglass World (3)
- Van Heusen (1)
- Vitamin World (8)
- Western Designers Outlet (2)

EATS & TREATS

- Java Hut (10)
- Marketplace Café (11)
- Taco Bell (11)

5 TEMPE

5A • Arizona Mills

www.millscorp.com

Address 500 Arizona Mills Cir *Phone* 480-491-7300 *Hours* Mon-Fri 10-9:30, Sat 9:30 -9:30, Sun 11-8 *Location* Only 9 miles southeast of downtown Phoenix. Located at the southeast corner of US 60 and I-10. From I-10, exit Baseline Road east. From US 60, exit Priest Drive south.

STORES

- 5-7-9 Outlet (1)
- A G Cheers Cards & Gifts (5)
- Aeropostale (1)
- Africana (4)
- Al Zuni Jewelers (3)
- AmeriSuites (9)
- Anchor Blue Clothing Co (1)
- Ann Taylor (1)
- Arizona Outfitters Gift Shop (5)
- As Seen On TV (5)
- Athlete's Foot (1)
- Awesome Atoms (5)
- Bag & Baggage (2)
- Bakers Shoes (1)
- Bass (1)
- Bath & Body Works (8)
- BCBG Max Azria (1)
- Beauty Express (8)
- Bebe Outlet (1)
- Big Dog Sportswear (1)
- Black Market Minerals (5)
- Bostonian Clarks (1)
- Burlington Coat Factory (1)
- California Luggage (2)
- Candleman Outlet (5)
- Capri Jewelers (3)
- Carter's Childrenswear (1)
- Casio (4)
- Charlotte Russe (1)
- Claire's Accessories (3)
- Clothestime (1)
- Converse (1)
- CR Jewelers Outlet (3)
- Dexter Shoe (1)
- Donna Karan (1)
- Dress Barn/Dress Barn Woman (1)
- Etienne Aigner (1)
- Eye Candy (1)
- Famous Brands Housewares (4)
- Famous Footwear (1)
- Fashion Nails (8)
- Florsheim (1)
- Foot Locker (1)
- Four Corners (4)
- Fragrance Outlet (8)
- Frederick's of Hollywood (1)
- Funzy's (5)
- GameWorks (9)
- Gap Outlet (1)
- GNC (8)
- Group USA (1)
- Guess? (1)
- Harkins Luxury 24 Theatre (9)
- Hat Club (1)
- Hat Company (1)
- Hi-Health World of Nutrition (8)
- Hillo Hattie Store of Hawaii (1)
- Hiphoptrendz (1)

- Imax Theatre (9)
- Imposters (3)
- Izod (1)
- JCPenney Outlet (1)
- Jewelers of Las Vegas (3)
- Journeys (1)
- Just for Feet (1)
- Just Sports (1)
- KB Toys (6)
- Kenneth Cole (1)
- Kiddie Kandids (9)
- Kits Camera 1 Hour Photo (7)
- Last Call Neiman Marcus (1)
- Leather Loft (2)
- Leather Mode (2)
- L'eggs Hanes Bali Playtex (1)
- Levi's Outlet by Most (1)
- Linen's N Things (4)
- Liz Claiborne Shoes (1)
- Marshalls (1)
- MasterCuts (8)
- Merlos Cutting Edge (4)
- Mikasa (4)
- Motherhood Maternity (1)
- Nine West (1)
- Off 5th-Saks Fifth Avenue (1)
- Off Rodeo Drive Beverly Hills (1)
- Old Navy (1)
- OshKosh B'Gosh (1)
- Oshman's SuperSports USA (6)
- Pacific Eyes & T's (1)
- Pacific Sunwear (1)
- Payless Shoe Source (1)
- Perfumania (8)
- Polo Jeans Co (1)
- Rack Room Shoes (1)
- Rampage (1)
- Recoton Electric Outlet (4)
- Red Eye (1)
- Reebok (1)
- Remington (4)
- Rockport (1)
- Ross Dress for Less (1)
- SA Farr Jewelers (3)
- Samsonite (2)
- Sanrio (9)
- Shemoni Jewelry (3)
- Shoe Cents (1)
- Signals Cellular & Paging (7)
- Skechers (1)
- Smart Scrubs (1)
- Spencer Gifts (5)
- Sports Cage (6)
- Stone Creek Furniture (4)
- Stop N Save Software (7)

- Styles For Less (1)
- Sunglass Hut (3)
- Sunglass Hut / Watch Station (3)
- Sun's Up (9)
- Swim N Sport (1)
- T-Shirts Plus (1)
- Tani Marra Boardshop (6)
- Two Lips Shoes (1)
- Ultra Diamond & Gold (3)
- Urban Planet (1)
- Van Heusen (1)
- Vans Shoes (1)
- Verizon Wireless (7)
- Virgin Megastore (5)
- Vista Optical (3)
- Vitamin World (8)
- Wallet Works (2)
- Warnaco (1)
- Way to Glow (5)
- Wild Wild Best! (5)
- Wilson's Leather (1)
- Windsor Outlet (1)
- Xi Clothing (1)
- Young Hui Imports (5)
- Zales The Diamond Store (3)
- Zap Create Your Own Cap (1)

EATS & TREATS

- Alcatraz Brewing Co (11)
- Auntie Anne's Pretzals (10)
- Bennigan's (11)
- Burger King (11)
- Cajan Grill (11)
- Chili Peppers (11)
- CinnaMonster (10)
- Claim Jumper (11)
- GameWorks Café (11)
- Gloria Jean's Gourmet Coffee (10)
- Haagen Dazs (10)
- Johnny Rockets (11)
- Krispy Kreme Doughnuts (10)
- Mrs Field's Bakery (11)
- Nathan's Famous (11)
- Panda Express (11)
- Paradis Bakery (11)
- Pretzelmaker (10)
- Rainforest Café (11)
- Renzio's (11)
- Rocky Mountain Chocolate (10)
- Rusty Pelican (11)
- Sbarro Italian Eatery (11)
- Starbucks Coffee (10)
- Steak Escape (11)
- Suki Hanna (11)
- Sweet Factory (10)

- Sweets From Heaven (10)
- Virgin Café (11)

6 TUCSON

6A • Factory Stores of America
www.chelseafactoryoutlets.com
Address 5120 S Juilan Dr *Phone*
520-889-4400 *Hours* Mon-Sat 10-
8, Sun 11-5 *Location* Traveling
west on I-10, take exit 264 north
(Palo Verde), turn left on Irvington
Rd to South Julian Dr, turn left.
Traveling east on I-10, take exit
264a to Ramada Inn. Turn right
onto South Julian Drive.

STORES
- Annie's & Frannie's Plus (1)
- Banister / Easy Spirit (1)
- Book Warehouse (5)
- Paper Factory (9)
- Samsonite (2)
- Toy Liquidators (6)
- Van Heusen (1)
- VF Factory Outlet (1)

EATS & TREATS
- Desert Deli (11)

6B • Foothills Mall
www.shopfoothillsmall
Address 7401 N La Cholla Blvd
Phone 520-219-0650 *Hours* Mon-
Sat 10-9, Sun 11-6 *Location* Just
north of Tucson off I-10, exit 248
(Ina Rd). Go east on Ina Rd to La
Cholla Blvd. Center is on your left.

STORES
- #1 Furniture Co (4)
- Aaron Bros Art & Framing (4)
- Adidas (1)
- Animations (5)
- Arizona Tourist News & Info (9)
- Banister Shoes (1)
- Barnes & Noble (5)
- Bath & Body Works (8)
- Big Dog Sportswear (1)
- Carter's For Kids (1)
- Claire's Boutique (3)
- Coldwater Creek Outlet (1)
- Corning Revere (4)
- Cost Cutters Salon (8)
- Dress Barn/Dress Barn Woman (1)
- E & J's Designer Shoe Outlet (1)
- Famous Footwear (1)
- Fiesta Gifts (5)
- Foxy Nails (8)
- GameZone (9)
- Haggar (1)
- In The Line Up (1)
- J B Wrangler & Co (4)
- KB Toys (6)
- Leather Loft (2)
- L'eggs Hanes Bali Playtex (1)
- Levi's Outlet by Most (1)
- Linen's N Things (4)
- Loews Cineplex Theater (9)
- Logo Wear (1)
- Mattress Firm (4)
- Mesa Verde Trading Co (9)
- Mikasa (4)
- Music 4 Less (5)
- Nike (1)
- Off 5th-Saks Fifth Avenue (1)
- Olga Warner (1)
- PacSun (1)
- Paper Warehouse (9)
- Quiksilver (1)
- Ross Dress for Less (1)
- Samsonite (2)
- Satellite City (9)
- Toni & Guy Hairdressing (8)
- Vitamin World (8)
- Zales The Diamond Store (3)

EATS & TREATS
- Applebee's (11)
- Ben & Jerry's (10)
- Cousins Subs (11)
- Domino's Pizza (11)
- French Loaf Bakery & Café (11)
- Gavi Italian Restaurant (11)
- Keaton's Arizona Grill (11)
- Orange Julius (10)
- Outback Steakhouse (11)
- Panda Express (11)
- Pretzel Maker (10)
- Rocky Mountain Chocolate (10)
- Thunder Canyon Brewery (11)
- Uncommon Grounds (10)

Arkansas

1 • Springdale

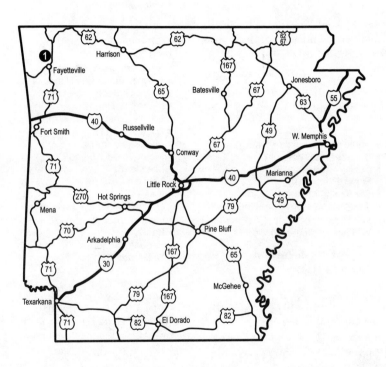

1 SPRINGDALE

1A • Ozark Center Point Place

Address 5320 W Sunset Ave *Phone* 800-927-1104 or 501-927-1100 *Hours* Mon-Sat 10-9, Sun 12-6 *Location* In northwest Arkansas, north of Fayetteville. Take exit 52 off US 71, then west on US 412.

STORES

- Big Lots (9)
- Bon Worth (1)
- Boots & Spurs (1)
- Cell Phone & Pager Station (7)
- Clothes Outs (1)
- Cookies by Design (9)
- Discount Bible (5)
- Dress Barn (1)
- Factory Brand Shoes (1)
- Fieldcrest Cannon (4)
- Freds Dollar Saver (9)
- Full Size Fashions (1)
- Gift Outlet (5)
- Hancock Fabrics (9)
- Nevada Bob's Discount Golf (6)
- North Carolina Furniture Mart (4)
- Outdoor America (9)
- Paper Factory (9)
- Puffs $12 Zoo (9)
- Robin's Nest (9)
- Rue 21 (1)

California

1 • Alpine
2 • Anderson
3 • Atascadero
4 • Barstow
5 • Cabazon
6 • Camarillo
7 • Carlsbad
8 • Commerce
9 • Folsom

10 • Gilroy
11 • Lake Arrowhead
12 • Lake Elsinore
13 • Lancaster
14 • Mammoth Lakes
15 • Milpitas
16 • Napa
17 • Ontario
18 • Orange
19 • Oxnard
20 • Pacific Grove
21 • Petaluma
22 • Pismo Beach
23 • San Diego
24 • San Leandro
25 • San Ysidro
26 • South Lake Tahoe
27 • St. Helena
28 • Tracy
29 • Tulare
30 • Vacaville

1 ALPINE

1A • Viejas Outlet Center
www.viejas.com
Address 5000 Willows Rd *Phone* 800-84Poker *Hours* Mon-Sat 10-9, Sun 10-7. The Viejas Casino is open 7 days a week, 24 hours a day. *Location* Just 30 minutes east of downtown San Diego. Take I-8 to the Willows Road exit in Alpine and go 1½ miles to Viejas.

STORES
- Aerosoles (1)
- American Brands (1)
- Bass (1)
- Big Dogs (1)
- Black & Decker (4)
- Bon Worth (1)
- Book Warehouse (5)
- Borrego Springs Bank (9)
- Carter's Childrenswear (1)
- Casual Corner Annex (1)
- Claire's Accessories (3)
- Corning Revere (4)
- Country Clutter (4)
- Dress Barn (1)
- Eddie Bauer (1)
- Factory Brand Shoes (1)
- Gap Outlet (1)
- Geoffrey Beene (1)
- GNC (8)
- Izod (1)
- Jones New York (1)
- Jones New York Country (1)
- KB Toys (6)
- Kitchen Collection (4)
- Koret (1)
- Leather Loft (2)
- L'eggs Hanes Bali Playtex (1)
- Levi's / Dockers (1)
- Linen Barn (4)
- Liz Claiborne (1)
- Liz Claiborne Shoes (1)
- Music For A Song (5)
- Naturalizer (1)
- Nautica (1)
- Nike (1)
- Nine West (1)
- Pacific Sunwear (1)

- Paper Factory (9)
- Perry Ellis (1)
- Polo Ralph Lauren (1)
- Reebok (1)
- Samsonite (2)
- San Diego's Visitor's Bureau (9)
- Shades International (3)
- Socks Galore (1)
- Sunglass Hut (3)
- Tommy Hilfiger (1)
- Ultra Jewelers (3)
- Van Heusen (1)
- Vans Shoes (1)
- Warnaco (1)
- Welcome Home (4)

EATS & TREATS
- Filippi's Pizza Grotto (11)
- McDonald's (11)
- Rocky Mountain Chocolate (10)
- Rubio's Baja Grill (11)
- Scatterbeans (11)
- Subway (11)

2 ANDERSON

2A • Prime Outlets Anderson
www.primeoutlets.com
Address 1699 Hwy 273 *Phone* 530-378-1000 *Hours* Mon-Sat 9:30-8, Sun 11-6 *Location* Northern California just south of Redding. Take I-5 to the Factory Outlets Drive exit (State Route 273). The center is on the west side of I-5.

STORES
- ATAZ (9)
- Big Dogs (1)
- Book Warehouse (5)
- Christian Supply (5)
- Claire's Accessories (3)
- Corning Revere (4)
- Corral West Ranchwear (1)
- Country Clutter (4)
- Dexter Shoe (1)
- Dress Barn/Dress Barn Woman (1)
- Famous Footwear (1)
- Fine Creations (4)
- Full Size Fashions (1)
- Gap Outlet (1)

- GNC (8)
- Halloween Outlet (9)
- Home Again (4)
- KB Toy Liquidators (6)
- Kitchen Collection (4)
- L'eggs Hanes Bali Playtex (1)
- Mikasa (4)
- Motherhood Maternity (1)
- Outdoor Outfitters (9)
- Paper Factory (9)
- Payless Shoe Source (1)
- Pendleton (1)
- Polo Ralph Lauren (1)
- Pro Image (1)
- Samsonite (2)
- Styles For Less (1)
- Tommy Hilfiger (1)
- Totes / Sunglass World (3)
- Van Heusen (1)
- Vans Shoes (1)
- VF Factory Outlet (1)
- Video Outlet (9)

Eats & Treats

- Big Town Hero (11)
- California Espresso Café (10)
- Honey Hill Yogurt (10)
- Long John Silvers (11)
- Patio Grill (11)
- Rocky Mountain Chocolate (10)

3 Atascadero

3A • Atascadero Factory Outlets
www.atascaderofactoryoutlets
Address US 101 & Del Rio Rd
Phone 805-461-5155 *Hours* Mon-
Sat 10-8, Sun 10-7 *Location* West-
central California, northwest of
San Luis Obispo. Follow US 101
to Del Rio Road, just north of
Atascadero.

Stores

- Banister Shoes (1)
- Bass (1)
- Big Dogs (1)
- Black & Decker (4)
- Bugle Boy (1)
- Canyonland Gifts (5)
- Casual Corner (1)

- Factory Brand Shoes (1)
- Jones New York (1)
- Kitchen Collection (4)
- Linen Barn (4)
- Nautica (1)
- Paper Outlet (9)
- Polo Ralph Lauren (1)
- Rue 21 (1)
- Styles For Less (1)
- Van Heusen (1)
- Welcome Home (4)
- Wine Outlet (9)

Eats & Treats

- Pretzels Popcorn & More (10)
- Rocky Mountain Chocolate (10)
- Subway (11)

4 Barstow

4A • Factory Merchants Barstow
www.factorymerchantsbarstow.com
Address 2552 Mercantile Way
Phone 760-253-7342 *Hours* Mon-
Sun 9-8 *Location* About 130 miles
east of Los Angeles. From I-15 take
the Lenwood Road exit, travel
south to Mercantile Way.

Stores

- Adidas (1)
- Ashworth (1)
- Balboa Beach Co (1)
- Bally Outlet (1)
- BCBG Max Azria (1)
- Big Dog Sportswear (1)
- Billabong (1)
- Book Warehouse (5)
- Brooks Brothers (1)
- Calvin Klein (1)
- Children's Place Outlet (1)
- Claire's Accessories (3)
- Coach (2)
- Danskin (1)
- Dexter Shoe (1)
- Donna Karan (1)
- Dress Barn (1)
- Dress Barn Woman (1)
- Esprit (1)
- Etienne Aigner (1)
- Etnies exs (1)

- Factory Brand Shoes (1)
- Famous Brands Housewares (4)
- Fanzz (1)
- Florsheim (1)
- Gap Outlet (1)
- Geoffrey Beene (1)
- Guess? (1)
- Hush Puppies & Family (1)
- Izod (1)
- Joe Boxer (1)
- Jones New York (1)
- Kitchen Collection (4)
- Leather Loft (2)
- L'eggs Hanes Bali Playtex (1)
- Levi's Outlet by Most (1)
- Luggage Factory (2)
- Maidenform (1)
- Music For A Song (5)
- Naturalizer (1)
- Nautica (1)
- Olga Warner (1)
- OshKosh B'Gosh (1)
- Pacific Sunwear (1)
- Paper Outlet (9)
- Perfumania (8)
- Polo Ralph Lauren (1)
- Puma (1)
- Quiksilver (1)
- Remington (4)
- Sak (2)
- Shoe Pavilion (1)
- Styles For Less (1)
- Sunglass Hut / Watch Station (3)
- Tehen (1)
- Timberland (1)
- Tommy Hilfiger (1)
- Tools & More (9)
- Totes / Sunglass World (3)
- Toys Unlimited (6)
- Ultra Diamond & Gold (3)
- Van Heusen (1)
- Vans Shoes (1)
- Vitamania (8)
- Vitamin Liquidators (8)
- Wilson's Leather (1)
- XOXO (1)
- Zales The Diamond Store (3)

EATS & TREATS

- Asian Express (11)
- Pretzelmaker (10)

4B • Tanger Outlet Center

www.tangeroutlets.com

Free Public Library of Monroe Township
306 S. Main Street
Williamstown, NJ 08094-1727

Address 2796 Tanger Way **Phone** 800-409-3175 or 760-253-4813 **Hours** Mon-Sun 9-8 **Location** Southern California, about 130 miles east of Los Angeles. From I-15 take the Lenwood Road exit, travel south to Mercantile Way.

STORES

- Ann Taylor (1)
- Bass (1)
- Beanie Heaven (9)
- California Market Place (9)
- California Welcome Center (9)
- Class Perfumes & Cosmetics (8)
- Harry & David (5)
- Heng Feng Center (9)
- Liz Claiborne (1)
- Mikasa (4)
- Nine West (1)
- Reebok (1)
- Reebok Kids (1)
- Rockport (1)
- Samsonite (2)
- Super Nu Life (9)
- Van Heusen (1)

EATS & TREATS

- Cinnamon Stop (10)
- Dreyer's Grand Ice Cream (10)
- Pizza Outlet (11)
- Sub King (11)

5   CABAZON

5A • Cabazon Outlets

www.cabazonoutlet.com
Address 48750 Seminole Dr **Phone** 909-922-3000 **Hours** Sun-Thu 10-8, Fri 10-9, Sat 9-9 **Location** Twenty minutes west of Palm Springs off I-10. Take the Apache Train Road exit, turn right, then left on Seminole Dr.

STORES

- Adidas (1)
- Brighton Outlet (1)

- Club Monaco Direct (1)
- Couture New York (2)
- Crate & Barrel (4)
- David Brooks (1)
- Greg Norman (1)
- Karen Kane (1)
- Le Creuset (4)
- Oakley Vault (1)
- Puma (1)
- Reebok (1)
- Sheridan Australia Linens (4)
- Sunglass Outlet (3)

EATS & TREATS

- Auntie Anne's Pretzals (10)
- Starbucks Coffee (10)

5B • Desert Hills Premium Outlets

www.premiumoutlets.com
Address 48400 Seminole Dr *Phone* 909-849-6641 *Hours* Sun-Thu 10-8, Fri 10-9, Sat 9-9 *Location* Twenty minuets west of Palm Springs in southern California. Take the Fields Road exit off I-10.

STORES

- A/X Armani Exchange (1)
- Andre's Jewelry & Repair (3)
- Ann Taylor (1)
- Anne Klein (1)
- Barneys New York (1)
- Bass (1)
- BCBG Max Azria (1)
- Bebe Outlet (1)
- Big Dog Sportswear (1)
- Billabong (1)
- Bon Bonsai (9)
- Book Warehouse (5)
- Bose Factory Store (4)
- Brooks Brothers (1)
- Burberry (1)
- Carter's Childrenswear (1)
- Cingular Wireless (7)
- Coach (2)
- Cole-Haan (1)
- Corning Revere (4)
- Cosmetics Company Store (8)
- Crabtree & Evelyn (5)
- Creation Therapy (9)
- Dana Buchman (1)
- Designer Brands Accessories (2)
- Dexter Shoe (1)
- Dockers Outlet by Most (1)
- Donna Karan (1)
- Dress Barn (1)
- Eddie Bauer (1)
- Ellen Tracy (1)
- Escada Company Store (1)
- Esprit (1)
- Etienne Aigner (1)
- Eye Zoo Sunglass Menagerie (3)
- Famous Footwear (1)
- Fantasy Glass & Gifts (5)
- Florsheim (1)
- Four Seasons Designer Eyewear (3)
- Furla (2)
- Gap Outlet (1)
- Geoffrey Beene Men's & Women's (1)
- Giorgio Armani (1)
- Gucci (1)
- Guess? (1)
- Hair for Her (8)
- Harry & David (5)
- Hugo Boss (1)
- Izod (1)
- J Crew (1)
- Jhane Barnes Xtras (1)
- Jockey (1)
- Jones New York (1)
- Jones New York Country (1)
- Judith Leiber (5)
- Karen Kane (1)
- Kasper ASL (1)
- KB Toys (6)
- Kenneth Cole (1)
- Kitchen Collection (4)
- Lacoste (1)
- Laundry by Shelli Segal (1)
- Le Gourmet Chef (4)
- Leather Loft (2)
- L'eggs Hanes Bali Playtex (1)
- Lenox (4)
- Levi's Outlet by Most (1)
- Liz Claiborne (1)
- Maidenform (1)
- Mario's of Palm Springs (9)
- Max Mara (1)
- Max Studio (1)
- Mikasa (4)
- Mothertime Maternity (1)
- Movado (2)
- Music For A Song (5)
- Nautica (1)
- Nike (1)
- Nine West (1)

- North Face (1)
- Off 5th-Saks Fifth Avenue (1)
- Oneida (4)
- OshKosh B'Gosh (1)
- PacSun (1)
- Parallel (1)
- Perry Ellis (1)
- Polo Jeans Co (1)
- Polo Ralph Lauren (1)
- Premier Fine Jewelry (3)
- PS Elegant Pets (9)
- Quiksilver (1)
- Rockport (1)
- Royal Doulton (4)
- Samsonite (2)
- Silver Outlet (3)
- Skechers (1)
- Smokes Cigars & Gifts (9)
- Socks Galore (1)
- Southwest Cellular Accessories (7)
- Space (Prada, Miu Miu) (1)
- St John Company Store (1)
- Stride Rite Keds Sperry (1)
- Sundance Hat Company (1)
- TAG Heuer (2)
- Timberland (1)
- Tod's (1)
- Tommy Hilfiger (1)
- TSE (1)
- Ultra Diamond Outlet (3)
- Umbro (1)
- Van Heusen (1)
- Vans Shoes (1)
- Versace (1)
- Villeroy & Boch (4)
- Watch Boutique (3)
- Waterford Wedgwood (4)
- Welcome Home (4)
- WestPoint Stevens (4)
- Wilson's Leather (1)
- Yard Art (9)
- Zegna Outlet Store (1)

EATS & TREATS

- Bakery at Desert Hills (11)
- Baron's Burgers (11)
- Coffee / Scrubbed Potato (11)
- Coffee II (10)
- Dragon Chef (11)
- Emperor's Café (11)
- Godiva Chocolatier (10)
- Ichiban Express (11)
- Miss Mary's Candy Apples (10)
- Pepperoni's Pizza / Surf City Squeeze (11)

- Pizzicotto West (11)
- Salsa the Border (11)
- Surf City Squeeze (10)

6 CAMARILLO

6A • Camarillo Premium Outlets

www.premiumoutlets.com
Address 740 E Ventura Blvd *Phone* 805-445-8520 *Hours* Mon-Sat 10-9, Sun 10-6 *Location* Southern California between Los Angeles and Santa Barbara. Take Hwy 101 to Camarillo, exit Las Posas Rd.

STORES

- Adidas (1)
- Ann Taylor (1)
- Anne Klein (1)
- Asics (1)
- Attitudes (1)
- Balboa Beach Co (1)
- Banana Republic (1)
- Barneys New York (1)
- Bass (1)
- BCBG Max Azria (1)
- Bebe Outlet (1)
- Betsey Johnson (1)
- Big & Tall Factory Store (1)
- Big Dog Sportswear (1)
- Black & Decker (4)
- Bombay Outlet (4)
- Book Warehouse (5)
- Bose Factory Store (4)
- Brooks Brothers (1)
- Calvin Klein (1)
- Card America (5)
- Carter's Childrenswear (1)
- Charles David (1)
- Claire's Accessories (3)
- Coach (2)
- Cole-Haan (1)
- Cosmetics Company Store (8)
- Country Clutter (4)
- Dansk (4)
- Designer Brands Accessories (2)
- Designer Fragrance/Cosmetics (8)
- Donna Karan (1)
- Dress Barn (1)
- Easy Spirit (1)
- Ellen Tracy (1)

- Esprit (1)
- Factory Brand Shoes (1)
- Four Seasons Designer Eyewear (3)
- Gap Outlet (1)
- Geoffrey Beene (1)
- Guess? (1)
- Harry & David (5)
- Hartman Factory Store (2)
- Hugo Boss (1)
- Hush Puppies & Family (1)
- Izod (1)
- Jhane Barnes Xtras (1)
- Jockey (1)
- Jones New York (1)
- Jones New York Country (1)
- Just Sports (1)
- Karen Kane (1)
- Kasper ASL (1)
- KB Toys (6)
- Kenneth Cole (1)
- Las Vegas Discount Golf/Tennis (6)
- Laundry by Shelli Segal (1)
- Le Gourmet Chef (4)
- Leather Loft (2)
- L'eggs Hanes Bali Playtex (1)
- Lenox (4)
- Levi's Outlet by Most (1)
- Liz Claiborne (1)
- Liz Claiborne Shoes (1)
- London Fog (1)
- Luggage Factory (2)
- Maidenform (1)
- Maternity Works (1)
- Max Studio (1)
- Mikasa (4)
- Movado (2)
- Music For A Song (5)
- Naturalizer (1)
- Nautica (1)
- Nike (1)
- Nine West (1)
- Off 5th-Saks Fifth Avenue (1)
- OshKosh B'Gosh (1)
- Pacific Bell PCS Store (7)
- PacSun (1)
- Perfumania (8)
- Perry Ellis (1)
- Polo Jeans Co (1)
- Polo Ralph Lauren (1)
- Prime Cell (7)
- Puma (1)
- Reebok (1)
- Remington (4)
- Rizo Art Glass (4)
- Rockport (1)

- Royal Doulton (4)
- Samsonite (2)
- Skechers (1)
- So Fun! Kids (1)
- St John Company Store (1)
- Stone Mountain (2)
- Stride Rite Keds Sperry (1)
- Sunglass Hut (3)
- Sunshine Sunglasses (3)
- T&M Gift Co (5)
- Territory Ahead (1)
- Timberland (1)
- Tommy Hilfiger (1)
- Tribal Market Sterling Silver (3)
- Tupperware (4)
- Two Lips Shoes (1)
- Ultra Diamond Outlet (3)
- Van Heusen (1)
- Vans Shoes (1)
- Versace (1)
- Villeroy & Boch (4)
- Vitamin World (8)
- Walking Company (1)
- Wallet Works (2)
- Waterford Wedgwood (4)
- Welcome Home (4)
- WestPoint Stevens (4)
- Zales The Diamond Store (3)

EATS & TREATS

- Auntie Anne's Pretzels (10)
- Cappucino Club (10)
- Flamers Charbroiled (11)
- Fresh Tortilla (11)
- La Trattoria Italian Café (11)
- Little Thai (11)
- Pyro's Homestyle Rotisserie (11)
- Rocky Mountain Chocolate (10)
- Subway / TCBY (11)
- Terri's Chocolate Chippery Cookies (10)

7 CARLSBAD

7A • Carlsbad Company Stores

www.carlsbadcompanystores.com
Address Paseo Del Norte & Palomar Airport Rd *Phone* 760-804-9000 or 888-790-Shop *Hours* Mon-Sun 10-8 *Location* Thirty minutes north of downtown San

Diego. From I-5 north, exit Palomar Airport Road and turn right. Turn left at the first stop light onto Paseo del Norte.

STORES

- Adidas (1)
- Banana Republic (1)
- Barneys New York (1)
- BCBG Max Azria (1)
- Bebe Outlet (1)
- Big Dog Sportswear (1)
- Bose Factory Store (4)
- Brooks Brothers (1)
- California Luggage (2)
- Calvin Klein (1)
- Carlsbad Book Co (5)
- Carlsbad Visitor Info (9)
- Carter's Childrenswear (1)
- Cashmere Elite (1)
- Cingular Wireless (7)
- Coach (2)
- Cole-Haan (1)
- Cosmetics Company Store (8)
- Country Clutter (4)
- Couture New York (2)
- Crate & Barrel (4)
- Donna Karan (1)
- Easy Spirit (1)
- Ellen Tracy (1)
- Factory Brand Shoes (1)
- Four Seasons Sunglasses (3)
- Gap Outlet (1)
- Gift Basket Shoppe (5)
- Guess? (1)
- Harry & David (5)
- Hush Puppies & Family (1)
- Izod (1)
- Jockey (1)
- Johnston & Murphy (1)
- Jones New York (1)
- Jones New York Country (1)
- Kasper ASL (1)
- Kenneth Cole (1)
- Kitchen Collection (4)
- Le Creuset (4)
- Learning Express (4)
- L'eggs Hanes Bali Playtex (1)
- Lenox (4)
- Maternity Works (1)
- Nature's Touch (9)
- Nine West (1)
- No Fear (1)
- North Face (1)

- Olga Warner (1)
- Ooh La La (1)
- OshKosh B'Gosh (1)
- Pacific Sunwear (1)
- Pauling Blue Fire Diamonds (3)
- Polo Ralph Lauren (1)
- Postal Annex + (9)
- Puma (1)
- Reebok (1)
- Right Start (1)
- Robert Scott & David Brooks (1)
- Rockport (1)
- Royal Doulton (4)
- Samsonite (2)
- Strasburg Children (1)
- Stride Rite (1)
- Sunglass Outlet (3)
- Territory Ahead (1)
- Thousand Mile Outdoor Wear (1)
- Timberland (1)
- Tommy Hilfiger (1)
- Vans Shoes (1)
- Vitamin World (8)
- Waterford Wedgwood (4)
- WestPoint Stevens (4)
- Zales The Diamond Store (3)

EATS & TREATS

- Bellefleur Winery & Restaurant (11)
- Garden State Bagels (11)
- Juice It Up (10)
- Panda Panda (11)
- Rocky Mountain Chocolate (10)
- Ruby's Diner (11)
- Starbucks Coffee (10)
- Sweet Factory (10)
- Wetzel's Pretzels (10)

8   COMMERCE

8A • Citadel Factory Stores

www.citadelfactorystores.com
Address 5675 E Telegraph Rd *Phone* 323-888-1724 or 323-888-1220 *Hours* Mon-Sat 10-8, Sun 10-6 *Location* Just 20 minutes south of downtown Los Angeles. Take the Atlantic Blvd North exit off I-5 to Telegraph Rd. Go south to Citadel Dr.

Stores

- A & Y Leather (2)
- Ann Taylor (1)
- Attitudes (1)
- Balboa Beach Co (1)
- Bass (1)
- BCBG Footwear (1)
- BCBG Max Azria (1)
- Benetton (1)
- Big Dog Sportswear (1)
- Bijoux Bijoux (9)
- Book Warehouse (5)
- Carter's Childrenswear (1)
- Corning Revere (4)
- Designer Brands Accessories (2)
- Eddie Bauer (1)
- Fragrance Outlet (8)
- Geoffrey Beene (1)
- GH q (1)
- Izod (1)
- Kitchen Collection (4)
- Leather Loft (2)
- Leather Revolution (2)
- L'eggs Hanes Bali Playtex (1)
- Linen Club (4)
- London Fog (1)
- Maidenform (1)
- Max Studio (1)
- Nine West (1)
- Old Navy (1)
- Paolo Giardini (1)
- Prime Time Jewelry (3)
- Quiksilver (1)
- Samsonite (2)
- SUO (1)
- Toy Liquidators (6)
- Two Lips Shoes (1)
- Van Heusen (1)
- Vans Shoes (1)
- Vitamin World (8)

Eats & Treats

- Juice Time (10)
- Pachanga Mexican Grill (11)
- Sbarro Italian Eatery (11)
- Subway (11)
- Taipan Express (11)

9 Folsom

9A • Folsom Premium Outlets
www.premiumoutlets.com

Address 13000 Folsom Blvd *Phone* 916-985-0312 *Hours* Mon-Sat 10-9, Sun 10-6 *Location* Just 15 minutes east of Sacramento. Take the Folsom Blvd exit from US 50 and go north.

Stores

- Balboa Beach Co (1)
- Bass (1)
- Bebe Outlet (1)
- Big & Tall Factory Store (1)
- Big Dog Sportswear (1)
- Bombay Outlet (4)
- Bon Worth (1)
- Book Warehouse (5)
- Bose Factory Store (4)
- Carter's Childrenswear (1)
- Casual Corner (1)
- Claire's Accessories (3)
- Clothestime (1)
- Corning Revere (4)
- Country Clutter (4)
- Dexter Shoe (1)
- Donna Karan (1)
- Dress Barn (1)
- Dress Barn Woman (1)
- Eddie Bauer (1)
- Factory Brand Shoes (1)
- Farberware (4)
- Fossil (2)
- Gadgets & More (4)
- Gap Outlet (1)
- Geoffrey Beene (1)
- Gilchrist Gallery (4)
- Glassware House (4)
- Harry & David (5)
- Home Again (4)
- Home Design (4)
- Hush Puppies & Family (1)
- Izod (1)
- Jockey (1)
- Kasper ASL (1)
- Kenneth Cole (1)
- Koret (1)
- Le Gourmet Chef (4)
- Leather Loft (2)
- L'eggs Hanes Bali Playtex (1)
- Levi's Outlet by Most (1)
- Linen Barn (4)
- Liz Claiborne (1)
- Liz Claiborne Shoes (1)
- London Fog (1)

- Music For A Song (5)
- Naturalizer (1)
- Nike (1)
- Nine West (1)
- Off 5th-Saks Fifth Avenue (1)
- OshKosh B'Gosh (1)
- PacSun (1)
- Paper Factory (9)
- Perfumania (8)
- Rue 21 (1)
- Samsonite (2)
- Skechers (1)
- Socks Galore (1)
- Stride Rite Keds Sperry (1)
- Styles For Less (1)
- Sunglass Hut / Watch Station (3)
- Totes Isotoner Sunglass World (3)
- Toy Liquidators (6)
- Ultra Diamond Outlet (3)
- Van Heusen (1)
- Vans Shoes (1)
- Vitamin World (8)
- Warnaco (1)
- Waterford Wedgwood (4)
- Wilson's Leather (1)
- Zales The Diamond Store (3)

EATS & TREATS
- Hof Brau (11)
- Java Station Café (11)
- Mrs Fields Cookies (10)
- Pretzel Time / TCBY (10)
- Rocky Mountain Chocolate (10)
- Taco Bell (11)

10 GILROY

10A • Gilroy Premium Outlets
www.premiumoutlets.com
Address 681 Leavesley Rd *Phone*
408-842-3729 *Hours* Mon-Sat 10-
9, Sun 10-6 *Location* West-central
California, south of San Jose.
Follow US 101 south from San Jose
to Leavesley Road, go east.

STORES
- Adidas (1)
- Ann Taylor (1)
- Anne Klein (1)
- Balboa Beach Co (1)

- Bass (1)
- Bath & Body Works (8)
- Big Dog Sportswear (1)
- Billabong (1)
- Birkenstock (1)
- Bon Worth (1)
- Book Warehouse (5)
- Bose Factory Store (4)
- Brooks Brothers (1)
- California Luggage (2)
- Calvin Klein (1)
- Carter's Childrenswear (1)
- Casual Corner (1)
- Casual Corner Woman (1)
- Claire's Accessories (3)
- Clothestime (1)
- Coach (2)
- Corning Revere (4)
- Cosmetics Company Store (8)
- Country Clutter (4)
- Crabtree & Evelyn (5)
- Danskin (1)
- Designer Brands Accessories (2)
- Designer Fragrance/Cosmetics (8)
- Dexter Shoe (1)
- DKNY Jeans (1)
- Dress Barn/Dress Barn Woman (1)
- Easy Spirit (1)
- Eddie Bauer (1)
- Elegant Illusions (3)
- Esprit (1)
- Etienne Aigner (1)
- Factory Brand Shoes (1)
- Famous Brands Housewares (4)
- Farberware (4)
- Fila (1)
- Foot Locker (1)
- Fossil (2)
- Gap Outlet (1)
- Geoffrey Beene (1)
- Greg Norman (1)
- Guess? (1)
- Haggar (1)
- Harry & David (5)
- Home Again (4)
- Hoover Outlet (4)
- Hush Puppies & Family (1)
- Izod (1)
- J Crew (1)
- Jockey (1)
- Joe Boxer (1)
- Jones New York (1)
- Jones New York Country (1)
- Jones New York Sport (1)
- Jones New York Woman (1)

- Kasper ASL (1)
- Kenneth Cole (1)
- Kitchen Collection (4)
- Koret (1)
- Las Vegas Discount Golf/Tennis (6)
- Le Creuset (4)
- Le Gourmet Chef (4)
- Leather Loft (2)
- Leather Mode (2)
- L'eggs Hanes Bali Playtex (1)
- Lenox (4)
- Levi's Outlet by Most (1)
- Linen Barn (4)
- Liz Claiborne (1)
- Liz Claiborne Shoes (1)
- London Fog (1)
- Lucia (1)
- Luggage Center (2)
- Maidenform (1)
- Max Studio (1)
- Mikasa (4)
- Motherhood Maternity (1)
- Music For A Song (5)
- Naturalizer (1)
- Nautica (1)
- New York Jewelry Outlet (3)
- Nike (1)
- Nine West (1)
- No Fear (1)
- NordicTrack (8)
- Noritake (4)
- Oneida (4)
- OshKosh B'Gosh (1)
- PacSun (1)
- Paper Outlet (9)
- PCS Smartmart (7)
- Pearl Izumi (1)
- Perfumania (8)
- Perry Ellis (1)
- Petite Sophisticate (1)
- Pfaltzgraff (4)
- Polo Jeans Co (1)
- Polo Ralph Lauren (1)
- Puma (1)
- Reebok (1)
- Remington (4)
- Robert Scott & David Brooks (1)
- Rockport (1)
- Royal Doulton (4)
- Rue 21 (1)
- Rug Decor (4)
- Samsonite (2)
- Sanrio (9)
- SAS Factory Shoes (1)
- Shoe Pavilion (1)

- Skechers (1)
- Socks Galore (1)
- Springmaid Wamsutta (4)
- Stride Rite Keds Sperry (1)
- Styles For Less (1)
- Sunglass Hut (3)
- Sunglass Outlet (3)
- Timberland (1)
- Tommy Hilfiger (1)
- Toys Unlimited (6)
- Ultra Diamond Outlet (3)
- Van Heusen (1)
- Vans Shoes (1)
- Versace (1)
- VF Factory Outlet (1)
- Vitamin World (8)
- Waterford Wedgwood (4)
- Wilson's Leather (1)
- Zales The Diamond Store (3)

EATS & TREATS
- Auntie Anne's Pretzals (10)
- Erik's Deli Café (11)
- Erik's Deli Marketplace (11)
- Garlic Grocery (10)
- Garlic Shoppe (10)
- Gilroy Café (11)
- Rocky Mountain Chocolate (10)
- Starbucks Coffee (10)

11   LAKE ARROWHEAD

11A • Lake Arrowhead Village
www.lakearrowheadvillage.com
Address 28200 Hwy 189 *Phone*
909-337-2533 *Hours* Mon-Sun
10-5:30 *Location* Midway between
Los Angeles and Palm Springs.
From San Bernardino follow Hwy
18 to Lake Arrowhead.

STORES
- Angel Wings (5)
- Arrowhead Gallery (4)
- Bass (1)
- Big Dog Sportswear (1)
- Christine's Village Beauty Supply (8)
- Coach (2)
- Coastal Cotton (1)
- Factory Brand Shoes (1)

- Geoffrey Beene (1)
- GNC (8)
- Goose Pond Company (9)
- Harry & David (5)
- Harvest (4)
- Heart's Desire (5)
- Izod (1)
- Jockey (1)
- Just Browsing (5)
- Just Browsing Books (5)
- Lake Arrowhead Visitors Center (9)
- Last Stop (5)
- Leroy's Sports (1)
- Lowe Gallery (4)
- Miss Kitty's (5)
- Mountain Haus Interiors (4)
- Mr G's for Toys (6)
- Photo Express & Studio (7)
- Postal Connection (9)
- Promenade On The Lake (9)
- Sondra's (1)
- Sunglass Hut (3)
- Tattle Tails (1)
- Thomas Kinkade Gallery (4)
- Timberland (1)
- US Post Office (9)
- Van Heusen (1)
- Village Christmas Shoppe (9)
- Village Jewelers (3)
- Welcome Home (4)
- What In The World (9)
- Wildflowers (9)
- Wishing Well (4)

EATS & TREATS
- Belgian Waffle Works (11)
- Casa Coyote Grill and Cantina (11)
- Chili Chompers (11)
- Green Burrito (11)
- Lake Arrowhead Deli & Pizza (11)
- McDonald's (11)
- Razzbearies Cookies (10)
- Rocky Mountain Chocolate (10)
- Subway (11)
- Village Ice Cream & Sweets (10)
- Woody's Boathouse (11)

12 LAKE ELSINORE

12A • Lake Elsinore Outlets
www.lakeelsinoreoutlet.com
Address 17600 Collier Ave *Phone*
909-245-4989 or 866-306-Shop

Hours Man-Sat 10-8, Sun 10-7
Location Southern California, south of San Bernardino. Take the Nichols Road exit off I-15, west to Collier Ave.

STORES
- A & Y Leather (2)
- Amani Boutique (1)
- American Brands (1)
- Arbi Jewelers (3)
- Balboa Beach Co (1)
- Bass (1)
- Bath & Body Works (8)
- Bayside Watch (3)
- Big Dogs (1)
- Billabong (1)
- Casual Male Big & Tall (1)
- Claire's Accessories (3)
- Corning Clearance (4)
- Corning Revere (4)
- Dress Barn (1)
- Elisabeth (1)
- Esprit (1)
- Factory Brand Shoes (1)
- Farberware (4)
- Farmer Brown's Gifts (5)
- Furniture Factory (4)
- Gap Outlet (1)
- Geoffrey Beene (1)
- Haggar (1)
- Hobbies Toys & More (6)
- Hush Puppies & Family (1)
- Izod (1)
- Jockey (1)
- Jones New York (1)
- Kasper ASL (1)
- Kathy's House (4)
- KB Toys (6)
- Kenwood Factory Outlet (4)
- Kitchen Collection (4)
- Koret (1)
- L'eggs Hanes Bali Playtex (1)
- Levi's Outlet by Most (1)
- Lil' Bit Country (9)
- Liz Claiborne (1)
- Maidenform (1)
- Mary's Fashion (1)
- Mikasa (4)
- Motorsport Trader (9)
- Naturalizer (1)
- Nike (1)
- Nike Kids (1)

- Old Navy (1)
- OshKosk B'Gosh / Baby B'Gosh (1)
- Pacific Shore (1)
- Paper Factory (9)
- Payless Shoes (1)
- Perfumania (8)
- Publishers Warehouse (5)
- Reebok (1)
- Royal Doulton (4)
- Samsonite (2)
- SAS Factory Shoes (1)
- Software Plus (7)
- Sony (4)
- Stoud's Linen (4)
- Styles For Less (1)
- Sunglass Hut / Watch Station (3)
- Tools & More (9)
- Van Heusen (1)
- Vans Shoes (1)
- VF Factory Outlet (1)
- Vitamin World (8)
- Welcome Home (4)

EATS & TREATS

- Aruba Juice N' Java (10)
- Dairy Queen (11)
- Rocky Mountain Chocolate (10)

13 LANCASTER

13A • Lancaster Marketplace
www.lancastermarketplace.com
Address 44950 Valley Central Way
Phone 661-942-7897 *Hours* Mon-
Sat 10-8, Sun 11-7 *Location* North
of Los Angeles between I-5 and I-15.
Travel north on Hwy 14 (Antelope
Valley Freeway), take Avenue I exit,
go west to Valley Central Way.

STORES

- Angels Among Us (5)
- Biehn Fitness Equipment (6)
- Big Dog Sportswear (1)
- BNC Brand Name Clothing (1)
- Bo D Tuxedo Rentals (9)
- Brat Active Wear (1)
- Claire's Accessories (3)
- Complete Computer Care (7)
- Corning Clearance (4)
- Corning Revere (4)

- Designer Outlet (1)
- Dress Barn (1)
- Factory Brand Shoes (1)
- Finer Things (9)
- Furniture Gallery (4)
- High Tide (9)
- K-Swiss Outlet (9)
- Kitchen Collection (4)
- Kuki's Bridal (1)
- Levi's Outlet by Most (1)
- Make It Sew (9)
- Mercantile (9)
- Montage Salon (9)
- Reebok / Rockport (1)
- Rossanas Bridal Cottage (1)
- S & Y Furniture (4)
- S & Y Kids Corner (1)
- Scentzations (8)
- Scrooge's (9)
- Sora Fashions (1)
- Spirit Halloween Store (9)
- Sunglass Hut (3)
- Teaching Supplies (9)
- Total Soccer (6)
- Toy Liquidators (6)
- US Imports (9)
- Vitamin Liquidators (8)
- Vitamin World (8)

EATS & TREATS

- Le Bon Café (11)
- Super King Buffet (11)
- Tastee's Fine Yogurt/Ice Cream (10)

14 MAMMOTH LAKES

14A • Mammoth Premium Outlets
Address 3343 Main St *Phone* 760-
934-9771 *Hours* In Season: Sun-
Thu 10-8, Fri-Sat 10-9. Off
Season: Sun-Thu 10-6, Fri-Sat 10-
8 *Location* Forty miles west of
Bishop via US 395 and State Hwy
203. Center is on Main St in
Mammoth Lakes.

STORES

- Bass (1)
- Big Dog Sportswear (1)
- Boby Works Mountain Spa (8)
- Book Warehouse (5)

- Coach (2)
- Graphic Conclusions (1)
- Great Outdoor Clothing (1)
- Haute Looks (9)
- Polo Ralph Lauren (1)
- Sun Mountain Sport (6)
- Uphill Sports (9)
- Van Heusen (1)

EATS & TREATS
- Perry's Italian Café (11)

15 MILPITAS

15A • Great Mall of the Bay Area
www.greatmallbayarea.com
Address 447 Great Mall Dr *Phone* 800-Mall-Bay or 408-956-2033 *Hours* Mon-Sat 10-9, Sun 11-8 *Location* In Silicon Valley, just north of San Jose. The mall is at the interesction of Montague Expressway and Great Mall Parkway between highways 680 and 880. From 880 take the Great Mall Parkway exit and proceed east, the mall will be on your left.

STORES
- 5-7-9 Outlet (1)
- ABC Toys (6)
- Afterthoughts (3)
- Almart (5)
- Alpaca Petes (1)
- Anchor Blue Clothing Co (1)
- Apparel Plus (1)
- Ariana Gift Collection (5)
- Art of Candles (5)
- Art Portraits by Yvette (4)
- As Seen on Screen (5)
- Athlete's Foot (1)
- Atomic Garage (1)
- Bath & Body Works (8)
- Bayside Watch (3)
- BCBG Max Azria (1)
- Beauty Express (8)
- Bebe Outlet (1)
- Berioni (1)
- BFO-Byer Factory Outlet (1)

- Big Dog Sportswear (1)
- Black Market Minerals (5)
- Blacy's Fine Jewelers (3)
- Borsa Fine Leather Outlet (2)
- Bossini Fine Menswear (1)
- Bowl by the Bay (9)
- Burlington Coat Factory (1)
- Calvin Klein (1)
- Cambridge SoundWorks (4)
- Cardsmart (5)
- Carpet Club (4)
- Carter's Childrenswear (1)
- Casual Corner (1)
- Cellular Warehouse (7)
- Century Theaters (9)
- Charlotte Russe (1)
- Children's Place Outlet (1)
- Choice Beauty Supply & Salon (8)
- Choice Plus (1)
- Choo Choo Time Train (9)
- Citilink Wireless (7)
- Claire's Accessories (3)
- Classic for Ladies (1)
- Collectibles of Asia (4)
- Corning Revere (4)
- Country Clutter (4)
- Crescent Jewelers (3)
- D. Valentine, Optometrist (3)
- Delicate Balance Health Care (8)
- Designer Rugs (4)
- Donna Karan (1)
- Dress Barn/Dress Barn Woman (1)
- Dynasty Jewelers (3)
- Eddie Bauer (1)
- Edward's Luggage Outlet (2)
- Eiffel Handbags (2)
- Electronics Boutique (4)
- Elements (1)
- EOS (1)
- Esprit (1)
- Eye Candy (1)
- Factory Brand Shoes (1)
- Famous Brands Housewares (4)
- Famous Footwear (1)
- Fantasy Beauty Spa (8)
- FitMe.com (9)
- Florsheim (1)
- Foot Locker (1)
- FootAction USA (1)
- Fornarina (1)
- Fragrance Shoppe (8)
- Futon Depot (4)
- Game Stop (9)
- Games & More (9)
- Gap Outlet (1)

- Generations (4)
- Georgiou Outlet (1)
- GHQ Outlet (1)
- GNC (8)
- Gold & Diamond Outlet (3)
- Grandeur Art Gallery (4)
- Great Nails (8)
- Group USA (1)
- Guess? (1)
- Hat Club (1)
- Hot Topic (1)
- Innovative Products Outlet (9)
- Italo Menswear (1)
- Izod (1)
- Jewelry Palace (3)
- Joe Boxer (1)
- Journeys (1)
- Just for Kids (1)
- KB Toys (6)
- Leather by Michael Lawrence (2)
- Leather Company (2)
- Leather Loft (2)
- Leather Mode (2)
- L'eggs Hanes Bali Playtex (1)
- Let's Talk Cellular (7)
- Levi's Outlet by Most (1)
- Linen's N Things (4)
- Little Angel (1)
- Magic Magic (9)
- Maidenform (1)
- Marshalls (1)
- MasterCuts (8)
- MCI WorldCom (7)
- Media Play (5)
- Mikasa (4)
- Mojos Surf & Skate Shop (6)
- Motherhood Maternity (1)
- Music For A Song (5)
- Naturalizer (1)
- Nine West (1)
- No Fear (1)
- NordicTrack (8)
- Nu Pair (1)
- Oakley Vault (1)
- Off 5th-Saks Fifth Avenue (1)
- Old Navy (1)
- Orchid Women's (1)
- OshKosh B'Gosh (1)
- Oshman's SuperSports USA (6)
- PacSun (1)
- Pager & Cellular Outlet (7)
- Paper Outlet (9)
- Payless Kids Shoe Source (1)
- Payless Shoe Source (1)
- Pegasus Gymnastics (6)

- Perfumania (8)
- Perry Ellis (1)
- Petite Sophisticate (1)
- Piercing Pagoda (3)
- Planting Art Center (9)
- Plumb Gold (3)
- Polo Jeans Co (1)
- Pro Star Sports (6)
- Radio Shack (7)
- Raider Locker Room (1)
- Remington (4)
- Reversity (1)
- Ritz Camera 1 Hour Photo (7)
- Samsonite (2)
- San Francisco Music Box (9)
- Sanrio (9)
- Sarda Jewelry & Interiors (3)
- Sharper Image Outlet (9)
- Sheikh Shoes (1)
- Shirtique (1)
- Shoe Pavilion (1)
- Silver Silver (3)
- Skechers (1)
- Smart Scrubs (1)
- Spencer Gifts (5)
- St John Knits (1)
- Star Shots (9)
- Styles For Less (1)
- Sun & Ski Sports (1)
- Sun Shade Optique (9)
- Sweet Things Candy & Gifts (5)
- Tiny Computers (6)
- Together (1)
- Tommy Hilfiger (1)
- Tuxedo Wearhouse (1)
- Ultra Diamond Outlet (3)
- Urban Leather (1)
- Van Heusen (1)
- Vans Shoes (1)
- Vans SkatePark (9)
- VIP Menswear (1)
- Vitamin World (8)
- Wilson's Leather (1)
- Zales The Diamond Store (3)
- Zumiez (1)

EATS & TREATS

- Arby's Roast Beef (11)
- Auntie Anne's Pretzals (10)
- Burger King (11)
- Cajun Grill (11)
- California Golden Cookies (10)
- Cinnabon (10)
- Coffee Bean (10)
- Cold Stone Creamery (10)

- Dave & Buster's (11)
- Florentine (11)
- Fresh Choice (11)
- Fujisan Restaurant (11)
- Gloria Jean's Gourmet Coffee (10)
- Grain D'Or (11)
- Great Mall Mayflower (11)
- Great Steak & Potato (11)
- Hot Dog on a Stick (11)
- Johnny Rockets (11)
- La Salsa Fresh Mexican Grill (11)
- Little Tokyo (11)
- McDonald's (11)
- Mr Wu's Chinese (11)
- Mrs Fields Cookies (10)
- Outback Steakhouse (11)
- Sbarro Italian Eatery (11)
- Sorabol (11)
- Starbucks Coffee (10)
- Subway (11)
- Super Scoop Ice Cream (10)
- Surf City Squeeze (10)
- Swagat (11)
- TCBY (10)
- Wetzel's Pretzels (10)

16 NAPA

16A • Napa Premium Outlets
www.premiumoutlets.com
Address 629 Factory Stores Dr
Phone 707-226-9876 *Hours* Mon-Sat 10-8, Sun 10-6 *Location* Northern California, north of San Francisco. The center is located at the First Street exit off Hwy 29.

STORES
- Ann Taylor (1)
- Barneys New York (1)
- BCBG Max Azria (1)
- Big Dog Sportswear (1)
- Billabong (1)
- Book Warehouse (5)
- California Luggage (2)
- Calvin Klein (1)
- Cole-Haan (1)
- Cosmetics Company Store (8)
- Dansk (4)
- DKNY Jeans (1)
- Dockers Outlet (1)

- Easy Spirit (1)
- Ellen Tracy (1)
- Esprit (1)
- Factory Brand Shoes (1)
- Geoffrey Beene (1)
- Illuminations (5)
- Izod (1)
- J Crew (1)
- Johnston & Murphy (1)
- Jones New York (1)
- Jones New York Country (1)
- Jones New York Sport (1)
- Karen Kane (1)
- Kenneth Cole (1)
- Le Gourmet Chef (4)
- Levi's (1)
- Liz Claiborne (1)
- Maidenform (1)
- Max Studio (1)
- Mikasa (4)
- Nautica (1)
- Nine West (1)
- Perry Ellis (1)
- Quiksilver (1)
- Robert Scott & David Brooks (1)
- Sunglass Hut / Watch World (3)
- Timberland (1)
- Tommy Hilfiger (1)
- TSE (1)
- Ultra Diamond Outlet (3)
- Wilson's Leather (1)

EATS & TREATS
- Caffe Siena (11)
- Fujiya Restaurant (11)
- Hunan Restaurant (11)
- Italia Mex Cucina (11)
- Just Another Joe's (11)

17 ONTARIO

17A • Ontario Mills
www.millscorp.com
Address One Mills Cir *Phone* 909-484-8300 *Hours* Mon-Fri 10-9:30, Sat 9:30-9:30, Sun 10-8 *Location* In the Riverside and San Bernardino metropolitan areas at the intersection of I-10 and I-15. From I-10, exit Haven Avenue North. From I-15, exit 4th Street West.

Stores

- 5-7-9 Outlet (1)
- A & Y Leather (2)
- AMC 30 Theatres (9)
- Anchor Blue Clothing Co (1)
- Angles Colors Cuts & Perms (8)
- Ann Taylor (1)
- Athlete's Foot (1)
- Bakers Shoes (1)
- Banister Shoes (1)
- Bass (1)
- Bath & Body Works (8)
- Beauty Express (8)
- Bebe Outlet (1)
- Bed Bath & Beyond (4)
- Benetton (1)
- Beyond the Beach (1)
- Big Dog Sportswear (1)
- Black & Decker (4)
- Black Market Minerals (5)
- Bose Factory Store (4)
- Bostonian Clarks (1)
- Bugle Boy (1)
- Burlington Coat Factory (1)
- Carter's For Kids (1)
- Casio (4)
- Casual Male Big & Tall (1)
- Charlotte Russe (1)
- Cingular Wireless (7)
- Citi Music (5)
- Claire's Accessories (3)
- Converse (1)
- Corning Revere (4)
- Cost Plus World Market (4)
- Country Clutter (4)
- CR Jewelers Outlet (3)
- Cutting Edge Outlet (4)
- David's Gifts & Tobacco (5)
- Day Runner Outlet (5)
- Designer Fragrance/Cosmetics (8)
- Dockers Outlet (1)
- Dress Barn/Dress Barn Woman (1)
- Electronics Boutique (4)
- Etienne Aigner (1)
- Eye Candy (1)
- Factory Brand Shoes (1)
- Famous Brands Housewares (4)
- Famous Footwear (1)
- Florsheim (1)
- Foot Locker (1)
- Foozles Bookstore (5)
- Fossil (2)
- GameWorks (9)
- Gap Outlet (1)
- Georgiou Outlet (1)
- Glow (5)
- GNC (8)
- Gotcha (1)
- Grand Jewelers (3)
- Group USA (1)
- Guess? (1)
- Hat Club (1)
- Hot Topic (1)
- Hugo Boss (1)
- Hush Puppies & Family (1)
- I S Interstate (1)
- Icing (3)
- JCPenney Outlet (1)
- Jewelers of Las Vegas (3)
- JNCO (1)
- Journeys (1)
- Just Sports (1)
- Kasper ASL (1)
- KB Toys (6)
- Learning Express (4)
- Leather Loft (2)
- Leather Mode (2)
- L'eggs Hanes Bali Playtex (1)
- LensCrafters (3)
- Let's Talk Cellular (7)
- Levi's (1)
- Lids (9)
- Liz Claiborne (1)
- Lucky Brand Dungarees (1)
- Maidenform (1)
- Marshalls (1)
- MasterCuts (8)
- Michael's Cards & Gifts (5)
- Mikasa (4)
- Morgan-Paris (1)
- Movado (2)
- Nail Trix (8)
- Nautica (1)
- Nine West (1)
- Off 5th-Saks Fifth Avenue (1)
- Off Rodeo Drive Beverly Hills (1)
- Old Navy (1)
- OshKosh B'Gosh Super Store (1)
- Outdoors (1)
- Pacific Sunwear (1)
- Papaya Clothing (1)
- Paper Outlet (9)
- Payless Shoe Source (1)
- Perfumania (8)
- Perfumania Plus (8)
- Players II (1)
- Premier Fine Jewelry (3)
- Red Eye (1)
- Remington (4)
- Ritz Camera 1 Hour Photo (7)

- Samsonite/American Tourister (2)
- Sanrio (9)
- Saving Time (9)
- Shemoni Sterling Silver (3)
- Shoe Pavilion (1)
- Skechers (1)
- Smart Scrubs (1)
- Sophia (1)
- Spencer Gifts (5)
- Sports Authority (6)
- Star Shots (9)
- Sterling Optical (3)
- Stride Rite Keds Sperry (1)
- Sunglass Hut (3)
- Tic Time Watch Specialists (3)
- Tilly's (1)
- TJ Maxx (1)
- Totally 4 Kids (1)
- ToyCo (6)
- Two Lips Shoes (1)
- Ultra Jewelers (3)
- Van Heusen (1)
- Vans Shoes (1)
- Vans SkatePark (9)
- Virgin Megastore (5)
- Vista Optical (3)
- Vitamin World (8)
- Warnaco (1)
- Westport Ltd/Westport Woman (1)
- Wilson's Leather (1)
- Windsor Outlet (1)
- World of Flags (9)
- World of Hats (1)
- XOXO (1)
- Young Hui Imports (5)
- Zales The Diamond Store (3)

EATS & TREATS

- Auntie Anne's Pretzals (10)
- Banana's Ultimate Juice Bar (10)
- Bruegger's Bagels (11)
- Burger King (11)
- Cheesecake Factory Bakery Café (11)
- Cinnabon (10)
- Dave & Buster's (11)
- Everything Yogurt & Salad Café (11)
- GameWorks Café (11)
- Gloria Jean's Gourmet Coffee (10)
- Haagen Dazs (10)
- Keily's Cajun Grill (11)
- Kenny Rogers Roasters (11)
- La Salsa Fresh Mexican Grill (11)
- Market Broiler (11)

- Panda Express (11)
- Rainforest Café (11)
- Rocky Mountain Chocolate (10)
- Sbarro Italian Eatery (11)
- Starbucks Coffee (10)
- Sweet Factory (10)
- Wolfgang Puck Café (11)
- World Links (11)

18 ORANGE

18A • Block at Orange
www.millscorp.com
Address 20 City Blvd W *Phone* 714-769-4000 or 877-2TheBlock *Hours* Mon-Thu 10-9:30, Fri-Sat 10-11, Sun 10-9:30 *Location* At the intersection of I-5 and Hwy 22 in the city of Orange.

STORES

- Afterthoughts (3)
- AMC 30 Theatres (9)
- Anchor Blue Clothing Co (1)
- Angles Colors Cuts & Perms (8)
- Ann Taylor (1)
- Art Center Gallery (4)
- Athlete's Foot (1)
- Atomic Garage (1)
- Bakers Shoes (1)
- Bath & Body Works (8)
- Big Dog Sportswear (1)
- Borders Books (5)
- Bose Factory Store (4)
- Burke Williams Day Spa (8)
- Claire's Accessories (3)
- Classic Kicks (1)
- Cohiba (9)
- Conspiracy (1)
- Cool 94.3 (5)
- Earthbound Trading Co (5)
- Electronics Boutique (4)
- Eye Candy (1)
- Fashion Nails (8)
- Frederick's of Hollywood (1)
- Games Workshop (9)
- Glow (5)
- GNC (8)
- Hallmark Creations (9)
- Hillo Hattie Store of Hawaii (1)

- I S Interstate (1)
- Imposters (3)
- Just Sports (1)
- LA Fitness (8)
- Leather Mode (2)
- Manga House (9)
- Mars Music (5)
- Money Man Gallery (9)
- New York Cargo (1)
- Nextel (7)
- No Fear (1)
- O2 Café (9)
- Off 5th-Saks Fifth Avenue (1)
- Old Navy (1)
- O'My Sole (1)
- Past Tense (9)
- Pearl Factory (3)
- Perfumania (8)
- Planet Beauty (8)
- Powerhouse Luggage (2)
- Red Eye (1)
- Robert Wayne Footwear (1)
- Ron Jon Surf Shop (6)
- Shemoni Sterling Silver (3)
- Sirens (1)
- Skechers (1)
- Spencer Gifts (5)
- Sun's Up (9)
- Tilly's (1)
- Ultra Diamond & Gold (3)
- Ultra House (9)
- Vans SkatePark (9)
- Virgin Megastore (5)
- Vitamin World (8)
- Watch Works (3)
- Windsor Outlet (1)
- Wizards of the Coast (4)
- World of Flags (9)
- Zap Create Your Own Cap (1)

EATS & TREATS

- Alcatraz Brewing Co (11)
- Auntie Anne's Pretzals (10)
- Ben & Jerry's (10)
- Bourban Street Cajun Cuisine (11)
- Café Tu Tu Tango (11)
- Carl's Jr (11)
- Cool Planet (11)
- Corner Bakery Café (11)
- Dave & Buster's (11)
- El Torito (11)
- Jamba Juice (10)
- Jody Maroni's Italian Sausage (11)
- Johnny Rockets (11)
- Koji's Sushi & Shabu Shabu (11)

- Krispy Kreme Doughnuts (10)
- Left At Albuquerque (11)
- Market Broiler (11)
- Pasta Bravo (11)
- Quizno's Classic Subs (11)
- Richie's Neighborhood Pizzeria (11)
- Rocky Mountain Chocolate (10)
- Rubio's Baja Grill (11)
- Starbucks Coffee (10)
- Sweets From Heaven (10)
- TGI Fridays (11)
- Twin Dragon (11)
- Wetzel's Pretzels (10)
- Wolfgang Puck Café (11)

19 OXNARD

19A • Oxnard Factory Outlet
www.oxnardfactoryoutlet.com
Address 2000 Outlet Center Dr
Phone 805-485-2244 *Hours* Mon-Sat 10-8, Sun 11-6 *Location* Between Los Angeles and Santa Barbara off US 101. Take the Ventura 101 Freeway to the Rose Avenue exit. Go south on Rose Ave to Gonzales Rd, turn left and the center will be on your left.

STORES

- Alfresco Patio Outlet (4)
- Baby's Room Kid's Room (4)
- Carpets Direct (4)
- Diamond Communications (9)
- Easy Spirit (1)
- Factory Brand Shoes (1)
- Florsheim (1)
- Furniture Expo (4)
- Harman Audio (4)
- Kitchen Collection (4)
- L'eggs Hanes Bali Playtex (1)
- Mar Vac Electronics (4)
- Oxnard Visitors Center (9)
- Paper Outlet (9)
- Pro Sports (1)
- Sit n Sleep (4)
- Straight A's (1)
- TLC Uniforms (1)
- Via Vai Favorite Linens to Wear (1)
- Vitamin Liquidators (8)

EATS & TREATS
- American Pizza (11)
- Bread Connection (11)

20 PACIFIC GROVE

20A • American Tin Cannery Premium Outlets

www.premiumoutlets.com
Address 125 Ocean View Blvd *Phone* 831-372-1442 *Hours* Sun-Thu 10-6, Fri-Sat 10-8 *Location* Across from the Montery Bay Aquarium. Take scenic Route 1 to the Pacific Grove exit, then follow signs to the aquarium.

STORES
- Adventure Comics & Toys (6)
- Anne Klein (1)
- Bass (1)
- Big Dog Sportswear (1)
- Bon Worth (1)
- Book Warehouse (5)
- Danskin (1)
- Designer Brands Accessories (2)
- Dress Barn (1)
- Eye Zoo Sunglass Menagerie (3)
- Factory Brand Shoes (1)
- Geoffrey Beene (1)
- Izod (1)
- Kitchen Collection (4)
- L'eggs Hanes Bali Playtex (1)
- Maidenform (1)
- Mr Z's Fine Jewelry (3)
- Mrs Z's Gemological Lab (3)
- Nine West (1)
- OshKosh B'Gosh (1)
- Reebok (1)
- Rockport (1)
- Samsonite (2)
- Synchronicity Studio (5)
- Totes Isotoner Sunglass World (3)
- Van Heusen (1)
- Vans Shoes (1)
- Vitamin World (8)
- Warnaco (1)
- WestPoint Stevens (4)
- Winborne Kites Express (9)
- Woolrich (1)

EATS & TREATS
- Archie's American Diner (11)
- First Awakenings (11)
- Inaka Japanese Restaurant (11)
- SweetZee's (10)

21 PETALUMA

21A • Petaluma Village Premium Outlets

www.premiumoutlets.com
Address 2200 Petaluma Blvd N *Phone* 707-778-9300 *Hours* Mon-Sat 10-8, Sun 10-6 *Location* About 35 minutes north of San Francisco off Hwy 101. Take the Old Redwood Highway exit and travel west 1.3 miles.

STORES
- Ann Taylor (1)
- Anne Klein (1)
- Balboa Beach Co (1)
- Bass (1)
- Big Dog Sportswear (1)
- Bon Worth (1)
- Book Warehouse (5)
- Bose Factory Store (4)
- Bostonian Clarks (1)
- Brooks Brothers (1)
- Carter's Childrenswear (1)
- Claire's Accessories (3)
- Coach (2)
- Corning Revere (4)
- Country Clutter (4)
- Dexter Shoe (1)
- Donna Karan (1)
- Factory Brand Shoes (1)
- Gap Outlet (1)
- Harry & David (5)
- Jones New York (1)
- KB Toys (6)
- Le Gourmet Chef (4)
- Leather Loft (2)
- L'eggs Hanes Bali Playtex (1)
- Linen Barn (4)
- Liz Claiborne (1)
- Mikasa (4)
- Motherhood Maternity (1)
- Music For A Song (5)

- Nine West (1)
- Off 5th-Saks Fifth Avenue (1)
- OshKosh B'Gosh (1)
- Perfumania (8)
- Puma (1)
- Reebok (1)
- Samsonite (2)
- Sunglass Hut (3)
- Totes Isotoner Sunglass World (3)
- Ultra Diamond Outlet (3)
- Van Heusen (1)
- Vans Shoes (1)
- Villeroy & Boch (4)
- Vitamin World (8)
- Warnaco (1)
- Wilson's Leather (1)
- Zales The Diamond Store (3)

EATS & TREATS

- Columbo Yogurt (10)
- Dreyer's Grand Ice Cream (10)
- Fog City Pizza (11)
- Rocky Mountain Chocolate (10)
- Sonoma Grill (11)

22 PISMO BEACH

22A • Prime Outlets Pismo Beach
www.primeoutlets.com
Address 333 Five Cities Dr *Phone* 805-773-4661 *Hours* Mon-Sat 10-8, Sun 11-6 *Location* Midway between San Luis Obispo and Santa Maria, just off Hwy 101 in Pismo Beach.

STORES

- Anne Klein (1)
- Bass (1)
- Big Dogs (1)
- Canyonland Gifts (5)
- Casual Corner (1)
- Claire's Accessories (3)
- Corning Revere (4)
- Country Clutter (4)
- Dress Barn (1)
- Factory Brand Shoes (1)
- Famous Brands Housewares (4)
- Geoffrey Beene (1)
- Harry & David (5)
- Izod (1)

- Jockey (1)
- Jones New York (1)
- Kitchen Collection (4)
- Koret (1)
- Leather Loft (2)
- L'eggs Hanes Bali Playtex (1)
- Levi's Outlet by Most (1)
- Maidenform (1)
- Mikasa (4)
- Nine West (1)
- Pacific Sunwear (1)
- Paper Factory (9)
- Perfumania (8)
- Publishers Warehouse (5)
- Rue 21 (1)
- Samsonite (2)
- Shoe Pavilion (1)
- Styles For Less (1)
- Sunglass Hut / Watch Station (3)
- Tommy Hilfiger (1)
- Van Heusen (1)
- Vans Shoes (1)
- Vitamin World (8)
- Welcome Home (4)

EATS & TREATS

- Rocky Mountain Chocolate (10)

23 SAN DIEGO

23A • Las Americas
www.internationalgatewayofthe
americas.com
Address U.S.-Mexico border *Phone* 619-934-8400 *Hours* Mon-Sat 10-8, Sun 10-6 *Location* U.S.-Mexico border in San Diego, west of I-5 off the Camino de la Plaza exit.

STORES

- Baja Duty Free (9)
- Banana Republic (1)
- Bass (1)
- Benzene (1)
- Brooks Brothers (1)
- Casual Corner (1)
- Charlotte Russe (1)
- Claire's Accessories (3)
- Designer Studio (1)
- Dress Barn (1)
- Ezera (1)
- Factory Brand Shoes (1)

- Fragrance Salon (8)
- Gap Outlet (1)
- Geoffrey Beene (1)
- GNC (8)
- Good Companies (1)
- Guess? (1)
- Haggar (1)
- Hush Puppies & Family (1)
- Izod (1)
- Joe Boxer (1)
- Kitchen Collection (4)
- Levi's (1)
- Liz Claiborne (1)
- Maidenform (1)
- Maternity World (1)
- Naturalizer (1)
- Nautica (1)
- New York Cargo (1)
- Nike (1)
- Old Navy (1)
- Pacific Sunwear (1)
- Papaya Clothing (1)
- Payless Shoe Source (1)
- Polo Ralph Lauren (1)
- Reference (9)
- Rivisto (1)
- Sally's Beauty Supply (8)
- Samsonite (2)
- Skechers (1)
- Springmaid Wamsutta (4)
- Stride Rite (1)
- Sunglass Hut (3)
- Swimsuit Outlet (1)
- Tommy Hilfiger Jeans (1)
- Van Heusen (1)
- Vitamin World (8)
- Wet Seal Outlet (1)
- Wilson's Leather (1)
- World Channel Showcase (9)
- Zales The Diamond Store (3)

EATS & TREATS
- A & W Restaurant (11)
- Church's Chicken (11)
- Dairy Queen (11)
- E & J Grill (11)
- Great Steak & Potato (11)
- IHOP (11)
- La Famiglia (11)
- McDonald's (11)
- Mexican Grill (11)
- Outback Steakhouse (11)
- Rice Garden (11)
- Starbucks Coffee (10)
- Subway (11)

24 SAN LEANDRO

24A • Marina Square Mall
www.marinasquaremall.com
Address I-880 at Marina Blvd E
Hours Mon-Fri 10-9, Sat 10-7, Sun 11-6 **Location** Only 10 minutes from downtown Oakland. Take the I-880 freeway south to Marina Blvd East. Exit and merge onto Marina Blvd. The mall will be on your right.

STORES
- Ann Taylor (1)
- Anna's Linens (4)
- Bath & Body Works (8)
- Big Dog Sportswear (1)
- Dress Barn (1)
- Eddie Bauer (1)
- Kinko's (9)
- Marshalls (1)
- Mikasa (4)
- Nine West (1)
- Nordstrom Rack (1)
- Office Max (9)
- Old Navy (1)
- Radio Shack (7)
- Shoe Pavilion (1)
- Sprint PCS Center (7)
- SuperVision (9)
- Talbots (1)

EATS & TREATS
- La Salsa Fresh Mexican Grill (11)
- Quizno's Classic Subs (11)
- Starbucks Coffee (10)
- TCBY (10)

25 SAN YSIDRO

25A • San Diego Factory Outlet
www.sandiegofactoryoutlet.com
Address 4498 Camino De La Plaza **Phone** 619-690-2999 **Hours** Mon-Fri 10-8, Sat 10-7, Sun 10-6 **Location** Fifteen miles from downtown San Diego. Follow I-5

or I-805 south to the Camino de la Plaza exit, turn right. Go one block and the center is on your right.

STORES
- American Brands (1)
- Ashworth (1)
- Bass (1)
- California Luggage (2)
- Calvin Klein (1)
- Carter's Childrenswear (1)
- Designer Brands Accessories (2)
- Designer Studio (1)
- Dockers Outlet by Most (1)
- Essence Perfume & Beauty (8)
- Famous Brands Housewares (4)
- Georgiou Outlet (1)
- Guess? (1)
- Jockey (1)
- KB Toy Liquidators (6)
- Levi's Outlet by Most (1)
- Maidenform (1)
- Mikasa (4)
- Nike (1)
- Nine West (1)
- OshKosh B'Gosh (1)
- Postal Center (9)
- Sunglass Hut (3)
- Swimwear Outlet (1)
- Van Heusen (1)
- Vans Shoes (1)
- Vitamin World (8)

EATS & TREATS
- Rocky Mountain Chocolate (10)
- Tasty China Express (11)

26   SOUTH LAKE TAHOE

26A • Factory Stores at the Y
www.tahoefactorystores.com
Address US 50 & Hwy 89 *Phone* 530-573-5545 *Hours* Mon-Sun 9-7 *Location* East of Sacramento, near the Nevada border. The center is located at the junction of US 50 and Hwy 89.

STORES
- Adidas (1)

- Bass (1)
- Big Dogs (1)
- Fragrance Outlet (8)
- Geoffrey Beene (1)
- Gold Store (3)
- Great Outdoor Clothing (1)
- Hi-Tec (1)
- Home Again (4)
- Izod (1)
- Oneida (4)
- Pazazz (1)
- Samsonite (2)
- Sealed with a Kiss (1)
- Sierra Shirts (1)
- Sunglass Hut / Watch Station (3)
- Van Heusen (1)
- Vitamin World (8)

EATS & TREATS
- Rocky Mountain Chocolate (10)

27   ST. HELENA

27A • St. Helena Premium Outlets
www.premiumoutlets.com
Address 3111 N St. Helena Hwy *Phone* 707-226-9876 *Hours* Mon-Sun 10-6 *Location* Northern California, north of Napa. The center is two miles north of downtown St. Helena, on Hwy 29.

STORES
- Brooks Brothers (1)
- Coach (2)
- Donna Karan (1)
- Escada Company Store (1)
- Jones New York (1)
- Movado (2)
- Spirits In Stone Gallery (5)
- Sunglass Outlet (3)
- Tumi (2)

28   TRACY

28A • Prime Outlets Tracy
www.primeoutlets.com
Address 1005 Pescadero Dr *Phone* 209-833-1895 *Hours* Mon-Sat 10-

8, Sun 10-6 *Location* Northern California, one hour east of San Francisco. Head east from San Francisco on I-580 to I-205 east. The center is at the last Tracy exit, MacArthur Drive.

STORES

- Bass (1)
- Big Dogs (1)
- Bon Worth (1)
- Casual Corner (1)
- Casual Male Big & Tall (1)
- Corning Revere (4)
- Dress Barn (1)
- Factory Brand Shoes (1)
- Famous Brands Housewares (4)
- GNC (8)
- Leather Mode (2)
- Levi's Outlet by Most (1)
- Liz Claiborne (1)
- Mikasa (4)
- Nine West (1)
- OshKosh B'Gosh (1)
- Paper Factory (9)
- Perfumania (8)
- Picture Perfect (4)
- Publishers Warehouse (5)
- Reebok (1)
- Rockport (1)
- Rue 21 (1)
- Samsonite (2)
- Shoe Pavilion (1)
- Software Outlet (7)
- Sony (4)
- Stoud's Linen (4)
- Toys Etc (6)
- Van Heusen (1)
- Vans Shoes (1)

EATS & TREATS

- LA Deli & Espresso (11)

29 TULARE

29A • Horizon Outlet Center
www.horizongroup.com
Address 1407 Retherford St *Phone* 559-684-9091 *Hours* Mon-Sat 10-8, Sun 10-6 *Location* Between

Fresno and Bakersfield. Take Hwy 63 east off Hwy 99.

STORES

- AT&T Wireless (7)
- Bass (1)
- Big Dogs (1)
- Claire's Boutique (3)
- Corning Revere (4)
- Country Clutter (4)
- Dress Barn (1)
- Factory Brand Shoes (1)
- Gap Outlet (1)
- Greetings 'n More (5)
- Kitchen Collection (4)
- L'eggs Hanes Bali Playtex (1)
- Linen Barn (4)
- Mikasa (4)
- OshKosh B'Gosh (1)
- PacSun (1)
- Perfumania (8)
- Polo Ralph Lauren (1)
- Publishers Warehouse (5)
- Quiksilver (1)
- Reebok (1)
- Rue 21 (1)
- Samsonite (2)
- Shoe Pavilion (1)
- Styles For Less (1)
- Sunglass Hut (3)
- Van Heusen (1)
- Vitamin World (8)
- Welcome Home (4)
- Zales The Diamond Store (3)

EATS & TREATS

- Auntie Anne's Pretzals (10)
- Rocky Mountain Chocolate (10)

30 VACAVILLE

30A • Factory Stores at Vacaville
www.chelseafactoryoutlets.com
Address 321-2 Nut Tree Rd *Phone* 707-447-5755 *Hours* Mon-Sat 10-8, Sun 10-6 *Location* Midway between San Francisco and Sacramento off I-80. Westbound travelers take Monte Vista Ave and turn right. Turn right on Nut Tree

Rd and follow to center. I-80 eastbound take Nut Tree Rd exit and turn right. Follow to center, which is on your right.

STORES

- Adidas (1)
- Ashworth (1)
- Bass (1)
- Bath & Body Works (8)
- Beeswax Candles (5)
- Big & Tall Factory Store (1)
- Big Dogs (1)
- Black & Decker (4)
- Black Hills Gold (3)
- Book Market (5)
- Book Warehouse (5)
- Boot Factory (1)
- California Luggage (2)
- Carter's Childrenswear (1)
- Casual Corner (1)
- Chico's (1)
- Christian Supply (5)
- Claire's Accessories (3)
- Clothestime (1)
- Corning Revere (4)
- Country Clutter (4)
- Danskin (1)
- Designer Brands Accessories (2)
- Designer Fragrance/Cosmetics (8)
- Diamonds Direct (3)
- Dress Barn (1)
- Dress Barn Woman (1)
- Easy Spirit (1)
- Eddie Bauer (1)
- Etienne Aigner (1)
- Factory Brand Shoes (1)
- Famous Brand Electronics (4)
- Famous Brands Housewares (4)
- Famous Footwear (1)
- Farberware (4)
- Florsheim (1)
- Full Size Fashions (1)
- Gap Outlet (1)
- Geoffrey Beene (1)
- Georgiou Outlet (1)
- Haggar (1)
- Harry & David (5)
- Hit or Miss (1)
- Home Again (4)
- Izod (1)
- Jelly Belly Store (9)
- Jockey (1)
- Johari's Aki (1)
- Johnston & Murphy (1)
- Kitchen Collection (4)
- Koret (1)
- Le Creuset (4)
- Leather Loft (2)
- L'eggs Hanes Bali Playtex (1)
- Lenox (4)
- Levi's Outlet by Most (1)
- Liz Claiborne Shoes (1)
- London Fog (1)
- Luggage Center (2)
- Mikasa (4)
- Motherhood Maternity (1)
- Music For A Song (5)
- Naturalizer (1)
- Nike (1)
- Nine West (1)
- Oneida (4)
- OshKosh B'Gosh (1)
- Paper Outlet (9)
- Paper Plus (9)
- Perfumania (8)
- Petite Sophisticate (1)
- Pfaltzgraff (4)
- Reebok (1)
- Remington (4)
- Royal Doulton (4)
- Rue 21 (1)
- Samsonite (2)
- San Francisco Music Box (9)
- Sanrio (9)
- Shoe Pavilion (1)
- Socks Galore (1)
- Software Outlet (7)
- Springmaid Wamsutta (4)
- Stoud's Linen (4)
- Styles For Less (1)
- Sunbeam & Oster (4)
- Sunglass Hut (3)
- Totes / Sunglass World (3)
- Toy Liquidators (6)
- Van Heusen (1)
- Vans Shoes (1)
- VF Factory Outlet (1)
- Vitamin World (8)
- Westport Limited (1)
- Westport Woman (1)
- ZapCity Laser Games (9)

EATS & TREATS

- A & W Restaurant (11)
- California Food Court (11)
- Rocky Mountain Chocolate (10)

Colorado

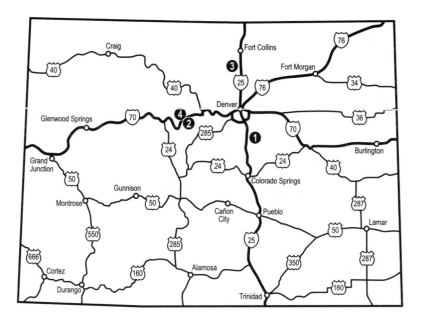

1   CASTLE ROCK

1A • Prime Outlets Castle Rock

www.primeoutlets.com
Address 5050 Factory Shops Blvd
Phone 800-245-8351 *Hours* Mon-Sat 10-9, Sun 11-6 *Location* Fifteen minutes south of Denver off I-25, exit 184 (Meadows Parkway / Founders Parkway), and turn right.

STORES

- Ann Taylor (1)
- Anne Klein (1)
- Bass (1)
- Bath & Body Works (8)
- Big Dogs (1)
- Blowout Video (9)
- Bombay Outlet (4)
- Book Warehouse (5)
- Brooks Brothers (1)
- Bugle Boy (1)
- Calendar Club (5)
- Calvin Klein (1)
- Camp Coleman (6)
- Carter's Childrenswear (1)
- Casual Corner (1)
- Casual Corner Woman (1)
- Casual Male Big & Tall (1)
- Chicago Cutlery (4)
- Claire's Accessories (3)
- Coach (2)
- Cole-Haan (1)
- Corning Revere (4)
- Cost Cutters Salon (8)
- Country Clutter (4)
- Danskin (1)
- Dockers Outlet by Most (1)
- Dress Barn (1)
- Eddie Bauer (1)
- Etienne Aigner (1)
- Factory Brand Shoes (1)
- Famous Brands Housewares (4)
- Fanzz (1)
- Farberware (4)
- Forget Me Not by American Greetings (5)
- Fossil (2)
- Fresh Produce (1)
- From the Woods (4)
- Gap Outlet (1)
- Geoffrey Beene (1)
- Global Wireless (7)
- Grace Christian Bookstore (5)
- Great Outdoor Clothing (1)
- Guess? (1)
- Haggar (1)
- Harry & David (5)
- Hartstrings (1)
- Heritage Lace (4)
- Hoover Outlet (4)
- Hush Puppies & Family (1)
- Izod (1)
- Jeffrey Rein Gallery (9)
- Jockey (1)
- Jones New York Country (1)
- Kitchen Collection (4)
- Koret (1)
- Leather Mode (2)
- L'eggs Hanes Bali Playtex (1)
- Levi's Outlet by Most (1)
- Maidenform (1)
- Maternity Works (1)
- Mikasa (4)
- Music 4 Less (5)
- Musician's Choice (5)
- Napier (2)
- Naturalizer (1)
- Nautica (1)
- Nike (1)
- Nine West (1)
- Off 5th-Saks Fifth Avenue (1)
- Olga Warner (1)
- Oneida (4)
- OshKosh B'Gosh (1)
- Pacific Sunwear (1)
- Paper Factory (9)
- Perfumania (8)
- Petite Sophisticate (1)
- Pfaltzgraff (4)
- Phones Plus (7)
- Quiksilver (1)
- Reebok (1)
- Remington (4)
- Robert Scott & David Brooks (1)
- Royal Doulton (4)
- Rue 21 (1)
- Rug Decor (4)
- Samsonite (2)
- Samsonite At Work (2)
- Santa Fe Collection (1)
- SAS Factory Shoes (1)
- Scrubs Select (1)
- Silverheels Jewelry (3)
- Socks Galore (1)
- Sony (4)
- Springmaid Wamsutta (4)
- St Nick's (9)
- Stillwaters (4)

- Stone Mountain (2)
- Sunee Wig Botik (8)
- Sunglass Outfitters (3)
- Sunglass Outlet (3)
- Times Square Clothing (1)
- Tommy Hilfiger (1)
- Tools 4 Less (9)
- Totes Isotoner Sunglass World (3)
- Toy Liquidators (6)
- Ultra Diamond & Gold (3)
- Van Heusen (1)
- Vans Shoes (1)
- VF Factory Outlet (1)
- Villeroy & Boch (4)
- Vitamin World (8)
- Watch Station (3)
- Waterford Wedgwood (4)
- Welcome Home (4)
- Wilson's Leather (1)
- Woolrich (1)
- Ye Olde Shoppe (9)
- Zales The Diamond Store (3)

EATS & TREATS

- Branding Iron BBQ (11)
- Burger King (11)
- Chinese Combo Express (11)
- CinnaMonster (10)
- Gloria Jean's Gourmet Coffee (10)
- Great Steak & Potato (11)
- Rocky Mountain Chocolate (10)
- Subway (11)
- Taco Bell (11)
- Ultimo Espresso (10)
- Villa Pizza (11)

2 DILLON

2A • Dillon Factory Stores
Address 765 Anemone Trail *Phone* 303-938-9946 *Hours* Mon-Sat 10-7, Sun 10-6 *Location* West of Denver, near Frisco. From I-70 take exit 205, two blocks east to Anemone Trail.

STORES

- Coach (2)
- Donna Karan (1)
- Flapdoodles (1)
- Nautica (1)
- Sunglass Hut (3)
- Timberland (1)

3 LOVELAND

3A • Prime Outlets Loveland
www.primeoutlets.com
Address 5661 McWhinney Blvd *Phone* 888-255-1273 *Hours* Mon-Sat 10-9, Sun 11-6 *Location* Thirty miles east of Rocky Mountain National Park. I-25 at US 34, exit 257B.

STORES

- Airwalk (1)
- Amish Furniture Showcase (4)
- Bass (1)
- Bear's Den (4)
- Beds "r" Us (4)
- Big Dogs (1)
- Book Warehouse (5)
- Bose Factory Store (4)
- Camp Coleman (6)
- Carter's Childrenswear (1)
- Casual Corner (1)
- Casual Corner Woman (1)
- Casual Male Big & Tall (1)
- Claire's Accessories (3)
- Concepts Direct (4)
- Corning Revere (4)
- Cost Cutters Salon (8)
- Dansk (4)
- Dress Barn (1)
- Dress Barn Woman (1)
- Enchanted Gardens and Gifts (5)
- Esprit (1)
- Factory Brand Shoes (1)
- Famous Brands Housewares (4)
- Farberware (4)
- Florsheim (1)
- Fossil (2)
- Full Size Fashions (1)
- Gems 'n Gold (3)
- Geoffrey Beene (1)
- Great Outdoor Clothing (1)
- Haggar (1)
- Harry & David (5)
- Izod (1)
- J Crew (1)
- Jockey (1)
- KB Toys (6)
- Kitchen Collection (4)
- Koret (1)
- Leather Loft (2)
- Leather Mode (2)
- L'eggs Hanes Bali Playtex (1)

- Lenox (4)
- Levi's Outlet by Most (1)
- Liz Claiborne (1)
- Maidenform (1)
- Michael Ricker Pewter (9)
- Mikasa (4)
- Music For A Song (5)
- Naturalizer (1)
- OshKosh B'Gosh (1)
- Paper Outlet (9)
- Petite Sophisticate (1)
- Pfaltzgraff (4)
- Phones Plus (7)
- Reebok (1)
- Rockport (1)
- Rocky Mountain Perfumery (8)
- Rue 21 (1)
- Samsonite (2)
- SAS Factory Shoes (1)
- Spiegel Outlet (1)
- Sports Fans (6)
- Springmaid Wamsutta (4)
- Sunee Wig Botik (8)
- Sunglass Hut (3)
- Tommy Hilfiger (1)
- Totes / Sunglass World (3)
- Ultra Diamond & Gold (3)
- Van Heusen (1)
- Vitamin World (8)
- Welcome Home (4)

EATS & TREATS

- Dairy Queen / Orange Julius (11)
- East Coast Pizza (11)
- Rocky Mountain Chocolate (10)

4 SILVERTHORNE

4A • Silverthorne Factory Stores
Address 145 Stephens Way *Phone* 970-468-9440 *Hours* Mon-Sat 10-8, Sun 10-6 *Location* West of Denver, near Frisco. From Denver travel west on I-70 to exit 205, Silverthorne / Dillon exit.

STORES

- Ashworth (1)
- Banister Shoes (1)
- Bass (1)
- Big Dogs (1)
- Book Discounters (5)
- Calvin Klein / Olga Warner's (1)

- Camp Coleman (6)
- Carter's Childrenswear (1)
- Casual Corner (1)
- Claire's Boutique (3)
- Colorado Hat (1)
- Corral West Ranchwear (1)
- Cosmetics Company Store (8)
- Crabtree & Evelyn (5)
- Dansk (4)
- Denby (9)
- Dexter Shoe (1)
- Dress Barn (1)
- Eddie Bauer (1)
- Famous Brands Housewares (4)
- Farberware (4)
- Gap Outlet (1)
- Geoffrey Beene (1)
- Great Outdoor Clothing (1)
- Haggar (1)
- Harry & David (5)
- Izod (1)
- J Crew (1)
- Jockey (1)
- Jones New York Career (1)
- Jones New York Country (1)
- Jones New York Sport (1)
- Le Creuset (4)
- Leather Loft (2)
- L'eggs Hanes Bali Playtex (1)
- Levi's Outlet by Most (1)
- Liz Claiborne (1)
- Maidenform (1)
- Mikasa (4)
- Nike (1)
- Nine West (1)
- OshKosh B'Gosh (1)
- Pearl Izumi (1)
- Perfumania (8)
- Petite Sophisticate (1)
- Pfaltzgraff (4)
- Rue 21 (1)
- Samsonite (2)
- Sunglass Broker (3)
- Tommy Hilfiger (1)
- Totes / Sunglass World (3)
- Van Heusen (1)
- Vitamin World (8)
- Watch Works (3)
- Welcome Home (4)
- Ye Olde Family Name (9)

EATS & TREATS

- Barney's Café / CinnaMonster (11)
- Dotes Café (11)
- Rocky Mountain Chocolate (10)

Connecticut

1 • Clinton
2 • Westbrook

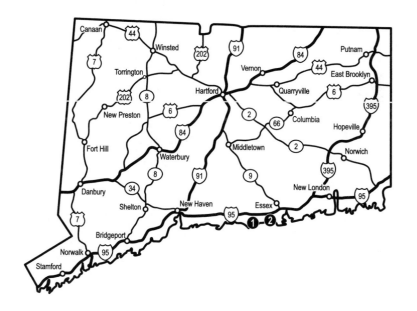

1   CLINTON

1A • Clinton Crossing Premium Outlets

www.premiumoutlets.com
Address 20-A Killingworth Tpk
Phone 860-664-0700 **Hours** Mon-Sat 10-9, Sun 10-6 **Location** Just 20 miles east of New Haven on I-95, exit 63.

STORES

- Anne Klein (1)
- Barneys New York (1)
- Bass (1)
- BCBG Max Azria (1)
- Bombay Outlet (4)
- Book Warehouse (5)
- Bose Factory Store (4)
- Bostonian Clarks (1)
- Brooks Brothers (1)
- Calvin Klein (1)
- Coach (2)
- Cole-Haan (1)
- Cosmetics Company Store (8)
- Crate & Barrel (4)
- Danskin (1)
- Donna Karan (1)
- Dooney & Bourke (2)
- Dress Barn (1)
- Escada Company Store (1)
- Etienne Aigner (1)
- Fila (1)
- Fossil (2)
- Gap Outlet (1)
- Geoffrey Beene (1)
- Harry & David (5)
- Izod (1)
- Jones New York (1)
- Jones New York Country (1)
- Jones New York Men (1)
- Jones New York Sport (1)
- Kasper ASL (1)
- Kenneth Cole (1)
- Le Creuset (4)
- Le Gourmet Chef (4)
- Lenox (4)
- Little Big Dogs (1)
- Liz Claiborne (1)
- Liz Claiborne Shoes (1)
- Maidenform (1)
- Malo (1)
- Mikasa (4)
- Nautica (1)
- Nike (1)
- Nine West (1)
- Off 5th-Saks Fifth Avenue (1)
- Panasonic (4)
- Perfumania (8)
- Perry Ellis (1)
- Polo Jeans Co (1)
- Polo Ralph Lauren (1)
- Quiksilver (1)
- Ralph Lauren Home (4)
- Reed & Barton (4)
- Royal Doulton (4)
- So Fun! Kids (1)
- Sunglasses USA (3)
- Tommy Hilfiger (1)
- Van Heusen (1)
- Versace (1)
- Waterford Wedgwood (4)
- WestPoint Stevens (4)
- Zales The Diamond Store (3)

EATS & TREATS

- Bristol Café (11)
- Food Court (11)
- Fuzziwig's Candy Factory (10)
- Rocky Mountain Chocolate (10)

2   WESTBROOK

2A • Westbrook Factory Stores

www.shopwestbrook.com
Address 314 Flat Rock Pl **Phone** 860-399-8656 **Hours** Jan-Mar: Mon-Wed 10-6, Thu-Sat 10-9, Sun 11-6. Apr-Dec: Mon-Sat 10-9, Sun 11-6 **Location** Midway between New Haven and New London off I-95. From I-95 take exit 65, go south to Flat Rock Place and turn left. The center is straight ahead.

STORES

- Bargain Books (5)
- Bass (1)
- Big & Tall Factory Store (1)
- Big Dog Sportswear (1)

- Black & Decker (4)
- Bon Worth (1)
- Carter's For Kids (1)
- Casual Corner (1)
- Casual Corner Woman (1)
- Claire's Accessories (3)
- Corning Revere (4)
- Cost Cutters Salon (8)
- Craftworks (4)
- Dockers Outlet (1)
- Dress Barn (1)
- Dress Barn Woman (1)
- Easy Spirit (1)
- Eddie Bauer (1)
- Factory Brand Shoes (1)
- Famous Brands Housewares (4)
- Haggar (1)
- J Crew (1)
- Jockey (1)
- Kitchen Collection (4)
- Leather Loft (2)
- L'eggs Hanes Bali Playtex (1)
- Levi's (1)
- Madison Furniture Barn (4)
- Maternity Works (1)
- Music For A Song (5)
- Naturalizer (1)
- Nautica Jeans (1)
- Nine West (1)
- Old Navy (1)
- Oneida (4)
- O'Neil's Westbrook Cinema 12 (9)
- OshKosh B'Gosh (1)
- Paper Factory (9)
- Petite Sophisticate (1)
- Pfaltzgraff (4)
- Reebok (1)
- Remington (4)
- Rockport (1)
- Rue 21 (1)
- Samsonite (2)
- Soccer Mainea (1)
- Springmaid Wamsutta (4)
- Sunglass Hut (3)
- TAG Menswear / Enro (1)
- Timberland (1)
- Time Factory Watch (3)
- Totes / Sunglass World (3)
- Toy Liquidators (6)
- Ultra Fine Jewelry (3)
- US Post Office (9)
- Van Heusen (1)
- VF Factory Outlet (1)
- Vitamin World (8)
- Welcome Home (4)

- Woolrich (1)

Eats & Treats
- BW's Coffee Station (10)
- Rocky Mountain Chocolate (10)

Delaware

1 • Rehoboth Beach
2 • Wilmington

1 REHOBOTH BEACH

1A • Rehoboth Outlets
www.shoprehoboth.com
Address 1600 Ocean Outlets *Phone*
302-226-9223 or 888-Shop333
Hours Jan-Apr: Sun-Thu 10-6, Fri-
Sat 10-9. May-Dec: Mon-Sat 10-
9, Sun 10-6 *Location* On the
eastern shore less than 2 miles from
the ocean. Follow Route 1 to
Rehoboth Beach. The outlets
consists of three shopping centers
located near each other on Rt 1.

STORES
- Ann Taylor (1)
- Athlete by Vernon Powell (1)
- Athlete's Foot (1)
- Banana Republic (1)
- Banister Shoes (1)
- Bass (1)
- Big Dog Sportswear (1)
- Black & Decker (4)
- Bon Worth (1)
- Book Cellar (5)
- Book Warehouse (5)
- Bose Factory Store (4)
- Britches (1)
- Brooks Brothers (1)
- California Sunshine Shops (1)
- Carter's Childrenswear (1)
- Casual Corner (1)
- Casual Corner Woman (1)
- Christmas Goose LTD (9)
- Christmas Tree Hill (9)
- Claiborne Menswear (1)
- Claire's Accessories (3)
- Coach (2)
- Coastal Cotton (1)
- Corning Revere (4)
- Cosmetics Company Store (8)
- Craftworks (4)
- Creative Impressions (9)
- Danskin (1)
- Designer Fragrance/Cosmetics (8)
- Dexter Shoe (1)
- Disney Catalog Outlet (5)
- Dockers Outlet (1)
- Donna Karan (1)

- Dress Barn (1)
- Dress Barn Woman (1)
- Eddie Bauer (1)
- Enzo Angiolini (1)
- Etienne Aigner (1)
- Factory Brand Shoes (1)
- Famous Brands Housewares (4)
- Fragrance Outlet (8)
- Gap Outlet (1)
- Geoffrey Beene (1)
- GNC (8)
- Gold Mine (3)
- Greetings 'n More (5)
- Guess? (1)
- Haggar (1)
- Harley Davidson Outlet (9)
- Harry & David (5)
- Hartstrings (1)
- Hush Puppies & Family (1)
- Izod (1)
- J Crew (1)
- Jockey (1)
- Jones New York (1)
- Jones New York Country (1)
- Jones New York Sport (1)
- Kasper ASL (1)
- KB Toys (6)
- Khalsa Jewelry (3)
- Kitchen Collection (4)
- Koret (1)
- L.L. Bean Factory Store (1)
- Leather Loft (2)
- L'eggs Hanes Bali Playtex (1)
- Lenox (4)
- Levi's (1)
- Lillian Vernon (9)
- Little Big Dogs (1)
- Little Me (1)
- Liz Claiborne (1)
- Liz Claiborne Shoes (1)
- London Fog (1)
- Lots of Linens (4)
- Lucia (1)
- M R Ducks (1)
- Maidenform (1)
- Midwest Feather & Down (4)
- Mikasa (4)
- Music For A Song (5)
- Naturalizer (1)
- Nautica (1)
- Nike (1)
- Nine West (1)
- Old Navy (1)
- Olga Warner (1)
- Oneida (4)

- OshKosh B'Gosh (1)
- Pacific Sunwear (1)
- Paper Factory (9)
- Pepper's (9)
- Perfumania (8)
- Perry Ellis (1)
- Petite Sophisticate (1)
- Pfaltzgraff (4)
- Polo Ralph Lauren (1)
- Rack Room Shoes (1)
- Reebok (1)
- Rockport (1)
- Royal Doulton (4)
- Rue 21 (1)
- Samsonite (2)
- Samsonite Travel Expo (2)
- SAS Factory Shoes (1)
- So Fun! Kids (1)
- Soccer Mainea (1)
- Socks Galore (1)
- Springmaid Wamsutta (4)
- Stride Rite Keds Sperry (1)
- Sunglass Hut (3)
- Terrific Toys (6)
- Timberland (1)
- Tommy Hilfiger (1)
- Totes / Sunglass World (3)
- Van Heusen (1)
- Vans Shoes (1)
- VF Factory Outlet (1)
- Virginia Metal Crafters (4)
- Vitamin World (8)
- Waterford Wedgwood (4)
- Westport Limited (1)
- Wicker Outlet (4)
- Wilson's Leather (1)

EATS & TREATS
- Applebee's (11)
- Bull on the Beach (11)
- Candy Kitchen Shoppes (10)
- Coffee Beanery (10)
- Grotto Food Court (11)
- Hot Diggity Dogs (11)
- Rocky Mountain Chocolate (10)

2 WILMINGTON

2A • Shipyard Shops
Address 900 S Madison St *Phone*
302-425-5000 *Hours* Jan-Apr:
Mon-Thu 10-6, Fri-Sat 10-9, Sun

11-5. May-Dec: Mon-Sat 10-9,
Sun 11-5 *Location* Minutes from
downtown Wilmington. Traveling
north on I-95 take exit 6 to Martin
Luther King Blvd, turn right onto
South Madison St. Follow black
and red signs to Riverfront and
Shipyards Shops.

STORES
- Big Dog Sportswear (1)
- Blair Catalog Outlet (1)
- Claire's Accessories (3)
- Coldwater Creek Outlet (1)
- Dress Barn (1)
- Dress Barn Woman (1)
- Factory Brand Shoes (1)
- Freeport Studio (4)
- Haband (1)
- L.L. Bean Factory Store (1)
- L'eggs Hanes Bali Playtex (1)
- Lillian Vernon (9)
- Nautica (1)
- Newport News Outlet (5)
- Totes Isotoner Sunglass World (3)
- WestPoint Stevens (4)

EATS & TREATS
- Molly's Ice Cream & Deli (11)
- Timothy's Riverfront Restaurant (11)

Florida

1 • Clearwater

2 • Destin

3 • Ellenton

4 • Estero

5 • Florida City

6 • Fort Myers

7 • Graceville

8 • Kissimmee

9 • Naples

10 • Orlando

11 • Saint Augustine

12 • Sunrise

13 • Vero Beach

1 CLEARWATER

1A • Crossroads Mall

www.crossroadsmallclearwater.com
Address 15579 US 19 N *Phone* 727-524-6540 *Hours* Mon-Sat 10-9, Sun 12-6 *Location* From Central Saint Petersburg take I-275 north to exit 16. Turn left and follow Rt 686 west towards Largo. Pass airport and go 2 miles to stoplight. Center is on your left.

STORES

- Bass (1)
- Beall's Outlet (1)
- Bobby Allison Cellular (7)
- Bon Worth (1)
- Casual Male Big & Tall (1)
- Claire's Accessories (3)
- Clothestime (1)
- Creations DKDA (1)
- Dexter Shoe (1)
- Dockside Imports (9)
- Dollar World (5)
- Dress Barn (1)
- Famous Footwear (1)
- Funny Farm (1)
- GNC (8)
- Jewelry Time (3)
- JIBAC Art & Framing (4)
- Kitchen Collection (4)
- Lasting Impressions (5)
- L'eggs Hanes Bali Playtex (1)
- Mis Young Fashions (1)
- Music 4 Less (5)
- MyGiftCottage.com (5)
- Nails Etc. (8)
- Optical Outlet (3)
- Pants Towne (1)
- Paper Factory (9)
- Premier Communications (7)
- Quik-Fix Jewelers (3)
- Rack Room Shoes (1)
- Reader's Outlet (5)
- Ross Dress for Less (1)
- Samsonite (2)
- Silky Beauty Supply (8)
- Simplicity (9)
- Sports Locker (6)
- Sunglass Hut (3)
- Swim Mart (1)
- Tee To Green (6)
- TJ Maxx (1)
- Today's Woman (1)
- Toy Liquidators (6)
- USA Gold & Silver (3)
- Van Heusen (1)
- Vitamin World (8)
- W&J Cards (5)

EATS & TREATS

- Chinese Egg Roll King (11)
- Granny's Country Kitchen (11)
- Havana Street Café (11)
- Mama's Italian Pizzeria (11)
- Mr Beans Coffee & Creams (10)
- Perry Scope's Sub Station (11)
- Uncle Sam's American Bar-B-Q (11)

2 DESTIN

2A • Silver Sands Factory Stores

www.silversandsfactorystores.com
Address 10562 Emerald Coast Pkwy W *Phone* 800-510-6255 or 850-654-9771 *Hours* Mon-Sat 10-9, Sun 10-6 *Location* Between Pensacola and Panama City, east of Fort Walton Beach. From Destin travel 8 miles east on Hwy 98.

STORES

- Allen Edmonds (1)
- Ann Taylor (1)
- Anne Klein (1)
- Baby Gap (1)
- Bally Outlet (1)
- Bass (1)
- Big Dog Sportswear (1)
- Black & Decker (4)
- Bose Factory Store (4)
- Brooks Brothers (1)
- Calvin Klein (1)
- Carter's For Kids (1)
- Coach (2)
- Cole-Haan (1)
- Cosmetics Company Store (8)
- Dansk (4)
- Danskin (1)
- Designer Fragrance/Cosmetics (8)
- Dockers Outlet (1)
- Donna Karan (1)
- Dooney & Bourke (2)

- Duck Head (1)
- Eagle's Eye (1)
- Eagle's Eye Ladies (1)
- Ellen Tracy (1)
- Etienne Aigner (1)
- Famous Brands Housewares (4)
- Famous Footwear (1)
- Fossil (2)
- Gap Kids (1)
- Gap Outlet (1)
- Geoffrey Beene (1)
- GNC (8)
- Greg Norman (1)
- Haggar (1)
- Harry & David (5)
- Hartman Factory Store (2)
- Hartstrings (1)
- Il Gelato (9)
- Izod (1)
- J Crew (1)
- Jockey (1)
- Johnston & Murphy (1)
- Jones New York (1)
- Jones New York Country (1)
- Jones New York Men (1)
- Jones New York Sport (1)
- Kasper ASL (1)
- KB Toys (6)
- Kenneth Cole (1)
- L'eggs Hanes Bali Playtex (1)
- Lenox (4)
- Levi's (1)
- Linens by Dan River (4)
- Liz & Jane Clothes (1)
- Liz Claiborne Shoes (1)
- Maidenform (1)
- Maternity Works (1)
- Mikasa (4)
- Movado (2)
- Music 4 Less (5)
- Nap Outlet (9)
- Naturalizer (1)
- Nautica (1)
- New York Jewelry Outlet (3)
- Nike (1)
- Nine West (1)
- Oneida (4)
- OshKosh B'Gosh (1)
- PacSun (1)
- Paper Factory (9)
- Perry Ellis (1)
- Pfaltzgraff (4)
- Polo Jeans Co (1)
- Polo Ralph Lauren (1)
- Publishers Warehouse (5)

- Reebok (1)
- Robert Scott & David Brooks (1)
- Rockport (1)
- Socks Galore (1)
- Springmaid Wamsutta (4)
- Stone Mountain (2)
- Strasburg Children (1)
- Stride Rite Keds Sperry (1)
- Sunglass Hut (3)
- Timberland (1)
- Tommy Hilfiger (1)
- Umbro (1)
- Van Heusen (1)
- Vans Shoes (1)
- Welcome Home (4)
- WestPoint Stevens (4)
- Westport Limited (1)
- Westport Woman (1)
- Woolrich (1)

EATS & TREATS

- Morgan's (11)
- Mrs Fields Cookies (10)
- Rocky Mountain Chocolate (10)

3   ELLENTON

3A • Prime Outlets Ellenton
www.primeoutlets.com
Address 5461 Factory Shops Blvd
Phone 888-260-7608 *Hours* Mon-
Sat 10-9, Sun 11-6 *Location* Thirty
miles south of Tampa. From I-75
take exit 43, head east two blocks
to 60th Ave, turn left.

STORES

- Ann Taylor (1)
- Anne Klein (1)
- Bag & Baggage (2)
- Bass (1)
- Big Dogs (1)
- Black & Decker (4)
- Book Warehouse (5)
- Bose Factory Store (4)
- Bostonian Clarks (1)
- Brooks Brothers (1)
- Bruce Alan Bags (2)
- Casual Corner (1)
- Chicago Cutlery (4)
- Chico's (1)
- Claiborne Menswear (1)

- Claire's Accessories (3)
- Coach (2)
- Coastal Cotton (1)
- Corning Revere (4)
- Cosmetics Company Store (8)
- Cost Cutters Salon (8)
- Dalton Rug (4)
- Dana Buchman (1)
- Danskin (1)
- Designer Brands Accessories (2)
- Designer Fragrance/Cosmetics (8)
- Dexter Shoe (1)
- DKNY Jeans (1)
- Donna Karan (1)
- Dress Barn/Dress Barn Woman (1)
- Easy Spirit (1)
- Elisabeth (1)
- Ellen Tracy (1)
- Escada Company Store (1)
- Etienne Aigner (1)
- Factory Brand Shoes (1)
- Famous Brands Housewares (4)
- Farberware (4)
- Fine Jewelry & Watches (3)
- Florsheim (1)
- Fragrance Outlet (8)
- Gap Outlet (1)
- Geoffrey Beene (1)
- Geoffrey Beene Ladies (1)
- Golf Manufacturer's Outlet (6)
- Haggar (1)
- Harry & David (5)
- Hartstrings (1)
- Home Style (4)
- Izod (1)
- Jockey (1)
- Jones New York Woman (1)
- Kasper ASL (1)
- KB Toys (6)
- Kipling (2)
- Kitchen Collection (4)
- Le Creuset (4)
- Le Gourmet Chef (4)
- L'eggs Hanes Bali Playtex (1)
- Levi's (1)
- Liz Claiborne (1)
- Liz Claiborne Shoes (1)
- Louis Feraud Paris (1)
- Maidenform (1)
- Mark, Fore & Strike Catalog Outlet (1)
- Mikasa (4)
- Motherhood Maternity (1)
- Movado (2)
- Music For A Song (5)
- Napier (2)

- Naturalizer (1)
- Nautica (1)
- Nike (1)
- Nine West (1)
- Off 5th-Saks Fifth Avenue (1)
- OshKosh B'Gosh (1)
- PacSun (1)
- Paper Factory (9)
- Perfumania (8)
- Perry Ellis (1)
- Petite Sophisticate (1)
- Pfaltzgraff (4)
- Polo Ralph Lauren (1)
- Quiksilver (1)
- Rack Room Shoes (1)
- Ralph Lauren Footwear (1)
- Reebok (1)
- Remington (4)
- Rockport (1)
- Royal Doulton (4)
- Rue 21 (1)
- S & K Menswear (1)
- Samsonite (2)
- SAS Factory Shoes (1)
- Saucony (1)
- SBX (1)
- Seiko (3)
- Springmaid Wamsutta (4)
- Sunglass Hut / Watch Station (3)
- Swank (2)
- Swim Mart (1)
- Time Factory Watch (3)
- Tommy Hilfiger (1)
- Totes Isotoner Sunglass World (3)
- Ultra Diamond & Gold (3)
- Unisa (1)
- Van Heusen (1)
- Versace (1)
- VF Factory Outlet (1)
- Villeroy & Boch (4)
- Vitamin World (8)
- Warnaco (1)
- Waterford Wedgwood (4)
- Welcome Home (4)
- Wilson's Leather (1)
- Zales The Diamond Store (3)

EATS & TREATS
- Bakery Shop (11)
- Burger Works (11)
- Joffrey's Coffee Co (10)
- New Orleans Grill (11)
- Old El Paso Café (11)
- Rocky Mountain Chocolate (10)
- Sweet Shoppe (10)

- Villa Pizza (11)
- Vittles (11)
- Wok Master (11)

4 ESTERO

4A • Miromar Outlets

www.euraminc.com/miromar
Address 10801 Corkscrew Rd
Phone 941-948-3766 *Hours* Mon-Sat 10-9, Sun 11-6 *Location*
Southwest Florida between Naples and Fort Myers. Take exit 19 (Corkscrew Rd) off I-75.

STORES

- Adidas (1)
- Bagmakers (2)
- Banister / Easy Spirit (1)
- Baron d'Orr Designer Jewelry (3)
- Bass (1)
- Beach House (1)
- Big & Tall Factory Store (1)
- Black & Decker (4)
- Bose Factory Store (4)
- Brooks Brothers (1)
- Calvin Klein Jeanswear (1)
- Carter's Childrenswear (1)
- Centex Homes (9)
- Chico's (1)
- Claire's Boutique (3)
- Coast Clutter (4)
- Coastal Cotton (1)
- Cole-Haan (1)
- Country Clutter (4)
- Croscill (4)
- Dress Barn (1)
- Fila (1)
- Florsheim (1)
- Forget Me Not by American Greetings (5)
- Fragrance Outlet (8)
- Geoffrey Beene (1)
- Haggar (1)
- Harry & David (5)
- Jockey (1)
- Lenox (4)
- Levi's (1)
- Maidenform (1)
- Marikita Home Decor (4)
- Music 4 Less (5)
- Nautica (1)

- Nike (1)
- OshKosh B'Gosh (1)
- Paper Factory (9)
- Perfumania (8)
- Perry Ellis (1)
- Picture Outlet (9)
- Polo Ralph Lauren (1)
- Pottery Row (4)
- Rack Room Shoes (1)
- Reebok (1)
- Rockport (1)
- Royal Doulton (4)
- Samsonite (2)
- Sheridan Australia Linens (4)
- St John Company Store (1)
- Sunglass Outlet (3)
- Sunworks (9)
- Time Factory Watch (3)
- Ultra Diamond & Gold (3)
- Victor Alexander Glass (4)
- Waves Music (5)
- Zales The Diamond Store (3)

EATS & TREATS

- Auntie Anne's Pretzals (10)
- Blue Heron Tropical Café (11)
- Don's Famous Hot Dog (11)
- Fabian's Pizzeria (11)
- La Bamba Mexican Restaurant (11)
- Luna Rossa Italian Restaurant (11)
- Ristorante Pasta Pasta (11)
- Rocky Mountain Chocolate (10)

5 FLORIDA CITY

5A • Prime Outlets Florida City

www.primeoutlets.com
Address 250 E Palm Dr *Phone* 305-248-4727 *Hours* Mon-Sat 10-9, Sun 11-6 *Location* South of Miami near Homestead. From Miami travel south on the Florida Turnpike to junction of US 1 in Florida City. Turn left on Palm Drive (SW 344th St).

STORES

- Baby B'Gosh (1)
- Bass (1)
- Battaglia Outlet (1)
- Beepers & Watches Plus (3)

- Big Dogs (1)
- Bugle Boy (1)
- Carter's For Kids (1)
- Claire's Boutique (3)
- Classic Characters (9)
- Cost Cutters Salon (8)
- Danskin (1)
- Dress Barn (1)
- Factory Brand Shoes (1)
- Famous Brands Housewares (4)
- Gap Outlet (1)
- Geoffrey Beene (1)
- Hush Puppies & Family (1)
- Izod (1)
- L'eggs Hanes Bali Playtex (1)
- Levi's (1)
- Lily of France (1)
- Mikasa (4)
- Music For A Song (5)
- New York Designe's Outlet (1)
- Nike (1)
- Nine West (1)
- OshKosh B'Gosh (1)
- Perfumania (8)
- Rack Room Shoes (1)
- Rue 21 (1)
- Samsonite (2)
- SAS Factory Shoes (1)
- Skate 2000 (9)
- Sunglass Hut (3)
- Totes / Sunglass World (3)
- Van Heusen (1)
- Vitamin World (8)
- Welcome Home (4)
- World Crafts (9)

Eats & Treats

- Freddie's Fresh Cup (10)
- Great Steak & Potato (11)
- Villa Pizza (11)

6 Fort Myers

6A • Tanger Ft. Myers
www.tangeroutlets.com
Address 20350 Summerlin Rd
Phone 888-471-3939 or 941-454-
1974 *Hours* Mon-Sat 10-9, Sun
11-6 *Location* Southern Florida
just minutes from the beaches.
From I-75 take exit 21, go west.
Take Daniels Pkwy to Summerlin

Rd, turn left and follow signs
toward Sanibel Island. The center
is on your right beyond intersection
of John Morris Rd.

Stores

- Bass (1)
- Big Dog Sportswear (1)
- Bon Worth (1)
- Caribbean Traders (1)
- Carter's Childrenswear (1)
- Claire's Accessories (3)
- Coach (2)
- Coastal Cotton (1)
- Corning Revere (4)
- Dexter Shoe (1)
- Dockers Outlet (1)
- Dress Barn (1)
- Elisabeth (1)
- Etienne Aigner (1)
- Factory Brand Shoes (1)
- Fieldcrest Cannon (4)
- Fossil (2)
- Gap Outlet (1)
- Geoffrey Beene (1)
- Gold Toe (1)
- Greg Norman (1)
- Izod (1)
- Jockey (1)
- Jones New York (1)
- Jones New York Sport (1)
- Kasper ASL (1)
- Kitchen Collection (4)
- Koret (1)
- L'eggs Hanes Bali Playtex (1)
- Levi's Outlet by Designs (1)
- Liz Claiborne (1)
- Maidenform (1)
- Mikasa (4)
- Naturalizer (1)
- OshKosh B'Gosh (1)
- Rack Room Shoes (1)
- Reebok (1)
- Reed & Barton (4)
- Rockport (1)
- Rue 21 (1)
- Samsonite (2)
- Sanibel Gems and Treasures (5)
- Sanibel Soap Factory (9)
- SAS Factory Shoes (1)
- Special Brands by Liz Claiborne (1)
- Swim Mart (1)
- Totes / Sunglass World (3)
- Van Heusen (1)

- Vitamin World (8)
- Wallet Works (2)
- Welcome Home (4)
- Zales The Diamond Store (3)

EATS & TREATS

- Fudgery (10)

7 GRACEVILLE

7A • Factory Stores of America
www.chelseafactoryoutlets.com
Address 950 Prim Ave *Phone* 850-263-3207 *Hours* Jan-Oct: Mon-Thu 9-7, Fri-Sat 9-8, Sun 12-6. Nov-Dec: Mon-Sat 9-8, Sun 12-6 *Location* Northwest Florida near Alabama border. From I-10 take exit 18 (Chipley), go north on Hwy 77 about 15 miles.

STORES

- Banister / Easy Spirit (1)
- Bon Worth (1)
- Brand Name Closeouts (1)
- Capacity (1)
- Corning Revere (4)
- Factory Brand Shoes (1)
- Ocean Graphics (9)
- Paper Factory (9)
- Van Heusen (1)
- VF Factory Outlet (1)

EATS & TREATS

- Dante's Café & Deli (11)

8 KISSIMMEE

8A • Kissimmee Value Outlet Shops
www.floridaoutlets.com
Address 4673 W Irlo Bronson Hwy (Hyw 192) *Phone* 407-396-8900 *Hours* Mon-Sat 10-9, Sun 11-5 *Location* Only 5 miles east of Disney World resort. From I-4 go east on Hwy192 to Kissimmee.

STORES

- Bon Worth (1)

- Brand Name Shoes (1)
- Capacity (1)
- Denim USA (1)
- Discount Tickets (9)
- Dress Barn (1)
- Nike (1)
- Publishers Outlet (5)
- Samsonite (2)
- Totes / Sunglass Station (3)
- Van Heusen (1)

EATS & TREATS

- Snax America (10)

9 NAPLES

9A • Prime Outlets Naples
www.primeoutlets.com
Address 6060 Collier Blvd *Phone* 888-545-7196 *Hours* Mon-Sat 10-8, Sun 11-6 *Location* Seven miles southeast of Naples. From I-75 take exit 15, go 8 miles south on Hwy 951. Center is on your left.

STORES

- Anne Klein (1)
- Bagmakers (2)
- Bass (1)
- Bon Worth (1)
- Capezio (1)
- Caribbean Traders (1)
- Claire's Boutique (3)
- Coach (2)
- Colours & Scents (8)
- Dalton Rug (4)
- Damon Enro (1)
- Dansk (4)
- Dress Barn (1)
- Etienne Aigner (1)
- Factory Brand Shoes (1)
- Fieldcrest Cannon (4)
- Geoffrey Beene (1)
- Harry & David (5)
- Island Gear (1)
- Izod (1)
- Jones New York (1)
- Kitchen Collection (4)
- L'eggs Hanes Bali Playtex (1)
- Liz Claiborne (1)
- Maidenform (1)
- Make-Up Scents (8)

- Mikasa (4)
- Pole Kat Golf (6)
- Pottery Connection (4)
- Publishers Warehouse (5)
- Quiet Storm (1)
- Rack Room Shoes (1)
- S & K Menswear (1)
- Samsonite (2)
- SAS Factory Shoes (1)
- Swim Mart (1)
- Totes Isotoner Sunglass Station (3)
- Van Heusen (1)
- Vitamin World (8)
- Welcome Home (4)

EATS & TREATS
- Mermaid Café (11)

10 ORLANDO

10A • Belz Designer Outlet Centre
www.belz.com
Address 5211 International Dr
Phone 407-352-3632 *Hours* Mon-
Sat 10-9, Sun 11-6 *Location* From
I-4 take exit 30A (Kirkman Rd),
go south to International Dr and
take a left.

STORES
- Ann Taylor (1)
- Anne Klein (1)
- Big Dog Sportswear (1)
- Bose Factory Store (4)
- Brooks Brothers (1)
- Casio (4)
- Coach (2)
- Cole-Haan (1)
- Danskin (1)
- Designer Fragrance/Cosmetics (8)
- Designer Jewelry (3)
- DKNY (1)
- Donna Karan (1)
- Esprit (1)
- Etienne Aigner (1)
- Fila (1)
- Fossil (2)
- Geoffrey Beene (1)
- Group USA (1)
- Guess? (1)
- Jones New York (1)
- Jones New York Country (1)

- Jones New York Sport (1)
- Kenneth Cole (1)
- Lenox (4)
- Liz Claiborne Shoes (1)
- Maternity Works (1)
- Max Studio (1)
- Movado (2)
- Nine West (1)
- Off 5th-Saks Fifth Avenue (1)
- Polo Ralph Lauren (1)
- SAS Factory Shoes (1)
- Stone Mountain (2)
- Sunglass Hut (3)
- Tools & More (9)
- Top Camera (7)
- Vitamin World (8)
- Waterford Wedgwood (4)
- WestPoint Pepperell (4)
- Zales The Diamond Store (3)

EATS & TREATS
- Gourmet Dippin Bread Café (11)
- Rocky Mountain Chocolate (10)

10B • Belz Factory Outlet World
www.belz.com
Address 5401 W Oak Ridge Rd
Phone 407-354-0126 or 407-352-
9611 *Hours* Mon-Sat 10-9, Sun
10-6 *Location* From I-4 take exit
30A (Kirkman Rd), go south to
International Dr and take a left.
Follow International Dr to Oak
Ridge Rd.

STORES
- $9.99 Stockroom (1)
- A & K Gift (5)
- Adidas (1)
- Bag & Baggage (2)
- Bass (1)
- Bible Factory Outlet (5)
- Birkenstock (1)
- Bon Worth (1)
- Books-A-Million (5)
- Burlington Brands (1)
- Buster Brown (1)
- Buy Best (8)
- Calvin Klein (1)
- Capers (1)
- Carter's Childrenswear (1)
- Casual Corner (1)

- Character Premier (1)
- Character Warehouse (1)
- Claire's Boutique (3)
- Computer Pictures & Portraits (9)
- Corning Revere (4)
- Country Clutter (4)
- Crown Jewels of Nature (3)
- Danskin (1)
- Dexter Shoe (1)
- Diamonds Unlimited (3)
- Dickies (1)
- Dockers Outlet (1)
- Dress Barn (1)
- Dress Barn Woman (1)
- Easy Spirit (1)
- Electronics Outlet Store (4)
- Elisabeth (1)
- Etienne Aigner (1)
- Everything But Water (1)
- Eye Candy (1)
- Factory Brand Shoes (1)
- Famous Brands Housewares (4)
- Fitz & Floyd (4)
- Foot Locker (1)
- Gap Outlet (1)
- Geoffrey Beene (1)
- Group USA (1)
- Guess? (1)
- Haggar (1)
- Import-Export Exchange (2)
- Izod (1)
- Jarmen Shoe (1)
- Jewelers (3)
- Jewelry Factory Outlet (3)
- Jewelry Factory Store (3)
- Jewelry Time (3)
- Jockey (1)
- Kasper ASL (1)
- Knife Factory (9)
- Koret (1)
- L'eggs Hanes Bali Playtex (1)
- Levi's / Dockers (1)
- Liz Claiborne (1)
- London Fog (1)
- Maidenform (1)
- Mikasa (4)
- Moda Fina (1)
- Music 4 Less (5)
- Nautica (1)
- Nike (1)
- Olga Warner (1)
- Oneida (4)
- Optical Outlet (3)
- OshKosh B'Gosh (1)
- Pacific Sunwear (1)

- Payless Shoe Source (1)
- Perfumania (8)
- Pfaltzgraff (4)
- Piercing Pagoda (3)
- Planet Hollywood (5)
- Puma (1)
- Rack Room Shoes (1)
- Reebok (1)
- Remington (4)
- Rockport (1)
- S & K Menswear (1)
- Samsonite (2)
- San Francisco Music Box (9)
- Saucony (1)
- SBX (1)
- Skechers (1)
- Socks Galore (1)
- Springmaid Wamsutta (4)
- Stride Rite (1)
- Styles For Less (1)
- Sunglass Hut (3)
- Surf Jungle (1)
- Swank (2)
- T-Shirt Factory (1)
- Timberland (1)
- Time Square Watches (3)
- Tinder Box (9)
- Today's Woman (1)
- Tommy Hilfiger (1)
- Toy Liquidators (6)
- Traffic Shoes (1)
- Umbro (1)
- Universal Studios Outlet (9)
- Van Heusen (1)
- Vans Shoes (1)
- Vitamin World (8)
- Wallet Works (2)
- Welcome Home (4)
- Westport Limited (1)
- Wolf Camera & Video (7)
- Woolrich (1)
- XOXO (1)

EATS & TREATS

- All American Burgers & Dogs (11)
- Buddy's Bakery (11)
- Buddy's Cinnamon Buns (10)
- Carnival Of Food (11)
- Carousel Grill (11)
- Coffee Café (10)
- Edy's Grand Ice Cream (10)
- Frontier Fruit & Nut (10)
- Lucy Ho's (11)
- Mom's Best Cookies (10)
- Pretzel Twister (10)

- Sbarro Italian Eatery (11)
- Snack World (10)
- Subway (11)
- Tic Taco (11)
- World Café (11)

10C • Lake Buena Vista Factory Stores

www.lbvfs.com
Address 15591 State Road 535 *Phone* 407-238-9301 *Hours* Mon-Sat 9:30- 9:30, Sun 10-6 *Location* Take exit 27 off I-4, go south on State Road 535 for two miles.

STORES

- Adidas (1)
- Big Dog Sportswear (1)
- Blowout Video (9)
- Carter's For Kids (1)
- Casio (4)
- Casuals (1)
- Claire's Accessories (3)
- Dexter Shoe (1)
- Disney Character Corner (5)
- Dress Barn (1)
- Dress Barn Woman (1)
- Factory Brand Shoes (1)
- Farberware (4)
- Fossil (2)
- Gap Outlet (1)
- Jockey (1)
- Kappa (1)
- KB Toys (6)
- Liz Claiborne (1)
- Manhattan Diamonds (3)
- Murano Glass Factory Store (9)
- Nine West (1)
- Oneida (4)
- Orlando.com (9)
- OshKosh B'Gosh Super Store (1)
- Paper Factory (9)
- Publishers Outlet (5)
- Reebok (1)
- Samsonite (2)
- Sony / JVC (4)
- Sunglass Hut (3)
- Sunglass Station (3)
- Swim Mart (1)
- VF Factory Outlet (1)
- Vitamin World (8)

EATS & TREATS

- Melitta Coffee (10)
- Reese Food Court (11)

10D • Orlando Premium Outlets

www.premiumoutlets.com
Address 8200 Vineland Ave *Phone* 407-238-7787 *Hours* Mon-Sat 10-10, Sun 10-9 *Location* Traveling east on I-4 take exit 27. Go straight across light at end of ramp onto Vineland Ave, continue 1 mile.

STORES

- Adidas (1)
- Aerosoles (1)
- American Swimwear (1)
- Anne Klein (1)
- Banana Republic (1)
- Barneys New York (1)
- Bass (1)
- BCBG Max Azria (1)
- Beauty Express (8)
- Bebe Outlet (1)
- Big & Tall Factory Store (1)
- Big Dog Sportswear (1)
- Bose Factory Store (4)
- Bostonian Clarks (1)
- Bottega Veneta (1)
- Brooks Brothers (1)
- Burberry (1)
- Calvin Klein (1)
- Candie's (1)
- Carter's Childrenswear (1)
- Claire's Accessories (3)
- Clothestime (1)
- Coach (2)
- Cole-Haan (1)
- Cosmetics Company Store (8)
- Country Clutter (4)
- Designer Brands Accessories (2)
- Designer Fragrance/Cosmetics (8)
- Disney's Character Premier (5)
- DKNY (1)
- Dockers Outlet by Designs (1)
- Donald J Pliner (1)
- Dooney & Bourke (2)
- Dress Barn/Dress Barn Woman (1)
- El Portal Last Stop (2)
- Escada Company Store (1)
- Etienne Aigner (1)
- Factory Brand Shoes (1)
- French Connection (1)

- Fubu (1)
- Geoffrey Beene (1)
- Giorgio Armani (1)
- Guess? (1)
- Hartstrings (1)
- Hugo Boss (1)
- Hush Puppies & Family (1)
- Izod (1)
- J M Originals (1)
- Johnston & Murphy (1)
- Jones New York (1)
- Journeys (1)
- Kenneth Cole (1)
- La Perla (1)
- Le Creuset (4)
- Le Gourmet Chef (4)
- L'eggs Hanes Bali Playtex (1)
- Levi's Outlet by Designs (1)
- Liz Claiborne Shoes (1)
- Louis Feraud Paris (1)
- Maidenform (1)
- Max Mara (1)
- Max Studio (1)
- Mikasa (4)
- Motherhood Maternity (1)
- Movado (2)
- Music For A Song (5)
- Naturalizer (1)
- Nautica (1)
- Nike (1)
- Oilily (1)
- OshKosh B'Gosh (1)
- PacSun (1)
- Papaya Clothing (1)
- Perfumania (8)
- Perry Ellis (1)
- Polo Ralph Lauren (1)
- Puma (1)
- Ralph Lauren Footwear (1)
- Reebok (1)
- Salvatore Ferragamo (1)
- Samsonite (2)
- Saucony (1)
- Skechers (1)
- Strasburg Children (1)
- Stride Rite Keds Sperry (1)
- Sunglass Outlet (3)
- Sunglass Shop (3)
- Timberland (1)
- Time Factory Watch (3)
- Tod's (1)
- Tommy Hilfiger (1)
- TSE (1)
- Ultra Diamond Outlet (3)
- Universal Studios Outlet (9)

- Van Heusen (1)
- Versace (1)
- Vitamin World (8)
- Warnaco (1)
- WestPoint Stevens (4)
- Wilson's Leather (1)
- Zales The Diamond Store (3)
- Zegna Outlet Store (1)

EATS & TREATS
- A & W Restaurant (11)
- Auntie Anne's Pretzals (10)
- Fudgery (10)
- Fuzziwig's Candy Factory (10)
- JR Steakery (11)
- Juice It Up (10)
- Maki of Japan (11)
- Max Orient (11)
- Mrs Fields Cookies (10)
- Starbucks Coffee (10)
- Subway (11)
- Villa Pizza (11)

11   SAINT AUGUSTINE

11A • Belz Factory Outlet World
www.belz.com
Address 500 Belz Outlet Roas
Phone 904-826-1311 *Hours* Mon-Sat 9-9, Sun 10-6 *Location* South of Jacksonville off I-95, exit 95. Head east on Hwy 16, follow sings to center.

STORES
- Adidas (1)
- Beauty Express (8)
- Big Dogs (1)
- Black & Decker (4)
- Buster Brown (1)
- Camp Coleman (6)
- Country Clutter (4)
- Croscill (4)
- Dansk (4)
- Danskin (1)
- Designer Fragrance/Cosmetics (8)
- Disney's Character Premier (5)
- Dress Barn (1)
- Earthbound Trading Co (5)
- Easy Spirit (1)
- Eye Candy Jr's (1)
- Factory Brand Shoes (1)

- Fossil (2)
- Guess? (1)
- Hamilton Luggage (2)
- Hartstrings (1)
- Home Style (4)
- Hush Puppies & Family (1)
- Jones New York (1)
- Kitchen Collection (4)
- Knife Factory (9)
- Le Creuset (4)
- Le Gourmet Chef (4)
- Lenox (4)
- Liz Claiborne & Elisabeth (1)
- Mobile Telesys (9)
- Music 4 Less (5)
- Nike (1)
- Pacific Sunwear (1)
- Perfumania (8)
- Pfaltzgraff (4)
- Piercing Pagoda (3)
- Polo Ralph Lauren (1)
- Puma (1)
- Remington (4)
- Royal Doulton (4)
- Rue 21 (1)
- Samsonite (2)
- Saucony (1)
- Silver & Gemstone Gallery (3)
- Silver and Gold Connections (3)
- Sock World (1)
- Special Brands by Liz Claiborne (1)
- Springmaid Wamsutta (4)
- Stride Rite (1)
- Styles For Less (1)
- Timberland (1)
- Time Square Watches (3)
- Tommy Hilfiger (1)
- Totes (3)
- Ultra Diamond & Gold (3)
- Vans Shoes (1)
- Vitamin World (8)
- Waterford Wedgwood (4)
- Wilson's Accessories (9)
- XOXO (1)
- Zales The Diamond Store (3)

EATS & TREATS

- Burger Boys (11)
- Edy's Grand Ice Cream (10)
- Gloria Jean's Gourmet Coffee (10)
- Golden Cajun Grill (11)
- Lucy Ho's (11)
- Nature's Best Subs (11)
- Pretzel Twister (10)
- Rocky Mountain Chocolate (10)
- Sbarro's Pizza (11)

11B • St. Augustine Outlet Center

www.staugustineoutlets.com
Address 2700 State Road 16 **Phone** 904-825-1555 **Hours** Mon-Sat 9-9, Sun 10-6 **Location** Northeast Florida, south of Jacksonville. Take exit 95 off I-95. Go east to center.

STORES

- Alan Stuart Menswear (1)
- Ann Taylor (1)
- Banister Shoes (1)
- Bass (1)
- Bible Factory Outlet (5)
- Big & Tall Factory Store (1)
- Big Dog Sportswear (1)
- Bon Worth (1)
- Bose Factory Store (4)
- Brooks Brothers (1)
- Calvin Klein (1)
- Capacity (1)
- Carter's Childrenswear (1)
- Casual Corner (1)
- Chico's (1)
- Claire's Accessories (3)
- Coach (2)
- Coastal Cotton (1)
- Corning Revere (4)
- Craftworks (4)
- Deanna's Gold & Diamond (3)
- Designer Brands Accessories (2)
- Dexter Shoe (1)
- Donna Karan (1)
- Dress Barn (1)
- Etienne Aigner (1)
- Factory Brand Shoes (1)
- Famous Brands Housewares (4)
- Farberware (4)
- Florsheim (1)
- Gap Outlet (1)
- Geoffrey Beene (1)
- Geoffrey Beene Women (1)
- GNC (8)
- Haggar (1)
- Harry & David (5)
- Hoover Outlet (4)
- J Crew (1)
- Jockey (1)
- Kasper ASL (1)
- Kitchen Collection (4)
- Koret (1)
- Leather Factory (2)
- Leather Loft (2)

- L'eggs Hanes Bali Playtex (1)
- Levi's (1)
- Liz Claiborne Shoes (1)
- Maidenform (1)
- Mikasa (4)
- Motherhood Maternity (1)
- Movado (2)
- National Book Warehouse (5)
- Naturalizer (1)
- Nautica (1)
- Nine West (1)
- Olga Warner (1)
- Oneida (4)
- OshKosh B'Gosh (1)
- Otto Collection (9)
- Paper Factory (9)
- Reebok (1)
- Rockport (1)
- S & K Menswear (1)
- Samsonite (2)
- SAS Factory Shoes (1)
- Seiko (3)
- Shadowline (1)
- So Fun! Kids (1)
- Strasburg Children (1)
- Styles For Less (1)
- Sunglass Hut (3)
- Thomas House (4)
- Tommy Bahamas (1)
- Tools & More (9)
- Toy Liquidators (6)
- Trend Club (1)
- Van Heusen (1)
- Welcome Home (4)
- WestPoint Stevens (4)

EATS & TREATS

- Burger King (11)
- Conch House Café (11)
- Dragon Hut (11)
- Rocky Mountain Chocolate (10)
- Rufino's Pizza (11)

12 SUNRISE

12A • Sawgrass Mills
www.millscorp.com
Address 12801 West Sunrise Blvd
Phone 954-846-2300 or 800-FL-Mills *Hours* Mon-Fri 10-9:30, Sat 9:30-9:30, Sun 11-8 *Location* Ten miles west of Fort Lauderdale.

Travel west on I-595 to the Flamingo Road exit. Go north on Flamingo Road and cross Sunrise Blvd. The mall is on your left.

STORES

- 5-7-9 Outlet (1)
- Accentables (2)
- Aerosoles (1)
- American Newstand (5)
- Ann Taylor (1)
- Anne Klein (1)
- Art Treasures (4)
- Athlete's Foot (1)
- Athletic Footwear (1)
- Auto Optical (9)
- B-Fashion (9)
- B2000 (1)
- Baby Gap (1)
- Banana Republic (1)
- Baron's Menswear (1)
- Bass (1)
- Battaglia Shoes (1)
- Bayside Brush (9)
- BCBG Max Azria (1)
- Beall's Outlet (1)
- Bebe Outlet (1)
- Bed Bath & Beyond (4)
- Benetton (1)
- Bentley's Luggage (2)
- Best Wishes (5)
- Beyond Electronics (5)
- Big & Tall Factory Store (1)
- Body Shop (8)
- Bomba Jeans (1)
- Bon Worth (1)
- Books-A-Million (5)
- Bose Factory Store (4)
- Bostonian Clarks (1)
- BrandsMart USA (4)
- Brief Encounters (1)
- Brooks Brothers (1)
- Buckle-Up Accessories (2)
- Burlington Coat Factory (1)
- Cache Outlet (1)
- Calvin Klein (1)
- Camelot Music (5)
- Carter's Childrenswear (1)
- Casual Corner (1)
- Chediak (1)
- Children's Place Outlet (1)
- Claire's Boutique (3)
- Class Perfumes & Cosmetics (8)
- Coastal Cotton (1)

- Cohen's Fashion Optical (3)
- Cole-Haan (1)
- Concept Store (4)
- Corning Revere (4)
- CR Jewelers Outlet (3)
- Dalton Rug (4)
- Damiani Outlet (1)
- Danskin (1)
- DB of South Beach (1)
- Designer Boot Outlet (1)
- Designers Row (1)
- Dexter Shoe (1)
- Diamond Centre (3)
- Discount Luggage (2)
- Disney's Character Premier (5)
- Dollar Star (5)
- Dome International (1)
- Donna Karan (1)
- Dress Barn (1)
- Dress Barn Woman (1)
- Easy Spirit (1)
- Electronics Boutique (4)
- Endless Summer (1)
- Enrico Uomo (1)
- Erdos Cashmere (1)
- Escada Company Store (1)
- Etienne Aigner (1)
- Express & Structure Warehouse (1)
- Factory Brand Shoes (1)
- Farberware (4)
- Fashion II (9)
- Field of Dreams (6)
- Flag Shop (9)
- Foot Locker (1)
- FootAction USA (1)
- Fossil (2)
- Fragrance Outlet (8)
- Freddy's Jewelers (3)
- Game Stop (9)
- GameWorks (9)
- Gap Kids (1)
- Gap Outlet (1)
- Geoffrey Beene (1)
- Glamour Shots (9)
- GNC (8)
- Group USA (1)
- Guess Kids (1)
- Guess? (1)
- Hilda Werth (1)
- Hugo Boss (1)
- Hush Puppies & Family (1)
- Icing (3)
- Ike Behar (1)
- Imposters (3)
- Infinity Fashions (1)
- Italia Sport (1)
- Izod (1)
- J Crew (1)
- Jalan Jalan (1)
- JCPenney Outlet (1)
- Jockey (1)
- Johnston & Murphy (1)
- Joseph Abboud (1)
- Kaiser (1)
- Kandlestix (4)
- Kappa (1)
- Kasper ASL (1)
- KB Toys (6)
- Kenneth Cole (1)
- Kipling (2)
- Kirkland's (4)
- Laminage Art & Frame (4)
- Last Call Neiman Marcus (1)
- Laughing Lizards (1)
- Le Boss (1)
- Leather Limited (2)
- L'eggs Hanes Bali Playtex (1)
- LensCrafters (3)
- Levi's / Dockers (1)
- Lexington Handbags (2)
- Lids (9)
- Lily of France (1)
- Limited Too (1)
- Liz Claiborne (1)
- Liz Claiborne Shoes (1)
- London Fog (1)
- Luggage Express (2)
- Maidenform (1)
- Manhattan Jewelry Exchange (3)
- Marshalls (1)
- MasterCuts (8)
- Max Mara (1)
- Mikasa (4)
- Mondo Collections (1)
- Motherhood Maternity (1)
- My Emotions (8)
- Nail Trix (8)
- Nautica (1)
- Net-CRT (9)
- Nextel (7)
- Nine West (1)
- Off 5th-Saks Fifth Avenue (1)
- On Time (3)
- One Stop Fashions (1)
- Optica (9)
- OshKosh B'Gosh (1)
- Pacific Sunwear (1)
- Palm Produce (1)
- Parade of Shoes (1)
- Perfumania (8)

- Perry Ellis (1)
- Perry Ellis America & More (1)
- Point of View (9)
- Polo Jeans Co (1)
- Polo Ralph Lauren (1)
- Pro Image (1)
- Psychic Fair (9)
- Puma (1)
- Rack Room Shoes (1)
- Radio Shack (7)
- Rave Girl (1)
- Reebok (1)
- Regal 23 Cinemas (9)
- Remington (4)
- Revlon Inspirations (8)
- Ritz Camera 1 Hour Photo (7)
- Rockport (1)
- Roma (1)
- Ron Jon Surf Shop (6)
- S & K Menswear (1)
- Samsonite (2)
- Samsonite Travel Expo (2)
- Sanrio (9)
- Saucony (1)
- Security World (9)
- Service Merchandise (9)
- Sharper Image Outlet (9)
- Silver Mill (3)
- Sirens (1)
- Specs Music & Movies (5)
- Spencer Gifts (5)
- Spiegel Outlet (1)
- Sportive (1)
- Sports Authority (6)
- Sportswear Unlimited Outlet (1)
- St John Knits (1)
- Streetcorner News (5)
- Sun & Ski Sports (1)
- Sundook Art Galleries (4)
- Sunglass Hut (3)
- Sunny Eyes (3)
- Surreys Menswear (1)
- Swim N Sport (1)
- Tahari (1)
- Target Greatland (9)
- Timberland (1)
- Time Factory Watch (3)
- Time World (3)
- TJ Maxx (1)
- Tommy Hilfiger (1)
- Top of the Line Fragrances & Cosmetics (8)
- Topper Outlet (1)
- Totto (2)
- Toy Works (6)

- Traffic Shoes (1)
- Trend Club (1)
- Tropical View (9)
- Ultra Jewelers (3)
- Underground Station (1)
- Urban Planet (1)
- US Post Office (9)
- US Tops (1)
- Valeriano Collection (9)
- Van Heusen (1)
- Vans Shoes (1)
- Vertigo (1)
- VF Factory Outlet (1)
- Vitamin World (8)
- Voice Stream Wireless (7)
- Watch Mart (3)
- Watch Me (9)
- Westport Limited (1)
- Westport Woman (1)
- Wet Seal Outlet (1)
- Wilderness Country (1)
- Wilson's Leather (1)
- Wolf Camera & Video (7)
- World Art (4)
- X'Andrini (9)
- XOXO (1)
- XX Me Outlet (1)
- Zales The Diamond Store (3)
- Zap Electronics (4)

EATS & TREATS

- Arthur Treacher's Fish & Chips (11)
- Auntie Anne's Pretzals (10)
- Burger King (11)
- Cajun Grill (11)
- Cheesecake Factory Bakery Café (11)
- Chicken Central (11)
- Churrisimo (11)
- Crepes de Paris (11)
- Dairy Queen / Orange Julius (11)
- Dippin Dots (11)
- Eye of the Hurricane (11)
- GameWorks Café (11)
- Ghirardelli Soda Fountain (11)
- Gloria Jean's Gourmet Coffee (10)
- Great American Cookie (10)
- Haagen Dazs (10)
- Hard Rock Café (11)
- Hot Cins (10)
- Italian Terrace Bistro (11)
- Jamba Juice (10)
- Japan Café - Asian Grill (11)
- Kohr Brothers Frozen Custard (10)
- Las Delicias (11)

- Legal Sea Foods (11)
- Los Ranchos (11)
- Miami Subs (11)
- My Favorite Muffin (11)
- Nathan's International Eatery (11)
- Palm Beach Confectioners (11)
- Panda Express (11)
- Rainforest Café (11)
- RayJay's Garden Cafe (11)
- Ruby Tuesday (11)
- Sbarro Italian Eatery (11)
- Sweets From Heaven (10)
- Taco Bell (11)
- Time Out At The Blimp (11)
- Tropical Café (10)
- Tropical Oasis (10)
- Wolfgang Puck Café (11)

13   VERO BEACH

13A • Prime Outlets Vero Beach
www.primeoutlets.com
Address 1824 94th Dr *Phone* 561-770-6171 *Hours* Mon-Sat 10-8, Sun 11-6 *Location* North of Fort Pierce in southeastern Florida. Take exit 68 off I-95.

STORES
- Ann Taylor (1)
- Anne Klein (1)
- Bagmakers (2)
- Bass (1)
- Big & Beautiful (1)
- Big Dogs (1)
- Bombay Outlet (4)
- Bon Worth (1)
- Book Warehouse (5)
- Bose Factory Store (4)
- Bugle Boy (1)
- Carter's Childrenswear (1)
- Casual Corner (1)
- Casual Corner Woman (1)
- Casual Male Big & Tall (1)
- Claire's Accessories (3)
- Coastal Cotton (1)
- Corning Revere (4)
- Cost Cutters Salon (8)
- Dexter Shoe (1)
- Dooney & Bourke (2)
- Dress Barn (1)

- Easy Spirit (1)
- Etienne Aigner (1)
- Factory Brand Shoes (1)
- Famous Brands Housewares (4)
- Famous Footwear (1)
- Farberware (4)
- Florsheim (1)
- Geoffrey Beene (1)
- Hush Puppies & Family (1)
- Izod (1)
- Jockey (1)
- Jones New York (1)
- Kasper ASL (1)
- Kitchen Collection (4)
- L'eggs Hanes Bali Playtex (1)
- Lenox (4)
- Levi's (1)
- Liz Claiborne (1)
- Lloyd Middleton Dolls (9)
- Maternity Works (1)
- Mikasa (4)
- Music For A Song (5)
- Nautica (1)
- Nine West (1)
- Nook & Cranny (9)
- Olga Warner (1)
- Oneida (4)
- OshKosh B'Gosh (1)
- Perfumania (8)
- Petite Sophisticate (1)
- Polo Ralph Lauren (1)
- Prestige Fragrance/Cosmetics (8)
- Reebok (1)
- Remington (4)
- Samsonite (2)
- SAS Factory Shoes (1)
- Savane (1)
- Silk Silk Silk (4)
- Springmaid Wamsutta (4)
- Sunglass Hut (3)
- Totes Isotoner Sunglass Station (3)
- Toy Liquidators (6)
- Van Heusen (1)
- Versace (1)
- Vitamin World (8)
- Welcome Home (4)
- Zales The Diamond Store (3)

EATS & TREATS
- Grill (11)
- Guisseppe's Pizza (11)
- Rocky Mountain Chocolate (10)
- Subway (11)
- TCBY (10)

Georgia

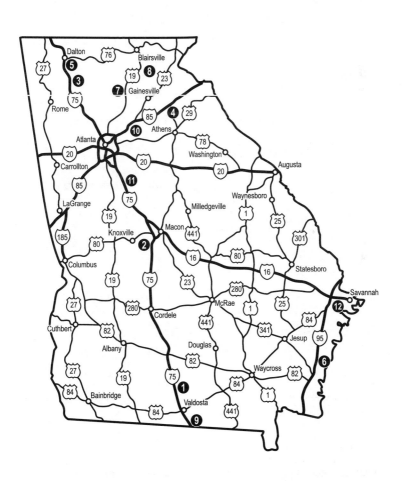

1 ADEL

1A • Factory Stores at Adel
www.kingfrogfactorystores.com
Address I-75 & exit 39 *Phone* 229-896-4848 *Hours* Mon-Sat 9-8, Sun 11-7 *Location* North of Valdosta off I-75, exit 39.

STORES
- $12 R Less (9)
- Bon Worth (1)
- Boots 'N Brims (1)
- Cali Nails (8)
- Christmas Factory (9)
- Clearance Warehouse (1)
- Country Home (4)
- Famous Footwear (1)
- Fashion Stop (1)
- Fieldcrest Cannon (4)
- FL-GA Welcome Center (9)
- Hush Puppies & Family (1)
- King Frog Factory Outlet (1)
- King Frog Furniture Mart (4)
- Kitchen Collection (4)
- Van Heusen (1)

2 BYRON

2A • Peach Factory Stores
www.peachfactorystores.com
Address 311 Hwy 49 *Phone* 478-956-1855 *Hours* Mon-Sat 10-9, Sun 11-6 *Location* South of Macon off I-75, exit 149.

STORES
- Bible Factory Outlet (5)
- Bon Worth (1)
- Book Warehouse (5)
- Capacity (1)
- Dress Barn (1)
- Dress Barn Woman (1)
- Duck Head (1)
- Factory Brand Shoes (1)
- GNC (8)
- Hush Puppies & Family (1)
- Kitchen Collection (4)
- L'eggs Hanes Bali Playtex (1)
- Levi's (1)

- Paper Factory (9)
- Rack Room Shoes (1)
- S & K Menswear (1)
- Toy Liquidators (6)
- Uniform Outlet (1)

EATS & TREATS
- Casa Mexico (11)
- Hickory House (11)

3 CALHOUN

3A • Prime Outlets Calhoun
www.primeoutlets.com
Address 455 Belwood Rd *Phone* 706-602-1300 *Hours* Mon-Sat 10-9, Sun 12-6 *Location* Sixty miles north of Atlanta off I-75, exit 312.

STORES
- Bass (1)
- Big Dog Sportswear (1)
- Black & Decker (4)
- Bon Worth (1)
- Book Warehouse (5)
- Buster Brown (1)
- Capacity (1)
- Carol's Fashions (1)
- Carter's Childrenswear (1)
- Casey's Corner (4)
- Casual Corner (1)
- Casual Corner Woman (1)
- Casual Male Big & Tall (1)
- Claire's Accessories (3)
- Dress Barn (1)
- Factory Brand Shoes (1)
- Farberware (4)
- Gap Outlet (1)
- Geoffrey Beene (1)
- Izod (1)
- J Crew (1)
- Jacob's Well (9)
- Jones New York (1)
- Leather Loft (2)
- L'eggs Hanes Bali Playtex (1)
- Liz Claiborne (1)
- Maidenform (1)
- Mikasa (4)
- Naturalizer (1)
- Nike (1)
- Nine West (1)
- Old Navy (1)
- Paper Factory (9)

- Perfumania (8)
- Petite Sophisticate (1)
- Pro Golf (6)
- Rue 21 (1)
- Springmaid Wamsutta (4)
- Sunglass Hut (3)
- Tommy Hilfiger (1)
- Van Heusen (1)
- VF Factory Outlet (1)
- Vitamin World (8)
- Welcome Home (4)

EATS & TREATS
- Rocky Mountain Chocolate (10)

4   COMMERCE

4A • Commerce Factory Stores
Address 199 Pottery Factory Dr
Phone 706-335-6352 *Hours* Mon-Sat 9-9, Sun 12-6 *Location* Northeast Georgia, north of Athens. From I-85 take exit 149, Hwy 441 south.

STORES
- Book Warehouse (5)
- Buffalo Rugs (4)
- Dan River (4)
- Dansk (4)
- Dress Barn (1)
- Dress Barn Woman (1)
- Furniture Market (4)
- GNC (8)
- Gold Toe (1)
- Hickory White Furniture (4)
- Home Furnishings & Patio (4)
- Imperial Class (4)
- Kitchen Collection (4)
- Lenox (4)
- Paper Factory (9)
- Patio Outlet (4)
- S & K Menswear (1)
- Southern Children (1)
- WestPoint Stevens (4)

4B • Tanger Outlet Center I
www.tangeroutlets.com
Address 111 Tanger Dr *Phone* 800-405-9828 or 706-335-3354 *Hours* Mon-Sat 9-9, Sun 12-6 *Location*

From Atlanta take I-85 north to exit 149, Commerce Banks Crossing. Turn right to center I, left for II.

STORES
- Banister Shoes (1)
- Bank One ATM (9)
- Bass (1)
- Black & Decker (4)
- Bon Worth (1)
- Britches (1)
- Bugle Boy (1)
- Capacity (1)
- Corning Revere (4)
- Elisabeth (1)
- Famous Brands Housewares (4)
- Farberware (4)
- Fieldcrest Cannon (4)
- Geoffrey Beene (1)
- Izod (1)
- L'eggs Hanes Bali Playtex (1)
- Levi's Outlet by Designs (1)
- Liz Claiborne (1)
- Maidenform (1)
- Mikasa (4)
- Motherhood Maternity (1)
- Naturalizer (1)
- Oneida (4)
- OshKosh B'Gosh (1)
- Perfumania (8)
- Publishers Warehouse (5)
- Rack Room Shoes (1)
- Reebok (1)
- Rockport (1)
- Samsonite (2)
- Socks Galore (1)
- Sunglass Outlet (3)
- Toy Liquidators (6)
- Van Heusen (1)
- Warnaco (1)
- Welcome Home (4)
- Woolrich (1)

EATS & TREATS
- Yummies (10)

4C • Tanger Outlet Center II
www.tangeroutlets.com
Address 111 Tanger Dr *Phone* 800-405-9828 or 706-335-3354 *Hours* Mon-Sat 9-9, Sun 12-6 *Location*

From Atlanta take I-85 north to exit 149, Commerce Banks Crossing. Turn right to center I, left for II.

Stores

- Adidas (1)
- American Outpost (1)
- Banana Republic (1)
- Bank One ATM (9)
- Bible Factory Outlet (5)
- Big Dog Sportswear (1)
- Bon Worth (1)
- Brooks Brothers (1)
- Bugle Boy (1)
- Calvin Klein (1)
- Camp Coleman (6)
- Carter's Childrenswear (1)
- Casual Corner (1)
- Casual Corner Woman (1)
- Casual Male Big & Tall (1)
- Children's Place Outlet (1)
- Claire's Boutique (3)
- Clothestime (1)
- Community Bank & Trust (9)
- Cost Cutters Salon (8)
- Country Clutter (4)
- Croscill (4)
- Dexter Shoe (1)
- DKNY Jeans (1)
- Easy Spirit (1)
- Etienne Aigner (1)
- Factory Brand Shoes (1)
- Florsheim (1)
- Fossil (2)
- Gap Outlet (1)
- Guess? (1)
- Haggar (1)
- Harry & David (5)
- Hoover Outlet (4)
- Hush Puppies & Family (1)
- J Crew (1)
- Jockey (1)
- Jones New York (1)
- Kasper ASL (1)
- Kirkland's (4)
- Koret (1)
- Le Gourmet Chef (4)
- Leather Loft (2)
- L'eggs Hanes Bali Playtex (1)
- Liz Claiborne Shoes (1)
- Music For A Song (5)
- Nautica (1)
- New York Jewelry (3)
- Nike (1)
- Nine West (1)
- Paul Harris (1)
- Peaches 'n Cream (1)
- Perfumania (8)
- Petite Sophisticate (1)
- Pfaltzgraff (4)
- Polo Jeans Co (1)
- Quilts & Such (4)
- Remington (4)
- Rue 21 (1)
- Samsonite (2)
- SAS Factory Shoes (1)
- Seiko (3)
- Springmaid Wamsutta (4)
- St Nick's (9)
- Stride Rite (1)
- Sunbeam & Oster (4)
- Timberland (1)
- Tommy Hilfiger Jeans (1)
- Tools & More (9)
- Totes / Sunglass World (3)
- Touch of Georgia (9)
- Vans Shoes (1)
- VF Factory Outlet (1)
- Vitamin World (8)
- We're Entertainment (4)
- Westport Limited (1)
- Wilson's Leather (1)
- Zales The Diamond Store (3)

Eats & Treats

- Denny's Diner (11)
- Main Street Eatery (11)
- Rocky Mountain Chocolate (10)

5 Dalton

5A • Tanger Outlet Center
www.tangeroutlets.com
Address 1001 Market Street **Phone** 800-409-7029 or 706-277-2688 **Hours** Mon-Sat 9-9, Sun 12-6 **Location** About 75 miles north of Atlanta. From I-75 north take exit 333 (Walnut Ave), turn right and follow to Market St, turn right.

Stores

- Bass (1)
- Bon Worth (1)
- Book Warehouse (5)

- Capacity (1)
- Carter's Childrenswear (1)
- Claire's Accessories (3)
- Corning Revere (4)
- Dress Barn (1)
- Dress Barn Woman (1)
- Duck Head (1)
- Etienne Aigner (1)
- Factory Brand Shoes (1)
- Izod (1)
- Jockey (1)
- Kitchen Collection (4)
- Koret (1)
- Leather Factory (2)
- L'eggs Hanes Bali Playtex (1)
- Nautica (1)
- Oneida (4)
- Paper Factory (9)
- Rack Room Shoes (1)
- Rue 21 (1)
- S & K Menswear (1)
- Samsonite (2)
- SAS Factory Shoes (1)
- Spiegel Outlet (1)
- Totes / Sunglass World (3)
- Toy Liquidators (6)
- Van Heusen (1)
- Vitamin World (8)
- Welcome Home (4)
- WestPoint Stevens (4)

EATS & TREATS

- Outback Steakhouse (11)
- Rocky Mountain Chocolate (10)

6   DARIEN

6A • Prime Outlets Darien

www.primeoutlets.com
Address 1 Magnolia Bluff Way
Phone 912-437-2700 *Hours* Mon-
Sat 10-8, Sun 11-6 *Location*
Southeastern Georgia, north of
Brunswick. The center is at exit 49
off I-95.

STORES

- Bass (1)
- Big Dog Sportswear (1)
- Black & Decker (4)
- Book Warehouse (5)
- Boot Emporium (1)

- Carter's Childrenswear (1)
- Casual Corner (1)
- Casual Corner Woman (1)
- Claire's Accessories (3)
- Coach (2)
- Cosmetics Company Store (8)
- Cost Cutters Salon (8)
- Dockers Outlet by Designs (1)
- Dress Barn/Dress Barn Woman (1)
- Duck Head (1)
- Etienne Aigner (1)
- Factory Brand Shoes (1)
- Farberware (4)
- Gap Outlet (1)
- GNC (8)
- Importers Liquidation (9)
- Jockey (1)
- Johnston & Murphy (1)
- KB Toys (6)
- Kitchen Collection (4)
- L'eggs Hanes Bali Playtex (1)
- Levi's Outlet by Designs (1)
- Liz Claiborne (1)
- Mikasa (4)
- Motherhood Maternity (1)
- Nautica (1)
- Nike (1)
- Perfumania (8)
- Petite Sophisticate (1)
- Polo Ralph Lauren (1)
- Quiksilver (1)
- Rack Room Shoes (1)
- Reebok (1)
- Robert Scott & David Brooks (1)
- Rockport (1)
- SAS Factory Shoes (1)
- Springmaid Wamsutta (4)
- Strasburg Children (1)
- Sunglass Hut (3)
- Tommy Hilfiger (1)
- Van Heusen (1)
- Welcome Home (4)
- Wilson's Leather (1)
- Woolrich (1)
- Zales The Diamond Store (3)

EATS & TREATS

- Oriental Food Fair (11)
- Rocky Mountain Chocolate (10)
- Subway (11)

7   DAWSONVILLE

7A • North Georgia Premium Outlets

www.premiumoutlets.com
Address 800 Hwy 400 S *Phone*
706-216-3609 *Hours* Mon-Sat 10-
9, Sun 12-6 *Location* Just 35
minutes north of Atlanta on State
Hwy 400/US 19.

STORES

- Adidas (1)
- Anne Klein (1)
- Banana Republic (1)
- Bass (1)
- BCBG Max Azria (1)
- Benetton (1)
- Bible Factory Outlet (5)
- Big & Tall Factory Store (1)
- Big Dog Sportswear (1)
- Bijoux Direct (3)
- Black & Decker (4)
- Bombay Outlet (4)
- Bon Worth (1)
- Book Warehouse (5)
- Bose Factory Store (4)
- Bostonian Clarks (1)
- Britches (1)
- Brooks Brothers (1)
- Calvin Klein (1)
- Carter's For Kids (1)
- Casual Corner (1)
- Casual Corner Woman (1)
- Charlotte Russe (1)
- Chattahoochee Candle Co (5)
- Claire's Accessories (3)
- Coach (2)
- Cole-Haan (1)
- Cosmetics Company Store (8)
- Cost Cutters Salon (8)
- Country Clutter (4)
- Crate & Barrel (4)
- Dalton Rug (4)
- Dansk (4)
- Danskin (1)
- Designer Brands Accessories (2)
- Designer Fragrance/Cosmetics (8)
- Dockers Outlet by Designs (1)
- Donna Karan (1)
- Dress Barn/Dress Barn Woman (1)
- Easy Spirit (1)
- EB Game World (9)
- Eddie Bauer (1)
- Elisabeth (1)
- Escada Company Store (1)
- Etienne Aigner (1)

- Factory Brand Shoes (1)
- Florsheim (1)
- Fossil (2)
- Four Seasons Designer Eyewear (3)
- Gap Outlet (1)
- Geoffrey Beene (1)
- GNC (8)
- Guess? (1)
- Harold's (1)
- Harry & David (5)
- Home Style (4)
- Hoover Outlet (4)
- Hugo Boss (1)
- Hush Puppies & Family (1)
- Izod (1)
- Jockey (1)
- Johnston & Murphy (1)
- Jones New York (1)
- Jones New York Country (1)
- Jones New York Sport (1)
- Jos A Bank Clothiers (1)
- Kasper ASL (1)
- KB Toys (6)
- Kenneth Cole (1)
- Le Creuset (4)
- Le Gourmet Chef (4)
- L'eggs Hanes Bali Playtex (1)
- Lego Outlet (6)
- Lenox (4)
- Levi's Outlet by Designs (1)
- Liz Claiborne (1)
- Liz Claiborne Shoes (1)
- LuxuryBeds (4)
- Maidenform (1)
- Maternity Works (1)
- Mori Luggage & Gifts (2)
- Movado (2)
- Music For A Song (5)
- Naturalizer (1)
- Nautica (1)
- Nike (1)
- Nine West (1)
- North Face (1)
- Off 5th-Saks Fifth Avenue (1)
- OshKosh B'Gosh (1)
- PacSun (1)
- Paper Factory (9)
- Perfumania (8)
- Perry Ellis (1)
- Petite Sophisticate (1)
- Pfaltzgraff (4)
- Polo Ralph Lauren (1)
- Pottery Barn Furniture (4)
- Quiksilver (1)
- Rack Room Shoes (1)

- Reebok (1)
- Reed & Barton (4)
- Remington (4)
- Rosalina Baby Collections (1)
- Royal Doulton (4)
- Rue 21 (1)
- S & K Menswear (1)
- Samsonite (2)
- Sigrid Olsen (1)
- So Fun! Kids (1)
- Springmaid Wamsutta (4)
- Stone Mountain (2)
- Strasburg Children (1)
- Stride Rite Keds Sperry (1)
- Sunglass Station (3)
- Tahari (1)
- Timberland (1)
- Time Factory Watch (3)
- Tommy Hilfiger (1)
- Totes Isotoner Sunglass World (3)
- UK Furniture Outlet (4)
- Ultra Diamond Outlet (3)
- Van Heusen (1)
- Vitamin World (8)
- Welcome Home (4)
- WestPoint Stevens (4)
- Williams-Sonoma Marketplace (4)
- Wilson's Leather (1)
- Zales The Diamond Store (3)

EATS & TREATS
- Food Pavilion (11)
- Fuzziwig's Candy Factory (10)

8 HELEN

8A • Alpine Village Shoppes
www.alpinevillageshoppes.com
Phone 800-755-1405 or 706-878-3016 *Hours* Mon-Thu 10-7 (Jan-May 10-6), Fri-Sat 10-9, Sun 12-6 *Location* Northern Georgia near the Chattahoochee National Forest. From Gainesville travel north on US 129 to Hwy 75 north into Helen on Hwy 75/17.

STORES
- Aunt Flossie's Attic (9)
- Bass (1)
- Capacity (1)

- Country Corner (1)
- Fieldcrest Cannon (4)
- Kitchen Collection (4)
- L'eggs Hanes Bali Playtex (1)
- Native Outpost (5)
- Roper's Clothing (1)
- Softglo Candle Shoppe (5)
- Totes / Sunglass World (3)

EATS & TREATS
- Jazzee Pizza (11)
- What's the Scoop (10)

9 LAKE PARK

9A • Lake Park Mill Store Plaza
www.shoplakepark.com
Address 5327 Mill Store Rd *Phone* 229-559-6822 *Hours* Mon-Sat 9-8, Sun 10-6 *Location* South of Valdosta near the state line. Take exit 5 off I-75, follow Hwy 376 east to Mill Store Rd, turn right.

STORES
- Baby Gap (1)
- Bass (1)
- Better Menswear (1)
- Big & Tall Factory Store (1)
- Big Dog Sportswear (1)
- Black & Decker (4)
- Bon Worth (1)
- Capacity (1)
- Corning Revere (4)
- Dansk (4)
- Dockers Outlet by Designs (1)
- Dress Barn/Dress Barn Woman (1)
- Duck Head (1)
- Famous Footwear (1)
- Gap Kids (1)
- Gap Outlet (1)
- Kitchen Collection (4)
- L'eggs Hanes Bali Playtex (1)
- Lenox (4)
- Levi's Outlet by Designs (1)
- Linens by Dan River (4)
- Oneida (4)
- Paper Factory (9)
- Pfaltzgraff (4)
- Polo Ralph Lauren (1)
- Rack Room Shoes (1)
- S & K Menswear (1)

- Samsonite (2)
- SAS Factory Shoes (1)
- Totes / Sunglass World (3)
- Van Heusen (1)
- WestPoint Stevens (4)

10 LAWRENCEVILLE

10A • Discover Mills
www.millscorp.com
Address 5900 Sugarloaf Pkwy *Phone* 678-847-5201 *Hours* Mon-Sat 10-9:30, Sun 11-7 *Location* 25 miles northeast of downtown Atlanta off I-85 exit 108 (Sugarloaf Pkwy) or exit 107 (State Hwy 120).

STORES
- Adidas (1)
- All About Cellular (7)
- American Greetings (5)
- Anne Hathaway (4)
- AquaMassage (8)
- Art Show (4)
- Artful Living (4)
- Artists' Loft (4)
- Athlete's Foot (1)
- Babies Breath (1)
- Bass Pro Shops Outdoor World (6)
- Bath & Body Works (8)
- Bear Cave (4)
- Beauty Express (8)
- Bebe Outlet (1)
- Bible Factory Outlet (5)
- Big Dog Sportswear (1)
- Bijoux Direct (3)
- Blacklion (4)
- Bobby Allison Wireless (7)
- Books-A-Million (5)
- Bose Factory Store (4)
- Brass and Crafts Imports (4)
- Brookstone Outlet (4)
- Burlington Coat Factory (1)
- Carnivale (4)
- Carter's Childrenswear (1)
- Casual Corner Annex (1)
- Casual Corner Annex Petite (1)
- Casual Corner Annex Woman (1)
- Charlotte Russe (1)
- Charming Gifts, Collectibles & Jewelry (5)
- Chico's (1)
- Coach House Gifts (4)
- Corning Revere (4)
- Cotton Salsa (1)
- Country Clutter (4)
- Dalton Rug (4)
- Date Place Calendar (5)
- Dish Networks (4)
- Dollar Store (9)
- Dress Barn/Dress Barn Woman (1)
- Earthbound Trading Co (5)
- Easy Spirit (1)
- EB Outlet (4)
- Eclectic Furnature (4)
- Eddie Bauer (1)
- ESPN X Games Skatepark (9)
- European Living Interiors (4)
- Eye Candy (1)
- Famous Footwear (1)
- Farberware (4)
- Flag Shop (9)
- Foot Locker (1)
- Fragrance Depot (8)
- Frederick's of Hollywood (1)
- Gadgets & More (4)
- Games Workshop (9)
- Gateway Newstand (5)
- GNC (8)
- Golf America (6)
- Haggar (1)
- Harley Davidson Outlet (9)
- Hensmark Jewelers (3)
- Home Co - Fine Furniture Direct (4)
- Home Impressions (4)
- Hot Wax Candles (5)
- Icing (3)
- Illuminations (5)
- J Crew (1)
- Jewelry Box Outlet (3)
- Joan Vass USA (1)
- Jones New York Country (1)
- Journeys (1)
- Just Sports (1)
- KB Toy Express (6)
- KB Toys (6)
- Kenneth Cole (1)
- La Mode (3)
- Lang Company Store (9)
- Last Call Neiman Marcus (1)
- Leather Limited (2)
- L'eggs Hanes Bali Playtex (1)
- Lego Outlet (6)
- Levi's / Dockers (1)
- Limited Too (1)
- Magnets & Logos (5)

- Mamma Ro' (4)
- Manhattans (1)
- Marco Polo Trading (4)
- MasterCuts (8)
- Mattress Expo (4)
- Mikasa (4)
- Mills Music Café (9)
- Motherhood Maternity (1)
- Nail Pro (8)
- Nail Trix (8)
- New York Cargo (1)
- Nine West (1)
- NordicTrack (8)
- Off 5th-Saks Fifth Avenue (1)
- Off Broadway Shoes (1)
- Oneida (4)
- OshKosh B'Gosh (1)
- Pad (4)
- Papaya Clothing (1)
- Past & Present (9)
- Payless Shoe Source (1)
- Perry Ellis (1)
- Pro Image (1)
- Puzzle World (4)
- Rack Room Shoes (1)
- Radio Shack (7)
- Relish (4)
- Remington (4)
- S & K Menswear (1)
- S Claus (9)
- Safe Warehouse (4)
- Sam Goody (5)
- Samsonite (2)
- Sanrio (9)
- SciTrek (9)
- Scrubs & Beyond (1)
- See (3)
- Seen on Screen/As Seen on TV (5)
- Select Comfort (4)
- Siblings (1)
- Silly Dilly's (6)
- Sirens (1)
- Skechers (1)
- Spa Sydell (8)
- Spencer Gifts (5)
- Splash Perfume (8)
- Sports Memories (6)
- Springmaid Wamsutta (4)
- Stone Mountain (2)
- Strasburg Children (1)
- Stride Rite Keds Sperry (1)
- Summer Classics (4)
- Sun & Ski Sports (1)
- Sunglass Hut (3)
- Sunglass Shop (3)

- SuperTel Wireless (7)
- Swank (2)
- Swim N Sport (1)
- Tommy Hilfiger (1)
- Underground Station (1)
- Vitamin World (8)
- Watches Etc (3)
- Well Suited (1)
- WestPoint Stevens (4)
- Wilson's Leather (1)
- Zales The Diamond Store (3)

EATS & TREATS

- Burger King (11)
- Chili's Too (11)
- Cinnabon (10)
- Cold Stone Creamery (10)
- Dairy Queen / Orange Julius (11)
- Great American Cookie (10)
- Great Steak & Potato (11)
- Great Wraps (11)
- Haagen Dazs (10)
- Hibachi-San Japanese Grill (11)
- Hickory Farms (10)
- Java Joe's (10)
- Jillian's (11)
- Johnny Rockets (11)
- Muscle Beach Lemonade (10)
- Nestle Toll House by Chip (10)
- Panda Express (11)
- Popeye's (11)
- Rocky Mountain Chocolate (10)
- Sbarro Italian Eatery (11)
- Smoothy Bee (10)
- Sweets From Heaven (10)
- Thai Diner (11)
- Wetzel's Pretzels (10)

11   LOCUST GROVE

11A • Tanger Outlet Center
www.tangeroutlets.com
Address 1000 Tanger Dr *Phone*
800-406-0833 or 770-957-5310
Hours Mon-Sat 9-9, Sun 12-6
Location Thirty minutes south of
Atlanta. Take I-75 south to exit
212. Turn left onto Bill Gardner
Pkwy. The center is on your right.

STORES

- Bass (1)
- Bible Factory Outlet (5)
- Big Dog Sportswear (1)
- Bill Hardin Music (5)
- Bon Worth (1)
- Capacity (1)
- Carter's Childrenswear (1)
- Casual Corner (1)
- Casual Corner Woman (1)
- Claire's Accessories (3)
- Corning Clearance (4)
- Corning Revere (4)
- Country Clutter (4)
- Dockers Outlet (1)
- Dress Barn/Dress Barn Woman (1)
- Duck Head (1)
- Eddie Bauer (1)
- Etienne Aigner (1)
- Express Warehouse (1)
- Factory Brand Shoes (1)
- Fossil (2)
- Gap Outlet (1)
- GNC (8)
- Haggar (1)
- Heritage Candle (5)
- Hush Puppies & Family (1)
- Jockey (1)
- Kitchen Collection (4)
- Koret (1)
- Leather Loft (2)
- L'eggs Hanes Bali Playtex (1)
- Levi's Outlet by Designs (1)
- Liz Claiborne (1)
- Mikasa (4)
- Morgan & Company (9)
- Music For A Song (5)
- Naturalizer (1)
- Nine West (1)
- Old Navy (1)
- OshKosh B'Gosh (1)
- Paper Factory (9)
- Perfumania (8)
- Petite Sophisticate (1)
- Publishers Warehouse (5)
- Rack Room Shoes (1)
- Reebok (1)
- Rockport (1)
- Rue 21 (1)
- Samsonite (2)
- SAS Factory Shoes (1)
- Springmaid Wamsutta (4)
- Tools & More (9)
- Totes / Sunglass World (3)
- Toy Liquidators (6)
- Ultra Diamond Outlet (3)
- Van Heusen (1)
- Welcome Home (4)
- Wilson's Leather (1)
- Zales The Diamond Store (3)

EATS & TREATS

- Denny's Diner (11)
- O.B.'s BBQ (11)
- Rocky Mountain Chocolate (10)

12   SAVANNAH

12A • Savannah Festival Factory Stores

www.savannahshopping.com
Address 11 Gateway Blvd S *Phone* 912-925-3089 *Hours* Mon-Sat 9-9, Sun 11-6 *Location* Eastern Georgia, just west of Savannah. Take exit 94 off I-95, follow Hwy 204 east to Gateway Blvd south.

STORES

- All Size Fashions (1)
- Bass (1)
- Beall's Outlet (1)
- Bible Factory Outlet (5)
- Book Warehouse (5)
- Bridal Mart (9)
- Claire's Accessories (3)
- Corning Revere (4)
- Dress Barn (1)
- Duck Head (1)
- Famous Footwear (1)
- GNC (8)
- KB Toys (6)
- Kitchen Collection (4)
- Leather Factory (2)
- L'eggs Hanes Bali Playtex (1)
- Levi's / Dockers (1)
- Paper Factory (9)
- Rack Room Shoes (1)
- Reebok (1)
- S & K Menswear (1)
- Samsonite (2)
- Springmaid Wamsutta (4)
- T-Shirts Plus (1)
- Uniform Outlet (1)
- Van Heusen (1)

Hawaii

1 • Waipahu

1   WAIPAHU

1A • Waikele Premium Outlets

www.premiumoutlets.com
Address 94-790 Lurniaina St *Phone* 808-676-5656 *Hours* Mon-Sat 10-9, Sun 10-6 *Location* Just 15 miles west of Honolulu directly off H-1 Freeway, exit 7.

STORES

- Aloha Gift (5)
- Anne Klein (1)
- Banana Republic (1)
- Barneys New York (1)
- Bass (1)
- BCBG Max Azria (1)
- Bebe Outlet (1)
- Benetton (1)
- Big Dog Sportswear (1)
- Blue Wave (1)
- Bose Factory Store (4)
- Brooks Brothers (1)
- California Luggage (2)
- Caree Image (1)
- Carter's For Kids (1)
- Crazy Shirts (1)
- Danny First (9)
- Donna Karan (1)
- Dressy Keiki (9)
- Ever Blue (1)
- Famous Footwear (1)
- Fantastic Sewing (9)
- Fragrance Outlet (8)
- Geoffrey Beene (1)
- Guess? (1)
- Hawaiian Kine Gifts (5)
- Hawaiian Moon (1)
- Head & Feet (1)
- Hibiscus Collection (9)
- Izod (1)
- Jockey (1)
- Kenneth Cole (1)
- Levi's Outlet by Most (1)
- Local Fever (1)
- Local Motion (1)
- Logo Logo (9)
- Lulu's Hawaiian Collection (5)
- Max Mara (1)
- Max Studio (1)
- Mikasa (4)
- Nine West (1)
- Off 5th-Saks Fifth Avenue (1)
- Olga Warner (1)
- OshKosh B'Gosh (1)
- Paris Fashions (1)
- Perfumania (8)
- Polo Jeans Co (1)
- Samsonite (2)
- Skechers (1)
- Sunglass Hut (3)
- Tommy Hilfiger (1)
- Universal Time Outlet (3)
- Van Heusen (1)
- Vans Shoes (1)
- Villeroy & Boch (4)
- Vitamin World (8)
- Waikele Jewelry Mart (3)

EATS & TREATS

- Oasis Café (11)
- Rocky Mountain Chocolate (10)
- Waikele Coffee (10)

Idaho

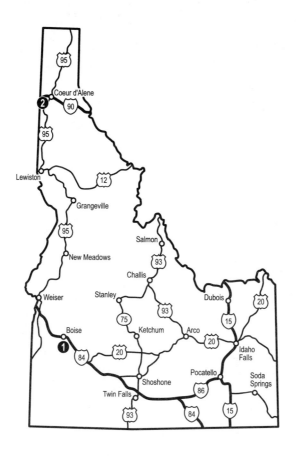

1 BOISE

1A • Boise Factory Outlets

www.boisefactoryoutlets.com
Address 7032 S Eisenman Rd
Phone 208-331-5000 *Hours* Mon-Sat 10-8, Sun 11-6 *Location* I-84 exit 57 (Gowen Rd), west to Eiseman Rd and south to center.

STORES

- Bass (1)
- Big Dog Sportswear (1)
- Book Warehouse (5)
- Carter's Childrenswear (1)
- Coldwater Creek Outlet (1)
- Dress Barn (1)
- Dress Barn Woman (1)
- Eddie Bauer (1)
- Factory Brand Shoes (1)
- Foot Locker (1)
- Full Size Fashions (1)
- Harry & David (5)
- KB Toy Liquidators (6)
- Kitchen Collection (4)
- Levi's (1)
- Paper Factory (9)
- Payless Shoe Source (1)
- Perfect Look Outlet Salon (8)
- Sunglass Hut / Watch Station (3)
- Van Heusen (1)
- Vitamin World (8)
- Welcome Home (4)

EATS & TREATS

- Rocky Mountain Chocolate (10)

2 POST FALLS

2A • Post Falls Factory Stores

www.idahooutlets.com
Address 4037 Riverbend Ave *Phone* 208-773-1329 *Hours* Mon-Sat 9:30-8 (Jan-Mar 9:30-6), Sun 11-6 *Location* Eight miles west of Coeur d'Alene off I-90, exit 2.

STORES

- Beauty Express (8)
- Black & Decker (4)
- Casual Corner (1)
- Christian Tree Of Life Outlet (5)
- Collectors Zone (9)
- Dress Barn (1)
- Farberware (4)
- Fieldcrest Cannon (4)
- Northwest Gift Outlet (5)
- Oneida (4)
- OshKosh B'Gosh (1)
- Riverbend Art Gallery (4)

EATS & TREATS

- Cabin Restaurant (11)

2B • Prime Outlets Post Falls

www.primeoutlets.com
Address 4300 W Riverbend Ave
Phone 208-773-4556 or 888-678-9847 *Hours* Mon-Sat 9:30-8, Sun 11-6 *Location* Eight miles west of Coeur d'Alene off I-90, exit 2.

STORES

- Antiques (4)
- Bass (1)
- Big Dogs (1)
- Bodies in Training (9)
- Book Warehouse (5)
- Corning Revere (4)
- Country Elegance (4)
- Dansk (4)
- Famous Brands Housewares (4)
- Famous Footwear (1)
- Full Size Fashions (1)
- GNC (8)
- Kitchen Collection (4)
- Leather Loft (2)
- L'eggs Hanes Bali Playtex (1)
- Levi's Outlet by Most (1)
- Mikasa (4)
- Oriental Gifts & Food (5)
- Paper Factory (9)
- Perfumania (8)
- Pfaltzgraff (4)
- Reebok (1)
- Samsonite/American Tourister (2)
- Socks Galore (1)
- Sunglass Hut (3)
- Super Silver Jewelry (3)
- Toy Liquidators (6)
- Van Heusen (1)
- Welcome Home (4)
- Wireless Etc (7)
- World Of Art (9)

EATS & TREATS

- Fuzziwig's Candy Factory (10)
- Rocky Mountain Chocolate (10)

Illinois

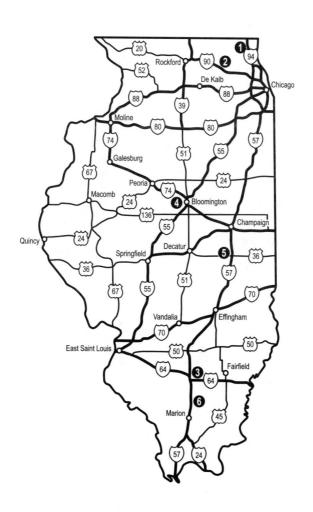

1 GURNEE

1A • Gurnee Mills

www.millscorp.com
Address 6170 W Grand Ave *Phone*
847-263-7500 *Hours* Mon-Fri 10-
9, Sat 9:30-9, Sun 10-7 *Location*
Forty minutes north of Chicago.
Take I-94 west (heading north) to
Hwy 132 west, Grand Ave.

STORES

- $9.99 Stockroom (1)
- Abercrombie & Fitch (1)
- Affordable Optical (3)
- All That's Natural (8)
- American Vision Center (3)
- Aromas Cigars (9)
- Athlete's Foot (1)
- Babbage's Software (7)
- Baja Hut (1)
- Bally Outlet (1)
- Banana Republic (1)
- Bank One (9)
- Bargain Books (5)
- Bass (1)
- Bass Pro Shops Outdoor World (6)
- Bath & Body Works (8)
- Beauty Express (8)
- Bed Bath & Beyond (4)
- Belvidere Blues (1)
- Bentley's Luggage (2)
- Bestcom (9)
- Big Dog Sportswear (1)
- Black Market Minerals (5)
- Burlington Coat Factory (1)
- Burlington Shoes (1)
- Camelot Music (5)
- Cancer Resource Center (9)
- Capers (1)
- Carter's Childrenswear (1)
- Casual Corner (1)
- Casual Corner Woman (1)
- Casual Male Big & Tall (1)
- Charlotte Russe (1)
- Chenice of Beverly Hills (8)
- Chicago Shop (9)
- Chico's (1)
- Children's Place Outlet (1)
- Christian Bernard (3)
- Claire's Boutique (3)
- Clothestime (1)
- Comics & Cards (5)
- Corning Revere (4)
- Cost Cutters Salon (8)
- Cristopher & Banks (1)
- Cunningham Research (9)
- Dara Michelle (2)
- Dockers Outlet by Designs (1)
- Dress Barn/Dress Barn Woman (1)
- Electronics Boutique (4)
- Etienne Aigner (1)
- Ev's Cottage Collectibles (4)
- Express Warehouse (1)
- Eye Candy (1)
- Factory Brand Shoes (1)
- Fancy Fakes (2)
- Finish Line (1)
- First Class Male (1)
- Flag Shop (9)
- Florsheim (1)
- Foot Locker (1)
- FootAction USA (1)
- Fossil (2)
- Games Workshop (9)
- Gap Outlet (1)
- Gateway Newstand (5)
- Geoffrey Beene (1)
- GNC (8)
- Goodstone Jewelers (3)
- Group USA (1)
- Guess? (1)
- Gurnee Marcus Cinema (9)
- Happy Kids (1)
- Harley Davidson Outlet (9)
- Home Shopping Network (1)
- Icing (3)
- Izod (1)
- JCPenney Outlet (1)
- Jockey (1)
- Journeys (1)
- Just Sports (1)
- Kasper ASL (1)
- KB Toys (6)
- Kirkland's (4)
- Leather Limited (2)
- Leather Mode (2)
- Lee Nails (8)
- L'eggs Hanes Bali Playtex (1)
- Let's Talk Cellular (7)
- Levi's Outlet by Designs (1)
- Lids (9)
- Liz Claiborne (1)
- Maidenform (1)
- Manhattan Diamonds (3)
- Marshalls Megastore (1)
- MasterCuts (8)

- Maternity Works (1)
- Metro Watch (3)
- Military Benefit Association (9)
- Movado (2)
- Music Recyclery (5)
- Naturalizer (1)
- Nautica (1)
- Nine West (1)
- Off 5th-Saks Fifth Avenue (1)
- OshKosh B'Gosh (1)
- Pacific Sunwear (1)
- Paper Factory (9)
- Parade of Shoes (1)
- Payless Shoe Source (1)
- Perfumania (8)
- Picture People (9)
- Picture Us (4)
- Polo Jeans Co (1)
- Premier Fine Jewelry (3)
- Radio Shack (7)
- Remington (4)
- Rink Side Sports (6)
- Ritz Camera 1 Hour Photo (7)
- Robin Marie's Tiki Hut (4)
- Runkel Bros American Greetings (5)
- Salton Retail Outlet (4)
- Sam Goody (5)
- Samsonite (2)
- San Francisco Music Box (9)
- Sanrio (9)
- Serpent Safari (9)
- Shoe Carnival (1)
- Sirens (1)
- Spencer Gifts (5)
- Spiegel Outlet (1)
- Sports Authority (6)
- Sterling Works (3)
- Stop 'N Out Shoe Repair/Tailor (9)
- Suncoast Motion Picture Co (9)
- Sunglass Hut (3)
- Sunglass World (3)
- T-Nails (8)
- Time Factory Watch (3)
- TJ Maxx (1)
- Tommy Hilfiger Jeans (1)
- Totes / Isotoner (3)
- ToyCo (6)
- Track N' Trail Outlet (1)
- Ultra Diamond & Gold (3)
- Underground Station (1)
- Urban Planet (1)
- Value City (9)
- Van Heusen (1)
- VF Factory Outlet (1)
- Vitamin World (8)

- Warnaco (1)
- Westport Ltd/Westport Woman (1)
- Whispers (9)
- Wilson's Leather (1)
- XOXO (1)
- Young Hui Imports (5)
- Zales The Diamond Store (3)

EATS & TREATS

- A & W Restaurant (11)
- Auntie Anne's Pretzals (10)
- Boardwalk Fries (11)
- Bresler's (10)
- Burger King (11)
- Cajan Grill (11)
- Charley's Steakery (11)
- China Kitchen (11)
- Corner Bakery Café (11)
- Edy's Grand Ice Cream (10)
- Fannie May Candies (10)
- Frullati Café (11)
- Fuzziwig's Candy Factory (10)
- Gloria Jean's Gourmet Coffee (10)
- Great American Cookie (10)
- Great Steak & Potato (11)
- Little Tokyo (11)
- Manchu Wok (11)
- McDonald's (11)
- Pizzahh! (11)
- Quencher Smoothies (10)
- Rainforest Café (11)
- Ruby Tuesday (11)
- Sbarro Italian Eatery (11)
- Starbucks Coffee (10)
- Subway (11)
- Taco Bell (11)
- Tropik Sun Fruit & Nut (10)
- Villa Pizza (11)

2 HUNTLEY

2A • Prime Outlets Huntley
www.primeoutlets.com
Address 11800 Factory Shops Blvd
Phone 888-545-7222 *Hours* Mon-
Sat 10-8, Sun 11-6 *Location*
Northern Illinois, between
Chicago and Rockford. Traveling
westbound on I-90 take Rt 47
north. Eastbound travelers can take

Rt 20 east to Rt 47 north.

STORES
- Amish Oak By Yoder (4)
- Bass (1)
- Big Dogs (1)
- Bon Worth (1)
- Book Warehouse (5)
- Bose Factory Store (4)
- Calendar Club (5)
- Carter's Childrenswear (1)
- Casual Corner (1)
- Casual Corner Woman (1)
- Claire's Boutique (3)
- Corning Revere (4)
- Dress Barn/Dress Barn Woman (1)
- Factory Brand Shoes (1)
- Gap Outlet (1)
- Giftmart (5)
- Interior Alternative (4)
- Izod (1)
- Jockey (1)
- KB Toys (6)
- Kitchen Collection (4)
- Koret (1)
- L'eggs Hanes Bali Playtex (1)
- Levi's Outlet by Designs (1)
- Linen Barn (4)
- London Fog (1)
- Mikasa (4)
- Nine West (1)
- OshKosh B'Gosh (1)
- Paper Factory (9)
- Petite Sophisticate (1)
- Pfaltzgraff (4)
- Reebok / Rockport (1)
- S & K Menswear (1)
- Samsonite (2)
- SAS Factory Shoes (1)
- Shoebilee (1)
- Sunglass Hut (3)
- Ultra Diamond & Gold (3)
- Van Heusen (1)
- VF Factory Outlet (1)
- Welcome Home (4)
- Wilson's Leather (1)

EATS & TREATS
- CinnaMonster (10)
- Fudgie Puppies (11)
- Great Steak & Potato (11)
- Rocky Mountain Chocolate (10)
- Subway (11)
- Taco John's (11)
- Villa Pizza (11)

3 MOUNT VERNON

3A • Rend Lake College Market Place
Address 200 Outlet Ave *Phone* 618-244-9525 *Hours* Mon-Sat 9-9, Sun 11-7 *Location* Southern Illinois, north of Rend Lake recreation area. Take exit 95 off I-64/57.

STORES
- Bon Worth (1)
- Brass Factory (4)
- Capers (1)
- Dress Barn (1)
- Dress Barn Woman (1)
- Kountry Depot (5)
- Pro Golf (6)
- Rack Room Shoes (1)

EATS & TREATS
- Fannie May Candies (10)
- Lonestar Steakhouse (11)

4 NORMAL

4A • Bloomington-Normal Factory Stores
Address 310 Wylie Dr *Phone* 309-452-7888 *Hours* Mon-Sat 10-9, Sun 11-6 *Location* Central Illinois, east of Peoria. From I-74/55 take exit 160B (Market St/Rt 9) westbound to Wylie Dr.

STORES
- Bass (1)
- Big Dogs (1)
- Casual Corner (1)
- Dollar General (9)
- Dress Barn (1)
- Dress Barn Woman (1)
- Famous Footwear (1)
- Full Size Fashions (1)
- Gazing Globe (9)
- KB Toys (6)

- Kitchen Collection (4)
- Nike (1)
- Party Concepts (9)
- Publishers Warehouse (5)
- Rue 21 (1)
- Totes (3)
- Van Heusen (1)
- VF Factory Outlet (1)
- Vitamin World (8)
- Welcome Home (4)

EATS & TREATS
- Fannie May Candies (10)

5 TUSCOLA

5A • Factory Stores at Tuscola
www.shoptuscola.com
Address Tuscola Blvd *Phone* 217-253-2282 *Hours* Jan-Feb: Mon-Thu 10-6, Fri-Sat 10-9, Sun 11-6. Mar-Dec: Mon-Sat 10-9, Sun 11-6 *Location* Just 20 minutes south of Champaign. Take exit 212 (US 36) off I-57.

STORES
- Bass (1)
- Big Dog Sportswear (1)
- Black & Decker (4)
- Bon Worth (1)
- Book Warehouse (5)
- Capacity (1)
- Carter's Childrenswear (1)
- Casual Corner (1)
- Casual Corner Woman (1)
- Claire's Accessories (3)
- Coach (2)
- Corning Revere (4)
- Dress Barn/Dress Barn Woman (1)
- Factory Brand Shoes (1)
- Gap Outlet (1)
- Geoffrey Beene (1)
- Harry & David (5)
- Hush Puppies & Family (1)
- Jockey (1)
- KB Toys (6)
- Kitchen Collection (4)
- Korean War Veterans National Museum & Library (9)
- Koret (1)
- Leather Loft (2)

- L'eggs Hanes Bali Playtex (1)
- Lenox (4)
- Levi's Outlet by Designs (1)
- Linen Barn (4)
- Mikasa (4)
- Music For A Song (5)
- Nautica (1)
- OshKosh B'Gosh (1)
- Paper Factory (9)
- Perfumania (8)
- Petite Sophisticate (1)
- Polo Ralph Lauren (1)
- Rockport (1)
- Rue 21 (1)
- S & K Menswear (1)
- Samsonite (2)
- SAS Factory Shoes (1)
- Sunglass Hut (3)
- Tommy Hilfiger (1)
- Totes / Sunglass World (3)
- Van Heusen (1)
- VF Factory Outlet (1)
- Vitamin World (8)
- Welcome Home (4)
- Wilson's Leather (1)
- Zales The Diamond Store (3)

EATS & TREATS
- Rocky Mountain Chocolate (10)

6 WEST FRANKFORT

6A • Factory Stores of America
www.chelseafactoryoutlets.com
Address 1000 Factory Outlet Dr *Phone* 618-937-3536 *Hours* Mon-Thu 9-8 (Jan-Feb 9-7), Fri-Sat 9-9, Sun 12-6 *Location* Southern Illinois, south of Rend Lake recreation area. Take exit 65 (Hwy 149) off I-57.

STORES
- Banister / Easy Spirit (1)
- Bon Worth (1)
- Capacity (1)
- Flash (9)
- Kountry Klutter Krafts (5)
- Miracle Ear (8)
- Paper Factory (9)
- VF Factory Outlet (1)

Indiana

1 • Daleville
2 • Edinburgh
3 • Fremont
4 • Michigan City
5 • Seymour

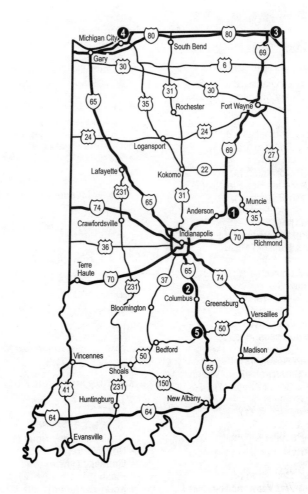

1 DALEVILLE

1A • Indiana Factory Shops

www.horizongroup.com
Address 9401 S Factory Shops Blvd
Phone 888-545-7223 or 765-378-1300 *Hours* Mon-Sat 10-9, Sun 11-6 *Location* Eastern Indiana between Anderson and Muncie. Take exit 34 off I-69/Rt67.

STORES

- Bass (1)
- Best Deal Home Furniture (4)
- Big Dogs (1)
- Bon Worth (1)
- Book Warehouse (5)
- Casual Corner (1)
- Casual Corner Woman (1)
- Corning Revere (4)
- Dress Barn/Dress Barn Woman (1)
- Factory Brand Shoes (1)
- KB Toy Liquidators (6)
- Kitchen Collection (4)
- L'eggs Hanes Bali Playtex (1)
- OshKosh B'Gosh (1)
- Petite Sophisticate (1)
- Pfaltzgraff (4)
- Polo Ralph Lauren (1)
- Racer's Edge (6)
- Rue 21 (1)
- SAS Factory Shoes (1)
- Springmaid Wamsutta (4)
- Sunglass Hut (3)
- Van Heusen (1)
- Vitamin World (8)
- Welcome Home (4)

EATS & TREATS

- CinnaMonster (10)

2 EDINBURGH

2A • Prime Outlets Edinburgh

www.primeoutlets.com
Address 3026 Outlet Dr *Phone* 812-526-9764 *Hours* Mon-Sat 10-9, Sun 11-6 *Location* Just 35 minutes south of Indianapolis.

Take the Edinburgh exit off I-65.

STORES

- Ann Taylor (1)
- Bass (1)
- Big Dogs (1)
- Black & Decker (4)
- Bon Worth (1)
- Carter's Childrenswear (1)
- Casual Corner (1)
- Casual Corner Woman (1)
- Casual Male Big & Tall (1)
- Christian Factory Outlet (5)
- Claire's Accessories (3)
- Corning Revere (4)
- Cosco (9)
- Cosmetics Company Store (8)
- Country Lace Gallery (4)
- Dress Barn (1)
- Easy Spirit (1)
- Eddie Bauer (1)
- Esprit (1)
- Factory Brand Shoes (1)
- Farberware (4)
- Fieldcrest Cannon (4)
- Florsheim (1)
- Gap Outlet (1)
- Geoffrey Beene (1)
- Golf Outlet (6)
- Haggar (1)
- Harry & David (5)
- Hush Puppies & Family (1)
- Izod (1)
- Jockey (1)
- Jones New York (1)
- Kasper ASL (1)
- KB Toys (6)
- Kitchen Collection (4)
- Koret (1)
- Leather Loft (2)
- L'eggs Hanes Bali Playtex (1)
- Lenox (4)
- Levi's Outlet by Designs (1)
- Motherhood Maternity (1)
- Music For A Song (5)
- Naturalizer (1)
- Nautica (1)
- Nike (1)
- Nine West (1)
- OshKosh B'Gosh (1)
- Pacific Sunwear (1)
- Paper Factory (9)
- Perfumania (8)
- Petite Sophisticate (1)
- Pfaltzgraff (4)

- Rue 21 (1)
- Samsonite (2)
- Spiegel Outlet (1)
- Sunglass Hut (3)
- Tommy Hilfiger (1)
- Tool Warehouse (9)
- Ultra Fine Jewelry (3)
- Van Heusen (1)
- Vitamin World (8)
- Welcome Home (4)
- Zales The Diamond Store (3)

EATS & TREATS

- Burrito Shack (11)
- Chill 'N Grill (11)
- Little Italy (11)
- Rocky Mountain Chocolate (10)

3 FREMONT

3A • Prime Outlets Fremont

www.primeoutlets.com
Address 6245 N Old 27 *Phone*
219-833-1684 *Hours* Mon-Sat 9-
8, Sun 11-6 *Location* Northeast
corner of the state. From I-80/90
take exit 144, follow signs to State
Rt 120. From I-69 take exit 157,
follow signs to State Rt 120.

STORES

- Ann Taylor (1)
- Bass (1)
- Big Dogs (1)
- Bon Worth (1)
- Book Warehouse (5)
- Carter's Childrenswear (1)
- Casual Corner (1)
- Chef's Outlet (4)
- Coach (2)
- Corning Revere (4)
- Cosmetics Company Store (8)
- Dress Barn (1)
- Easy Spirit (1)
- Factory Brand Shoes (1)
- Fieldcrest Cannon (4)
- Gap Outlet (1)
- Geoffrey Beene (1)
- GNC (8)
- Gold N Stone (3)
- Hush Puppies & Family (1)

- Jockey (1)
- Jones New York (1)
- KB Toys (6)
- Kitchen Collection (4)
- Leather Manor (2)
- L'eggs Hanes Bali Playtex (1)
- Levi's Outlet by Designs (1)
- Mikasa (4)
- Nautica (1)
- Oneida (4)
- OshKosh B'Gosh (1)
- Paper Factory (9)
- Pickle Factory (9)
- Polo Ralph Lauren (1)
- Reebok (1)
- Rue 21 (1)
- Samsonite (2)
- Smileys (4)
- Socks Galore (1)
- Sunglass Hut (3)
- Tommy Hilfiger (1)
- Totes / Sunglass World (3)
- Van Heusen (1)
- Welcome Home (4)

EATS & TREATS

- Bubba's (11)
- Rocky Mountain Chocolate (10)

4 MICHIGAN CITY

4A • Lighthouse Place Premium Outlets

www.premiumoutlets.com
Address 601 Wabash St *Phone* 219-
879-6506 *Hours* Mon-Sat 9-9, Sun
10-6 *Location* Northern Indiana,
west of South Bend. From I-80/90
take exit 39, US 421 north. Follow
US 421 north for 9 miles to 6th
St, turn left; two blocks to center.

STORES

- All Stars / Small Stars (1)
- Ann Taylor (1)
- Banister Shoes (1)
- Bass (1)
- Bass Kids (1)
- Big Dog Sportswear (1)
- Bombay Outlet (4)

- Bon Worth (1)
- Bookstore In The Works (5)
- Bose Factory Store (4)
- Brooks Brothers (1)
- Burberry (1)
- Calendar Club (5)
- Carpenter's Candle & Lace (5)
- Carter's For Kids (1)
- Casual Corner (1)
- Chef's Outlet (4)
- Chico's (1)
- Claire's Accessories (3)
- Coach (2)
- Corning Revere (4)
- Corning Revere Warehouse (4)
- Cosmetics Company Store (8)
- Crate & Barrel (4)
- Dansk (4)
- Designer Brands Accessories (2)
- Designer Fragrance/Cosmetics (8)
- Dinger's Dog Bakery (9)
- DKNY Jeans (1)
- Donna Karan (1)
- Doolittles (5)
- Dress Barn/Dress Barn Woman (1)
- Easy Spirit (1)
- Eddie Bauer (1)
- Elegant Illusions (3)
- Elisabeth (1)
- Ellen Tracy (1)
- Esprit (1)
- Etienne Aigner (1)
- Factory Brand Shoes (1)
- Famous Brands Housewares (4)
- Farberware (4)
- Fila (1)
- Gap Outlet (1)
- Geoffrey Beene (1)
- Good Ship (9)
- Guess? (1)
- Haggar (1)
- Hanna Andersson Outlet (1)
- Harry & David (5)
- Hartmarx Brands Outlet (1)
- Hugo Boss (1)
- Hush Puppies & Family (1)
- Izod (1)
- J Crew (1)
- Jockey (1)
- Jones New York (1)
- Jones New York Country (1)
- Kasper ASL (1)
- Kitchen Collection (4)
- Koret (1)
- Leather Loft (2)

- L'eggs Hanes Bali Playtex (1)
- Lenox (4)
- Levi's Outlet by Designs (1)
- Liz Claiborne (1)
- London Fog (1)
- Maidenform (1)
- Mikasa (4)
- Motherhood Maternity (1)
- Movado (2)
- Music For A Song (5)
- Naturalizer (1)
- Nautica (1)
- Nine West (1)
- Oilily (1)
- Olga Warner (1)
- OshKosh B'Gosh (1)
- Paper Factory (9)
- Payless Shoe Source (1)
- Perfumania (8)
- Pfaltzgraff (4)
- Polo Jeans Co (1)
- Polo Ralph Lauren (1)
- Reebok (1)
- Reebok / Rockport (1)
- Remington (4)
- Royal Doulton (4)
- Rue 21 (1)
- Rug Decor (4)
- S & K Menswear (1)
- Samsonite (2)
- Sassafras (4)
- Socks Galore (1)
- Spiegel Outlet (1)
- Sunglass Source (3)
- Timberland (1)
- Tommy Hilfiger (1)
- Tools & More (9)
- Totes / Sunglass World (3)
- Toy Liquidators (6)
- Ultra Diamond Outlet (3)
- Van Heusen (1)
- Vitamin World (8)
- Waterford Wedgwood (4)
- Wilson's Leather (1)

EATS & TREATS

- Bristol Café (11)
- Fannie May Candies (10)
- Fuzziwig's Candy Factory (10)
- Hammer's Pasta & Pizza (11)
- Jo-C's Gourmet Café (11)
- Pepperidge Farm (10)
- Pullman Café/Club Car Lounge (11)
- Scoops Ice Cream (10)
- Subway (11)

5 SEYMOUR

5A • Tanger Outlet Center
www.tangeroutlets.com
Address 357 Tanger Blvd *Phone*
800-406-1154 or 812-524-0917
Hours Mon-Sat 9-9, Sun 11-6
Location About 1 hour south of
Indianapolis. Take exit 50A off I-65.

STORES
- Bass (1)
- Bon Worth (1)
- Christian Factory Outlet (5)
- Claire's Accessories (3)
- Factory Brand Shoes (1)
- Full Size Fashions (1)
- Gap Outlet (1)
- Great Escape Theater (9)
- J Crew (1)
- KB Toys (6)
- L'eggs Hanes Bali Playtex (1)
- Liz Claiborne (1)
- Mikasa (4)
- Old Navy (1)
- Polo Ralph Lauren (1)
- Reebok (1)
- Rue 21 (1)
- S & K Menswear (1)
- Samsonite (2)
- Van Heusen (1)
- Visitors Center Jackson Cty (9)
- Vitamin World (8)

EATS & TREATS
- Dairy Mart (11)
- McDonald's (11)

Iowa

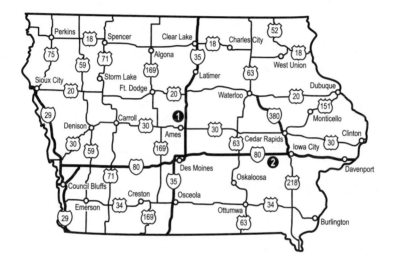

1 STORY CITY

1A • Factory Stores of America
www.chelseafactoryoutlets.com
Address 324 Factory Outlet Dr
Phone 515-733-5242 *Hours* Mon-
Sat 9-8 (Jan-Apr 9-7), Sun 11-5
Location North of Des Moines off
I-35, exit 124.

STORES

- Banister Shoes (1)
- Bass (1)
- Bon Worth (1)
- Claire's Accessories (3)
- KB Toy Liquidators (6)
- L'eggs Hanes Bali Playtex (1)
- M&J Sports Collectibles (6)
- Paper Factory (9)
- Phoenix Rising (9)
- Rue 21 (1)
- Van Heusen (1)
- VF Factory Outlet (1)

2 WILLIAMSBURG

2A • Tanger Outlet Center
www.tangeroutlets.com
Address 150 Tanger Dr *Phone* 800-
406-2887 or 319-668-2885 *Hours*
Mon-Sat 9-9, Sun 12-6 *Location*
Eastern Iowa, southwest of Cedar
Rapids. Take exit 220 off I-80.

STORES

- Bass (1)
- Bass Kids (1)
- Big & Tall Factory Store (1)
- Big Dog Sportswear (1)
- Black & Decker (4)
- Brooks Brothers (1)
- Calendar Club (5)
- Carter's Childrenswear (1)
- Claire's Accessories (3)
- Coach (2)
- Corning Revere (4)
- Cosmetics Company Store (8)
- Dansk (4)
- Dress Barn (1)
- Eddie Bauer (1)
- Factory Brand Shoes (1)
- Fieldcrest Cannon (4)
- Florsheim (1)
- Full Size Fashions (1)
- Gap Outlet (1)
- Geoffrey Beene (1)
- GNC (8)
- Haggar (1)
- Heritage Lace (4)
- Jockey (1)
- Kitchen Collection (4)
- Koret (1)
- L'eggs Hanes Bali Playtex (1)
- Levi's Outlet by Most (1)
- Liz Claiborne (1)
- Mikasa (1)
- Motherhood Maternity (1)
- Music For A Song (5)
- Nautica (1)
- Nike (1)
- Old Navy (1)
- Oneida (4)
- OshKosh B'Gosh (1)
- Paper Factory (9)
- Pfaltzgraff (4)
- Polo Ralph Lauren (1)
- Publishers Warehouse (5)
- Reebok (1)
- Rockport (1)
- Rue 21 (1)
- Samsonite (2)
- Socks Galore (1)
- Tommy Hilfiger (1)
- Totes / Sunglass World (3)
- Toy Liquidators (6)
- Ultra Diamond Outlet (3)
- Van Heusen (1)
- VF Factory Outlet (1)
- Welcome Home (4)
- Wilson's Leather (1)
- Woolrich (1)

EATS & TREATS

- Rocky Mountain Chocolate (10)
- Subway (11)
- Taste of China (11)

Kansas

1 • Newton
2 • Olathe

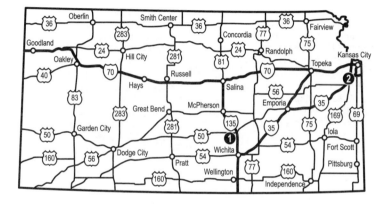

1 NEWTON

1A • Newton Factory Outlet Stores
www.shopnewton.com
Address I-135 at exit 28 *Phone* 316-282-1518 *Hours* Mon-Sat 10-9, Sun 12-6 *Location* South-central Kansas, 16 miles north of Wichita. The center is at exit 28 off I-135.

STORES

- Big Dogs (1)
- Bon Worth (1)
- Book Warehouse (5)
- Carter's For Kids (1)
- Claire's Boutique (3)
- Dress Barn/Dress Barn Woman (1)
- Factory Brand Shoes (1)
- Farberware (4)
- Full Size Fashions (1)
- Gap Outlet (1)
- Harbor View Miniature Golf (9)
- KB Toys (6)
- Kitchen Collection (4)
- Paper Factory (9)
- Pfaltzgraff (4)
- Royale 8 Cinemas (9)
- Rue 21 (1)
- Samsonite (2)
- Tools & More (9)
- Totes / Sunglass World (3)
- Van Heusen (1)
- VF Factory Outlet (1)
- Vitamin World (8)

EATS & TREATS

- Creole Hut (11)
- Hong Kong Garden (11)
- Rocky Mountain Chocolate (10)
- Subway (11)
- Sunset Bar & Grill (11)
- Taste of New Orleans (11)

2 OLATHE

2A • The Great Mall of the Great Plains
www.greatmallgreatplains
Address 20700 W 151st St *Phone* 913-829-6277 or 888-Fun-Mall *Hours* Mon-Sat 10-9, Sun 12-6 *Location* Southwest of Kansas City in eastern Kansas. Take exit 215 (151st St) off I-35.

STORES

- 31st Century (5)
- Afterthoughts (3)
- As Seen On TV (5)
- Auto Fun Shop (5)
- Banister Shoes (1)
- Bass (1)
- Bath & Body Works (8)
- Beauty Express (8)
- Big Dogs (1)
- Black & Decker (4)
- Bon Worth (1)
- Brown Wrappings (5)
- Bungee Ball (5)
- Burlington Coat Factory (1)
- Calendar Club (5)
- Carter's Childrenswear (1)
- Casual Corner Annex (1)
- Casual Male Big & Tall (1)
- Chai's Tailor (9)
- Claire's Boutique (3)
- Classic Glass (4)
- Classic Sports (6)
- Clay Café (4)
- Corning Clearance (4)
- Corning Revere (4)
- Country Clutter (4)
- Deb (1)
- Designer Rugs (4)
- Dickinson Theaters (9)
- Dress Barn (1)
- DSW Shoe Warehouse (1)
- Eddie Bauer (1)
- Egg Cetera (5)
- Elegant Jewelers (3)
- Endless Editions (1)
- Everything for a dollar (5)
- Exquisite Art (4)
- Factory Brand Shoes (1)
- Famous Footwear (1)
- Fashion Outlet (1)
- Finish Line (1)
- Florsheim (1)
- Foot Locker (1)
- Foozles Bookstore (5)
- Foto Fantasy (9)
- Gameco Video Games (9)
- Gear Zone (1)
- GNC (8)

- Go - The Game Store (9)
- Gold Plus (3)
- Gone Racing (9)
- Group USA (1)
- Handbags 'N More (2)
- Hat Zone (1)
- Hot Topic (1)
- Jewel Time (3)
- Jewelry Jungle (3)
- Just Sports (1)
- KB Toys (6)
- Leather Collection (2)
- L'eggs Hanes Bali Playtex (1)
- Levi's (1)
- Lids (9)
- Linen's N Things (4)
- Magic Pens (5)
- Manhattans (1)
- Marshalls (1)
- MasterCuts (8)
- Motherhood Maternity (1)
- Nail Citi (8)
- Nail Shop (8)
- National Jewelry Outlet (3)
- Nautica (1)
- Nextel (7)
- Noble House Jewelry (3)
- NordicTrack / Healthrider (8)
- Northport Crossing (5)
- Off 5th-Saks Fifth Avenue (1)
- Old Navy (1)
- On The Run (9)
- Oshman's SuperSports USA (6)
- Paper Factory (9)
- Payless Shoe Source (1)
- Perfumania (8)
- Piercing Pagoda (3)
- Radio Shack (7)
- Remington (4)
- Rice Man (3)
- RP Bonsai (9)
- Rue 21 (1)
- Russian Gifts & Collectibles (5)
- Santa's Pen (9)
- Simply Southwest (5)
- Snyder's Spas (4)
- Spencer Gifts (5)
- Sports Fans (6)
- Stop N Save Software (7)
- Street Company (1)
- Suit Mart (1)
- Sun Lizard (3)
- Sunglass Hut (3)
- Superior Sound (4)
- T-Shirts Plus (1)

- Taylor's Treasure Trove (5)
- Tools & More (9)
- Toy Works (6)
- Trendwest (9)
- Van Heusen (1)
- VF Factory Outlet (1)
- Vitamin World (8)
- Waves Music (5)
- Westport Ltd/Westport Woman (1)
- Wilson's Leather (1)
- Wireless Accessories (7)

EATS & TREATS

- A & W Restaurant (11)
- Auntie Anne's Pretzals (10)
- Cajun Grill (11)
- Cinnabon (10)
- Dairy Queen (11)
- Delect-a-Rama (11)
- Dippin Dots (11)
- Flamers Charbroiled (11)
- Great Steak & Potato (11)
- Hickory Farms (10)
- Java Jive (10)
- Jeepers! (11)
- King BBQ (11)
- Mr Bulky Treats and Gifts (10)
- New York Deli (11)
- Nuts for You (10)
- Original Pizza (11)
- Rocky Mountain Chocolate (10)
- Sweet Stop (10)
- Topsy's Popcorn (10)
- Villa Perez Cantina and Restaurant (11)
- Wetzel's Pretzels (10)
- Yeung's Lotus Express (11)

Kentucky

1 • Eddyville
2 • Georgetown
3 • Hanson

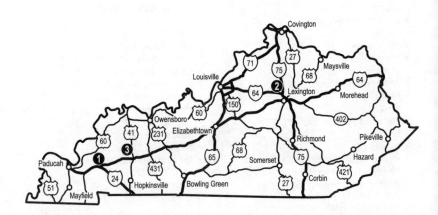

1 EDDYVILLE

1A • West Kentucky Factory Outlets

Address 100 Outlet Ave *Phone* 270-388-7379 *Hours* Jan-Mar: Mon-Sat 10-7, Sun 12-5. Apr-Dec: Mon-Sat 9-9, Sun 11-6 *Location* Western Kentucky, east of Paducah. From I-24 take exit 40 (US 62/421 east) to Eddyville.

STORES

- Arrow Shirt (1)
- Bon Worth (1)
- Brass Factory (4)
- Capacity (1)
- Capers (1)
- Corning Revere (4)
- Discount Jewelry (3)
- Dress-Ups/Tie Factory (1)
- Dress Barn (1)
- Dress Barn Woman (1)
- House of Books (5)
- Interiors For Less (4)
- KB Toy Liquidators (6)
- Kitchen Collection (4)
- L'eggs Hanes Bali Playtex (1)
- Mama Mia's (9)
- Naturalizer (1)
- Paper Factory (9)
- Rack Room Shoes (1)
- Sports Outlet (6)
- Wallet Works (2)
- Walnut Bowl / Chicago Cutlery (4)
- Welcome Home (4)

EATS & TREATS

- Rocky Mountain Chocolate (10)

2 GEORGETOWN

2A • Factory Stores of America
www.chelseafactoryoutlets.com
Address 401 Outlet Center Dr *Phone* 502-868-0682 *Hours* Jan 1-Mar 11: Mon-Sat 10-7, Sun 12-6. Mar 11-Dec 31: Mon-Thu 10-9, Sun 12-6 *Location* About 15 miles north of Lexington. Take exit 126 off I-75.

STORES

- Angel Hair and Nails (8)
- Bass (1)
- Bell's Honda (9)
- Bon Worth (1)
- Book Warehouse (5)
- Carolina Pottery (4)
- Casual Corner (1)
- Claire's Boutique (3)
- Corning Revere (4)
- Dress Barn (1)
- Dress Barn Woman (1)
- GNC (8)
- Golf Etc (6)
- Habitat for Humanity Yard Sale (9)
- L'eggs Hanes Bali Playtex (1)
- Levi's (1)
- Paper Factory (9)
- Rack Room Shoes (1)
- Rue 21 (1)
- Theatres of Georgetown (9)
- Toy Liquidators (6)
- Van Heusen (1)
- Wireless Warehouse (7)

3 HANSON

3A • Factory Stores of America
www.chelseafactoryoutlets.com
Address 100 Factory Outlet Dr *Phone* 270-322-8480 *Hours* Mon-Thu 9-8 (Jan 1-Mar 3 9-7), Fri-Sat 9-9, Sun 12-6 *Location* Western Kentucky, north of Madisonville. Take exit 49 off the Pennyrile Parkway.

STORES

- Banister / Easy Spirit (1)
- Bon Worth (1)
- Mid City Art Gallery (4)
- Van Heusen (1)
- VF Factory Outlet (1)

Louisiana

1 • Arcadia
2 • Gonzales
3 • Iowa

1 ARCADIA

1A • Factory Stores of America
www.chelseafactoryoutlets.com
Address 700 Factory Outlet Dr
Phone 318-263-8553 *Hours* Mon-Fri 9-7, Sat 9-9, Sun 12-6 *Location* Between Shreveport and Monroe. Take exit 69 off I-20.

STORES
- Ashley's (1)
- Banister / Easy Spirit (1)
- Bass (1)
- Bon Worth (1)
- Book Warehouse (5)
- Capacity (1)
- Friends (1)
- Ivy Cottage (9)
- L'eggs Hanes Bali Playtex (1)
- Van Heusen (1)
- VF Factory Outlet (1)

2 GONZALES

2A • Tanger Outlet Center
www.tangeroutlets.com
Address 2410 Tanger Blvd *Phone* 800-406-2112 or 225-647-9383 *Hours* Mon-Sat 10-9, Sun 12-6 *Location* Southeast of Baton Rouge off I-10 east, exit 177.

STORES
- Bass (1)
- Big Dog Sportswear (1)
- Bon Worth (1)
- Book Warehouse (5)
- Carter's Childrenswear (1)
- Chicago Cutlery (4)
- Claire's Accessories (3)
- Corning Revere (4)
- Danskin (1)
- Dexter Shoe (1)
- Dress Barn (1)
- Duck Head (1)
- Factory Brand Shoes (1)
- Fragrance Outlet (8)
- Fubu (1)
- Gap Outlet (1)
- Guess? (1)
- Izod (1)
- Jockey (1)
- Jones New York (1)
- Kasper ASL (1)
- Kitchen Collection (4)
- Koret (1)
- L'eggs Hanes Bali Playtex (1)
- Lenox (4)
- Levi's Outlet by Most (1)
- Liz Claiborne (1)
- Maidenform (1)
- Malone Outfitters (9)
- Mikasa (4)
- Naturalizer (1)
- Nine West (1)
- Old Navy (1)
- OshKosh B'Gosh (1)
- Paper Factory (9)
- Rack Room Shoes (1)
- Reebok (1)
- Rue 21 (1)
- S & K Menswear (1)
- Samsonite (2)
- Sports World (6)
- Tommy Hilfiger (1)
- Totes / Sunglass World (3)
- Toy Liquidators (6)
- Van Heusen (1)
- VF Factory Outlet (1)
- Vitamin World (8)
- Welcome Home (4)
- Wilson's Leather (1)
- Zales The Diamond Store (3)

EATS & TREATS
- Cracker Barrel (11)
- Smoothie King (10)
- Subway (11)

3 IOWA

3A • Factory Stores of America
www.chelseafactoryoutlets.com
Address 800 Factory Outlet Dr
Phone 337-582-8800 *Hours* Mon-Fri 9-7, Sat 9-9, Sun 12-6 *Location* East of Lake Charles off I-10, exit 43.

STORES

- Bass (1)
- Bon Worth (1)
- Book Warehouse (5)
- Burke's Outlet (1)
- Capacity (1)
- Easy Spirit (1)
- Factory Brand Shoes (1)
- KB Toy Liquidators (6)
- L'eggs Hanes Bali Playtex (1)
- Noreen's (1)
- Parker's Boots & Clothing (1)
- Van Heusen (1)
- VF Factory Outlet (1)

Maine

1 • Freeport
2 • Kittery

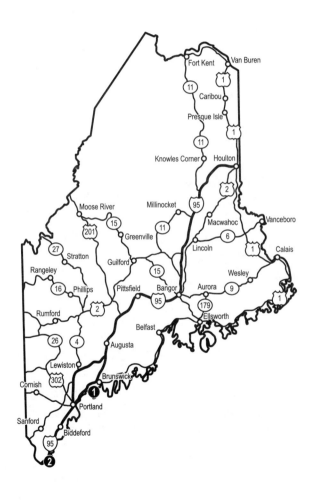

1 FREEPORT

Freeport offers a unique mix of shopping, from outlets to company stores to small gift shops. The best way to find your way around the shopping district is to pick up a Freeport Map and Visitor Guide, available at most downtown stores. Most shops are along a 2-mile strip of US 1 (Main St), but are within walking distance of each other. From the north take exit 17, 19 or 20 off I-95, all lead directly to US 1.

1A • Freeport Outlets
www.freeportusa.com
Address US 1 *Phone* 800-865-1994
Hours Vary by store *Location* See Freeport introduction.

STORES
- Abacus American Crafts (4)
- American History Center (5)
- Antiquarius / Caswell Massey (5)
- B & B Wood Products (5)
- Banana Republic (1)
- Beadin' Path (5)
- Bridgham and Cook (5)
- Brooks Brothers (1)
- Brown Goldsmiths (3)
- Burberry (1)
- Buttons & Things (5)
- Cannon Sheets Towels & More (4)
- Carter's Childrenswear (1)
- Chaudier Cookware (4)
- Children's Place Outlet (1)
- Chilton Furniture & Shaker (4)
- Christmas Magic (9)
- Claire Murray (4)
- Clarks England (1)
- Clothes Tree Thrift Shop (1)
- Coach (2)
- Cole-Haan (1)
- Cool As A Moose (1)
- Cosmetics Company Store (8)
- Cuddledown of Maine (4)
- Dansk (4)
- Desert Dunes Gift Shop (5)
- Dexter Shoe (1)
- Dooney & Bourke (2)
- DownEast Treasures from Thomas Kinkade (4)
- Earrings & Co. (3)
- Edgecomb Potters Galleries (4)
- Fairbanks, Frost & Lowe Fine Jewelers (3)
- Foreside Company (4)
- Freeport Knife Co (4)
- Gap Outlet (1)
- Heritage Lace (4)
- J Crew (1)
- J L Coombs Footwear & Fine Casuals (1)
- Jockey (1)
- Johnston & Murphy (1)
- Jones New York (1)
- Jones New York Country (1)
- L.L. Bean Factory Store (1)
- L.L. Kids (1)
- Levi's Outlet by Designs (1)
- Maidenform (1)
- Maine Bear Factory (5)
- Maine Wreath & Flower (4)
- Mangy Moose (5)
- Mostly Maine (5)
- Nine West (1)
- North Face (1)
- Off-Season Elves (5)
- OshKosh B'Gosh (1)
- Patagonia (1)
- Perfumania (8)
- Pet Pantry (9)
- Play and Learn (5)
- Polo Ralph Lauren (1)
- R D Allen Jewelry (3)
- Reebok (1)
- S & K Menswear (1)
- Sherman's Book & Stationery (5)
- Soccer Mainea (1)
- Stone Mountain (2)
- Sunglass Shop (3)
- Thomas Moser Cabinetmakers (4)
- Village Candle Factory Store (5)
- Wilson's Leather (1)
- Yankee Candle (5)
- Zales The Diamond Store (3)

EATS & TREATS
- A Wilbur's Candy Shoppe (10)
- Ben & Jerry's (10)

- Broad Arrow Tavern (11)
- Chowder Express & Sandwich (11)
- Conundrum-Wine & Martini Bistro (11)
- Corsican Restaurant (11)
- Crickets Restaurant (11)
- Dunkin Donuts (10)
- Freeport Inn & Café (11)
- Gritty McDuff's Brewpub (11)
- Harraseeket Lunch & Lobster (11)
- Isabella's Sticky Buns Bakery & Café (11)
- Jamesom Tavern (11)
- Mister Bagel (11)
- Muddy Rudder Restaurant (11)
- Royal River Natural Foods (11)
- Subway (11)
- Village Nut Shoppe (10)
- Wolfe's Neck Farm (11)

2 KITTERY

Kittery is home to more than 120 outlet stores, the Weathervane Seafood Restaurant & Shops, and the Kittery Trading Post. The stores are along a one mile strip of US 1 in southern Maine, one hour south of Portland. From I-95 south take exit 4 (York/Berwicks) and turn left at the end of the exit ramp. At the next intersection turn right onto Coastal Route 1 south. The outlets are 4 1/2 miles.

2A • Dansk Square
www.thekitteryoutlets.com
Address 275 US 1 *Phone* 888-Kittery *Hours* Sun-Thu 9:30-6, Fri-Sat 9:30-8 *Location* See introduction to Kittery.

STORES
- Dansk (4)
- Florsheim (1)
- Soccer Mainea (1)
- Sportshoe Center (1)
- Toy Liquidators (6)

2B • Dexter Factory Store
www.thekitteryoutlets.com
Address US 1 *Phone* 207-439-3667 or 888-Kittery *Hours* Mon-Sat 9-9, Sun 10-7 *Location* See Kittery introduction.

STORES
- Dexter Shoe (1)

2C • Factory Stores of America
www.thekitteryoutlets.com
Address 325 US 1 *Phone* 888-Kittery *Hours* Mon-Sat 10-8, Sun 106 *Location* See introduction to Kittery.

STORES
- Cambridge SoundWorks (4)
- Factory Brand Shoes (1)
- London Fog (1)

2D • Kittery Outlet Center
www.thekitteryoutlets.com
Address 340 US 1 *Phone* 888-Kittery *Hours* Mon-Sat 9:30-9, Sun 9:30-6 *Location* See Kittery introduction.

STORES
- Book Warehouse (5)
- Harry & David (5)
- Levi's Outlet by Designs (1)
- Mostly Maine (5)
- Ross-Simons Jewelers (3)
- Royal Doulton (4)
- Rue 21 (1)
- Seiko (3)
- Stride Rite Keds Sperry (1)
- Sunglass World (3)
- Totes / Sunglass World (3)
- Van Heusen (1)

2E • Kittery Outlet Village

www.thekitteryoutlets.com
Address 294 US 1 *Phone* 888-Kittery *Hours* Mon-Sat 9:30-9, Sun 10-6 *Location* See Kittery introduction.

STORES

- Crate & Barrel (4)
- Easentials by Etienne Aigner (1)
- Etienne Aigner (1)
- J Crew (1)
- Jones NY Men's/Women's Suits (1)
- Polo Ralph Lauren (1)
- Tumi (2)

2F • Kittery Place

www.thekitteryoutlets.com
Address 336 US 1 *Phone* 888-Kittery *Hours* Sun-Thu 10-6, Fri-Sat 10-8 *Location* See Kittery introduction.

STORES

- Esprit (1)
- Geoffrey Beene (1)
- Nautica Jeans (1)
- Sunglasses USA (3)
- Vitamin World (8)

EATS & TREATS

- Burger King (11)

2G • Kittery Premium Outlets

www.premiumoutlets.com
www.thekitteryoutlets.com
Address US 1 *Phone* 888-Kittery
Hours Apr-Dec: Mon-Sat 9:30-9, Sun 10-6. Jan-Mar: Sun-Thu 10-6, Fri-Sat 10-8 *Location* See introduction to Kittery.

STORES

- Banana Republic (1)
- Bose Factory Store (4)
- Bostonian Clarks (1)
- Cambridge SoundWorks (4)
- Coach (2)
- Crate & Barrel (4)
- Etienne Aigner (1)
- Factory Brand Shoes (1)
- Foreside Company (4)
- Gap Outlet (1)
- Hanna Andersson Outlet (1)
- Hickey Freeman (1)
- J Crew (1)
- Jones New York (1)
- Jones NY Men's/Women's Suits (1)
- Lenox (4)
- London Fog (1)
- Old Navy (1)
- PacSun (1)
- Pfaltzgraff (4)
- Polo Ralph Lauren (1)
- Reebok / Rockport (1)
- Reed & Barton (4)
- Saucony (1)
- Tumi (2)
- Villeroy & Boch (4)
- Yankee Candle (5)
- Zales The Diamond Store (3)

2H • Kittery Trading Post

www.kitterytradingpost.com
www.thekitteryoutlets.com
Address 301 US 1 *Phone* 207-439-2700 or 888-Kittery *Hours* Mon-Sat 9-9, Sun 10-6 *Location* See introduction to Kittery.

STORES

- Kittery Trading Post (9)

2I • Maine Gate Outlet Center

www.thekitteryoutlets.com
Address US 1 *Phone* 888-Kittery
Hours Mon-Sat 9-9, Sun 10-6
Location See Kittery introduction.

STORES

- Corning Revere (4)
- Eddie Bauer (1)

2J • Manufacture's Outlet

www.thekitteryoutlets.com
Address 318 US 1 *Phone* 888-Kittery *Hours* Mon-Sat 9:30-9, Sun 10-6 *Location* See Kittery introduction.

STORES
- Bose Factory Store (4)
- Jones New York (1)
- Saucony (1)
- Villeroy & Boch (4)
- Yankee Candle (5)

2K • Outlet Mall of Kittery

www.thekitteryoutlets.com
Address US 1 *Phone* 888-Kittery *Hours* Mon-Sat 9-9, Sun 10-6 *Location* See Kittery introduction.

STORES
- Big Dog Sportswear (1)
- Cape Cod Crafters (4)
- Casual Male Big & Tall (1)
- Hartstrings (1)
- Sox Market (1)
- Sweatshirt Shop (1)

2L • Tanger Outlet Center I

www.tangeroutlets.com
www.thekitteryoutlets.com
Address 283 US 1 *Phone* 800-406-4490 or 207-439-6822 *Hours* Mon-Sat 9:30-9, Sun 10-6 *Location* See Kittery introduction.

STORES
- Anne Klein (1)
- Bass (1)
- Black & Decker (4)
- Carter's Childrenswear (1)
- Coldwater Creek Outlet (1)
- Dana Buchman (1)
- Elisabeth (1)

- Le Creuset (4)
- L'eggs Hanes Bali Playtex (1)
- Liz Claiborne (1)
- OshKosh B'Gosh (1)
- Van Heusen (1)

2M • Tanger Outlet Center II

www.tangeroutlets.com
www.thekitteryoutlets.com
Address 360 US 1 *Phone* 800-406-4490 or 207-439-6822 *Hours* Mon-Sat 9:30-9, Sun 10-6 *Location* See Kittery introduction.

STORES
- Brooks Brothers (1)
- Calvin Klein (1)
- Jones New York Country (1)
- Nautica (1)
- Samsonite (2)

2N • The Maine Outlet

www.thekitteryoutlets.com
Address 345 US 1 *Phone* 888-Kittery *Hours* Jan-Apr: Sun-Thu 10-6, Fri-Sat 10-8. May-Dec: Mon-Sat 9:30-9, Sun 10-6 *Location* See Kittery introduction.

STORES
- Brookstone Outlet (4)
- Children's Place Outlet (1)
- Cole-Haan (1)
- Cosmetics Company Store (8)
- Donna Karan (1)
- Dress Barn/Dress Barn Woman (1)
- Easy Spirit (1)
- Fuller Brush (8)
- Izod (1)
- Jockey (1)
- L'eggs Hanes Bali Playtex (1)
- Linen's N Things (4)
- Mikasa (4)
- Motherhood Maternity (1)
- Movado (2)
- Music 4 Less (5)

- Naturalizer (1)
- Nine West (1)
- Oneida (4)
- Perfumania (8)
- Samsonite (2)
- SharpKids (9)
- Stone Mountain (2)
- Sunglass Hut (3)
- Timberland (1)
- Tommy Hilfiger (1)
- Waterford Wedgwood (4)
- Welcome Center (9)
- Wilson's Leather (1)

- Coach (2)
- Foreside Company (4)
- Gap Outlet (1)
- Hanna Andersson Outlet (1)
- Hickey Freeman (1)
- Lenox (4)
- Old Navy (1)
- Pacific Sunwear (1)
- Pfaltzgraff (4)
- Reebok / Rockport (1)
- Reed & Barton (4)
- Zales The Diamond Store (3)

EATS & TREATS
- McDonald's (11)
- Noel's Restaurant (11)

2O • The Shops at Weathervane
www.thekitteryoutlets.com
Address 306 US 1 *Phone* 888-Kittery *Hours* Mon-Sat 9-9, Sun 9-6 *Location* See introduction to Kittery.

STORES
- Cape Cod Crafters (4)
- Kittery Outlet Association (9)

EATS & TREATS
- Hebert Candies (10)
- Pepperidge Farm (10)
- Weathervane Seafood Market (11)
- Weathervane Seafood Restaurant (11)

2P • Tidewater Outlet Mall
www.thekitteryoutlets.com
Address 375 US 1 *Phone* 888-Kittery *Hours* Mon-Sat 9:30-9, Sun 10-6 *Location* See Kittery introduction.

STORES
- Banana Republic (1)
- Bostonian Clarks (1)

Maryland

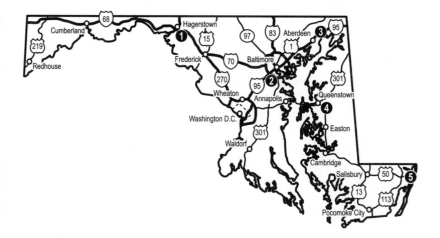

1 HAGERSTOWN

1A • Prime Outlets Hagerstown

www.primeoutlets.com

Address 495 Prime Outlets Blvd
Phone 888-883-6288 *Hours* Mon-
Sat 10-9, Sun 11-6 *Location*
Northern Maryland between
Cumberland and Washington,
DC. From I-70 take exit 29, Rt 65
north. Entrance sign to center is
on your left.

STORES

- Adidas (1)
- American Outpost (1)
- April Cornell (1)
- Banana Republic (1)
- Bass (1)
- Beauty Express (8)
- Big & Tall Factory Store (1)
- Big Dogs (1)
- Black & Decker (4)
- Bombay Outlet (4)
- Book Cellar (5)
- Bose Factory Store (4)
- Britches (1)
- Brooks Brothers (1)
- Camp Coleman (6)
- Carter's For Kids (1)
- Casual Corner (1)
- Casual Corner Woman (1)
- Children's Place Outlet (1)
- Claire's Accessories (3)
- Clothestime (1)
- Coach (2)
- Corning Revere (4)
- Cosmetics Company Store (8)
- David Brooks (1)
- Designer Fragrance/Cosmetics (8)
- Dexter Shoe (1)
- Dockers Outlet (1)
- Dress Barn/Dress Barn Woman (1)
- Eddie Bauer (1)
- Etienne Aigner (1)
- Factory Brand Shoes (1)
- Famous Brands Housewares (4)
- Fuller Brush (8)
- Gap Outlet (1)
- Geoffrey Beene (1)
- Guess? (1)
- Haggar (1)
- Harry & David (5)
- Home Co - Fine Furniture Direct (4)
- Hush Puppies & Family (1)
- Izod (1)
- J Crew (1)
- Jockey (1)
- Johnston & Murphy (1)
- Jones New York (1)
- Jones New York Country (1)
- Kasper ASL (1)
- KB Toys (6)
- King's Jewelry (3)
- Kitchen Collection (4)
- Koret (1)
- L.L. Bean Factory Store (1)
- Le Gourmet Chef (4)
- L'eggs Hanes Bali Playtex (1)
- Lenox (4)
- Levi's (1)
- Little Me (1)
- Liz Claiborne (1)
- Liz Claiborne Shoes (1)
- London Fog (1)
- Maidenform (1)
- Mikasa (4)
- Motherhood Maternity (1)
- Music For A Song (5)
- National Wildlife Federation (9)
- Naturalizer (1)
- Nautica (1)
- Nike (1)
- Nine West (1)
- Oneida (4)
- OshKosh B'Gosh (1)
- Paper Factory (9)
- Perfumania (8)
- Petite Sophisticate (1)
- Pfaltzgraff (4)
- Polo Ralph Lauren (1)
- Rack Room Shoes (1)
- Reebok (1)
- Rockport (1)
- Royce Hosiery (1)
- Rue 21 (1)
- S & K Menswear (1)
- Samsonite (2)
- SAS Factory Shoes (1)
- Springmaid Wamsutta (4)
- Stride Rite Family Footwear (1)
- Sunglass Outlet (3)
- Timberland (1)
- Time Factory Watch (3)
- Tommy Hilfiger (1)
- Totes Isotoner Sunglass World (3)

- Ultra Diamond & Gold (3)
- Van Heusen (1)
- Vans Shoes (1)
- Vitamin World (8)
- Warnaco (1)
- Welcome Home (4)
- Wilson's Leather (1)
- Woolrich (1)
- Zales The Diamond Store (3)

EATS & TREATS
- Auntie Anne's Pretzals (10)
- Coffee House (10)
- Flamers Charbroiled (11)
- Great Steak & Potato (11)
- Panda China (11)
- Subway (11)
- TCBY / Nathan's Hot Dog (11)
- Villa Pizza (11)

2 HANOVER

2A • Arundel Mills
www.millscorp.com
Address 7000 Arundel Mills Cir
Phone 410-540-5100 *Hours* Mon-
Fri 10-9:30, Sat 9:30-9:30, Sun 11-
8 *Location* Just southwest of the
downtown Baltimore area. Travel
south on I-95 to exit 43A (Rt 100
E) to exit 10A, Arundel Mills Blvd.
The mall is on the right.

STORES
- Aeropostale (1)
- Afterthoughts (3)
- All About Cellular (7)
- Ann Taylor (1)
- AT&T Wireless (7)
- Athlete's Foot (1)
- Avenue (1)
- Banana Republic (1)
- Bass (1)
- Bass Pro Shops Outdoor World (6)
- Bath & Body Works (8)
- Beauty Express (8)
- Bed Bath & Beyond (4)
- Big Dog Sportswear (1)
- Black Market Minerals (5)
- Body Shop (8)
- Books-A-Million (5)

- Burlington Coat Factory (1)
- Carter's For Kids (1)
- Casual Corner Annex (1)
- Casual Corner Annex Petite (1)
- Casual Corner Woman (1)
- Changes (1)
- Charlotte Russe (1)
- Children's Place Outlet (1)
- Claire's Accessories (3)
- Cole-Haan (1)
- Country Clutter (4)
- CR Jewelers Outlet (3)
- Dress Barn/Dress Barn Woman (1)
- Eddie Bauer (1)
- Etienne Aigner (1)
- Eye Candy (1)
- Factory Brand Shoes (1)
- Flag Shop (9)
- Foot Locker (1)
- Foto Image 1 Hour (7)
- Fragrance Depot (8)
- Fubu (1)
- FYE - For Your Entertainment (4)
- Gadgets & More (4)
- Game Stop (9)
- Games Workshop (9)
- Gap Outlet (1)
- GNC (8)
- Golf America (6)
- Great Chesapeake Bay (9)
- Guess? (1)
- Haggar (1)
- Hot Topic (1)
- Hot Wax Candles (5)
- Hugo Boss (1)
- International Exchange (1)
- Island Rattan (4)
- Jarmen Shoe (1)
- Jewelry Box Outlet (3)
- Jewelry Service Center (3)
- Jones New York Country (1)
- Journeys (1)
- Just Sports (1)
- Kasper ASL (1)
- KB Toys (6)
- Kenneth Cole (1)
- Kirkland's (4)
- Le Creuset (4)
- Leather Limited (2)
- L'eggs Hanes Bali Playtex (1)
- Levi's / Dockers Outlet by Design (1)
- Lids (9)
- Limited Too (1)
- Liz Claiborne (1)
- Liz Claiborne Shoes (1)

- LVL X Direct (1)
- Manhattan Jewelry Exchange (3)
- MasterCuts (8)
- Merlo's Cutting Edge (4)
- Mikasa (4)
- Motherhood Maternity (1)
- Muvico Egyptian 24 Theaters (9)
- Nail Trix (8)
- New York Perfumery (8)
- Nine West (1)
- North Arundel Hospital (9)
- Off 5th-Saks Fifth Avenue (1)
- Off Broadway Shoes (1)
- Old Navy (1)
- Oneida (4)
- OshKosh B'Gosh (1)
- PacSun (1)
- Payless Shoe Source (1)
- Perfumania (8)
- Perry Ellis (1)
- Picture People (9)
- Picture Perfect (4)
- Quiksilver (1)
- Radio Shack (7)
- Rave Girl (1)
- Reeds Jewelers (3)
- Ritz Camera 1 Hour Photo (7)
- S & K Menswear (1)
- Samsonite (2)
- Scrubs & Beyond (1)
- Shoe Carnival (1)
- Sirens (1)
- Skechers (1)
- Sleep Numbers Store (4)
- Spencer Gifts (5)
- Sports Zone (6)
- Stop N Save Software (7)
- Stride Rite Keds Sperry (1)
- Sun & Ski Sports (1)
- Sunglass Hut / Watch Station (3)
- Sunglass World (3)
- Swim N Sport (1)
- Time Factory Watch (3)
- TJ Maxx (1)
- Ultra Diamond & Gold (3)
- United Colors of Bennetton (1)
- Vans Shoes (1)
- Vitamin World (8)
- Voice Stream Wireless (7)
- Watch Station (3)
- White Barn Candle (5)
- Whitehall Co Jewelers (3)
- Wilson's Leather (1)
- Wizards of the Coast (4)
- World Accents (4)
- World Kitchen (4)
- Zales The Diamond Store (3)

EATS & TREATS

- Auntie Anne's Pretzals (10)
- Ben & Jerry's (10)
- Blue Chip Cookies (10)
- Burger King (11)
- Candy World (10)
- Carvel Ice Cream (10)
- Chevy's Fresh Mex (11)
- Chili's Too (11)
- Cinnabon (10)
- Dairy Queen / Orange Julius (11)
- DuClaw Brewing Co. (11)
- Great Steak & Potato (11)
- Jillian's (11)
- Johnny Rockets (11)
- Keily's Cajun Grill (11)
- Mrs Fields Cookies (10)
- Muscle Beach Lemonade & Hot Dogs (11)
- Popeye's (11)
- Remomo Café Italian (11)
- Sbarro Italian Eatery (11)
- Starbucks Coffee (10)
- Sweets From Heaven (10)
- Taco Bell (11)
- Wetzel's Pretzels / Cinnamonster (10)
- Yeung's Lotus Express (11)

3   PERRYVILLE

3A • Prime Outlets Perryville

www.primeoutlets.com
Address 68 Heather Ln *Phone* 410-378-9399 *Hours* Mon-Sat 10-9, Sun 11-6 *Location* Northeastern Maryland between Baltimore and Wilmington, DE. Take exit 93 off I-95.

STORES

- Bass (1)
- Beauty Express (8)
- Book Cellar (5)
- City Wear (1)
- Claire's Accessories (3)
- D & R Total Image Square Dance & Western Wear (1)
- Deckers Country Woods (9)
- Dollar House (9)

- Dress Barn (1)
- Elisabeth (1)
- Etienne Aigner (1)
- Factory Brand Shoes (1)
- Geoffrey Beene (1)
- Jones New York (1)
- Jones New York Sport (1)
- Jones New York Woman (1)
- Jos A Bank Clothiers (1)
- Kitchen Collection (4)
- L.L. Bean Factory Store (1)
- Leather Loft (2)
- L'eggs Hanes Bali Playtex (1)
- Liz Claiborne (1)
- Mikasa (4)
- Nike (1)
- Nine West (1)
- Northfork Country Crafts (5)
- OshKosh B'Gosh (1)
- Paper Factory (9)
- Perfumania (8)
- Peruvian Connection (1)
- Prime Time Jewelry (3)
- Rue 21 (1)
- Sun Cellular (7)
- Totes Isotoner Sunglass World (3)
- Van Heusen (1)

EATS & TREATS
- Chesapeake Food Works (11)

4 QUEENSTOWN

4A • Prime Outlets Queenstown
www.primeoutlets.com
Address 441 Outlet Center Dr
Phone 410-827-8699 *Hours* Jan-Feb: Mon-Thu 10-6, Fri-Sat 10-8, Sun 11-6. Mar-Dec: Mon-Sat 10-8, Sun 11-7 *Location* East of Annapolis, just 10 miles east of the Chesapeake Bay Bridge. Go across bridge to 50E/301N split.

STORES
- Banister / Easy Spirit (1)
- Bass (1)
- Big Dogs (1)
- Book Warehouse (5)
- Botanical Treasures (4)
- Britches (1)

- Brooks Brothers (1)
- Bruce Alan Bags (2)
- Bugle Boy (1)
- Carter's Childrenswear (1)
- Chesapeake Gourmet (4)
- Corning Revere (4)
- Craftworks (4)
- Dockers Outlet by Designs (1)
- Dress Barn (1)
- Etienne Aigner (1)
- Factory Brand Shoes (1)
- Famous Brands Housewares (4)
- Geoffrey Beene (1)
- Geoffrey Beene Women (1)
- Harve Benard (1)
- Izod (1)
- Jones New York (1)
- Jones New York Country (1)
- Jones New York Woman (1)
- Kasper ASL (1)
- KB Toys (6)
- L'eggs Hanes Bali Playtex (1)
- Lenox (4)
- Levi's Outlet by Designs (1)
- Liz Claiborne (1)
- Maidenform (1)
- Motherhood Maternity (1)
- Naturalizer (1)
- Nike (1)
- Nine West (1)
- Outlet Island Imports (9)
- Paper Factory (9)
- Pendleton (1)
- Perfumania (8)
- Pfaltzgraff (4)
- Queenstown Bank / ATM (9)
- Quiksilver (1)
- Rue 21 (1)
- Samsonite (2)
- Seiko (3)
- Springmaid Wamsutta (4)
- St John Knits (1)
- Sunglass Hut (3)
- Van Heusen (1)
- VF Factory Outlet (1)
- Vitamin World (8)
- Welcome Home (4)
- Wicker Outlet (4)

EATS & TREATS
- Chesapeake Gourmet (11)
- Pepperidge Farm (10)
- Rocky Mountain Chocolate (10)
- Wye River Seafood Co (11)

5 WEST OCEAN CITY

5A • Ocean City Factory Outlets
www.ocfactoryoutlets.com
Address Rt 50 and Golf Course Rd
Phone 800-625-6696 *Hours* Jan-Apr: Mon-Thu 10-6, Fri-Sat 10-9, Sun 10-6. May-Sep: Mon-Sat 10-9:30, Sun 10-6. Oct-Dec: Mon-Thu 10-8, Fri-Sat 10-9, Sun 10-6 *Location* Eastern Maryland, 35 miles east of Salisbury. Just one mile from Ocean City's beach and boardwalk on Rt 50 and Golf Course Rd.

STORES
- Ann Taylor (1)
- Bass (1)
- Big Dogs (1)
- Book Warehouse (5)
- Carter's For Kids (1)
- Casual Corner (1)
- Claire's Accessories (3)
- Dockers Outlet (1)
- Dress Barn (1)
- Dress Barn Woman (1)
- Factory Brand Shoes (1)
- Famous Brands Housewares (4)
- Gap Outlet (1)
- Geoffrey Beene (1)
- GNC (8)
- Harry & David (5)
- Jockey (1)
- Jones New York (1)
- Jos A Bank Clothiers (1)
- L'eggs Hanes Bali Playtex (1)
- Levi's (1)
- Nautica (1)
- Nine West (1)
- OshKosh B'Gosh (1)
- Park Place Jewelers (3)
- Perfumania (8)
- Rack Room Shoes (1)
- Reebok (1)
- Rue 21 (1)
- Sports Zone (6)
- Sunglass Hut (3)
- Super Fresh (9)
- Tommy Hilfiger (1)
- Van Heusen (1)
- Welcome Home (4)
- Wicker Outlet (4)

EATS & TREATS
- Mione's Italian Restaurant (11)
- Outback Steakhouse (11)
- Rocky Mountain Chocolate (10)

Massachusetts

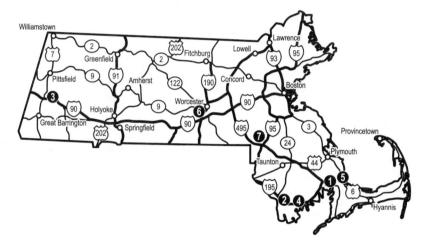

1   BUZZARDS BAY

1A • Tanger Outlet Center
www.tangeroutlets.com
Address 2 Burne Bridge *Phone* 800-406-8435 or 207-439-6822 *Hours* Mon-Sat 9:30-9, Sun 10-6 *Location* One hour south of Boston. Travel south on Rt 3 to US 6 west. Center is on US 6 at the Buzzards Bay Rotary.

STORES
- Elisabeth (1)
- Izod (1)
- Levi's Outlet by Designs (1)
- Liz Claiborne (1)
- Nine West (1)

2   FALL RIVER

2A • Tower Place
Address 657 Quarry St *Phone* 508-674-4672 *Hours* Mon-Fri 10-6, Sat 9-6, Sun 12-5 *Location* Southern Massachusetts, west of New Bedford. From I-195 take exit 8A (Rt 24 south) to exit 2. Take a left at bottom of ramp and a right at first traffic light.

STORES
- Baby Depot (1)
- Bag Outlet (2)
- Burlington Coat Factory (1)
- L'eggs Hanes Bali Playtex (1)
- Luxury Linens (4)
- Northeast Knitting Mill (9)
- Remodelers Outlet (9)
- Savvy Image (1)
- TSI Jewelry (3)

EATS & TREATS
- Candy & Nut Center (10)

3   LEE

3A • Prime Outlets Lee
www.primeoutlets.com
Address 50 Water St *Phone* 413-243-8186 *Hours* Mon-Sat 10-9, Sun 11-6 *Location* South of Pittsfield in western Massachusetts. Take exit 2 off I-90.

STORES
- Anne Klein (1)
- Banister / Easy Spirit (1)
- Bass (1)
- Big Dogs (1)
- Brooks Brothers (1)
- Card America (5)
- Carter's Childrenswear (1)
- Claire's Boutique (3)
- Coach (2)
- Corning Revere (4)
- Cosmetics Company Store (8)
- Crane & Company (9)
- Dockers Outlet (1)
- Dress Barn/Dress Barn Woman (1)
- Etienne Aigner (1)
- Factory Brand Shoes (1)
- Factory to U (9)
- Fila (1)
- Gap Outlet (1)
- Geoffrey Beene (1)
- Haggar (1)
- Harry & David (5)
- Harve Benard (1)
- J Crew (1)
- Jockey (1)
- Johnston & Murphy (1)
- Jones New York (1)
- Jones New York Country (1)
- Kasper ASL (1)
- KB Toys (6)
- Leather Loft (2)
- Lechter's Housewares (4)
- L'eggs Hanes Bali Playtex (1)
- Levi's (1)
- Liz Claiborne (1)
- Log Cabin Candle Company (5)
- London Fog (1)
- Maidenform (1)
- Media Merchant (9)

- Mikasa (4)
- Nautica (1)
- Nine West (1)
- Perry Ellis (1)
- Pfaltzgraff (4)
- Polo Ralph Lauren (1)
- Ragamuffin (1)
- Reebok / Rockport (1)
- Samsonite (2)
- Saucony (1)
- So Fun! Kids (1)
- Socks Galore (1)
- Sunglass Hut (3)
- Timberland (1)
- Tommy Hilfiger (1)
- Van Heusen (1)
- Vitamin World (8)
- Waterford Wedgwood (4)
- Wilson's Leather (1)
- Zales The Diamond Store (3)

EATS & TREATS

- Ben & Jerry's (10)
- Cinnamon Café (10)
- Flamers Charbroiled (11)
- Orientaste (11)
- Subway (11)
- Villa Pizza (11)

4 NORTH DARTMOUTH

4A • VF Factory Outlet Mall

www.vffo.com

Address 375 Faunce Corner Rd **Phone** 508-998-3917 **Hours** Jan-Feb: Mon-Thu 9-8, Fri-Sat 9-9, Sun 11-5. Mar-Dec: Mon-Sat 9-9, Sun 11-6 **Location** Southeastern Massachusetts just outside New Bedford. From I-95 take exit 12, Faunce Corner Rd.

STORES

- ABC Fashion Outlet (1)
- Bag & Coat Outlet (1)
- Bass (1)
- Beauty Bargains (8)
- Bon Worth (1)
- Book Warehouse (5)
- Dress Barn (1)

- Easy Spirit (1)
- Izod (1)
- Paper Factory (9)
- Samsonite (2)
- Van Heusen (1)
- VF Factory Outlet (1)

5 SAGAMORE

5A • Cape Cod Factory Outlet Mall

www.capecodoutletmall.com

Address Factory Outlet Rd **Phone** 508-888-8417 **Hours** Jan-Mar: Mon-Wed 9:30-6, Thu-Sat 9:30-9, Sun 9:30-6. Apr-Dec: Mon-Sat 9:30-9, Sun 9:30-6 **Location** One hour south of Boston. Travel south on Rt 3 to Sagamore Bridge (Rt 6), cross bridge and take right at exit 1. At blinking yellow light take a right onto Factory Outlet Rd.

STORES

- Bass (1)
- Buck A Book (5)
- Carter's Childrenswear (1)
- Casual Corner (1)
- CFO (1)
- Corning Revere (4)
- Dress Barn (1)
- Easy Spirit (1)
- Grandma's Attic (5)
- Home Decor (4)
- Izod (1)
- L'eggs Hanes Bali Playtex (1)
- Museum Of Fine Arts, Boston Catalog (9)
- Oneida (4)
- OshKosh B'Gosh (1)
- Petite Sophisticate (1)
- Reebok (1)
- Samsonite (2)
- Soft As A Grape (1)
- Super Nail Salon (8)
- Van Heusen (1)

EATS & TREATS

- Sbarro Italian Eatery (11)

6 WORCESTER

6A • Worcester Common Outlets
www.worcestercommonoutlets.com
Address 100 Front St *Phone* 508-798-2581 *Hours* Mon-Sat 10-7:30, Sun 12-6 *Location* Midway between Boston and Springfield. From I-90 take exit 10, follow I-290 east (heading north) to exit 16.

STORES
- A Dollar Store (9)
- Afro Beauty Supply (8)
- Aldo Shoes (1)
- Almoda (3)
- Ann Taylor (1)
- Bass (1)
- Bed Bath & Beyond (4)
- Better Living Patio (4)
- Big Dogs (1)
- Bijou Cinema (9)
- Bon Worth (1)
- Braids and Barbering Castle (8)
- Carter's For Kids (1)
- Children's Place Outlet (1)
- Claire's Accessories (3)
- Cosmetics Plus (8)
- Country Candle (5)
- CVS Pharmacy (8)
- Donna Karan (1)
- Erata Sports (6)
- Factory Brand Shoes (1)
- Flagship Bank (9)
- Foothills Theatre (9)
- Geoffrey Beene (1)
- Gifts & Half Price Cards (5)
- GNC (8)
- GTI Leather (1)
- Henry M Gifts (5)
- Kasper ASL (1)
- KB Toys (6)
- Kid's Clubhouse (9)
- Levi's Outlet by Designs (1)
- London Fog (1)
- Lord's & Lady's (8)
- Media Play (5)
- Moa (2)
- Motherhood Maternity (1)

- Nautica (1)
- Nineties Nails (8)
- Off 5th-Saks Fifth Avenue (1)
- Panda Pearl (3)
- Payless Shoe Source (1)
- PCX Exchange (1)
- Piercing Pagoda (3)
- Pref Caps (1)
- Radio Shack (7)
- Rainbow Apparel (1)
- Reebok (1)
- Ritz Camera 1 Hour Photo (7)
- Samantha's Cards & Gifts (5)
- Sharfmans Jewelry (3)
- Software Etc (7)
- Sports Authority (6)
- Sunglass Hut (3)
- Ultra Diamond & Gold (3)
- Van Heusen (1)
- VF Factory Outlet (1)
- Vitamin World (8)
- Voice Stream Wireless (7)

EATS & TREATS
- Applebee's (11)
- Au Bon Pan Bakery Café (11)
- Burger King (11)
- Candy Country Warehouse (10)
- Genji Express (11)
- Panda Express (11)
- Preferred Café (11)
- Sbarro Italian Eatery (11)
- Subway (11)
- Water Lily Café (11)

7 WRENTHAM

7A • Wrentham Village Premium Outlets
www.premiumoutlets.com
Address One Premium Outlets Blvd *Phone* 508-384-0600 *Hours* Mon-Sat 10-9, Sun 10-6 *Location* South of Boston off I-495. Traveling north or south on I-95 take I-495 north to exit 15, Rt 1A.

STORES
- Aerosoles (1)

- American Outpost (1)
- American Tourister (2)
- Andrew Marc (1)
- Anne Klein (1)
- Avenue (1)
- Banana Republic (1)
- Barneys New York (1)
- Bass (1)
- BCBG Max Azria (1)
- Bebe Outlet (1)
- Big & Tall Factory Store (1)
- Big Dog Sportswear (1)
- Birkenstock (1)
- Black & Decker (4)
- Bombay Outlet (4)
- Book Warehouse (5)
- Bose Factory Store (4)
- Bostonian Clarks (1)
- Brooks Brothers (1)
- California Sunshine Swimwear (1)
- Calvin Klein (1)
- Camp Coleman (6)
- Candie's (1)
- Card America (5)
- Carter's Baby (1)
- Carter's Childrenswear (1)
- Casio (4)
- Casual Corner (1)
- Casual Corner Woman (1)
- Children's Place Outlet (1)
- Claire's Accessories (3)
- Clothestime (1)
- Cole-Haan (1)
- Corning Revere (4)
- Cosmetics Company Store (8)
- Cost Cutters Salon (8)
- Country Clutter (4)
- Crabtree & Evelyn (5)
- Craftworks (4)
- Croscill (4)
- Cutter & Buck (1)
- Dansk (4)
- Designer Brands Accessories (2)
- Designer Fragrance/Cosmetics (8)
- DKNY Jeans (1)
- Dockers Outlet by Designs (1)
- Donna Karan (1)
- Dress Barn/Dress Barn Woman (1)
- Easentials by Etienne Aigner (1)
- Easy Spirit (1)
- Eddie Bauer (1)
- Elisabeth (1)

- Etienne Aigner (1)
- Factory Brand Shoes (1)
- Famous Brands Housewares (4)
- Fila (1)
- Fossil (2)
- Gap Outlet (1)
- Geoffrey Beene (1)
- Guess? (1)
- Harry & David (5)
- Harve Benard (1)
- Hoover Outlet (4)
- Hugo Boss (1)
- Hush Puppies & Family (1)
- Izod (1)
- J Jill (1)
- Jockey (1)
- Johnston & Murphy (1)
- Jones New York (1)
- Jones New York Country (1)
- Jones NY Men's/Women's Suits (1)
- Joseph Abboud (1)
- Kasper ASL (1)
- KB Toys (6)
- Kenneth Cole (1)
- Kitchen Collection (4)
- Lang Company Store (9)
- Le Creuset (1)
- Le Gourmet Chef (4)
- Leather Loft (2)
- L'eggs Hanes Bali Playtex (1)
- Levi's Outlet by Designs (1)
- Lids (9)
- Little Me (1)
- Liz Claiborne (1)
- Liz Claiborne Shoes (1)
- London Fog (1)
- Maidenform (1)
- Mark, Fore & Strike / Boston Proper (1)
- Mikasa (4)
- Motherhood Maternity (1)
- Movado (2)
- Music For A Song (5)
- Naturalizer (1)
- Nautica (1)
- Nike (1)
- Nine West (1)
- North Face (1)
- Off 5th-Saks Fifth Avenue (1)
- Oneida (4)
- OshKosh B'Gosh (1)
- PacSun (1)

- Paper Factory (9)
- Perfumania (8)
- Perry Ellis (1)
- Petite Sophisticate (1)
- Pfaltzgraff (4)
- Polo Jeans Co (1)
- Polo Ralph Lauren (1)
- Puma (1)
- Quiksilver (1)
- Ralph Lauren Footwear (1)
- Reebok (1)
- Reed & Barton (4)
- Remington (4)
- Robert Scott & David Brooks (1)
- Rockport (1)
- Ross-Simons Jewelers (3)
- Rue 21 (1)
- Samsonite (2)
- Saucony (1)
- Seiko (3)
- Sigrid Olsen (1)
- Skechers (1)
- So Fun! Kids (1)
- Sony (4)
- Springmaid Wamsutta (4)
- Strasburg Children (1)
- Stride Rite Keds Sperry (1)
- Sunglass Outlet (3)
- Sunglass Shop (3)
- Timberland (1)
- Time Factory Watch (3)
- Tommy Hilfiger (1)
- Totes Isotoner Sunglass World (3)
- TSE (1)
- Ultra Diamond Outlet (3)
- Understatements (1)
- Van Heusen (1)
- Vans Shoes (1)
- Versace (1)
- Villeroy & Boch (4)
- Vitamin World (8)
- Waterford Wedgwood (4)
- Welcome Home (4)
- WestPoint Stevens (4)
- Williams-Sonoma Marketplace (4)
- Wilson's Leather (1)
- Zales The Diamond Store (3)

EATS & TREATS

- Friendly's (11)
- Fuzziwig's Candy Factory (10)
- Lindt Chocolate (10)

- Main Street Eatery (11)
- Rocky Mountain Chocolate (10)
- Ruby Tuesday (11)

Michigan

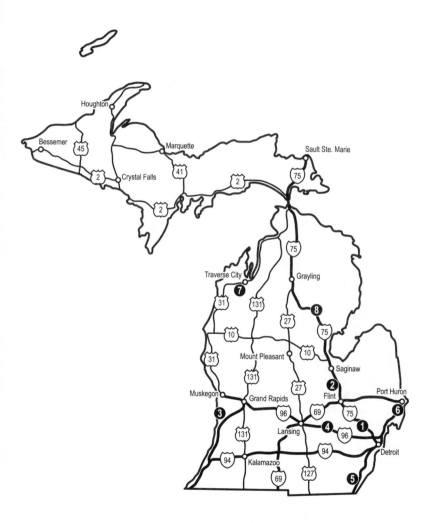

1 AUBURN HILLS

1A • Great Lakes Crossing
www.greatlakescrossing.com
Address 4000 Baldwin Rd *Phone* 877-Shop-GLC *Hours* Mon-Sat 9-10, Sun 11-8 *Location* Just north of Detroit. Follow I-75 north to exit 83, Joslyn Road. Turn left onto Joslyn Rd and travel 1/4 mile to Great Lakes Crossing Dr.

STORES

- 5-7-9 Outlet (1)
- Activate Cellular (7)
- Aeropostale (1)
- Afterthoughts (3)
- Alamo Flags (9)
- Always Classic (9)
- Ann Taylor (1)
- Avenue (1)
- Bakers Shoes (1)
- Bantam Racing (9)
- Bass (1)
- Bass Pro Shops Outdoor World (6)
- Bath & Body Works (8)
- Beauty Express (8)
- Bebe Outlet (1)
- Bed Bath & Beyond (4)
- Bentley's Luggage (2)
- Big Dogs (1)
- Bose Factory Store (4)
- Brooks Brothers (1)
- Burlington Coat Factory (1)
- Burlington Shoes (1)
- Carter's Childrenswear (1)
- Casual Corner Annex (1)
- Casual Corner Annex Petite (1)
- Casual Corner Annex Woman (1)
- Charlotte Russe (1)
- Children's Place Outlet (1)
- China Capital Arts (9)
- Christmas Decor (9)
- Claire's Accessories (3)
- Clothestime (1)
- Copper Creations (4)
- Corey's Jewel Box (3)
- Country Clutter (4)
- CR Jewelers Outlet (3)
- Crazy Rice (3)
- Custom Fit Tailor (9)
- Day By Day Calendar Co (5)
- DKNY (1)
- DOC Eyeworld (3)
- Donna Sacs Outlet (1)
- Dress Barn/Dress Barn Woman (1)
- Earthbound Trading Co (5)
- Eddie Bauer (1)
- Etienne Aigner (1)
- Eye Candy (1)
- Factory Brand Shoes (1)
- Fila (1)
- Finish Line (1)
- Footquarters (1)
- Forever 21 (1)
- Fragrance Depot (8)
- FYE - For Your Entertainment (4)
- Gags and Gifts (5)
- Game Stop (9)
- Games Workshop (9)
- GameWorks (9)
- Glow (5)
- GNC (8)
- Group USA (1)
- Haggar (1)
- Harley Davidson Outlet (9)
- Harry & David (5)
- Heart To Heart Fine Jewelers (3)
- Hill & Hill Tobacconists (9)
- Horn of Plenty (9)
- Hot Topic (1)
- Icing (3)
- In Touch Wireless (7)
- It's Perfume Oil (8)
- Jarmen Shoe (1)
- JCPenney Outlet (1)
- Jerusalem Crafts (5)
- Jewelry Palace (3)
- Jones New York (1)
- Just Sports (1)
- Kasper ASL (1)
- KB Toys (6)
- Kirkland's (4)
- Kitchen Collection (4)
- Last Call Neiman Marcus (1)
- Le Nails (8)
- Leather Limited (2)
- L'eggs Hanes Bali Playtex (1)
- Leno Leather (1)
- Levi's / Dockers (1)
- Lids (9)

- Limited Too (1)
- London Fog (1)
- Love from Michigan (9)
- Maidenform (1)
- Marshalls (1)
- MasterCuts (8)
- Merlo's Cutting Edge (4)
- Mikasa (4)
- Motherhood Maternity (1)
- Mr Rags (1)
- National Sports Liquidators (3)
- Naturalizer (1)
- New England Home (4)
- Nextel (7)
- Nine West (1)
- Northern Lights (5)
- Off 5th-Saks Fifth Avenue (1)
- OshKosh B'Gosh (1)
- Oshman's SuperSports USA (6)
- Pacific Sunwear (1)
- Palace Locker Room (1)
- Payless Shoe Source (1)
- Perfumania (8)
- Pfaltzgraff (4)
- Piercing Pagoda (3)
- Rack Room Shoes (1)
- Radio Shack (7)
- Rainbow Apparel (1)
- Rainbow Art (4)
- Ralph Marlin (1)
- Randazzo Tuxedo (1)
- Remington (4)
- Ritz Camera 1 Hour Photo (7)
- Robotoys (6)
- Roots (1)
- Rue 21 (1)
- S & K Menswear (1)
- Samsonite (2)
- San Francisco Music Box (9)
- Sanrio (9)
- Seen on Screen/As Seen on TV (5)
- Select Comfort (4)
- Sempliner's Tuxedo World (1)
- Sibley's Shoes (1)
- Silver Images (3)
- Spencer Gifts (5)
- Star Theatres (9)
- Start Climbing Walls (9)
- Steve and Barry's University Sportswear (1)
- Stop N Save Software (7)
- Sunglass Hut / Watch Station (3)

- Sunshine Products (9)
- T-Shirt Place (1)
- TCF Bank (9)
- Teddy Bear Factory (6)
- TJ Maxx (1)
- Tommy Hilfiger (1)
- Tupperware (4)
- Ultra Diamond & Gold (3)
- Urban Planet (1)
- Van Heusen (1)
- Vans Shoes (1)
- Venture Communications (9)
- Victoria's Secret (1)
- Victoria's Secret Fragrance (8)
- Vitamin World (8)
- Waldenbooks (5)
- Wallet Works (2)
- Welcome Home (4)
- Westport Limited (1)
- White Barn Candle (5)
- Wilson's Leather (1)
- Windsor Outlet (1)
- Wizards of the Coast (4)
- Xochitl (1)
- Zales The Diamond Store (3)
- Zoom (4)

EATS & TREATS

- A & W Restaurant (11)
- Alcatraz Brewing Co (11)
- Auntie Anne's Pretzals (10)
- Ben & Jerry's (10)
- Bigata Coffee (10)
- Chicken Connection (11)
- Cinnabon (10)
- Coffee Beanery (10)
- Dairy Queen / Orange Julius (11)
- Dick Clark's American Bandstand (11)
- Edy's Grand Ice Cream (10)
- Fudgery Fudge & Fun (10)
- GameWorks Café (11)
- Gloria Jean's Gourmet Coffee (10)
- Great Steak & Potato (11)
- Hot Dog on a Stick (11)
- Island Jimmy's (11)
- Japan Café (11)
- Jeepers! (11)
- Johnny Rockets (11)
- Keily's Cajun Grill (11)
- Kerby's Koney Island (11)
- Le Petit Bistro (11)
- Mediterranean Express (11)

- Mrs Fields Cookies (10)
- Panda Express (11)
- Pretzel Time (10)
- Rainforest Café (11)
- Real Sweets (10)
- Rocky Mountain Chocolate (10)
- Sbarro Italian Eatery (11)
- Stir Crazy Café (11)
- Texas Taco (11)
- Tropical Squeeze (10)

2 BIRCH RUN

2A • Prime Outlets Birch Run
www.primeoutlets.com
Address 12240 S Beyer Rd *Phone* 989-624-4868 *Hours* Mon-Sat 10-9, Sun 11-6 *Location* Eastern Michigan between Flint and Saginaw. From I-75 take exit 136, travel west two blocks.

STORES
- Adidas (1)
- All About Dogs (9)
- American Outpost (1)
- Bailey's Bridal and Prom (1)
- Bass (1)
- Bath & Body Works (8)
- Big Dogs (1)
- Black & Decker (4)
- Bombay Outlet (4)
- Bon Worth (1)
- Book Warehouse (5)
- Bose Factory Store (4)
- Boxes and Bears (9)
- Brass World (4)
- Brooks Brothers (1)
- Camp Coleman (6)
- Carter's Childrenswear (1)
- Casual Corner (1)
- Casual Corner Woman (1)
- Casual Male Big & Tall (1)
- Chef's Outlet (4)
- Claire's Accessories (3)
- Coldwater Creek Outlet (1)
- Columbia Sportswear (1)
- Corbin Menswear (1)
- Corning Clearance (4)
- Corning Revere (4)

- Cosmetics Company Store (8)
- Country Clutter (4)
- Crabtree & Evelyn (5)
- Damon Enro (1)
- Dansk (4)
- Designer Brands Accessories (2)
- Dexter Shoe (1)
- Dollars & Cents (4)
- Donna Karan (1)
- Dress Barn (1)
- Dress Barn Woman (1)
- Easy Spirit (1)
- Eddie Bauer (1)
- Elegant Illusions (3)
- Elisabeth (1)
- Esprit (1)
- Etienne Aigner (1)
- Exclusive's etc (9)
- Famous Footwear (1)
- Farberware (4)
- Fieldcrest Cannon (4)
- Florsheim (1)
- Forget Me Not by American Greetings (5)
- Fossil (2)
- Fragrance Outlet (8)
- Gap Outlet (1)
- Geoffrey Beene (1)
- GNC (8)
- Golf Liquidators (6)
- Guess? (1)
- Haggar (1)
- Hamilton Beach (4)
- Harry & David (5)
- Hoover Outlet (4)
- Hush Puppies & Family (1)
- Izod (1)
- J Crew (1)
- J T Webb (9)
- Jockey (1)
- Jones New York Country (1)
- Jones New York Woman (1)
- Jones NY Executive Suite (1)
- Kasper ASL (1)
- Kid Spot (1)
- Kitchen Collection (4)
- Le Creuset (4)
- Leather Manor (2)
- Lechter's Housewares (4)
- L'eggs Hanes Bali Playtex (1)
- Leno Leather (1)
- Lenox (4)

- Levi's Outlet by Designs (1)
- London Fog (1)
- Maidenform (1)
- Mikasa (4)
- Millennium Gear (1)
- Motherhood Outlet (1)
- Music 4 Less (5)
- Music For A Song (5)
- Naturalizer (1)
- Nautica (1)
- Nautica Jeans (1)
- Nike (1)
- Nine West (1)
- Noah's Cove (9)
- Noritake (4)
- North Face (1)
- Olga / Warner / Calvin Klein (1)
- Oneida (4)
- OshKosh B'Gosh (1)
- PacSun (1)
- Paper Factory (9)
- Pegasus Jewelry (3)
- Perfumania (8)
- Perry Ellis (1)
- Petite Sophisticate (1)
- Pfaltzgraff (4)
- Pilgrim Silks (4)
- Polo Jeans Co (1)
- Polo Ralph Lauren (1)
- Reebok (1)
- Remington (4)
- Rockport (1)
- Royal Doulton (4)
- Rue 21 (1)
- S & K Menswear (1)
- Samsonite (2)
- Socks Galore (1)
- Sony (4)
- Southwest Imports (9)
- Spiegel Outlet (1)
- Sports Collectors Haven (6)
- Sports Outlet (6)
- Springmaid Wamsutta (4)
- Steve and Barry's University Sportswear (1)
- Stone Mountain (2)
- Sunglass Outlet (3)
- Timberland (1)
- Tommy Hilfiger (1)
- Tools & More (9)
- Totes / Sunglass World (3)

- Toy Liquidators (6)
- Ultra Gold & Diamond (3)
- Van Heusen (1)
- Verizon Wireless (7)
- VF Factory Outlet (1)
- Vitamin World (8)
- Wall Deckers (4)
- Welcome Home (4)
- WestPoint Stevens (4)
- Woolrich (1)
- Zales The Diamond Store (3)

EATS & TREATS
- A & W Restaurant (11)
- Beijing Express (11)
- Bob Evans (11)
- D & D Deli (11)
- Goin' Nuts (10)
- Pepperidge Farm (10)
- Pizzeria Uno (11)
- Rocky Mountain Chocolate (10)
- Schlotzsky's Deli (11)
- Wendy's (11)

3 HOLLAND

3A • Holland Outlet Center
www.horizongroup.com
Address 12330 James St *Phone* 616-396-1808 *Hours* Mon-Sat 10-9, Sun 11-6 *Location* Near Lake Michigan, 35 miles southwest of Grand Rapids off I-196. On US 31 at James St.

STORES
- Bass (1)
- Bea's Gifts (5)
- Book Warehouse (5)
- Carter's Childrenswear (1)
- Casual Corner (1)
- Eddie Bauer (1)
- Famous Footwear (1)
- Gap Outlet (1)
- Harvest Antiques (4)
- KB Toys (6)
- Kitchen Collection (4)

- Leather Loft (2)
- Lost City (9)
- Pfaltzgraff (4)
- Reebok (1)
- S & K Menswear (1)
- Samsonite (2)
- Socks Galore (1)
- Sunglass Hut (3)
- Van Heusen (1)
- Vitamin World (8)

Eats & Treats

- Sveden House Buffet (11)

4 Howell

4A • Kensington Valley Factory Shops

www.kensingtonvalley.com

Address 1475 N Burkhart *Phone* 888-545-0565 *Hours* Jan-Feb: Mon-Thu 10-7, Fri-Sat 10-9, Sun 11-5. Mar-Dec: Mon-Sat 10-9, Sun 11-6 *Location* Eastern Michigan between Detroit and Lansing. From Detroit take I-96 west to exit 133 (Hwy 59/ Highland Rd), turn right off exit ramp. At traffic light, turn left onto N Burkhart Rd. The center is 1/4 mile on the left.

Stores

- Adidas (1)
- Banister Shoes (1)
- Bass (1)
- Big Dogs (1)
- Black & Decker (4)
- Bon Worth (1)
- Bose Factory Store (4)
- Carter's Childrenswear (1)
- Casual Corner Annex (1)
- Casual Corner Annex Petite (1)
- Casual Corner Annex Woman (1)
- Casual Male Big & Tall (1)
- Children's Place Outlet (1)

- Claire's Accessories (3)
- Corning Revere (4)
- Cost Cutters Salon (8)
- Dockers Outlet by Designs (1)
- Dress Barn/Dress Barn Woman (1)
- Factory Brand Shoes (1)
- Farberware (4)
- Fossil (2)
- Gap Outlet (1)
- Geoffrey Beene (1)
- Guess? (1)
- Haggar (1)
- Harry & David (5)
- Hoover Outlet (4)
- Hush Puppies & Family (1)
- Jockey (1)
- Jones New York (1)
- Jones New York Country (1)
- Kasper ASL (1)
- KB Toys (6)
- Kitchen Collection (4)
- Koret (1)
- Lechter's Housewares (4)
- L'eggs Hanes Bali Playtex (1)
- Leno Leather (1)
- Levi's Outlet by Designs (1)
- Liz Claiborne (1)
- London Fog (1)
- Mikasa (4)
- Music 4 Less (5)
- Nails First (8)
- Naturalizer (1)
- Nautica (1)
- Nautica Jeans (1)
- Nike (1)
- Nine West (1)
- Old Navy (1)
- PacSun (1)
- Palace Locker Room (1)
- Paper Factory (9)
- Polo Ralph Lauren (1)
- Publishers Warehouse (5)
- Rue 21 (1)
- Rug Decor (4)
- S & K Menswear (1)
- Samsonite/American Tourister (2)
- Soak N Relax Bath & Body (8)
- Springmaid Wamsutta (4)
- Stone Mountain (2)
- TCF Bank (9)
- Tommy Hilfiger (1)
- Tools & More (9)

- Totes Isotoner Sunglass World (3)
- Ultra Diamond & Gold (3)
- Van Heusen (1)
- VF Factory Outlet (1)
- Vitamin World (8)
- Wax Wonders (5)
- WestPoint Stevens (4)
- Wilson's Leather (1)

EATS & TREATS
- Freshens Yogurt (10)
- Grill It (11)
- Hot Dog Construction Co (11)
- MainStreet Deli (11)
- Mrs Fields Bakery (11)
- Sbarro Italian Eatery (11)

5 MONROE

5A • Horizon Outlet Center
www.horizongroup.com
Address 14500 LaPlaisance Rd
Phone 734-241-4813 *Hours* Jan-Feb: Mon-Thu 10-6, Fri-Sat 10-9, Sun 12-6. Mar-Dec: Mon-Sat 10-9, Sun 11-6 *Location* Forty miles south of Detroit. Take exit 11 (LaPlaisance Rd) off I-75.

STORES
- Banister Shoes (1)
- Bass (1)
- Big Dogs (1)
- Bon Worth (1)
- Book Warehouse (5)
- Brass Factory (4)
- Carter's Childrenswear (1)
- Casual Corner (1)
- Casual Male Big & Tall (1)
- Dress Barn (1)
- Factory Brand Shoes (1)
- Farberware (4)
- Gap Outlet (1)
- GNC (8)
- Kitchen Collection (4)
- Leather Manor (2)
- L'eggs Hanes Bali Playtex (1)
- Levi's (1)

- Linen Barn (4)
- Mikasa (4)
- Nike (1)
- Paper Factory (9)
- Perfumania (8)
- Rainbow Apparel (1)
- Rue 21 (1)
- Samsonite (2)
- Socks Galore (1)
- Steve and Barry's University Sportswear (1)
- Toy Liquidators (6)
- Van Heusen (1)

EATS & TREATS
- Pepperidge Farm (10)

6 PORT HURON

6A • Horizon Outlet Center
Address 1661 Range Rd *Phone* 810-364-7001 *Hours* Jan-Feb: Mon-Thu 10-6, Fri-Sat 10-9, Sun 12-6. Mar-Dec: Mon-Sat 10-9, Sun 11-6 *Location* Northeast of Detroit off I-94, exit 269 (Range Rd).

STORES
- Artistry Hair & Tanning Salon (8)
- Bass (1)
- Book Warehouse (5)
- Brass Werks (4)
- Capers (1)
- Carter's Childrenswear (1)
- Casual Corner (1)
- Casual Male Big & Tall (1)
- Corning Revere (4)
- Dress Barn (1)
- Dress Barn Woman (1)
- Famous Footwear (1)
- GNC (8)
- Hush Puppies & Family (1)
- L'eggs Hanes Bali Playtex (1)
- Levi's (1)
- Paper Factory (9)
- Toy Liquidators (6)
- Van Heusen (1)
- Welcome Home (4)

7   TRAVERSE CITY

7A • Horizon Outlet Center

www.horizongroup.com

Address 3639 Market Place Cir **Phone** 231-941-9211 **Hours** Jan-Feb: Mon-Thu 10-6, Fri-Sat 10-9, Sun 12-6. Mar-Dec: Mon-Sat 10-9, Sun 11-6 **Location** On US 31 in Northwestern Michigan, 4 miles south of downtown Traverse City.

STORES

- Bass (1)
- Book Warehouse (5)
- Brass World (4)
- Brew Zone (9)
- Dansk (4)
- Factory Brand Shoes (1)
- Gap Outlet (1)
- Granny's Attic (9)
- Hush Puppies & Family (1)
- Izod (1)
- Kitchen Collection (4)
- Koret (1)
- Ladies Designer Outlet (1)
- Levi's Outlet by Designs (1)
- Linen Barn (4)
- Old Navy (1)
- Paper Factory (9)
- Stamp'n Scrap'n (9)
- Van Heusen (1)

8   WEST BRANCH

8A • Tanger Outlet Center

www.tangeroutlets.com

Address 2990 Cook Rd **Phone** 800-406-8874 or 989-345-2594 **Hours** Mon-Sat 10-9, Sun 10-6 **Location** South of Huron National Forest in eastern Michigan. Traveling north on I-75 from the Midland/Bay City area take exit 212 (1st West Branch exit), follow signs.

STORES

- Bass (1)
- Big Dog Sportswear (1)
- Carter's Childrenswear (1)
- Coach (2)
- Dress Barn (1)
- Easy Spirit (1)
- Eddie Bauer (1)
- Factory Brand Shoes (1)
- Gap Outlet (1)
- Geoffrey Beene (1)
- Izod (1)
- Kitchen Collection (4)
- Koret (1)
- Lechter's Housewares (4)
- L'eggs Hanes Bali Playtex (1)
- Liz Claiborne (1)
- Paper Factory (9)
- Perfumania (8)
- Polo Ralph Lauren (1)
- Publishers Warehouse (5)
- Reebok (1)
- Rue 21 (1)
- Sports Collectors Haven (6)
- Tools & More (9)
- Van Heusen (1)
- Welcome Home (4)
- Zales The Diamond Store (3)

EATS & TREATS

- Coffee Bagle Café & Deli (11)

Minnesota

1 • Albertville
2 • Medford
3 • North Branch
4 • Red Wing
5 • Woodbury

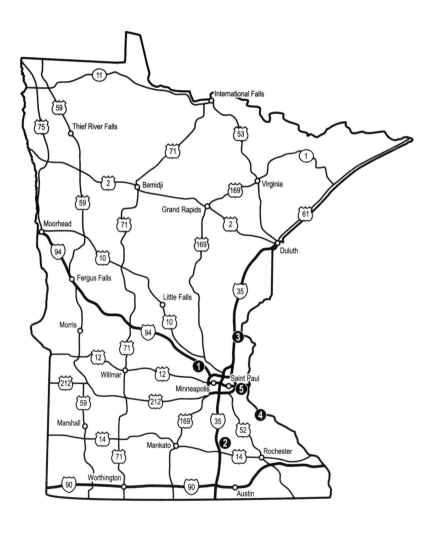

1 ALBERTVILLE

1A • Outlets at Albertville

www.outletinfo.com
Address 6415 Labeaux Ave NE
Phone 763-497-1911 *Hours* Mon-Sat 10-9 (Jan-Mar 10-8), Sun 11-6 *Location* Between St. Cloud and Minneapolis off I-94 at Hwy 19. Westbound travelers use exit 202, eastbound exit 201.

STORES

- Adidas (1)
- Banana Republic (1)
- Bass (1)
- Bath & Body Works (8)
- Big & Tall Factory Store (1)
- Big Dog Sportswear (1)
- Black & Decker (4)
- Bombay Outlet (4)
- Book Warehouse (5)
- Bose Factory Store (4)
- Brooks Brothers (1)
- Carter's Childrenswear (1)
- Casual Corner (1)
- Casual Corner Annex Petite (1)
- Casual Corner Woman (1)
- Claire's Accessories (3)
- Corning Revere (4)
- Cosmetics Company Store (8)
- Cost Cutters Salon (8)
- Dress Barn (1)
- Dress Barn Woman (1)
- Eddie Bauer (1)
- Etienne Aigner (1)
- Factory Brand Shoes (1)
- Gap Outlet (1)
- Geoffrey Beene (1)
- Guess? (1)
- Harry & David (5)
- Izod (1)
- Jockey (1)
- Jones New York (1)
- Jones New York Country (1)
- KB Toys (6)
- Kitchen Collection (4)
- L'eggs Hanes Bali Playtex (1)
- Liz Claiborne Shoes (1)
- Mikasa (4)
- Motherhood Maternity (1)
- Music For A Song (5)
- Naturalizer (1)
- Nautica (1)
- Nike (1)
- Old Navy (1)
- OshKosh B'Gosh (1)
- PacSun (1)
- Perry Ellis (1)
- Pfaltzgraff (4)
- Polo Ralph Lauren (1)
- Reebok (1)
- Rockport (1)
- Samsonite (2)
- SAS Factory Shoes (1)
- Springmaid Wamsutta (4)
- Tommy Hilfiger (1)
- Totes Isotoner Sunglass World (3)
- Ultra Gold & Diamond (3)
- Van Heusen (1)
- Vitamin World (8)
- Warnaco (1)
- Waterford Wedgwood (4)
- Welcome Home (4)
- WestPoint Stevens (4)
- Wicks 'N Sticks (5)
- Wilson's Leather (1)

EATS & TREATS

- Broadway Pizza (11)
- Food Court (11)
- Glorious Beans (10)
- Subway (11)

2 MEDFORD

2A • Medford Outlet Center

www.horizongroup.com
Address 6750 W Frontage Rd
Phone 507-455-4111 *Hours* Mon-Sat 10-8, Sun 11-6 *Location* Forty miles south of Minneapolis/St. Paul. Take exit 48 off I-35.

STORES

- Bass (1)
- Big Dog Sportswear (1)
- Black & Decker (4)
- Book Warehouse (5)
- Carter's Childrenswear (1)
- Casual Corner (1)
- Casual Corner Woman (1)
- Champion (1)

- Claire's Boutique (3)
- Columbia Sportswear (1)
- Corning Revere (4)
- Dress Barn (1)
- Dress Barn Woman (1)
- Eddie Bauer (1)
- Factory Brand Shoes (1)
- Food For Thought (9)
- Gap Outlet (1)
- Guess? (1)
- Harry & David (5)
- KB Toys (6)
- Kitchen Collection (4)
- Koret (1)
- Leather Loft (2)
- L'eggs Hanes Bali Playtex (1)
- Levi's (1)
- Linen Barn (4)
- Liz Claiborne (1)
- Mikasa (4)
- Naturalizer (1)
- Nike (1)
- OshKosh B'Gosh (1)
- Paper Factory (9)
- Payless Shoe Source (1)
- Petite Sophisticate (1)
- Pfaltzgraff (4)
- Rue 21 (1)
- SAS Factory Shoes (1)
- Totes (3)
- T's And Sweats (1)
- Van Heusen (1)
- Wilson's Leather (1)

EATS & TREATS

- Rocky Mountain Chocolate (10)

3 NORTH BRANCH

3A • Tanger Outlet Center
www.tangeroutlets.com
Address 38573 Tanger Dr **Phone** 800-409-3631 or 651-674-5886 **Hours** Mon-Sat 10-9, Sun 11-7 **Location** Less than 1 hour north of Minneapolis/St. Paul. Take I-35 north to Hwy 95, exit 147.

STORES

- Bass (1)
- Big Dog Sportswear (1)

- Carter's Childrenswear (1)
- Claire's Accessories (3)
- Corning Revere (4)
- Date Place Calendar (5)
- Dress Barn (1)
- Elisabeth (1)
- Factory Brand Shoes (1)
- Furniture Outlet (4)
- Gap Outlet (1)
- GNC (8)
- Kitchen Collection (4)
- Koret (1)
- L'eggs Hanes Bali Playtex (1)
- Levi's Outlet by Most (1)
- Liz Claiborne (1)
- Naturalizer (1)
- North Branch Cinema (9)
- Old Navy (1)
- OshKosh B'Gosh (1)
- Reebok (1)
- Rue 21 (1)
- Samsonite (2)
- Toy Liquidators (6)
- Van Heusen (1)
- Welcome Home (4)
- Wild Wings Catalog Outlet (9)
- Wilson's Leather (1)
- Woolrich (1)
- Zales The Diamond Store (3)

EATS & TREATS

- Burger King (11)
- Denny's Diner (11)
- O'Fudge Deli & Coffee (11)

4 RED WING

4A • Historic Pottery Place Mall
www.rwpotteryplace.com
Address 2000 W Main St **Phone** 651-388-1428 **Hours** Mon-Fri 10-7 (Nov-Memorial Day 10-6), Sat 10-6, Sun 11-5 **Location** Southeast of St. Paul near the state line off US 61, Withers Harbor Dr exit.

STORES

- Bed & Bath Treasures (4)
- Christmas Cupboard (9)
- Corning Revere (4)
- Full Size Fashions (1)

- Hush Puppies & Family (1)
- In The Woods (1)
- Life's Little Oasis (4)
- Old Main Street Antiques (4)
- Paper Factory (9)
- Parlour (8)
- Potter's Gold (3)
- Pottery Place Antiques (4)
- Van Heusen (1)
- Whimsy's Closet (1)

EATS & TREATS
- Godfather's Pizza (11)
- Tickle Yer Fancy Fine Candies (10)
- What's the Scoop (10)

5 WOODBURY

5A • Prime Outlets Woodbury
www.primeoutlets.com
Address 10150 Hudson Rd *Phone* 651-735-9060 *Hours* Mon-Sat 10-8, Sun 11-6 *Location* Near the state line, east of St. Paul. Take I-94 east to exit 251.

STORES
- Banister Shoes (1)
- Big Dogs (1)
- Book Warehouse (5)
- Casual Corner (1)
- Casual Corner Woman (1)
- Claire's Accessories (3)
- Corning Revere (4)
- Dress Barn (1)
- Dress Barn Woman (1)
- Eddie Bauer (1)
- Factory Brand Shoes (1)
- Five Day Golf Liquidation (6)
- Foot Locker (1)
- Geoffrey Beene (1)
- GNC (8)
- Hush Puppies & Family (1)
- Kasper ASL (1)
- Kitchen Collection (4)
- L'eggs Hanes Bali Playtex (1)
- Levi's Outlet by Most (1)
- Naturalizer (1)
- Paper Factory (9)
- Petite Sophisticate (1)
- Rue 21 (1)

- Samsonite (2)
- SAS Factory Shoes (1)
- Spiegel Outlet (1)
- Sterling Spas (8)
- Toy Liquidators (6)
- Van Heusen (1)
- Vivian Nails (8)
- Welcome Home (4)
- WestPoint Stevens (4)
- Wilson's Leather (1)

Mississippi

1 • Batesville
2 • Gulfport
3 • Robinsonville
4 • Tupelo
5 • Vicksburg

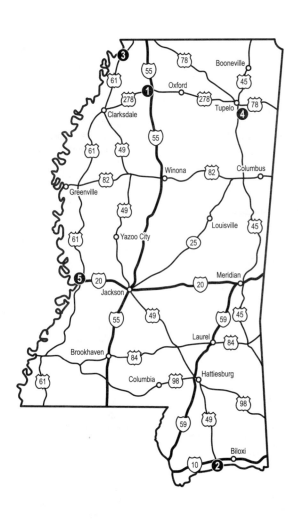

1 BATESVILLE

1A • Factory Stores of Mississippi
Address 325 Lakewood Dr *Phone* 662-563-5491 or 800-361-7406 *Hours* Mon-Sat 10-9 (Winter: Mon-Thu 10-6), Sun 12-6 *Location* Northwest Mississippi, west of Oxford. I-55 exit 243 (US 278) west to Lakewood Dr, then north to center.

STORES
- American Outpost (1)
- Bass (1)
- Big Dog Sportswear (1)
- Bon Worth (1)
- Capacity (1)
- Claire's Accessories (3)
- Dress Barn (1)
- Dress Barn Woman (1)
- Duck Head (1)
- Factory Brand Shoes (1)
- Farberware (4)
- Florsheim (1)
- Full Size Fashions (1)
- Holiday Fashions (9)
- It's Fashion (1)
- Kidz World (1)
- L'eggs Hanes Bali Playtex (1)
- National Book Warehouse (5)
- Paper Factory (9)
- Promises & Praise (9)
- Rue 21 (1)
- Simmons World of Sleep (4)
- Sports World (6)
- Sunglass Hut (3)
- Sussie's Of Mississippi (9)
- Uniquely Southern (9)
- Van Heusen (1)
- Vitamin World (8)
- Welcome Home (4)

2 GULFPORT

2A • Prime Outlets Gulfport
www.primeoutlets.com
Address 10000 Factory Shops Blvd
Phone 888-260-7609 *Hours* Mon-Sat 10-9, Sun 11-6 *Location* Southern Mississippi, west of Biloxi, along the Gulf of Mexico. From I-10 take exit 34A, Hwy 49 south, turn right on Creosote Rd.

STORES
- American Outpost (1)
- Banana Republic (1)
- Bass (1)
- Bath & Body Works (8)
- Bible Factory Outlet (5)
- Big Dog Sportswear (1)
- Bon Worth (1)
- Capacity (1)
- Carter's Childrenswear (1)
- Casual Corner (1)
- Casual Corner Woman (1)
- Casual Male Big & Tall (1)
- Claire's Accessories (3)
- Coach (2)
- Cost Cutters Salon (8)
- Dockers Outlet by Designs (1)
- Dress Barn (1)
- Duck Head (1)
- Factory Brand Shoes (1)
- Gap Outlet (1)
- Geoffrey Beene (1)
- Haggar (1)
- Jockey (1)
- Kitchen Collection (4)
- Koret (1)
- Leather Loft (2)
- L'eggs Hanes Bali Playtex (1)
- Levi's Outlet by Designs (1)
- Mikasa (4)
- Motherhood Maternity (1)
- Music 4 Less (5)
- Naturalizer (1)
- Nike (1)
- OshKosh B'Gosh (1)
- Perfumania (8)
- Petite Sophisticate (1)
- Polo Ralph Lauren (1)
- Rack Room Shoes (1)
- Reebok (1)
- Remington (4)
- Rockport (1)
- Rue 21 (1)
- Rug Decor (4)
- SAS Factory Shoes (1)
- Springmaid Wamsutta (4)
- Strasburg Children (1)

- Stride Rite Keds Sperry (1)
- Sunglass Outlet (3)
- Tommy Hilfiger (1)
- Totes Isotoner Sunglass World (3)
- Toy Liquidators (6)
- Ultra Diamond & Gold (3)
- Van Heusen (1)
- Verizon Wireless (7)
- VF Factory Outlet (1)
- Vitamin World (8)
- Welcome Home (4)
- Wilson's Leather (1)
- Wireless Age (7)
- Zales The Diamond Store (3)

EATS & TREATS

- Bean & Leaf (11)
- Blimpie Subs & Salads (11)
- China Garden Express (11)
- CinnaMonster (10)
- Frank & Stein Dogs & Drafts (11)
- Great Steak & Potato (11)
- Rocky Mountain Chocolate (10)
- Villa Pizza (11)

3 ROBINSONVILLE

3A • Casino Factory Shoppes
Address 13118 US Hwy 61 N
Phone 662-363-2200 *Hours* Mon-Thu 10-7, Fri-Sat 10-8, Sun 12-6
Location Northwest Mississippi, west of Senatobia. Center is on US 61 N, across the street from the main entrance to the Grand Casino Resort.

STORES

- Bass (1)
- Big Dogs (1)
- Calvin Klein Jeanswear (1)
- Capacity (1)
- Carter's Childrenswear (1)
- Case XX-Chicago Cutlery (4)
- Casual Corner Annex (1)
- Casual Corner Annex Petite (1)
- Casual Corner Annex Woman (1)
- Dress Barn (1)
- Duck Head (1)
- Etienne Aigner (1)

- Factory Brand Shoes (1)
- Gail Pittman Pottery (4)
- Gap Outlet (1)
- GNC (8)
- Izod (1)
- KB Toy Express (6)
- Kitchen Collection (4)
- Leather Outlet (2)
- L'eggs Hanes Bali Playtex (1)
- Nautica (1)
- OshKosh B'Gosh (1)
- Paper Factory (9)
- Pfaltzgraff (4)
- Rack Room Shoes (1)
- Reebok (1)
- Rue 21 (1)
- Totes / Sunglass World (3)
- Van Heusen (1)
- Zales The Diamond Store (3)

EATS & TREATS

- Rocky Mountain Chocolate (10)

4 TUPELO

4A • Factory Stores of America
www.chelseafactoryoutlets.com
Address 2824 S Eason Blvd *Phone* 662-844-5898 *Hours* Mon-Thu 9-8 (Jan- Jul 4th 9-7), Fri-Sat 9-9, Sun 12-6 *Location* Northeast Mississippi, east of Holly Springs National Forest. From US 45 take the Eason Blvd exit and travel east to center.

STORES

- Bass (1)
- Bon Worth (1)
- Capacity (1)
- Easy Spirit (1)
- Paper Factory (9)
- US Factory Outlet (9)
- Van Heusen (1)
- VF Factory Outlet (1)
- Wholesale Picture Outlet (4)

EATS & TREATS

- Topp's Deli (11)

5 VICKSBURG

5A • Vicksburg Factory Outlets
www.vicksburgfactoryoutlet.com
Address 4000 S Frontage Rd *Phone*
601-636-7434 *Hours* Mon-Thu
10-8, Fri-Sat 10-9, Sun 12-6
Location 45 minutes west of
Jackson. Eastbound on I-20 take
exit 4A, turn right to Frontage Rd.
I-20 westbound take exit 5A (Hwy
27 south) to East Clay St. Turn
right and follow to Frontage Rd.

STORES
- Bass (1)
- Bible Factory Outlet (5)
- Bon Worth (1)
- Book Warehouse (5)
- Boot Country (1)
- Capacity (1)
- Casual Corner (1)
- Christmas Corner (9)
- Claire's Boutique (3)
- Collage (1)
- Corning Revere (4)
- Dress Barn/Dress Barn Woman (1)
- Duck Head (1)
- Factory Brand Shoes (1)
- Factory Outlet Furniture (4)
- Florsheim (1)
- Full Size Fashions (1)
- Gap Outlet (1)
- L'eggs Hanes Bali Playtex (1)
- OshKosh B'Gosh (1)
- Paper Factory (9)
- Reebok (1)
- Rue 21 (1)
- Tots To Teens (1)
- Van Heusen (1)
- Vitamin World (8)
- Welcome Home (4)

EATS & TREATS
- Billy's Italian Restaurant (11)

Missouri

1 • Branson
2 • Lebanon
3 • Odessa
4 • Osage Beach
5 • Sikeston-Miner
6 • Warrenton

1 BRANSON

1A • Factory Merchants Branson

www.bransonoutlets.com
Address 1000 Pat Nash Dr *Phone* 417-335-6686 *Hours* Mon-Sat 9-9, Sun 9-9. Jan-Feb: 10-6 daily *Location* One hour south of Springfield. From US 65, take Hwy 76 west 4 miles to Pat Nash Dr.

STORES

- Alan Stuart Menswear (1)
- Bath Junkie (8)
- Black Hills Jewelry (3)
- Bon Worth (1)
- Book Warehouse (5)
- Boot Country (1)
- Brass Crafters (4)
- Buster Brown (1)
- Carter's Childrenswear (1)
- Casual Corner (1)
- Casual Corner Woman (1)
- Chase Clark Collection (2)
- Claire's Accessories (3)
- Clothes Outs (1)
- Coach (2)
- Corning Clearance (4)
- Corning Revere (4)
- Country Clutter (4)
- Damon Regular Big & Tall (1)
- Dexter Shoe (1)
- Discount Bible (5)
- Dress Barn (1)
- Dress Barn Woman (1)
- Easy Spirit (1)
- Famous Footwear (1)
- Fieldcrest Cannon (4)
- Florsheim (1)
- Full Size Fashions (1)
- Fuller Brush (8)
- GNC (8)
- Heritage Lace (4)
- Hush Puppies & Family (1)
- I Love Quilts (4)
- Izod (1)
- Jockey (1)
- Kitchen Collection (4)
- Koret (1)
- L'eggs Hanes Bali Playtex (1)
- Lenox (4)
- Little Big Dogs (1)

- Motherhood Maternity (1)
- Music 4 Less (5)
- Naturalizer (1)
- Nautica (1)
- Perfumania (8)
- Petite Sophisticate (1)
- Pfaltzgraff (4)
- Reebok (1)
- S & K Menswear (1)
- Samsonite (2)
- Shadowline Lingerie (1)
- Socks Galore (1)
- Stockroom (1)
- Sunglass Hut (3)
- Supermarket of Shoes (1)
- T-Shirt Souvenir & Gift (1)
- Tools & More (9)
- Totes / Sunglass World (3)
- Toys Unlimited (6)
- Van Heusen (1)
- Wallet Works (2)
- Walnut Bowl / Chicago Cutlery (4)
- WestPoint Stevens (4)

EATS & TREATS

- A & W Restaurant (11)
- Auntie Anne's Pretzals (10)
- Fudgery (10)
- Rocky Mountain Chocolate (10)

1B • Factory Shoppes at Branson Meadows

www.chelseafactoryoutlets.com
Address 4562 Gretna Rd *Phone* 417-339-2580 *Hours* Jan-Mar: Mon-Sun 10-6. Apr-Dec: Mon-Sat 9-9, Sun 10-6 *Location* One hour south of Springfield. From US 65, take Hwy 248 west to Gretna Rd.

STORES

- Art of Glynda Turley (4)
- Bon Worth (1)
- Bostonian Shoes (1)
- Branson Meadows Cinemas (9)
- Capacity (1)
- Casual Male Big & Tall (1)
- Christian Gift Outlet (5)
- Country Music USA (5)
- Dress Barn/Dress Barn Woman (1)

- Easy Spirit (1)
- Famous Jewelry Wearhouse (3)
- Foozles Bookstore (5)
- Golf USA (6)
- Hannah Candle Co (5)
- International Resort (9)
- J T Webb (9)
- Leather Factory (2)
- Lucky Red Wagon (9)
- Mountain Music Shop (5)
- Ozarks Quilts & More (4)
- Paper Factory (9)
- Quincee's (1)
- Rue 21 (1)
- Spiegel Outlet (1)
- Supermarket of Shoes (1)
- T-Shirts Plus (1)
- US Factory Outlet (9)
- Vasken's International Market (9)
- VF Factory Outlet (1)
- Watonga Cheese (9)
- World Wide Dream Vacations (9)

EATS & TREATS
- Mountain Man Fruit & Nut (10)

1C • Tanger Outlet Center
www.tangeroutlets.com
Address 300 Tanger Blvd *Phone* 800-407-2762 or 417-337-9328 *Hours* Mon-Sat 9-9, Sun 10-7 *Location* One hour south of Springfield. From US 65, take Hwy 76 west about two miles.

STORES
- American Outpost (1)
- Ann Taylor (1)
- Bass (1)
- Bath & Body Works (8)
- Bible Factory Outlet (5)
- Big Dog Sportswear (1)
- Black & Decker (4)
- Bombay Outlet (4)
- Bon Worth (1)
- Branson Hotline (9)
- Camp Coleman (6)
- Capacity (1)
- Children's Place Outlet (1)
- Class Perfumes & Cosmetics (8)
- Coach (2)
- Cosmetics Company Store (8)

- Disney Character Corner (5)
- Eddie Bauer (1)
- Extreme Discount Books (5)
- Factory Brand Shoes (1)
- Famous Brands Housewares (4)
- Fossil (2)
- Gap Outlet (1)
- Guess? (1)
- Haggar (1)
- Harry & David (5)
- Helwig Art Glass (4)
- Heritage Lace (4)
- Icing (3)
- Izod (1)
- J Crew (1)
- Jockey (1)
- Kitchen Collection (4)
- Koret (1)
- Leather Loft (2)
- L'eggs Hanes Bali Playtex (1)
- Levi's Outlet by Most (1)
- Liz Claiborne (1)
- Liz Claiborne Shoes (1)
- Maidenform (1)
- Mikasa (4)
- Music For A Song (5)
- Oneida (4)
- OshKosh B'Gosh (1)
- Polo Ralph Lauren (1)
- Publishers Warehouse (5)
- Quiksilver (1)
- Reebok (1)
- Rockport (1)
- Samsonite (2)
- SAS Factory Shoes (1)
- Seiko (3)
- Smith & Wesson (9)
- Springmaid Wamsutta (4)
- Stone Mountain (2)
- Sunglass Hut (3)
- Tommy Hilfiger (1)
- Tools 4 Less (9)
- Totes / Sunglass World (3)
- Ultra Diamond Outlet (3)
- Van Heusen (1)
- Vitamin World (8)
- Warnaco (1)
- Welcome Home (4)
- Wilson's Leather (1)
- Zales The Diamond Store (3)

EATS & TREATS
- A & W Restaurant (11)
- Fudgery (10)
- Hard Rock Café (11)

2 LEBANON

2A • Factory Stores of America

www.chelseafactoryoutlets.com
Address 2020 Industrial Dr *Phone* 417-588-4142 *Hours* Mon-Sat 9-8 (Jan-Mar 9-7), Sun 11-5 *Location* One hour northeast of Springfield. Take exit 129 off I-44.

STORES

- Banister / Easy Spirit (1)
- Bon Worth (1)
- Capacity (1)
- Dress Barn (1)
- Factory Brand Shoes (1)
- Kitchen Collection (4)
- Leather Factory (2)
- Paper Factory (9)
- Totes (3)
- Van Heusen (1)
- VF Factory Outlet (1)

EATS & TREATS

- Cornerstone Subs (11)

3 ODESSA

3A • Prime Outlets Odessa

www.primeoutlets.com
Address 1452 W Old Hwy 40 *Phone* 816-230-5662 *Hours* Mon-Sat 10-8, Sun 11-6 *Location* Twenty miles east of Kansas City on I-70, exit 37A.

STORES

- $1 Store (9)
- Bass (1)
- Big Dogs (1)
- Capacity (1)
- Casual Corner (1)
- Casual Corner Woman (1)
- Claire's Accessories (3)
- Clothes Closet (1)
- Dress Barn/Dress Barn Woman (1)
- Eddie Bauer (1)
- Factory Brand Shoes (1)
- Farberware (4)
- Ferrellgas (9)
- Gap Outlet (1)
- GNC (8)
- Haggar (1)
- Harry & David (5)
- Hometown Wireless (7)
- JBT Tobacco (9)
- KB Toys (6)
- Kitchen Collection (4)
- L'eggs Hanes Bali Playtex (1)
- Levi's Outlet by Most (1)
- Mikasa (4)
- Music For A Song (5)
- Odessa Pool & Patio (4)
- Odessa Visitor Info (9)
- OshKosh B'Gosh (1)
- Paper Factory (9)
- Petite Sophisticate (1)
- Premier Sports (6)
- Publishers Warehouse (5)
- Reebok (1)
- Rue 21 (1)
- Samsonite (2)
- SAS Factory Shoes (1)
- Something Old Something New (9)
- Sunglass Hut (3)
- Van Heusen (1)
- Vitamin World (8)
- Wehner Feed & Tack (9)
- Welcome Home (4)

EATS & TREATS

- Block and Barrel Deli (11)
- Izzy's Pizza (11)
- Rocky Mountain Chocolate (10)

4 OSAGE BEACH

4A • Factory Outlet Village

www.osageoutlets.com
Address 4540 Hwy 54 *Phone* 513-348-2065 *Hours* Jan-Feb: Mon-Sun 10-6. Mar-Dec: Mon-Sat 9-9, Sun 9-6 *Location* Central Missouri between Springfield and Jefferson City. Center is on the south side of Hwy 54 in Osage Beach.

STORES

- Baby Gap (1)

- Bass (1)
- Bass Kids (1)
- Bible Factory Outlet (5)
- Big Dogs (1)
- Black & Decker (4)
- Bombay Outlet (4)
- Bon Worth (1)
- Boot Country (1)
- Bose Factory Store (4)
- Brooks Brothers (1)
- Carter's Childrenswear (1)
- Casual Corner (1)
- Casual Corner Woman (1)
- Children's Place Outlet (1)
- Claire's Boutique (3)
- Coach (2)
- Corning Revere (4)
- Country Clutter (4)
- Dansk (4)
- Del Sol (1)
- Designer Brands Accessories (2)
- Dress Barn (1)
- Dress Barn Woman (1)
- Easy Spirit (1)
- Enro Mens (1)
- Etienne Aigner (1)
- Famous Brands Housewares (4)
- Famous Footwear (1)
- Farberware (4)
- Fragrance Outlet (8)
- Gap Outlet (1)
- Geoffrey Beene (1)
- Gold Toe (1)
- Guess? (1)
- Haggar (1)
- Harry & David (5)
- Heritage Lace (4)
- Hush Puppies & Family (1)
- I Love Quilts (4)
- Izod (1)
- Jaymar (1)
- Jockey (1)
- Johnston & Murphy (1)
- Jones New York (1)
- Kasper ASL (1)
- KB Toys (6)
- Kitchen Collection (4)
- Koret (1)
- Leather Loft (2)
- Leather Outlet (2)
- L'eggs Hanes Bali Playtex (1)
- Levi's / Dockers (1)
- Levi's Outlet by Designs (1)
- Liz Claiborne (1)
- Maidenform (1)

- Mikasa (4)
- Motherhood Maternity (1)
- Music 4 Less (5)
- Naturalizer (1)
- Nautica (1)
- Nautica Jeans (1)
- Nine West (1)
- Oneida (1)
- Oreck Vacuum & Home Care (4)
- OshKosh B'Gosh (1)
- PacSun (1)
- Paper Factory (9)
- Perfumania (8)
- Petite Sophisticate (1)
- Pfaltzgraff (4)
- Polo Ralph Lauren (1)
- Publishers Warehouse (5)
- Quiksilver (1)
- Reebok (1)
- Robert Scott & David Brooks (1)
- Rockport (1)
- Rue 21 (1)
- Samsonite (2)
- SAS Factory Shoes (1)
- Springmaid Wamsutta (4)
- Stride Rite (1)
- Sunglass Hut / Watch Station (3)
- T-Shirt Outlet (1)
- Tommy Hilfiger (1)
- Tools & More (9)
- Totes / Sunglass World (3)
- Ultra Diamond & Gold (3)
- Value Nutrition (8)
- Van Heusen (1)
- Wehrenberg - 5 Cine' (9)
- Welcome Home (4)
- Wilson's Leather (1)
- Zales The Diamond Store (3)

EATS & TREATS

- Auntie Anne's Pretzals (10)
- Chief's Food & Spirits (11)
- Dawg House (11)
- Main Street Eatery (11)
- Papa C's Pizza & Custard (11)
- Rocky Mountain Chocolate (10)

5 SIKESTON-MINER

5A • Sikeston Factory Outlet Stores
www.visitsikeston-miner.com
Address 100 Outlet Dr *Phone* 573-
472-2222 or 800-908-Shop *Hours*

Mon-Sat 9-9, Sun 12-6 *Location*
Southeast Missouri, south of Cape
Girardeau. Take exit 67 off I-55.

STORES

- $9.99 Stockroom (1)
- 50 Off (9)
- Bass (1)
- Bon Worth (1)
- Book Warehouse (5)
- Capacity (1)
- Carter's Childrenswear (1)
- Corning Clearance (4)
- Corning Revere (4)
- Country Music USA (5)
- Dress Barn (1)
- Dress Barn Woman (1)
- Duck Head (1)
- Famous Footwear (1)
- Fashion Nails (8)
- Fieldcrest Cannon (4)
- Full Size Fashions (1)
- Hush Puppies & Family (1)
- Kitchen Collection (4)
- Leather's by MJ (2)
- L'eggs Hanes Bali Playtex (1)
- Levi's Outlet by Most (1)
- MJ Jewelers (3)
- Paper Factory (9)
- Van Heusen (1)
- Welcome Home (4)

EATS & TREATS

- Main Street Eatery (11)

6   WARRENTON

6A • Warrenton Outlet Center
www.horizongroup.com
Address 1000 Warrenton Outlet
Center *Phone* 636-456-5045
Hours Mon-Sat 10-9, Sun 11-6
Location 45 miles west of St Louis.
Take exit 193 off I-70.

STORES

- Bass (1)
- Big Dog Sportswear (1)
- Bon Worth (1)
- Capacity (1)
- Carter's Childrenswear (1)
- Casual Male Big & Tall (1)
- Charming Gifts, Collectibles & Jewelry (5)
- Dress Barn (1)
- Easy Spirit (1)
- Factory Brand Shoes (1)
- Farberware (4)
- Full Size Fashions (1)
- Gap Outlet (1)
- GNC (8)
- Gold Connection (3)
- Izod (1)
- Jockey (1)
- KB Toys (6)
- Kitchen Collection (4)
- Koret (1)
- L'eggs Hanes Bali Playtex (1)
- Levi's (1)
- Linen Barn (4)
- Liz Claiborne (1)
- Mikasa (4)
- Music Outlet (5)
- Nike (1)
- Nine West (1)
- Novedades (9)
- Paper Factory (9)
- Pecoraro's (9)
- Perfumania (8)
- Publishers Warehouse (5)
- Radio Shack (7)
- Rue 21 (1)
- Samsonite (2)
- SAS Factory Shoes (1)
- Van Heusen (1)
- Welcome Home (4)

EATS & TREATS

- Blue's Café (11)
- Imo's Pizza (11)
- Rocky Mountain Chocolate (10)

Nebraska

1 • Gretna
2 • Nebraska City

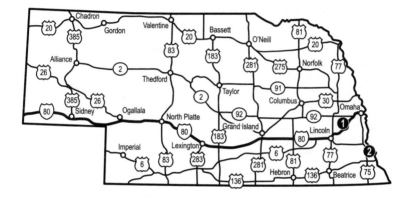

1 GRETNA

1A • Nebraska Crossings Factory Stores

www.horizongroup.com
Address 14333 S Hwy 31 *Phone* 402-332-4940 *Hours* Mon-Sat 10-8, Sun-11-6 *Location* Between Omaha and Lincoln off I-80, exit 432

STORES

- American Heroes (9)
- American Tourister (2)
- Banister Shoes (1)
- Bass (1)
- Bon Worth (1)
- Book Warehouse (5)
- Candy's Bouquet (1)
- Carter's Childrenswear (1)
- Casual Corner (1)
- Casual Corner Woman (1)
- Cherrie Anderson Dance Studio (9)
- Corning Revere (4)
- Curves for Women (1)
- Dress Barn (1)
- Dress Barn Woman (1)
- Factory Brand Shoes (1)
- Full Size Fashions (1)
- GNC (8)
- Grun's Sports Cage (3)
- Jazzercise (8)
- Kitchen Collection (4)
- Koret (1)
- Leather Loft (2)
- L'eggs Hanes Bali Playtex (1)
- Micole's (1)
- Midwest Kitchen Crafts (4)
- Mikasa (4)
- Naturalizer (1)
- OshKosh B'Gosh (1)
- Paper Factory (9)
- Petite Sophisticate (1)
- Rug Shop (4)
- T-Shirts Plus (1)
- Toy Liquidators (6)
- Tunes 4 Christ (5)
- Van Heusen (1)
- Walnut Bowl / Chicago Cutlery (4)
- Welcome Home (4)

2 NEBRASKA CITY

2A • Factory Stores of America

www.chelseafactoryoutlets.com
Address 1001 Hwy 2 *Phone* 402-873-7727 *Hours* Mon-Sat 9-8 (Jan-Mar 9-7), Sun 11-6 *Location* Southeast Nebraska, east of Lincoln. From I-29 (in Iowa), take Hwy 2 west.

STORES

- Bass (1)
- Bon Worth (1)
- Dress Barn (1)
- Easy Spirit (1)
- Leather Factory (2)
- Paper Factory (9)
- Toy Liquidators (6)
- Van Heusen (1)
- VF Factory Outlet (1)

Nevada

1 • Las Vegas
2 • Laughlin
3 • Primm

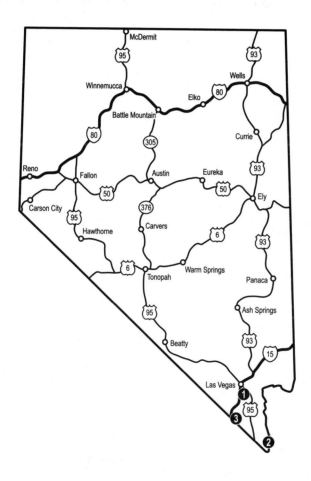

1 LAS VEGAS

1A • Belz Factory Outlet World

www.belz.com

Address 7400 Las Vegas Blvd S
Phone 702-896-5599 *Hours* Mon-Sat 10-9, Sun 10-6 *Location* I-15 exit 33, east to Las Vegas Blvd and north to center, which is on the right.

STORES

- 90 Park Ave (3)
- Afterthoughts (3)
- Ashworth (1)
- Bass (1)
- Big Dogs / Little Dogs (1)
- Black & Decker (4)
- Black Hills Gold (3)
- Blue Wave (1)
- Bon Worth (1)
- Bose Factory Store (4)
- Bostonian Clarks (1)
- Bruce Alan Bags (2)
- Burlington Brands (1)
- Buster Brown (1)
- California Luggage (2)
- Calvin Klein (1)
- Canyonland Gifts (5)
- Carter's Childrenswear (1)
- Casio (4)
- Casual Corner (1)
- Casual Corner Woman (1)
- Catherine's (1)
- Chez Magnifique (1)
- China Collection (5)
- Cigarmania (9)
- Claire's Accessories (3)
- Coastal Cotton (1)
- Corning Revere (4)
- Creative Travel (9)
- Dansk (4)
- Danskin (1)
- Designer Brands Accessories (2)
- Designer Fragrance/Cosmetics (8)
- Dexter Shoe (1)
- Diamond Exchange (3)
- Dress Barn/Dress Barn Woman (1)
- El Mundo (1)
- Emporio Armani (1)
- Esprit (1)
- Etienne Aigner (1)
- Famous Brands Housewares (4)
- Famous Footwear (1)
- Fila (1)
- Flashback (5)
- Florsheim (1)
- Fossil (2)
- Fragrance Outlet (8)
- Frenchy's (5)
- Fresh Produce (1)
- Furniture Factory (4)
- Geoffrey Beene (1)
- Greatful Thread (2)
- Greg Norman (1)
- Group USA (1)
- Haggar (1)
- Harris & Frank (1)
- Harry & David (5)
- Hat Company (1)
- Hunting World (6)
- Hush Puppies & Family (1)
- Izod (1)
- Jewelers (3)
- Jewelry Factory Outlet (3)
- Jockey (1)
- Joe Boxer (1)
- Jones New York (1)
- Jones New York Country (1)
- Kasper ASL (1)
- Kitchen Collection (4)
- Koret (1)
- Leather Mode (2)
- L'eggs Hanes Bali Playtex (1)
- Lenox (4)
- Levi's Outlet by Most (1)
- Linda Ray's Gifts (5)
- Liz Claiborne (1)
- Liz Claiborne Shoes (1)
- Loco Boutique (1)
- London Fog (1)
- Major T's (5)
- Mikasa (4)
- Momento (3)
- Motherhood Maternity (1)
- Music 4 Less (5)
- Naturalizer (1)
- Nautica (1)
- Nike (1)
- Nine West (1)
- Noritake (4)

- Off 5th-Saks Fifth Avenue (1)
- Olga Warner (1)
- Oneida (4)
- OshKosh B'Gosh (1)
- Pacific Sunwear (1)
- Paper Factory (9)
- Perfumania (8)
- Petite Sophisticate (1)
- Pfaltzgraff (4)
- Reebok (1)
- Rockport (1)
- Royal Doulton (4)
- Rue 21 (1)
- Samsonite/American Tourister (2)
- SAS Factory Shoes (1)
- SBX (1)
- Skechers (1)
- So Fun! Kids (1)
- Space Pens (9)
- Spiegel Outlet (1)
- Springmaid Wamsutta (4)
- Stone Mountain (2)
- Stride Rite Keds Sperry (1)
- Sunglass Hut (3)
- Tie One On (1)
- Tommy Hilfiger (1)
- Toy Liquidators (6)
- Ultra Jewelers (3)
- Valerie's Sterling Designs (5)
- Van Heusen (1)
- Vans Shoes (1)
- Vitamin World (8)
- Waterford Wedgwood (4)
- Welcome Home (4)
- Wilson's Accessories (9)
- Wizard of Eyes (8)
- Wolf Camera & Video (7)
- XOXO (1)
- Yes! Perfumes (8)

EATS & TREATS

- Bean Stalk (11)
- Burger King (11)
- Chao Praya (11)
- Dreyer's Grand Ice Cream (10)
- Great American Cookie (10)
- Pretzel Zone (10)
- Rocky Mountain Chocolate (10)
- Rocky's Philly Cheesesteaks
  Mediterranean Delight (11)
- Sbarro's Pizza (11)
- Steak & Spud (11)

- Subs n' Such (11)
- Sweet Zone (10)
- Umbertos (11)

2 LAUGHLIN

2A • Horizon Outlet Center

www.horizongroup.com
Address 1955 S Casino Dr *Phone* 702-298-3003 *Hours* Mon-Sat 9-8, Sun 10-6 *Location* 76 miles south of Boulder City via US 95 and State Hwy 163. Center is near the intersection of South Casino Dr and Edison Way.

STORES

- Ambiance (1)
- Asian Wrap (9)
- Bass (1)
- Big Dogs (1)
- Body Lights (9)
- Card Outlet (5)
- Carter's For Kids (1)
- Cecil's Market (9)
- Chez Magnifique (1)
- Copper Creations (4)
- Corning Revere (4)
- Corral West Ranchwear (1)
- Country Clutter (4)
- Custom Tees & More (1)
- Designer Bargains (1)
- Designer Brands Accessories (2)
- Dexter Shoe (1)
- Dr Douglas Lee, Optometry (3)
- Dress Barn (1)
- Elegant Illusions (3)
- Factory Brand Shoes (1)
- Famous Brands Housewares (4)
- Fox Creek (1)
- Full Size Fashions (1)
- Gap Outlet (1)
- Geoffrey Beene (1)
- Gifts & Souvenirs (5)
- Haley Sportswear (1)
- Healthy Vibes (8)
- Izod (1)
- KB Toy Express (6)

- Koret (1)
- Leather Loft (2)
- L'eggs Hanes Bali Playtex (1)
- Levi's Outlet by Most (1)
- Linen Barn (4)
- London Bridge Candle (5)
- Mad Dog Wireless (7)
- Maidenform (1)
- Main Attraction (1)
- Mikasa (4)
- Mr Biggle's Pad (9)
- Music 4 Less (5)
- Nature's Treasures (9)
- OshKosh B'Gosh (1)
- Perfumania (8)
- Personalized Creations (1)
- Piercing Pagoda (3)
- Polo Ralph Lauren (1)
- Publishers Warehouse (5)
- Queen's Nails (8)
- Ramada Information Booth (9)
- Reebok (1)
- Rockport (1)
- Rue 21 (1)
- SAS Factory Shoes (1)
- Stadium 9 Cinemas (9)
- Styles For Less (1)
- Sugar & Spice (9)
- Sunglass Hut (3)
- Ultra Gold & Diamond (3)
- Van Heusen (1)
- Vitamin World (8)
- Wild Things (1)
- Wonders of Eucalyptus (1)

EATS & TREATS
- Dairy Queen / Orange Julius (11)
- McDonald's (11)
- Muddy Rudder Pub (11)
- Quizno's Classic Subs (11)
- Rice Garden (11)
- Rocky Mountain Chocolate (10)

3 PRIMM

3A • Fashion Outlet Las Vegas
www.fashionoutletlasvegas.com
Address I-15 exit 1 *Phone* 702-874-1400 *Hours* Mon-Sat 10-9, Sun 10-8 *Location* 30 minutes south of

Las Vegas on the east side of I-15, exit 1 near the state line. The center is connected to the Primm Valley Resort & Casino.

STORES
- Accessoire Paris (3)
- Activewear Outlet (1)
- Alpaca Petes (1)
- Art of Mexico (4)
- Bally Outlet (1)
- Banana Republic (1)
- Bath & Body Works (8)
- BCBG Max Azria (1)
- Big Dog Sportswear (1)
- Bikini Bay (1)
- Brooks Brothers (1)
- Burberry (1)
- Calvin Klein (1)
- Canyonland Gifts (5)
- Clio Blue (3)
- Coach (2)
- Cole-Haan (1)
- Cosmetics Company Store (8)
- CR Jewelers Outlet (3)
- Donna Karan (1)
- Eddie Bauer (1)
- El Portal Last Stop (2)
- Escada Company Store (1)
- Euro Artistic Glass (4)
- Gap Outlet (1)
- Golden Cuffs (1)
- Guess? (1)
- Harley Davidson Outlet (9)
- Icing (3)
- Imposters (3)
- J Crew (1)
- J P Tod's (1)
- Jhane Barnes Xtras (1)
- Johnston & Murphy (1)
- Kenneth Cole (1)
- Krazy Kidz / Viva Las Vegas (1)
- Lacoste (1)
- Last Call Neiman Marcus (1)
- Le Gallerie Luministe (4)
- Le Sportsac (2)
- Money Company (9)
- Music 4 Less (5)
- Nautica (1)
- New York Diamond Exchange (3)
- Nine West (1)

- Oilily (1)
- Perfumania (8)
- Polo Ralph Lauren (1)
- Quiksilver (1)
- Reebok (1)
- Road Show (1)
- Schillaci Eyewear Store (3)
- Skechers (1)
- Smoker's Outlet (9)
- St John Company Store (1)
- St John Knits (1)
- Stop N Save Software (7)
- Styles For Less (1)
- Sunglass Hut (3)
- Tahari (1)
- That Jewelry Place (3)
- Timberland (1)
- Tommy Hilfiger (1)
- ToyCo (6)
- Tropical Tantrum (1)
- United Colors of Bennetton (1)
- Universal Time Outlet (3)
- Versace (1)
- Vitamin World (8)
- Walking Company (1)
- Williams-Sonoma Marketplace (4)
- Wilson's Leather (1)
- Zales The Diamond Store (3)

EATS & TREATS

- Carl's Jr (11)
- Denny's Diner (11)
- Great Khan's Mongolian Festival (11)
- Great Steak & Potato (11)
- Hot Dog on a Stick (11)
- Koraku Restaurant (11)
- Oasis Rose Sushi Bar (11)
- Panda Express (11)
- Planet Pretzel (10)
- Sbarro Italian Eatery (11)
- Starbucks Coffee (10)
- Sweet Factory (10)
- Taco Maker (11)

New Hampshire

1 • North Conway
2 • Tilton

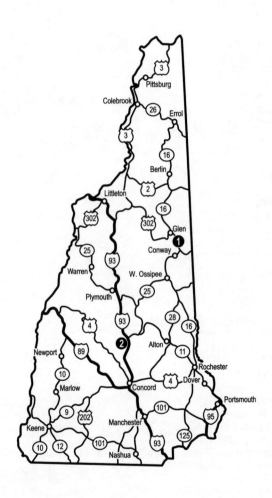

1 NORTH CONWAY

Located in eastern New Hampshire surrounded by the White Mountain National Forest. Shoppers here will find several outlet centers as well as some freestanding stores. Travelers have several options in driving to North Conway. From the north use Hwys 16 or 302. You can travel through the national forest on Rt 112 from the west, or Hwys 16 or 153 from the south.

1A • Settlers' Green Outlet Village Plus

www.settlersgreen.com
Address 13 Settler's Green, adjacent to Hwy 302 intersection. *Phone* 603-356-7031 *Hours* Jun-Sep: Mon-Sat 10-9, Sun 10-6. Oct-May: Mon-Thu & Sun 10-6, Fri-Sat 10-8 *Location* See North Conway introduction.

STORES

- Adidas (1)
- April Cornell (1)
- Banana Republic (1)
- Bass (1)
- Black & Decker (4)
- Brookstone Outlet (4)
- Cape Cod Crafters (4)
- Carter's Childrenswear (1)
- Claire's Accessories (3)
- Claire's Dress Barn (1)
- Dress Barn Woman (1)
- Eddie Bauer (1)
- Famous Footwear (1)
- Farberware (4)
- Foreside Company (4)
- Fuller Brush (8)
- Gap Outlet (1)
- Haggar (1)
- Harry & David (5)
- J Crew (1)
- J Jill (1)
- Jockey (1)
- Jones New York (1)
- KB Toys (6)
- Kitchen Collection (4)
- Levi's (1)
- Levi's / Dockers (1)
- Maidenform (1)
- Motherhood Maternity (1)
- Music 4 Less (5)
- Nike (1)
- Nine West (1)
- Oneida (4)
- Orvis Factory Store (1)
- OshKosh B'Gosh (1)
- Pacific Sunwear (1)
- Pfaltzgraff (4)
- Reebok (1)
- Reed & Barton (4)
- Rockport (1)
- Rue 21 (1)
- Rugged Bear (1)
- Seiko (3)
- Springmaid Wamsutta (4)
- Sunglass Hut (3)
- Van Heusen (1)
- Vitamin World (8)
- Warnaco (1)
- Wilson's Leather (1)
- Woolrich (1)
- Yankee Candle (5)

EATS & TREATS

- Brandli's Pasta, Pizza & Grille (11)
- Dancers Café (11)

1B • Tanger - Clover Center

www.tangeroutlets.con
Address 1672 White Mtn Hwy (Rt 16) *Phone* 800-407-4078 or 207-439-6822 *Hours* Sun-Thu 10-6, Fri-Sat 10-8 *Location* See North Conway introduction.

STORES

- Brooks Brothers (1)
- Liz Claiborne (1)
- Polo Ralph Lauren (1)

1C • Tanger - L.L. Bean Center

www.tangeroutlets.con
Address 1699 White Mtn Hwy (Rt

16) *Phone* 800-407-4078 or 207-439-6822 *Hours* Sun-Thu 10-6, Fri-Sat 10-8 *Location* See North Conway introduction.

Stores

- Big Dog Sportswear (1)
- Chuck Roast Outerwear (1)
- Cole-Haan (1)
- Freeport Studio (4)
- Geoffrey Beene (1)
- L.L. Bean Factory Store (1)
- L'eggs Hanes Bali Playtex (1)
- Nautica (1)
- Samsonite (2)

Eats & Treats

- Rocky Mountain Chocolate (10)

1D • Tanger - Red Barn Center

www.tangeroutlets.con
Address 1976 White Mtn Hwy (Rt 16) *Phone* 800-407-4078 or 207-439-6822 *Hours* Sun-Thu 10-6, Fri-Sat 10-8 *Location* See North Conway introduction.

Stores

- Aeropostale (1)
- Corning Revere (4)
- Danskin (1)
- Paper Factory (9)
- Socks Galore (1)
- Swank (2)

2 TILTON

2A • Lakes Region Factory Stores

www.shoplakesregion.com
Address 120 Laconia Rd *Phone* 603-286-7880 or 888-Shop-333 *Hours* Jan-Apr: Sun-Thu 10-6, Fri-Sat 10-8. May-Dec: Mon-Sat 10-9, Sun 10-6 *Location* North of Concord off I-93, exit 20 (Rt 3 east). Center is 1/4 mile on the left.

Stores

- Bass (1)
- Big Dogs (1)
- Black & Decker (4)
- Book Warehouse (5)
- BootLegger's (1)
- Brooks Brothers (1)
- Carter's Childrenswear (1)
- Casual Corner (1)
- Casual Male Big & Tall (1)
- Chuck Roast Outerwear (1)
- Claire's Accessories (3)
- Coach (2)
- Craftworks (4)
- Danskin (1)
- Dress Barn/Dress Barn Woman (1)
- Easy Spirit (1)
- Eddie Bauer (1)
- Factory Brand Shoes (1)
- Farberware (4)
- Gap Outlet (1)
- Geoffrey Beene (1)
- Hair Excitement (8)
- Harry & David (5)
- Hearth & Home (4)
- J Crew (1)
- J Jill (1)
- Jockey (1)
- Jones New York (1)
- KB Toys (6)
- Kitchen Collection (4)
- Leather Loft (2)
- L'eggs Hanes Bali Playtex (1)
- Levi's Outlet by Designs (1)
- Liz Claiborne Shoes (1)
- Mesa Home Factory Store (4)
- Mikasa (4)
- Nine West (1)
- OshKosh B'Gosh (1)
- Paper Factory (9)
- Polo Ralph Lauren (1)
- Reebok (1)
- Rue 21 (1)
- Samsonite (2)
- Springmaid Wamsutta (4)
- Totes / Sunglass World (3)
- Van Heusen (1)
- Vitamin World (8)
- Welcome Home (4)
- Wilson's Leather (1)

Eats & Treats

- Food Court (11)
- Rocky Mountain Chocolate (10)

New Jersey

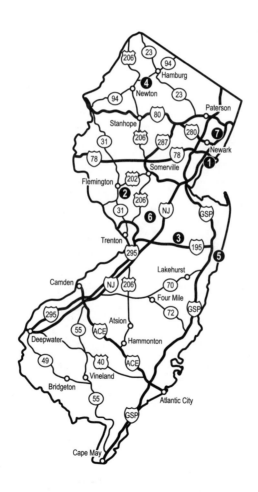

1 ELIZABETH

1A • Jersey Gardens

www.jerseygardens.com
Address 651 Kapkowski Rd *Phone*
877-Say-Valu *Hours* Mon-Sat 10-
9, Sun 11-7 *Location* The center is
located at exit 13A on the NJ
Turnpike. After passing through
the tollbooth, follow signs for
Jersey Gardens Blvd. From local
Rts 1 & 9, follow North Avenue
East-Elizabeth Seaport. Take Jersey
Gardens Blvd onto the property.

STORES

- Aeropostale (1)
- Aerosoles (1)
- Afaze (3)
- Afterthoughts (3)
- Against All Odds (1)
- Aldo Shoes (1)
- Alex & Alex Leather (1)
- Altrom Outlet (1)
- American Greetings (5)
- Ann Taylor (1)
- AquaMassage (8)
- As Seen On TV (5)
- Atlantic Book Warehouse (5)
- Bambini Italiani (1)
- Banana Republic (1)
- Bass (1)
- Bath & Body Works (8)
- BCBG Max Azria (1)
- Beauty Express (8)
- Bebe Outlet (1)
- Bed Bath & Beyond (4)
- Benetton (1)
- Bostonian Clarks (1)
- Bow Wow (5)
- Brooks Brothers (1)
- Bruno Magli (1)
- Burlington Coat Factory (1)
- Burlington Shoes (1)
- Candie's (1)
- Carter's Childrenswear (1)
- Casual Corner Annex (1)
- Charlotte Russe (1)
- Children's Place Outlet (1)
- Cinema Ride (9)
- Claire's Accessories (3)
- Club Monaco Direct (1)
- Cohen's Fashion Optical (3)
- Cohoes (1)
- Collezione (1)
- Corning Revere (4)
- Cosmetics Plus (8)
- CR Jewelers Outlet (3)
- Daffy's (1)
- Danskin (1)
- Deb (1)
- Dress Barn (1)
- Etienne Aigner (1)
- Executive Cellular (7)
- Eye Candy (1)
- Factory Brand Shoes (1)
- Feet First (1)
- Fila (1)
- Filene's Basement (1)
- FYE - For Your Entertainment (4)
- Gap Outlet (1)
- Gateway Newstand (5)
- Geoffrey Beene (1)
- GNC (8)
- Group USA (1)
- Guess? (1)
- H&M (1)
- Haggar (1)
- Harry & David (5)
- Her Highness Fine Jewelry (3)
- Hot Topic (1)
- Illuminations (5)
- Inspired by Nature (5)
- Izod (1)
- Jewelers on Fifth (3)
- Jhane Barnes Xtras (1)
- Jockey (1)
- Journeys (1)
- Just Sports (1)
- KB Toys (6)
- Keep in Touch Cellular (7)
- Kenneth Cole (1)
- Kids Outlet (1)
- Kidstown (1)
- Kirkland's (4)
- Kiziwoo (1)
- La Perfumerie (8)
- Last Call Neiman Marcus (1)
- L'eggs Hanes Bali Playtex (1)
- Lens Lab Express (3)
- Let's Talk Cellular (7)
- Levi's / Dockers (1)
- Lids (9)
- Loutie Outlet (1)
- Lowes Theatres (9)

- Lulu's Hawaiian Collection (5)
- Maidenform (1)
- Mandee (1)
- Marshalls Megastore (1)
- MasterCuts (8)
- Mickey Sportswear (1)
- Mikasa (4)
- Motherhood Maternity (1)
- Nail Pro (8)
- National Luggage Outlet (2)
- Naturalizer (1)
- Nautica (1)
- Nautica Jeans (1)
- Nike (1)
- Nine West (1)
- Norma Reed (1)
- Off 5th-Saks Fifth Avenue (1)
- Old Navy (1)
- Pacific Sunwear (1)
- Papaya Clothing (1)
- Payless Shoe Source (1)
- Perfumania (8)
- Perry Ellis (1)
- Perry Ellis Clearance Center (1)
- Pfaltzgraff (4)
- Piercing Pagoda (3)
- Polo Jeans Co (1)
- Prato Fine Men's Wear (1)
- Quiksilver (1)
- Reebok (1)
- Remington (4)
- Rockaway Bedding (4)
- Rue 21 (1)
- Samsonite (2)
- Shoot 'n Score (6)
- Siso Shoe Repair (9)
- Skechers (1)
- Software Etc (7)
- Square One (1)
- Steve and Barry's University Sportswear (1)
- Stop N Save Software (7)
- Stride Rite (1)
- Stylz (1)
- Sunglass Hut (3)
- Sunglass Hut / Watch Station (3)
- Tommy Hilfiger Jeans (1)
- Triple Five Soul (1)
- Ultra Diamond & Gold (3)
- Van Heusen (1)
- Vans Shoes (1)
- Verizon Wireless (7)
- Victoria's Beauty (8)
- Victoria's Secret (1)
- Vitamin World (8)
- Watch Station (3)
- Wilson's Leather (1)
- Windsor Outlet (1)
- Zales The Diamond Store (3)

EATS & TREATS

- Asian Islands (11)
- Auntie Anne's Pretzals (10)
- Burger King (11)
- Chili's Too (11)
- Cindy's Cinnamon Rolls (10)
- Cinnabon (10)
- Great Steak & Potato (11)
- Greenleaf Grille (11)
- Haagen Dazs (10)
- Jeepers! (11)
- Jersey Ice (11)
- Johnny Rockets (11)
- Keily's Cajun Grill (11)
- Nathan's Famous (11)
- Ranch 1 (11)
- Rocky Mountain Chocolate (10)
- Sbarro Italian Eatery (11)
- Yeung's Lotus Express (11)

2　FLEMINGTON

2A • Circle Outlet Center

www.lernerheidenberg.com

Address US 202 & SR 31 *Phone* 908-782-4100 *Hours* Mon-Fri 10-9, Sat 10-8, Sun 11-6 *Location* Western New Jersey, north of Trenton. Take Hwy 31 south off I-78 to Flemington. The center is at the intersection of Hwy 202/31 and Reaville Rd.

STORES

- Alwilk Music (5)
- Bed Bath & Beyond (4)
- Book Warehouse (5)
- Bugle Boy (1)
- Capers (1)
- Carter's Childrenswear (1)
- Company Store Outlet (1)
- Dress Barn (1)
- Famous Footwear (1)
- KB Toys (6)
- Lechter's Housewares (4)
- Paper Factory (9)
- Totes (3)

2B • Liberty Village Premium Outlets

www.premiumoutlets.com

Address One Church St *Phone* 908-782-8550 *Hours* Jan-Mar: Mon-Sun 10-6. Apr-Dec: Sun-Wed 10-6, Thu-Sat 10-9 *Location* Western New Jersey, north of Trenton. Take Hwy 31 south off I-78 to Flemington. Go west on Hwy 12 to center.

STORES

- Anne Klein (1)
- Artrageous (5)
- Bass (1)
- Brooks Brothers (1)
- Calvin Klein (1)
- Carter's Childrenswear (1)
- Claire's Accessories (3)
- Cole-Haan (1)
- Corning Revere (4)
- Country Clutter (4)
- Designer Fragrance/Cosmetics (8)
- Donna Karan (1)
- Ellen Tracy (1)
- Etienne Aigner (1)
- Euro Bebe (1)
- Fossil (2)
- Gem Vault (3)
- Geoffrey Beene (1)
- Harry & David (5)
- Izod (1)
- Jones New York (1)
- Jones New York Country (1)
- Jones New York Sport (1)
- Kasper ASL (1)
- Le Creuset (4)
- Le Gourmet Chef (4)
- L'eggs Hanes Bali Playtex (1)
- Limited Editions for Her (1)
- Liz Claiborne Shoes (1)
- Maidenform (1)
- Maternity Works (1)
- Nautica (1)
- Nine West (1)
- Oneida (4)
- OshKosh B'Gosh (1)
- Perry Ellis (1)
- Polo Ralph Lauren (1)

- Ralph Lauren Home (4)
- Royal Doulton (4)
- Shady Lamp Shop (4)
- Stride Rite Keds Sperry (1)
- Sunglass World (3)
- Timberland (1)
- Tommy Hilfiger (1)
- Totes / Isotoner (3)
- Van Heusen (1)
- Villeroy & Boch (4)
- Vitamin World (8)
- Waterford Wedgwood (4)
- World of Fun (1)
- Zales The Diamond Store (3)

EATS & TREATS

- Rocky Mountain Chocolate (10)

3   JACKSON

3A • Six Flags Factory Outlets

www.sixflagsfactoryoutlets.com

Address 537 Monmouth Rd *Phone* 732-833-0503 *Hours* Mon-Sat 10-9, Sun 11-7 *Location* East of Trenton near Six Flags Great Adventure Theme Park. From I-195 take exit 16B (westbound exit 16). Follow Rt 537 east, center is on the right.

STORES

- Bass (1)
- Big Dog Sportswear (1)
- Black & Decker (4)
- Brooks Brothers (1)
- California Sunshine Shops (1)
- Calvin Klein (1)
- Candie's (1)
- Carter's For Kids (1)
- Casual Corner (1)
- Casual Corner Woman (1)
- Chaps by Ralph Lauren (1)
- Children's Place Outlet (1)
- Claire's Accessories (3)
- Conair (4)
- Country Clutter (4)
- Delia's (1)
- Dockers Outlet by Designs (1)

- Donna Karan (1)
- Dress Barn (1)
- Dress Barn Woman (1)
- Ecko (1)
- Factory Brand Shoes (1)
- Famous Brands Housewares (4)
- Florsheim (1)
- Fossil (2)
- Gap Outlet (1)
- Guess? (1)
- Gund (9)
- Haggar (1)
- Harry & David (5)
- Izod (1)
- J Crew (1)
- Jockey (1)
- Jones New York (1)
- Jonte Jewelry (3)
- Kasper ASL (1)
- KB Toys (6)
- Le Gourmet Chef (4)
- L'eggs Hanes Bali Playtex (1)
- Levi's Outlet by Designs (1)
- Liz Claiborne Shoes (1)
- London Fog (1)
- Maidenform (1)
- Mikasa (4)
- Motherhood Maternity (1)
- Music For A Song (5)
- Naturalizer (1)
- Nature's Way (9)
- Nautica (1)
- Nike (1)
- Nine West (1)
- OshKosh B'Gosh (1)
- PacSun (1)
- Paper Factory (9)
- Pfaltzgraff (4)
- Reebok (1)
- Rockport (1)
- Samsonite (2)
- Sunglass Hut (3)
- T-Shirts Plus (1)
- Timberland (1)
- Tommy Hilfiger (1)
- Totes (3)
- Ultra Diamond & Gold (3)
- Van Heusen (1)
- Vans Shoes (1)
- Waterford Wedgwood (4)
- WestPoint Stevens (4)
- Wilson's Leather (1)
- XOXO (1)

EATS & TREATS

- Pizza Express & More (11)
- Ragin Cajun (11)
- Salad Café (11)
- South Philly Steaks & Fries (11)
- Treat Street (10)
- Uptown Deli (11)
- Wok & Roll (11)

4 LAFAYETTE

4A • Olde Lafayette Village

www.lafayettevillageshops.com
Address 75 State Rt 15 **Phone** 973-383-8323 **Hours** Mon-Wed 10-6, Thu-Fri 10-8, Sat 10-6, Sun 11-6 **Location** Midway between Newton and Franklin in northern New Jersey. The center is at the intersection of State Rts 15 and 94.

STORES

- American Craft Network (9)
- Barkery Boutique (9)
- Bass (1)
- Big Dog Sportswear (1)
- Bon Worth (1)
- Branchville Dance Center (9)
- Capacity (1)
- Classic Silver & Frangrances (3)
- Country Mugger (5)
- Depot (1)
- Geoffrey Beene (1)
- Historic Toy Soldier Shoppe (5)
- Izod (1)
- Luggage Co & Cigar Room (2)
- Maidenform (1)
- Marty's Shoes (1)
- North Country Outfitters (9)
- Rock & Gem (3)
- Rose Cottage (4)
- Samsonite (2)
- Van Heusen (1)
- Victoria's Embroidery (9)
- Village Mane (8)
- Vitamin World (8)

EATS & TREATS

- JellyRoll Café & Specialty Foods (11)
- Lafayette House (11)
- Oh! Heavenly Sweets (10)

5 MANASQUAN

5A • Circle Factory Outlet Center
Address 1407 W Atlantic Ave
Phone 732-223-2300 *Hours* Mon-Sat 10-9, Sun 10-6. Winter: Mon-Wed 10-6, Thu-Fri 10-9, Sat-Sun 10-6. *Location* On the eastern coast, south of Long Branch. From the Garden State Pkwy take exit 98 (Hwy 138 east), to Hwy 35 south. Follow Hwy 35 S to traffic circle. Take first road on right (Atlantic Ave) into parking lot.

STORES

- Bass (1)
- Bon Worth (1)
- Brass Plus (4)
- Capacity (1)
- Carter's Childrenswear (1)
- Corning Revere (4)
- Famous Brands Housewares (4)
- Fragrance Boutique (8)
- Geoffrey Beene (1)
- Haggar (1)
- Harry & David (5)
- Harve Benard (1)
- Izod (1)
- Jones New York (1)
- Jones New York Country (1)
- Jones New York Sport (1)
- L'eggs Hanes Bali Playtex (1)
- Marty's Shoes (1)
- Mikasa (4)
- OshKosh B'Gosh (1)
- Samsonite (2)
- Van Heusen (1)

6 PRINCETON

6A • Princeton Forrestal Village
www.princetonoutlets.com
Address Rt 1 at College Rd W
Phone 609-799-7400 *Hours* Mon-Wed 10-6, Thu-Fri 10-9, Sat 10-6, Sun 11-5 *Location* Northeast of Trenton, just off US 1 at College Rd West (behind the Marriott).

STORES

- Bass (1)
- Bon Worth (1)
- Card Max (5)
- Carter's Childrenswear (1)
- Casual Corner (1)
- Corning Revere (4)
- Dansk (4)
- Dress Barn (1)
- Dress Barn Woman (1)
- Famous Footwear (1)
- Geoffrey Beene (1)
- Izod (1)
- Leather Loft (2)
- L'eggs Hanes Bali Playtex (1)
- Monday Morning Flower & Balloon (9)
- Nine West (1)
- OshKosh B'Gosh (1)
- Perfume Prophecy (8)
- Pring Gallery & Framing (4)
- S & K Menswear (1)
- Terra Cotta (1)
- Van Heusen (1)
- Village Convenience Store (9)
- Vitamin World (8)
- WestPoint Stevens (4)
- Workbench (9)

EATS & TREATS

- Allie's American Grill (11)
- Ben & Jerry's (10)
- Boardwalk Seafood Grill (11)
- Mikado's Japanese Steakhouse (11)
- My Favorite Muffin (11)
- Teriyaki Boy (11)
- Valentino's Pizzeria (11)

7 SECAUCUS

Just north of Jersey City, Secaucus offers the shopper many choices. In addition to the centers listed here there are several freestanding stores spread out around the area. A free map showing the locations can be found at most stores, check near the entrance. To get started, take the Meadowlands Pkwy exit off Rt 3 in Secaucus. Most of the outlets are either on or just off Meadowlands Pkwy.

7A • Designer Outlet Gallery

www.hartzmountain.com
Address 55 Hartz Way *Phone* 877-Outlet2 or 201-348-4780 *Hours* Mon-Wed 10-6, Thu 10-8, Fri-Sat 10-7, Sun 11-6 *Location* See introduction to Secaucus.

STORES

- Anne Klein (1)
- Brooks Brothers (1)
- Chelsea Cambell (1)
- Contempo Casual (1)
- DKNY Jeans (1)
- Donna Karan (1)
- Fashion Point (1)
- Jones New York (1)
- Jones New York Country (1)
- Jones New York Sport (1)
- Jones New York Woman (1)
- Jones NY Executive Suite (1)
- La Chine Classic (1)
- Laundry by Shelli Segal (1)
- Maternity Works (1)
- OshKosh B'Gosh (1)

EATS & TREATS

- Cross Roads Café (11)

7B • Harmon Cove Outlet Center

www.hartzmountain.com
Address 20 Enterprise Ave *Phone* 877-Outlet2 or 201-348-4780 *Hours* Mon-Wed 10-6, Thu 10-8, Fri-Sat 10-7, Sun 11-6 *Location* See introduction to Secaucus.

STORES

- Aeropostale (1)
- Bally Outlet (1)
- Banister Shoes (1)
- Bass (1)
- Bed Bath & Beyond (4)
- Bon Worth (1)
- Carter's Childrenswear (1)
- Chaps by Ralph Lauren (1)
- Charles Jourdan (1)
- Children's Place Outlet (1)
- Cosmetics Plus (8)
- Crystal-Kobe KB Lawrence (1)
- Dimension New York Leather (1)

- Geoffrey Beene (1)
- Geoffrey Beene Women (1)
- Izod (1)
- Kup's Athlete's Outlet (1)
- Lechter's Housewares (4)
- L'eggs Hanes Bali Playtex (1)
- Lenox (4)
- Marty's Shoes (1)
- Noritake (4)
- Olga Warner (1)
- Oneida (4)
- Oriental Rug Outlet (4)
- Panasonic Technics (4)
- Perfect Time (3)
- Perfume Outlet (8)
- Perry Ellis (1)
- Rue 21 (1)
- Samsonite (2)
- Silver Hut (3)
- Speedo (1)
- Sunglass Outlet (3)
- Van Heusen (1)
- Vitamin World (8)

EATS & TREATS

- Candyland (10)
- Chinese Food (11)
- Cookies 'N Cream (10)
- Fowl Play (11)
- Reno's Pizza (11)
- Sandwiched Shop (11)
- Steaks & Dogs (11)

7C • Outlets at the Cove

www.hartzmountain.com
Address 45 Meadowlands Pkwy *Phone* 877-Outlet2 or 201-348-4780 *Hours* Mon-Wed 10-6, Thu 10-8, Fri-Sat 10-7, Sun 11-6 *Location* See introduction to Secaucus.

STORES

- Bass (1)
- Calvin Klein (1)
- Cee Dee Perfumes (8)
- Easy Spirit (1)
- Maidenform (1)
- Nine West (1)
- Van Heusen (1)

EATS & TREATS

- Cove Café (11)

New Mexico

1 • Santa Fe

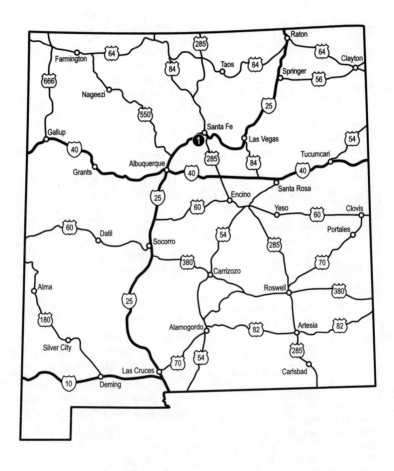

1 SANTA FE

1A • Santa Fe Premium Outlets
www.premiumoutlets.com
Address 8380 Cerrillos Rd *Phone*
505-474-4000 *Hours* Mon-Sat 10-
8 (Jan-Mar 10-6), Sun 11-6
Location Southern Santa Fe off I-
25, exit 278. Follow State Hwy 14
(Cerrillos Rd) north one mile.
Center is on the left.

STORES
- Bass (1)
- Big Dog Sportswear (1)
- Book Warehouse (5)
- Bose Factory Store (4)
- Brooks Brothers (1)
- Cellular Now (7)
- Coach (2)
- Dansk (4)
- Donna Karan (1)
- Eddie Bauer (1)
- Factory Brand Shoes (1)
- Famous Brands Housewares (4)
- Harry & David (5)
- Jockey (1)
- Johnston & Murphy (1)
- Jones New York (1)
- KB Toy Express (6)
- Leather Loft (2)
- L'eggs Hanes Bali Playtex (1)
- Liz Claiborne (1)
- Nautica (1)
- Nine West (1)
- OshKosh B'Gosh (1)
- Peruvian Connection (1)
- Samsonite (2)
- Seiko (3)
- Sissel's Indian Jewelry (3)
- Sunglass Hut (3)
- Van Heusen (1)
- Vitamin World (8)
- Wilson's Leather (1)
- Woodworkers Guild Gallery (4)
- Zales The Diamond Store (3)

EATS & TREATS
- Casa de Cecilia (11)
- Rocky Mountain Chocolate (10)

New York

1 • Bellport
2 • Central Valley
3 • Lake George
4 • Latham
5 • Mount Kisco
6 • Niagara Falls
7 • Riverhead
8 • Waterloo

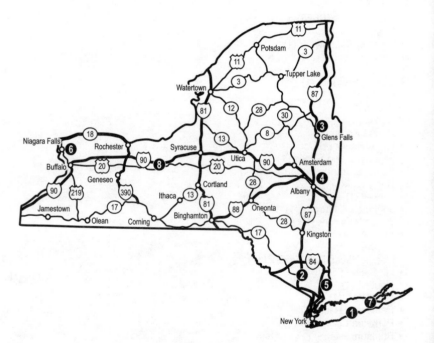

1   BELLPORT

1A • Prime Outlets Bellport

www.primeoutlets.com
Address 10 Farber Dr *Phone* 631-286-4952 *Hours* Jan-Feb: Mon-Thu 10-6, Fri-Sat 10-8, Sun 11-6. Mar-Dec: Mon-Sat 10-9, Sun 11-6 *Location* East of New York City on Long Island. Travel east on I-495 to exit 63 (Rt 83), travel south to Rt 27 (Sunrise Hwy). Take Rt 27 east to exit 56 (Station Rd). The center is on the north and south sides of the highway.

STORES

- Black & Decker (4)
- Carter's For Kids (1)
- Dexter Shoe (1)
- Dress Barn/Dress Barn Woman (1)
- Everlasting Candle (5)
- Famous Footwear (1)
- Fashion Outlet (1)
- Icing (3)
- Jockey (1)
- Kitchen Collection (4)
- L'eggs Hanes Bali Playtex (1)
- Little Big Dogs (1)
- OshKosh B'Gosh (1)
- Paper Factory (9)
- Pendleton (1)
- Pfaltzgraff (4)
- Platinum Hits (5)
- Reebok (1)
- Rue 21 (1)
- Springmaid Wamsutta (4)
- Sunglass Hut (3)
- Totes Isotoner Sunglass World (3)
- Vans Shoes (1)
- VF Factory Outlet (1)
- Vitamin World (8)

EATS & TREATS

- Milano Pizza (11)
- Pepperidge Farm (10)

2   CENTRAL VALLEY

2A • Woodbury Common Premium Outlets

www.premiumoutlets.com
Address 498 Red Apple Ct *Phone* 845-928-4000 *Hours* Mon-Sat 10-9, Sun 10-8 *Location* One hour north of New York City off I-87, exit 16.

STORES

- A Pea in the Pod (1)
- A/X Armani Exchange (1)
- Adidas (1)
- Aldo Shoes (1)
- American Tourister (2)
- Andrew Marc (1)
- Ann Taylor (1)
- Anne Klein (1)
- Arden B (1)
- Avenue (1)
- Bally Outlet (1)
- Banana Republic (1)
- Banister / Easy Spirit (1)
- Barneys New York (1)
- Bass (1)
- BCBG Max Azria (1)
- Bear Mountain Books (5)
- Bebe Outlet (1)
- Benetton (1)
- Betsey Johnson (1)
- Big Dog Sportswear (1)
- Bombay Outlet (4)
- Book Warehouse (5)
- Bose Factory Store (4)
- Bostonian Clarks (1)
- Bottega Veneta (1)
- Brooks Brothers (1)
- Burberry (1)
- Calvin Klein (1)
- Carter's Childrenswear (1)
- Casual Corner (1)
- Chanel (1)
- Children's Place Outlet (1)
- Christian Dior (1)
- Cinzia Rocca (1)
- Claiborne Menswear (1)
- Claire's Accessories (3)

- Club Monaco Direct (1)
- Coach (2)
- Cole-Haan (1)
- Corning Revere (4)
- Cosmetics Company Store (8)
- Dana Buchman (1)
- Dansk (4)
- Delia's (1)
- Designer Brands Accessories (2)
- Designer Fragrance/Cosmetics (8)
- DKNY Jeans (1)
- Dolce & Gabbana (1)
- Donald J Pliner (1)
- Donna Karan (1)
- Dooney & Bourke (2)
- Dr Martens (1)
- Dress Barn (1)
- Eddie Bauer (1)
- Eileen Fisher (1)
- Elisabeth (1)
- Ellen Tracy (1)
- Escada Company Store (1)
- Esprit (1)
- Etienne Aigner (1)
- Etro (1)
- Factory Brand Shoes (1)
- Farberware (4)
- Fendi (1)
- Fila (1)
- Florsheim (1)
- Fossil (2)
- French Connection (1)
- Frette (4)
- Fubu (1)
- Furla (2)
- Gap Outlet (1)
- Geoffrey Beene (1)
- Ghurka (2)
- Giorgio Armani (1)
- Greg Norman (1)
- Gucci (1)
- Guess? (1)
- Hard Rock Café Factory Gear (1)
- Harry & David (5)
- Hartman Factory Store (2)
- Harve Benard (1)
- Headline News (9)
- Hugo Boss (1)
- Hunting World (6)
- Hush Puppies & Family (1)
- Iceberg Factory Outlet (1)
- Izod (1)

- J Crew (1)
- J M Originals (1)
- Jockey (1)
- Johnston & Murphy (1)
- Jones New York (1)
- Jones New York Country (1)
- Jones New York Sport (1)
- Jones New York Woman (1)
- Jones NY Men's/Women's Suits (1)
- Joseph Abboud (1)
- Judith Leiber (5)
- Kasper ASL (1)
- Kate Spade (3)
- KB Toys (6)
- Kenneth Cole (1)
- Kipling (2)
- La Perla (1)
- Lacoste (1)
- Lancome The Company Outlet (8)
- Landau Costume Jeweller (3)
- Last Call Neiman Marcus (1)
- Laundry by Shelli Segal (1)
- Le Creuset (4)
- Le Gourmet Chef (4)
- Leather Loft (2)
- L'eggs Hanes Bali Playtex (1)
- Levi's Outlet by Designs (1)
- Lids (9)
- Little Me (1)
- Liz Claiborne (1)
- Liz Claiborne Shoes (1)
- London Fog (1)
- Louis Feraud Paris (1)
- Maidenform (1)
- Malo (1)
- Marina Rinaldi (1)
- Max Mara (1)
- Mikasa (4)
- Mom's Cigar Factory Outlet (9)
- Movado (2)
- Music 4 Less (5)
- Natori Outlet (1)
- Nautica (1)
- Nautica Jeans (1)
- Nike (1)
- Nine West (1)
- North Face (1)
- Off 5th-Saks Fifth Avenue (1)
- Oilily (1)
- Olga Warner (1)
- Oneida (4)
- OshKosh B'Gosh (1)

- PacSun (1)
- Perfumania (8)
- Perry Ellis (1)
- Petite Sophisticate (1)
- Polo Jeans Co (1)
- Polo Ralph Lauren (1)
- Quiksilver (1)
- Ralph Lauren Home (4)
- Reebok (1)
- Rockport (1)
- Royal Doulton (4)
- Salvatore Ferragamo (1)
- Samsonite (2)
- Seiko (3)
- Sheridan Australia Linens (4)
- Skechers (1)
- Socks Galore (1)
- Sony (4)
- Space (Prada, Miu Miu) (1)
- St John Company Store (1)
- Steve Madden Shoes (1)
- Stride Rite Keds Sperry (1)
- Studio 7 (1)
- Sunglass Outfitters (3)
- Sunglass Station (3)
- TAG Heuer (2)
- Tahari (1)
- Theory (1)
- Timberland (1)
- Time Factory Watch (3)
- Tod's (1)
- Tommy Hilfiger (1)
- Totes Isotoner Sunglass World (3)
- TSE (1)
- Tumi (2)
- Ultra Diamond Outlet (3)
- Unisa (1)
- Van Heusen (1)
- Vans Shoes (1)
- Variazioni (1)
- Ventilo Paris (1)
- Versace (1)
- Via Spiga & Co (1)
- Villeroy & Boch (4)
- Vitamin World (8)
- Waterford Wedgwood (4)
- WestPoint Stevens (4)
- Williams-Sonoma Marketplace (4)
- Wilson's Leather (1)
- Wolford (1)
- Woolrich (1)
- World of Fun (1)

- XOXO (1)
- Zales The Diamond Store (3)
- Zegna Outlet Store (1)

EATS & TREATS
- Applebee's (11)
- Au Bon Pan Bakery Café (11)
- Carvel / Nathan's (10)
- China Taste (11)
- Fuzziwig's Candy Factory (10)
- Godiva Chocolatier (10)
- Great American Cookie (10)
- Haagen Dazs (10)
- McDonald's (11)
- McSnacks (11)
- Nathan's International Eatery (11)
- New York Pretzel (10)
- Pari Pari Ko (11)
- Posa Posa Too Italian Restaurant (11)
- Rocky Mountain Chocolate (10)
- South Philly Steaks & Fries (11)
- Starbucks Coffee (10)
- Thyme to Eat (11)

3 LAKE GEORGE

Located in eastern New York, north of Albany. Lake George offers the shopper four main outlet centers, all within walking distance of each other. To reach the factory outlets take exit 20 off I-87north or exit 22 from I-87 south.

3A • Adirondack Outlet Mall
www.factoryoutletsoflakegeorge.com
Address 1454 Rt 9 *Phone* 518-793-2161 *Hours* Mon-Sat 9:30-9, Sun 10-6 *Location* See Lake George introduction.

STORES
- Big Dog Sportswear (1)
- Bon Worth (1)
- Book Warehouse (5)
- Champion (1)
- Corning Revere (4)

- Dress Barn/Dress Barn Woman (1)
- Easy Spirit (1)
- Eddie Bauer (1)
- Kitchen Collection (4)
- Paper Factory (9)
- Rue 21 (1)
- Sunglass World (3)
- Swank (2)
- Totes / Isotoner (3)
- Toy Liquidators (6)

EATS & TREATS
- CK's Eatery (11)

3B • Factory Stores of America
www.chelseafactoryoutlets.com
www.factoryoutletsoflakegeorge.com
Address 1476 Rt 9 *Phone* 518-792-
5316 *Hours* Jun-Sep 3: Mon-Sat
10-9. Sep 4-May: Mon-Thu 10-6,
Fri-Sat 10-8, Sun 11-5 *Location*
See Lake George introduction.

STORES
- Brand Name Closeouts (1)
- Carter's Childrenswear (1)
- Factory Brand Shoes (1)
- L'eggs Hanes Bali Playtex (1)
- Levi's Outlet by Designs (1)
- Sportshoe Center (1)

3C • French Mountain Commons
www.factoryoutletsoflakegeorge.com
Address 1439 Rt 9 *Phone* 518-792-
1483 *Hours* Jan-May: Sun-Thu
10-6, Fri-Sat 10-9. Jun-Dec: Mon-
Sat 9:30-9, Sun 10-6. *Location* See
Lake George introduction.

STORES
- Fieldcrest Cannon (4)
- Gap Outlet (1)
- Hush Puppies & Family (1)
- Jockey (1)
- Lillian Vernon (9)

- Nine West (1)
- Oneida (4)
- OshKosh B'Gosh (1)
- Pfaltzgraff (4)
- Sunglass Hut (3)
- Tommy Hilfiger (1)

EATS & TREATS
- Commons Deli (11)

3D • Lake George Plaza
www.factoryoutletsoflakegeorge.com
Address 1424 Rt 9 *Phone* 518-798-
7234 *Hours* Mon-Thu 10-6, Fri-
Sat 10-8, Sun 11-6. Jun-Aug: Mon-
Sat 10-9, Sun 10-6. *Location* See
Lake George introduction.

STORES
- Bass (1)
- Coach (2)
- Dansk (4)
- Designer Fragrance/Cosmetics (8)
- Harry & David (5)
- Izod (1)
- Jones New York (1)
- Maidenform (1)
- Nautica (1)
- PacSun (1)
- Perfumania (8)
- Polo Ralph Lauren (1)
- Stone Mountain (2)
- Timberland (1)
- Van Heusen (1)

4 LATHAM

4A • Prime Outlets at Latham
www.primeoutlets.com
Address 400 Old Loudon Rd
Phone 413-243-8186 *Hours* Jan-
Memorial Day: Mon-Thu 9-6, Fri
9-8, Sat 9-6, Sun 11-5. Memorial
Day-Dec: Mon-Fri 9-9, Sat 9-6,
Sun 11-5 *Location* Eastern New

York, just north of Albany. From I-87 take exit 7 (State Hwy 7) east to Old Louden Rd.

STORES

- Dansk (4)
- Lenox (4)
- Oneida (4)
- WestPoint Stevens (4)

5 MOUNT KISCO

5A • Manufacturer's Outlet Center
www.westchesterweb.com
Address 195 N Bedford Rd *Phone* 914-241-8503 *Hours* Mon-Sat 10-9, Sun 12-6 *Location* North of New York City and White Plains. From the Sawmill River Pkwy take the Kisco Ave exit (exit 37) and turn left. Follow to Preston Way and turn left to North Bedford Rd (State Hwy 117). Center is at the intersection of Preston Way and North Bedford Rd.

STORES

- A & R Silk Flowers (4)
- Adam & Eve (8)
- Antique On The Mall (4)
- Bass (1)
- Cappy's Travel Center (9)
- Casual Corner (1)
- Clear Connection (7)
- Corning Revere (4)
- Dress Barn Woman (1)
- EK Bags (2)
- Famous Brands Housewares (4)
- Famous Footwear (1)
- Farberware (4)
- Geoffrey Beene (1)
- Golf Outlet (6)
- Harry Ketchel (1)
- Hobby Craft Center (6)
- Jewelry Den (3)
- Leather Loft (2)
- Levi's Outlet by Designs (1)
- Michelle Danielle (8)
- Mikasa (4)
- Mount Kisco Cards & Collectables (5)
- Nine West (1)
- NRM Music (5)
- Outlet Wines & Liquors (9)
- Playscape Gymtime (6)
- Playscapes Fun & Games (4)
- Royal Book Outlet (5)
- Sam's Camera (7)
- Socks & More (1)
- Van Heusen (1)
- VIP Vision (3)
- Welcome Home (4)
- Westchester Apparel (1)

EATS & TREATS

- Applebee's (11)
- Bagel Nosh (11)
- Café Bongiorno (11)

6 NIAGARA FALLS

6A • Prime Outlets Niagara Falls
www.primeoutlets.com
Address 1900 Military Rd *Phone* 716-297-0933 *Hours* Mon-Sat 10-9, Sun 11-6 *Location* Thirty minutes north of Buffalo. Take I-190 to exit 22 (US 62 south), to Military Rd. Go left 1/2 mile.

STORES

- A Dollar Store (9)
- A Little Princess (1)
- Adelphia (9)
- Adidas (1)
- Afrika (9)
- Bass (1)
- Big Dogs (1)
- Bon Worth (1)
- Books Etc (5)
- Bose Factory Store (4)
- Brooks Brothers (1)
- Bruce Alan Bags (2)
- Burberry (1)

- Calvin Klein (1)
- Carter's Childrenswear (1)
- Casual Corner (1)
- Casual Male Big & Tall (1)
- Children's Place Outlet (1)
- Claire's Accessories (3)
- Coach (2)
- Corning Revere (4)
- Cosmetics Company Store (8)
- Cost Cutters Salon (8)
- CT News (9)
- Designer Outlet (1)
- Dexter Shoe (1)
- Donna Karan (1)
- Dress Barn (1)
- Drew Candle (5)
- Eddie Bauer (1)
- Factory Brand Shoes (1)
- Famous Brands Housewares (4)
- Fila (1)
- Flagtastics (9)
- Foot Locker (1)
- Fragrance Outlet (8)
- Gap Outlet (1)
- GNC (8)
- Green Onion (9)
- Guess? (1)
- Harley Davidson Outlet (9)
- Harry & David (5)
- Hartstrings (1)
- Homespun Country Store (9)
- Hush Puppies & Family (1)
- Izod (1)
- J Crew (1)
- Jockey (1)
- Johnston & Murphy (1)
- KB Toys (6)
- Kitchen Collection (4)
- L'eggs Hanes Bali Playtex (1)
- Levi's Outlet by Designs (1)
- Linen's N Things (4)
- Liz Claiborne (1)
- Lovely Nails (8)
- Maidenform (1)
- Marshalls (1)
- Mikasa (4)
- Morey's Jewelers (3)
- Motherhood Maternity (1)
- Music 4 Less (5)
- Naturalizer (1)
- Nautica (1)
- Nine West (1)

- Off 5th-Saks Fifth Avenue (1)
- Old Navy (1)
- Olsen Collection (1)
- OshKosh B'Gosh (1)
- PacSun (1)
- Paper Outlet (9)
- Payless Shoe Source (1)
- Perfumania (8)
- Perry Ellis (1)
- Petite Sophisticate (1)
- Pfaltzgraff (4)
- Piercing Pagoda (3)
- Polo Ralph Lauren (1)
- Reebok / Rockport (1)
- Remington (4)
- Rue 21 (1)
- S & K Menswear (1)
- Samsonite (2)
- Stride Rite Family Footwear (1)
- Sunglass Hut (3)
- Swank (2)
- Timberland (1)
- Tommy Hilfiger (1)
- Ultra Gold & Diamond (3)
- Van Heusen (1)
- Vitamin World (8)
- Wear House (1)
- Westport Ltd/Westport Woman (1)
- Woolrich (1)
- Zales The Diamond Store (3)

EATS & TREATS
- Applebee's (11)
- Ben & Jerry's (10)
- Burger King (11)
- CinnaMonster (10)
- Leon's Pizza (11)
- Nancy's Coffee Café (11)
- Panda Express (11)
- Pita Gourmet (11)
- Red Lobster (11)
- Steak Escape (11)
- Taco Bell (11)

7   RIVERHEAD

Riverhead is located about 80 miles east of New York City. Follow I-495 east to exit 73, the last exit.

Exit 73 is a direct entrance to the Tanger Outlet Center I parking lot. Shoppers can walk, drive, or take the trolley to access both outlets.

7A • Tanger Outlet Center I
www.tangeroutlets.com
Address 1770 W Main St **Phone** 800-407-4894 or 631-369-2732 **Hours** Mon-Sat 9-9, Sun 10-7 **Location** See introduction to Riverhead.

STORES
- Aeropostale (1)
- Ann Taylor (1)
- Bass (1)
- Bath & Body Works (8)
- Carter's Childrenswear (1)
- Casual Male Big & Tall (1)
- Claiborne Menswear (1)
- Clothestime (1)
- Coach (2)
- Corning Revere (4)
- Dana Buchman (1)
- Danskin (1)
- DKNY Jeans (1)
- Dress Barn (1)
- Dress Barn Woman (1)
- Eddie Bauer (1)
- Elisabeth (1)
- Etienne Aigner (1)
- Florsheim (1)
- Gap Outlet (1)
- Geoffrey Beene Men's & Women's (1)
- Greg Norman (1)
- Harry & David (5)
- Hoover Outlet (4)
- Izod (1)
- Jockey (1)
- Jones New York (1)
- Jones New York Men (1)
- Jones New York Sport (1)
- Kitchen Collection (4)
- Laundry by Shelli Segal (1)
- Leather Loft (2)
- Lechter's Housewares (4)
- L'eggs Hanes Bali Playtex (1)
- Levi's Outlet by Designs (1)
- Liz Claiborne (1)
- Liz Claiborne Shoes (1)
- London Fog (1)
- Maidenform (1)
- Maternity Works (1)
- Music 4 Less (5)
- New York Jewelry (3)
- Nine West (1)
- Olga Warner (1)
- Oneida (4)
- OshKosh B'Gosh (1)
- Perfumania (8)
- Pfaltzgraff (4)
- Polo Ralph Lauren (1)
- Reebok (1)
- Rena Rowan (1)
- Rue 21 (1)
- Samsonite (2)
- SAS Factory Shoes (1)
- Springmaid Wamsutta (4)
- Sprint PCS Center (7)
- Stride Rite Keds Sperry (1)
- Timberland (1)
- Time Factory Watch (3)
- Tommy Hilfiger (1)
- Totes / Sunglass World (3)
- Van Heusen (1)
- Vans Shoes (1)
- Welcome Home (4)
- Woolrich (1)
- Zales The Diamond Store (3)

EATS & TREATS
- Food Court (11)
- Pepperidge Farm (10)

7B • Tanger Outlet Center II
www.tangeroutlets.com
Address 1770 W Main St **Phone** 800-407-4894 or 631-369-2732 **Hours** Mon-Sat 9-9, Sun 10-7 **Location** See introduction to Riverhead.

STORES
- Adidas (1)
- Aerosoles (1)
- Aldo Shoes (1)

- Banana Republic (1)
- Banister Shoes (1)
- Barneys New York (1)
- BCBG Max Azria (1)
- Benetton (1)
- Big Dog Sportswear (1)
- Bose Factory Store (4)
- Bostonian Clarks (1)
- Britches (1)
- Brooks Brothers (1)
- Bugle Boy (1)
- California Sunshine Swimwear (1)
- Calvin Klein (1)
- Camp Coleman (6)
- Candie's (1)
- Casual Corner (1)
- Casual Corner Woman (1)
- Chelsea Watch Co (3)
- Children's Place Outlet (1)
- Claire's Accessories (3)
- Class Perfumes & Cosmetics (8)
- Club Monaco Direct (1)
- Cole-Haan (1)
- Cosmetics Company Store (8)
- Country Clutter (4)
- Craftworks (4)
- Delia's (1)
- Dexter Shoe (1)
- Donna Karan (1)
- Easy Spirit (1)
- Factory Brand Shoes (1)
- Farberware (4)
- Fila (1)
- Fossil (2)
- Guess? (1)
- Haggar (1)
- Hush Puppies & Family (1)
- J Crew (1)
- J Peterman Co. (1)
- Joseph Abboud (1)
- Kasper ASL (1)
- KB Toys (6)
- Kenneth Cole (1)
- Le Gourmet Chef (4)
- L'eggs Hanes Bali Playtex (1)
- Lenox (4)
- Lids (9)
- Lillian Vernon (9)
- Metabolife (8)
- Mikasa (4)
- Music 4 Less (5)
- Natori Outlet (1)

- Nautica (1)
- Nike (1)
- Noritake (4)
- Off 5th-Saks Fifth Avenue (1)
- Office Max (9)
- Old Navy (1)
- Pacific Sunwear (1)
- Paper Factory (9)
- Perry Ellis (1)
- Petite Sophisticate (1)
- Polo Jeans Co (1)
- Remington (4)
- Renfrew (1)
- Rockport (1)
- Royal Doulton (4)
- Samsonite (2)
- Sents For Less (8)
- Skechers (1)
- So Fun! Kids (1)
- Socks Galore (1)
- Steve Madden Shoes (1)
- Sunglass World (3)
- Tools & More (9)
- Ultra Diamond & Gold (3)
- Ultra Watch Outlet (3)
- Vitamin World (8)
- Waterford Wedgwood (4)
- We're Entertainment (4)
- WestPoint Stevens (4)
- Wilson's Leather (1)

EATS & TREATS
- Auntie Anne's Pretzals (10)
- CinnaMonster (10)
- Fuzziwig's Candy Factory (10)
- Great Steak & Potato (11)
- Lindt Chocolate (10)
- McDonald's (11)
- Ragin Cajun (11)
- Rocky Mountain Chocolate (10)
- Villa Pizza (11)
- Wiz (11)
- Wok & Roll (11)

8 WATERLOO

8A • Waterloo Premium Outlets
www.premiumoutlets.com
Address 655 Route 318 *Phone* 315-
539-1100 *Hours* Mon-Sat 10-9,

Sun 10-6 *Location* Between Rochester and Syracuse off I-90. From I-90 east take exit 42 to Rt 318 east. From I-90 west take exit 41, right onto Rt 414 to Rt 318 west.

STORES

- American Outpost (1)
- Banister Shoes (1)
- Bass (1)
- Beauty Express (8)
- Big Dog Sportswear (1)
- Black & Decker (4)
- Bon Worth (1)
- Bose Factory Store (4)
- Brooks Brothers (1)
- Calendar Club (5)
- Calvin Klein (1)
- Card America (5)
- Carter's Childrenswear (1)
- Casual Corner (1)
- Casual Corner Woman (1)
- Casual Male Big & Tall (1)
- Chef's Outlet (4)
- Claire's Accessories (3)
- Coach (2)
- Corning Revere (4)
- Cosmetics Company Store (8)
- Danskin (1)
- Dexter Shoe (1)
- Dockers Outlet by Designs (1)
- Dress Barn/Dress Barn Woman (1)
- Eddie Bauer (1)
- Erin's Way (1)
- Esprit (1)
- Etienne Aigner (1)
- Factory Brand Shoes (1)
- Famous Brands Housewares (4)
- Farberware (4)
- Fila (1)
- Gap Outlet (1)
- Geoffrey Beene (1)
- Haggar (1)
- Harry & David (5)
- Hoover Outlet (4)
- Hush Puppies & Family (1)
- Izod (1)
- J Crew (1)
- Jockey (1)
- Johnston & Murphy (1)
- Jones New York (1)
- Kasper ASL (1)
- KB Toys (6)
- King Ferry Winery (9)
- Kitchen Collection (4)
- Laurie's Lasting Memories (5)
- L'eggs Hanes Bali Playtex (1)
- Levi's Outlet by Designs (1)
- Liz Claiborne (1)
- London Fog (1)
- Maidenform (1)
- Mikasa (4)
- Motherhood Maternity (1)
- Music For A Song (5)
- Naturalizer (1)
- Nautica (1)
- Nine West (1)
- Oneida (4)
- OshKosh B'Gosh (1)
- PacSun (1)
- Paper Factory (9)
- Perfumania (8)
- Perry Ellis (1)
- Petite Sophisticate (1)
- Polo Ralph Lauren (1)
- Reebok (1)
- Rockport (1)
- Rue 21 (1)
- S & K Menswear (1)
- Samsonite (2)
- SAS Factory Shoes (1)
- Soft As A Grape (1)
- Springmaid Wamsutta (4)
- Stride Rite Keds Sperry (1)
- Sunglass Hut / Watch Station (3)
- Timberland (1)
- Totes Isotoner Sunglass World (3)
- Value Booksellers (5)
- Van Heusen (1)
- VF Factory Outlet (1)
- Vitamin World (8)
- Waterford Wedgwood (4)
- Welcome Home (4)
- Wilson's Leather (1)
- Yankee Candle (5)
- Zales The Diamond Store (3)

EATS & TREATS

- Arby's Roast Beef (11)
- Burger King (11)
- Rocky Mountain Chocolate (10)
- Subway (11)
- Sun Garden Grill (11)
- Villa Pizza (11)

North Carolina

1 • Blowing Rock
2 • Burlington
3 • Concord
4 • Hickory
5 • Kannapolis
6 • Morrisville
7 • Nags Head
8 • Smithfield

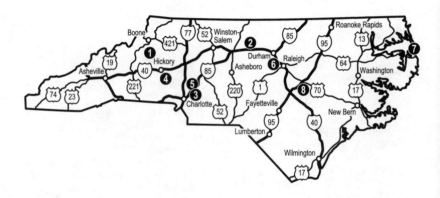

1 BLOWING ROCK

1A • Tanger Shoppes on the Parkway

www.tangeroutlets.com
Address US Hwy 321 *Phone* 800-720-6728 or 828-295-4444 *Hours* Mon-Sat 10-9 (Jan-Mar17: 10-6), Sun 12-6 *Location* North of Hickory, near the Pisgah National Forest. From Hickory take US 321 north to Blowing Rock. Then take US 321 bypass, center is on the left.

STORES
- Bass (1)
- Big Dog Sportswear (1)
- Capacity (1)
- Carter's Childrenswear (1)
- Christmas Market (9)
- Claire's Accessories (3)
- Coach (2)
- Corning Revere (4)
- Dress Barn (1)
- Easy Spirit (1)
- Gap Outlet (1)
- Geoffrey Beene (1)
- Izod (1)
- Jockey (1)
- Jones New York (1)
- Kasper ASL (1)
- Kitchen Collection (4)
- Leather Loft (2)
- L'eggs Hanes Bali Playtex (1)
- Liz Claiborne (1)
- London Fog (1)
- Nautica (1)
- Polo Ralph Lauren (1)
- Royal Doulton (4)
- Saslow's Jewelers (3)
- Seiko (3)
- Socks Galore (1)
- Sunglass Hut (3)
- Van Heusen (1)
- Vitamin World (8)
- Welcome Home (4)

EATS & TREATS
- Kilwins Chocolate & Ice Cream (10)
- Parkway Café (11)

2 BURLINGTON

2A • Burlington Manufacturer's Outlet Center

www.save-at-bmoc-outlets.com
Address 2389 Corporation Pkwy *Phone* 336-227-2872 *Hours* Mon-Sat 10-9, Sun 1-6 *Location* Between Greensboro and Durham. Take exit 145 off I-85/40, go north on Hwy 49.

STORES
- Allen Edmonds (1)
- Bass (1)
- Big Dog Sportswear (1)
- Bon Worth (1)
- Bridal Mart (9)
- Burlington Artist League (4)
- Burlington Brands (1)
- Burlington Coat Factory (1)
- Capacity (1)
- Carter's Childrenswear (1)
- Casual Male Big & Tall (1)
- Corning Revere (4)
- Croscill (4)
- Diamond P Western Store (1)
- Dress Barn (1)
- Dress Barn Woman (1)
- Elisabeth (1)
- Famous Footwear (1)
- Farberware (4)
- Finish Line (1)
- Great Buy Clothing (1)
- Hanes Mill Outlet (1)
- It's Fashion (1)
- Izod (1)
- Jockey (1)
- KB Toys (6)
- Kitchen Collection (4)
- L A Nails (8)
- Le Creuset (4)
- Liz Claiborne (1)
- Mikasa (4)
- Natural Nails (8)
- Naturalizer (1)
- Nine West (1)
- Paper Factory (9)
- Pfaltzgraff (4)
- Rack Room Shoes (1)
- Receptions (1)

- Riddle & Cockrell (1)
- Rolane (1)
- Rue 21 (1)
- S & K Menswear (1)
- Samsonite (2)
- Scent Saver Cosmetics & Fragrances (8)
- Shoe Show (1)
- Van Heusen (1)
- Vitamin World (8)
- WestPoint Stevens (4)

EATS & TREATS
- Pepperidge Farm (10)
- Sam's Cheeseburgers (11)
- Sara Lee Sandwich Shoppe (11)
- Tiha Of Japan (11)

2B • Tanger Outlet Center
www.tangeroutlets.com
Address I-85 & Hwy 49, exit 145
Phone 800-407-5005 *Hours* Mon-Sat 10-9 (Jan-Feb 10-6), Sun 12-6
Location Between Greensboro and Durham. Take exit 145 off I-85/40, go north on Hwy 49.

STORES
- Bible Factory Outlet (5)
- Big Dog Sportswear (1)
- Carter's Childrenswear (1)
- Elisabeth (1)
- Farberware (4)
- Finish Line (1)
- Hanes Mill Outlet (1)
- Izod (1)
- Kitchen Collection (4)
- Liz Claiborne (1)
- Naturalizer (1)
- Nine West (1)
- Samsonite (2)

3 CONCORD

3A • Concord Mills
www.millscorp.com
Address 8111 Concord Mills Blvd
Phone 704-979-3000 or 877-NC-Mills *Hours* Mon-Sat 10-9, Sat 9:30-9:30, Sun 11-8 *Location* Ten miles north of Charlotte off I-85, exit 49 (Concord Mills Blvd).

STORES
- AC Moore (1)
- ACC Communications (7)
- Aeropostale (1)
- All About Cellular (7)
- AMC 24 Theatres (9)
- Ann Taylor (1)
- Arden B (1)
- Athlete's Foot (1)
- Banana Republic (1)
- Bass (1)
- Bass Pro Shops Outdoor World (6)
- Bath & Body Works (8)
- Beauty Express (8)
- Bed Bath & Beyond (4)
- Bible Factory Outlet (5)
- Big Dogs (1)
- Black & Decker (4)
- Blacklion (4)
- Books-A-Million (5)
- Bose Factory Store (4)
- Brooks Brothers (1)
- Build-A-Bear Workshop (5)
- Burlington Coat Factory (1)
- Carter's Childrenswear (1)
- Casual Corner Annex (1)
- Casual Corner Annex Petite (1)
- Casual Corner Annex Woman (1)
- Charlotte Russe (1)
- Children's Place Outlet (1)
- Claire's Boutique (3)
- Corning Revere (4)
- Cosmetics Company Store (8)
- Country Clutter (4)
- CR Jewelers Outlet (3)
- CTC Wireless (7)
- Cutting Edge Outlet (4)
- Deck The Walls (4)
- Dress Barn/Dress Barn Woman (1)
- Earthbound Trading Co (5)
- Eddie Bauer (1)
- Etienne Aigner (1)
- Eye Candy (1)
- Factory Brand Shoes (1)
- Finish Line (1)
- Flag Shop (9)
- Forget Me Not by American Greetings (5)

- FYE - For Your Entertainment (4)
- Games Workshop (9)
- Gap Outlet (1)
- Glamour Nails (8)
- GNC (8)
- Golf America (6)
- Group USA (1)
- Haggar (1)
- Hot Topic (1)
- Hot Wax Candle (5)
- Icing (3)
- Jewelers of Las Vegas (3)
- Jockey (1)
- Jones New York (1)
- Journeys (1)
- Julie's (1)
- Kasper ASL (1)
- Kay Jewelers (3)
- Kirkland's (4)
- Leather Limited (2)
- Leather Loft (2)
- L'eggs Hanes Bali Playtex (1)
- Levi's / Dockers (1)
- Lids (9)
- Limited Too (1)
- Liz Claiborne (1)
- Liz Claiborne Shoes (1)
- Maidenform (1)
- MasterCuts (8)
- Mikasa (4)
- Motherhood Maternity (1)
- NASCAR Silicon Motor Speedway (6)
- Naturalizer (1)
- Nautica (1)
- Nike (1)
- Nine West (1)
- Off 5th-Saks Fifth Avenue (1)
- Old Navy (1)
- OshKosh B'Gosh (1)
- Pacific Sunwear (1)
- Payless Shoe Source (1)
- Perfumania (8)
- Perry Ellis (1)
- Picture People (9)
- Polo Jeans Co (1)
- Polo Ralph Lauren (1)
- Pro Image (1)
- Rack Room Shoes (1)
- Reebok / Rockport (1)
- Reeds Jewelers (3)
- Remington (4)
- Rue 21 (1)

- S & K Menswear (1)
- Sam's Clothier (1)
- Samsonite Travel Expo (2)
- San Francisco Music Box (9)
- Sanrio (9)
- Scrubs & Beyond (1)
- Select Comfort (4)
- Skechers (1)
- Spencer Gifts (5)
- Sports Memories (6)
- Stop N Save Software (7)
- Sun & Ski Sports (1)
- Sunglass Hut (3)
- Sunglass World (3)
- Swim N Sport (1)
- T-Shirts Plus (1)
- Time Factory Watch (3)
- TJ Maxx (1)
- Tommy Hilfiger (1)
- ToyCo (6)
- Underground Station (1)
- Urban Planet (1)
- Vans Shoes (1)
- Vitamin World (8)
- Warnaco (1)
- Watch World International (3)
- Waterford Wedgwood (4)
- Wet Seal Outlet (1)
- Wilson's Leather (1)
- Zales The Diamond Store (3)

EATS & TREATS

- Alabama Grill (11)
- Auntie Anne's Pretzals (10)
- Burger King (11)
- Cajun Grill (11)
- California Pizza Kitchen (11)
- Candy World (10)
- Carvel Ice Cream (10)
- Chili's Too (11)
- Cinnabon (10)
- Dairy Queen (11)
- Dickey's Barbecue Pit (11)
- Dive In (11)
- Fox Sky Box (11)
- Freshens Yogurt / Great American Cookie / Pretzel Time (10)
- Great Steak & Potato (11)
- Jeepers! (11)
- Jillian's (11)
- Macado's (11)
- Mrs Rich's Bakery (11)

- Ranch 1 (11)
- Rocky Mountain Chocolate (10)
- Sbarro Italian Eatery (11)
- Starbucks Coffee (10)
- Sweets From Heaven (10)
- Yeung's Lotus Express (11)

4 HICKORY

4A • Hickory Furniture Mart
www.hickoryfurniture.com
Address 2220 Hwy 70 SE *Phone*
800-462-Mart or 828-322-3510
Hours Mon-Sat 9-6 *Location*
Northwest of Charlotte off I-40.
Eastbound on I-40 take exit 125,
turn right onto Lenoir-Rhyne Blvd
then left onto Hwy 70 east. Center
is about 1 mile on the right. From
I-40 west take exit 126. Turn left
at the off-ramp, then right onto
Hwy 70 west.

STORES
- Bassett Furniture Direct (4)
- Boyles Galleries (4)
- Boyles Showcase (4)
- Broyhill Showcase (4)
- Century Factory Outlet (4)
- Comfort Zone (4)
- Councill Factory Outlet (4)
- Daydreams (4)
- Designing Women (4)
- Dinstinction Leather Gallery (4)
- Don Lamor (4)
- Drexel Heritage (4)
- Flexsteel Gallery (4)
- Franklin Place (4)
- Gallery of Lights (4)
- Generations (4)
- Grandfather Clock Gallery (4)
- Henredon Factory Outlet (4)
- Hickory Chair (4)
- Hickory Coffee Company (4)
- Hickory Park Furniture (4)
- Hickory White Furniture (4)
- Hollin Gate (4)
- Home Focus (4)
- House of Mirrors (4)

- Intro Outlet (4)
- Jessica's Veranda (4)
- La-Z-Boy Gallery (4)
- La Petite France (4)
- Leather Gallery (4)
- Lexington Gallery (4)
- Nostalgia (4)
- Pennsylvania House (4)
- Reflections (4)
- Resource Design (4)
- Rhoney (4)
- Robert Bergelin (4)
- Rowe Gallery (4)
- Rug Room (4)
- Seasons Outdoor Gallery (4)
- Sity Slicker (4)
- Southern Designs (4)
- Southern Furniture (4)
- Theodore Alexander (4)
- Timeless Interiors (4)
- Wild Pair (4)
- Work Station (4)
- Zagaroli Classics (4)

5 KANNAPOLIS

5A • Cannon Village
www.cannonvillage.com
Address 115 Oak Ave *Phone* 800-
438-6111 or 704-938-3200 *Hours*
Mon-Fri 9-5, Sat 10-6, Sun 1-6
Location 25 minutes north of
Charlotte off I-85. Take exits 58 or
63 and follow signs to Cannon
Village Home Furnishings Market.

STORES
- Antique Mall (4)
- Baker Furniture (4)
- Bashian Oriental Rug (4)
- Bon Worth (1)
- Book Gallery (5)
- Brass Exchange (4)
- Budget Blinds (4)
- Carolina Chandeliers (4)
- Carolina Interiors (4)
- Carolina Scents (5)
- CAWW Studios (4)
- Century Furniture Clearance (4)
- Churchill's (1)

- Crow's Nest Gallery (4)
- Diane Overcash Art Studio (4)
- Dress Barn (1)
- Falls Jewelers (3)
- Fieldcrest Cannon (4)
- First Union National Bank (9)
- Gem Theatre (9)
- Gift Corner (5)
- Goodnight Clothing Store (1)
- Jewel Shoppe (3)
- K-Town Furniture (4)
- Kidstyle (1)
- Kitchen Collection (4)
- Lee Clothing (1)
- L'eggs Hanes Bali Playtex (1)
- Maitland-Smith Outlet (4)
- Neta's Children Shop (1)
- Omega Graphics (1)
- Paoli and Tellus (4)
- Paper Factory (9)
- Potter's Mark (4)
- Regent's Corner (4)
- Southern Charm (5)
- Southern Charm Christmas Shoppe (9)
- Village Boutique (5)
- Village Furniture House (4)
- Virginia's (1)
- Wicker and Rattan Gallery (4)
- World Wide Furniture (4)

EATS & TREATS

- Bangkok Fried Rice (11)
- Curds & Whey Health Foods (11)
- Gee Willigaus Barbeque & General Store (11)
- Towel City Junction (11)
- Village Grill (11)
- Village Kiosk (11)

6 MORRISVILLE

6A • Prime Outlets Morrisville

www.primeoutlets.com
Address 1001 Airport Blvd *Phone* 919-380-8700 *Hours* Mon-Sat 10-9, Sun 12-6 *Location* Between Raleigh and Durham off I-40. From Raleigh take I-40 west to exit 284 (Airport Blvd). Turn left and the center will be on your right in the Concourse Plaza.

STORES

- Alltel (7)
- Artscapes (4)
- Bass (1)
- Big Dogs (1)
- Body Shop (8)
- Book Warehouse (5)
- Bruce Alan Bags (2)
- Capacity (1)
- Corning Revere (4)
- Desire Tree (2)
- Dress Barn Petites (1)
- Dress Barn/Dress Barn Woman (1)
- Famous Brands Housewares (4)
- Finish Line (1)
- Geoffrey Beene (1)
- Izod (1)
- KB Toys (6)
- L'eggs Hanes Bali Playtex (1)
- Levi's / Dockers (1)
- Naturalizer (1)
- Nine West (1)
- Off 5th-Saks Fifth Avenue (1)
- Paper Factory (9)
- Petite Sophisticate (1)
- Rack Room Shoes (1)
- S & K Menswear (1)
- Sam's Factory Outlet (1)
- Samsonite (2)
- Samsonite At Work (2)
- SAS Factory Shoes (1)
- Tanner (1)
- Totes / Sunglass World (3)
- Van Heusen (1)
- Vitamin World (8)
- Welcome Home (4)

EATS & TREATS

- Casbah Café (11)
- Edible Complex (11)
- Frank & Stein and US Bistro (11)
- Grandstand Grille & Tavern (11)
- Greek Fiesta (11)
- Keily's Cajun Grill (11)
- Mediterranean/American Cuisine (11)
- Philly Steaks Factory (11)
- Sorrento Italian Restaurant (11)
- Subway (11)
- Szechuan Express (11)
- Villa Pizza (11)
- Wall Street Grill (11)

7 NAGS HEAD

7A • Tanger Outlet Center
www.tangeroutlets.com
Address 7100 S Croatan Hwy
Phone 800-720-6747 or 252-441-5634 **Hours** Jan-Mar 17: Mon-Sat 10-7, Sun 12-6. Mar 18-Dec: Mon-Sat 9-9, Sun 11-6 **Location** Eastern North Carolina on the coast. Traveling east on Hwy 64 cross over the Washington Baum Bridge and continue through Manteo. Follow the signs to Hwy 158. Go through the intersection at Whalebone Junction, center is on your immediate left.

STORES
- Bass (1)
- Big Dog Sportswear (1)
- Cabin Creek Gifts (5)
- Claire's Accessories (3)
- Coach (2)
- Corning Revere (4)
- Donna Designs (1)
- Dress Barn (1)
- Dress Barn Woman (1)
- Gap Outlet (1)
- Geoffrey Beene (1)
- Izod (1)
- L'eggs Hanes Bali Playtex (1)
- London Fog (1)
- Michael's Gems & Glass (5)
- Nautica (1)
- Nine West (1)
- Pfaltzgraff (4)
- Polo Ralph Lauren (1)
- Publishers Warehouse (5)
- Rack Room Shoes (1)
- Sunglass Hut (3)
- Van Heusen (1)
- Vitamin World (8)
- Wilson's Leather (1)

EATS & TREATS
- Stone Oven Pizza (11)

8 SMITHFIELD

8A • Carolina Outlet Center
Address 1025 Industrial Park Dr **Phone** 919-989-8757 **Hours** Mon-Sat 10-9, Sun 12-6 **Location** South of Raleigh off I-95, exit 95.

STORES
- American Tourister (2)
- Bath & Body Works (8)
- Big Dog Sportswear (1)
- Black & Decker (4)
- Body Shop (8)
- Bombay Outlet (4)
- Bon Worth (1)
- Book Warehouse (5)
- Brooks Brothers (1)
- Camp Coleman (6)
- Carolina Linen (4)
- Carolina Pottery (4)
- Carter's Childrenswear (1)
- Casual Corner (1)
- Casual Corner Woman (1)
- Casual Male Big & Tall (1)
- Claire's Accessories (3)
- Cost Cutters Salon (8)
- Craftworks (4)
- DKNY Jeans (1)
- Dress Barn (1)
- Dress Barn Woman (1)
- Easy Spirit (1)
- Eddie Bauer (1)
- Expressions (1)
- Factory Brand Shoes (1)
- Farberware (4)
- Fossil (2)
- Gap Outlet (1)
- Geoffrey Beene (1)
- Haggar (1)
- Harry & David (5)
- Hoover Outlet (4)
- Izod (1)
- J Williams Jewelry (3)
- Jewelry World (3)
- Jockey (1)
- Kasper ASL (1)
- KB Toy Liquidators (6)
- Kitchen Collection (4)
- Koret (1)
- Le Creuset (4)

- Leather Factory (2)
- L'eggs Hanes Bali Playtex (1)
- Levi's (1)
- Liz Claiborne (1)
- Mikasa (4)
- Music For A Song (5)
- Naturalizer (1)
- Nike (1)
- Oneida (4)
- OshKosh B'Gosh (1)
- Paper Factory (9)
- Petite Sophisticate (1)
- Pfaltzgraff (4)
- Polo Ralph Lauren (1)
- Rack Room Shoes (1)
- Reebok (1)
- Rockport (1)
- Royal Doulton (4)
- S & K Menswear (1)
- SAS Factory Shoes (1)
- Stormin Norman's (9)
- Time Factory Watch (3)
- Tommy Hilfiger (1)
- Totes / Sunglass World (3)
- Van Heusen (1)
- Vitamin World (8)
- Welcome Home (4)
- Wilson's Leather (1)
- Yankee Candle (5)
- Zales The Diamond Store (3)

EATS & TREATS

- Davey's American Cuisine (11)

Ohio

1 • Aurora
2 • Burbank
3 • Jeffersonville

1 AURORA

1A • Aurora Premium Outlets
www.premiumoutlets.com
Address 549 S Chillicothe Rd
Phone 330-562-2000 *Hours* Mon-
Sat 10-9, Sun 10-6 *Location*
Between Cleveland and Akron.
From I-80 take exit 13, Rt 14
south. Follow Rt 14 a couple miles
to Rt 43 north into Aurora.

STORES
- Adidas (1)
- Al Root Candle (5)
- All About Time (9)
- Ann Taylor (1)
- Bass (1)
- Big Dog Sportswear (1)
- Bon Worth (1)
- Book Warehouse (5)
- Bose Factory Store (4)
- Brooks Brothers (1)
- Carter's Childrenswear (1)
- Casual Corner (1)
- Claire's Accessories (3)
- Corning Revere (4)
- Designer Fragrance/Cosmetics (8)
- DKNY Jeans (1)
- Doolittles (5)
- Dress Barn (1)
- Dress Barn Woman (1)
- Easy Spirit (1)
- Factory Brand Shoes (1)
- Gap Outlet (1)
- GNC (8)
- Haggar (1)
- Harry & David (5)
- Hugo Boss (1)
- Hush Puppies & Family (1)
- Jockey (1)
- Jones New York (1)
- KB Toys (6)
- Kitchen Collection (4)
- Le Gourmet Chef (4)
- Leather Loft (2)
- L'eggs Hanes Bali Playtex (1)
- Lenox (4)
- Levi's Outlet by Designs (1)
- Liz Claiborne (1)
- Maidenform (1)
- Mikasa (4)
- Music For A Song (5)
- Naturalizer (1)
- Nautica (1)
- Off 5th-Saks Fifth Avenue (1)
- Oneida (4)
- OshKosh B'Gosh (1)
- PacSun (1)
- Paper Factory (9)
- Pfaltzgraff (4)
- Polo Ralph Lauren (1)
- Rue 21 (1)
- Samsonite (2)
- So Fun! Kids (1)
- Stride Rite Keds Sperry (1)
- Tommy Hilfiger (1)
- Totes Isotoner Sunglass World (3)
- Ultra Diamond Outlet (3)
- Van Heusen (1)
- Wayside Workshop (4)
- Welcome Home (4)
- WestPoint Stevens (4)
- What On Earth (5)
- Zales The Diamond Store (3)

EATS & TREATS
- Aurora's Amish Style Restaurant (11)
- Farmer's Grill (11)
- Fuzziwig's Candy Factory (10)
- Malley's Chocolates (10)
- Subway (11)

2 BURBANK

2A • Prime Outlets Lodi
www.primeoutlets.com
Address 9911 Avon Lake Rd *Phone*
330-948-9929 or 888-746-7563
Hours Mon-Sat 10-9, Sun 11-6
Location West of Akron off I-71,
exit 204 (Rt 83).

STORES
- Adidas (1)
- Bass (1)
- Bath & Body Works (8)
- Big Dogs (1)
- Book Warehouse (5)
- Brooks Brothers (1)
- Calendar Club (5)
- Capacity (1)
- Carter's For Kids (1)
- Casual Corner (1)
- Casual Corner Woman (1)
- Claire's Accessories (3)
- Corning Revere (4)
- Cost Cutters Salon (8)
- Country Clutter (4)

- Dockers Outlet by Designs (1)
- Dress Barn/Dress Barn Woman (1)
- Eddie Bauer (1)
- Factory Brand Shoes (1)
- Farberware (4)
- Gap Outlet (1)
- Geoffrey Beene (1)
- Haggar (1)
- Hamilton Luggage (2)
- Harry & David (5)
- Hoover Outlet (4)
- Izod (1)
- J Marco Galleries (1)
- Jockey (1)
- Jones New York Country (1)
- Kasper ASL (1)
- KB Toys (6)
- King's Jewelry (3)
- Kitchen Collection (4)
- Koret (1)
- L'eggs Hanes Bali Playtex (1)
- Levi's Outlet by Designs (1)
- Liz Claiborne (1)
- Liz Claiborne Shoes (1)
- Mikasa (4)
- Music For A Song (5)
- Naturalizer (1)
- Nautica (1)
- New England Home (4)
- Nike (1)
- OshKosh B'Gosh (1)
- Paper Factory (9)
- Petite Sophisticate (1)
- Pfaltzgraff (4)
- Polo Ralph Lauren (1)
- Rack Room Shoes (1)
- Reebok (1)
- Root Candles (5)
- Rue 21 (1)
- S & K Menswear (1)
- Samsonite (2)
- SAS Factory Shoes (1)
- Springmaid Wamsutta (4)
- Sunglass Outlet (3)
- Tommy Hilfiger (1)
- Tools & More (9)
- Totes Isotoner Sunglass World (3)
- Ultra Gold & Diamond (3)
- US Post Office (9)
- Van Heusen (1)
- Vitamin World (8)
- Welcome Home (4)
- Wilson's Leather (1)

EATS & TREATS

- Arby's Roast Beef (11)
- Auntie Anne's Pretzals (10)

- Boardwalk Fries (11)
- Central Station (11)
- Great Steak & Potato (11)
- Rocky Mountain Chocolate (10)
- Subway (11)
- Villa Pizza (11)
- Wok & Roll (11)

3 JEFFERSONVILLE

3A • Prime Outlets Jeffersonville I
www.primeoutlets.com
Address 8000 Factory Shops Blvd
Phone 800-746-7644 *Hours* Mon-
Sat 10-9, Sun 11-6 *Location*
Between Dayton and Columbus
off I-71, exit 65 (US 35).

STORES

- A to Z Imports (9)
- Allen Edmonds (1)
- American Outpost (1)
- Austin 925 (3)
- Bass (1)
- Bath & Body Works (8)
- Big Dog Sportswear (1)
- Blowout Video (9)
- Bombay Outlet (4)
- Book Warehouse (5)
- Bose Factory Store (4)
- Brooks Brothers (1)
- Calendar Club (5)
- Carlisle Home (4)
- Casual Corner (1)
- Casual Corner Woman (1)
- Children's Place Outlet (1)
- Claire's Accessories (3)
- Coach (2)
- Corning Revere (4)
- Cosmetics Company Store (8)
- Dress Barn/Dress Barn Woman (1)
- Easy Spirit (1)
- Eddie Bauer (1)
- Esprit (1)
- Factory Brand Shoes (1)
- Famous Brands Housewares (4)
- Florsheim (1)
- Gap Outlet (1)
- Geoffrey Beene (1)
- GNC (8)
- Gold Toe (1)
- Gorant's Cards Plus (5)
- Guess? (1)
- Haggar (1)
- Hamilton Beach (4)

- Harry & David (5)
- Hartstone (4)
- Hartstrings (1)
- Hoover Outlet (4)
- Izod (1)
- Jockey (1)
- Johnston & Murphy (1)
- Jones New York (1)
- KB Toy Express (6)
- KB Toys (6)
- King's Jewelry (3)
- Kitchen Collection (4)
- Koret (1)
- Leather Loft (2)
- Lenox (4)
- Levi's / Dockers (1)
- Liz Claiborne Shoes (1)
- Maidenform (1)
- Motherhood Maternity (1)
- Music For A Song (5)
- Naturalizer (1)
- Nautica (1)
- Nautica Jeans (1)
- Nike (1)
- Nine West (1)
- Noritake (4)
- North Face (1)
- Oneida (4)
- PacSun (1)
- Paper Factory (9)
- Perfumania (8)
- Petite Sophisticate (1)
- Pfaltzgraff (4)
- Polo Jeans Co (1)
- Polo Ralph Lauren (1)
- Pottery Barn Furniture (4)
- Pro Image (1)
- Rack Room Shoes (1)
- Remington (4)
- Royal Doulton (4)
- Rue 21 (1)
- S & K Menswear (1)
- Samsonite (2)
- SAS Factory Shoes (1)
- Sony (4)
- Springmaid Wamsutta (4)
- Talbots (1)
- Tommy Hilfiger (1)
- Tools & More (9)
- Totes Isotoner Sunglass World (3)
- Trade Secret Beauty Salon (8)
- Ultra Diamond & Gold (3)
- Van Heusen (1)
- Vitamin World (8)
- Waterford Wedgwood (4)
- Welcome Home (4)
- Wilson's Leather (1)
- Woolrich (1)
- Yankee Candle (5)
- Zales The Diamond Store (3)

EATS & TREATS
- Blimpie Subs & Salads (11)
- CinnaMonster (10)
- Fuzziwig's Candy Factory (10)
- Gold Star Chili (11)
- Great Steak & Potato (11)
- Rocky Mountain Chocolate (10)
- Uncle Andy's Pretzels (10)
- Villa Pizza (11)
- Wok & Roll (11)

3B • Prime Outlets Jeffersonville II
www.primeoutlets.com
Address 8000 Factory Shops Blvd
Phone 800-746-7644 *Hours* Mon-Sat 10-9, Sun 11-6 *Location* Between Dayton and Columbus off I-71, exit 69 (Rt 41 north). Turn right at first traffic light, then right at next traffic light into center entrance.

STORES
- Bass (1)
- Book Warehouse (5)
- Carter's Childrenswear (1)
- Casual Male Big & Tall (1)
- Corning Clearance (4)
- Corning Revere (4)
- Dress Barn/Dress Barn Woman (1)
- Elisabeth (1)
- Factory Brand Shoes (1)
- Gap Clearance Store (1)
- Jones New York (1)
- L'eggs Hanes Bali Playtex (1)
- Liz Claiborne (1)
- Mikasa (4)
- OshKosh B'Gosh (1)
- Reebok / Rockport (1)
- Samsonite (2)
- Socks Galore (1)
- Van Heusen (1)
- Welcome Home (4)

EATS & TREATS
- Cindy's Café (11)
- Pepperidge Farm (10)

Oregon

1 • Bend
2 • Lincoln City
3 • Phoenix
4 • Seaside
5 • Troutdale
6 • Woodburn

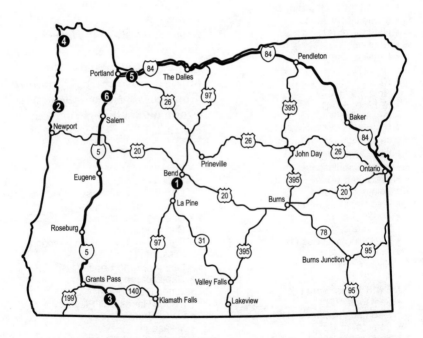

1 BEND

1A • Prime Outlets Bend

www.primeoutlets.com
Address 61300 S Hwy 97 *Phone* 541-382-4512 *Hours* Mon-Sat 9:30-8, Sun 11-6 *Location* In Bend off US 97, south of Powers Rd.

STORES

- Bass (1)
- Big Dogs (1)
- Carter's Childrenswear (1)
- Claire's Accessories (3)
- Coldwater Creek Outlet (1)
- Columbia Sportswear (1)
- Dansk (4)
- Eddie Bauer (1)
- Factory Brand Shoes (1)
- GNC (8)
- Harry & David (5)
- Izod (1)
- Kitchen Collection (4)
- L.L. Bean Factory Store (1)
- L'eggs Hanes Bali Playtex (1)
- Levi's Outlet by Most (1)
- Malone Outfitters (9)
- Nautica (1)
- Nike (1)
- Norm Thompson (1)
- North Face (1)
- Paper Factory (9)
- Sprint PCS Center (7)
- Sunglass Hut (3)
- Van Heusen (1)
- Wallet Works (2)
- Welcome Home (4)

EATS & TREATS

- Rocky Mountain Chocolate (10)

2 LINCOLN CITY

2A • Factory Stores @ Lincoln City

www.shoplincolncity.com
Address 1500 SE East Devils Lake Rd *Phone* 541-996-5000 or 888-Shop333 *Hours* Jan-Feb: Mon-Sun 10-6. Mar-Dec: Mon-Sat 10-8, Sun 10-6 *Location* Northwest Oregon on the coast. The center is on US 101 in the heart of Lincoln City.

STORES

- Banister / Easy Spirit (1)
- Bass (1)
- Beauty Express (8)
- Big Dog Sportswear (1)
- Book Warehouse (5)
- Calendar Club (5)
- Carter's Childrenswear (1)
- Christian Outlet (5)
- Christian Tree of Life Outlet (5)
- Claire's Accessories (3)
- Coach (2)
- Columbia Sportswear (1)
- Dress Barn (1)
- Dress Barn Woman (1)
- Eddie Bauer (1)
- Factory Brand Shoes (1)
- Famous Brands Housewares (4)
- Florsheim (1)
- Full Size Fashions (1)
- Gap Kids (1)
- Gap Outlet (1)
- Haggar (1)
- Harry & David (5)
- Helly Hansen (1)
- Jockey (1)
- Jones New York (1)
- Jones New York Country (1)
- KB Toy Liquidators (6)
- Kitchen Collection (4)
- Koret (1)
- Leather Loft (2)
- L'eggs Hanes Bali Playtex (1)
- Levi's Outlet by Most (1)
- Liz Claiborne (1)
- London Fog (1)
- Maidenform (1)
- Midwest Feather & Down (4)
- Mikasa (4)
- Nautica (1)
- Nine West (1)
- Norm Thompson (1)
- Old Navy (1)

- Oneida (4)
- OshKosh B'Gosh (1)
- Pacific Sunwear (1)
- Paper Factory (9)
- Perfumania (8)
- Pfaltzgraff (4)
- Polo Ralph Lauren (1)
- Quiksilver (1)
- Reebok (1)
- Rockport (1)
- Royal Doulton (4)
- Samsonite (2)
- Shutterbug (7)
- Springmaid Wamsutta (4)
- Tools & More (9)
- Totes / Sunglass World (3)
- Van Heusen (1)
- Vitamin World (8)
- Welcome Home (4)
- Wilson's Leather (1)
- Zales The Diamond Store (3)

EATS & TREATS

- Chateau Benoit (11)
- Snack City / Dreyer's (10)
- Sweeties (10)

3 PHOENIX

3A • Pacific Northwest Market Place & Outlet Mall

Address 205 Fern Valley Rd *Phone* 541-535-1194 *Hours* Mon-Sat 9:30-8, Sun 11-6 *Location* Between Medford and Ashland off I-5, exit 24.

STORES

- Bass (1)
- Corning Revere (4)
- Famous Footwear (1)
- Fieldcrest Cannon (4)
- Full Size Fashions (1)
- Glass And Art (5)
- Le Creuset (4)
- Leather Loft (2)
- Oregon's Best (9)
- Paper Factory (9)
- Phoenix Chamber Visitor Ctr (9)
- Publishers Warehouse (5)

- Van Heusen (1)
- Welcome Home (4)

EATS & TREATS

- Mello Coffee Shop (11)
- Michaels Courtyard Café (11)

4 SEASIDE

4A • Seaside Factory Outlet Center

www.seasidefactoryoutlet.com
Address 1111 N Roosevelt St *Phone* 503-717-1603 *Hours* Mon-Sat 10-8, Sun 10-7 *Location* Northwest corner of Oregon on the coast. The center is on US 101 at 12th Ave.

STORES

- Adidas (1)
- Big Dog Sportswear (1)
- Black & Decker (4)
- Book Warehouse (5)
- Christian Tree of Life Outlet (5)
- Coldwater Creek Outlet (1)
- Dress Barn (1)
- Dress Barn Woman (1)
- Factory Brand Shoes (1)
- GNC (8)
- Harry & David (5)
- Jones New York (1)
- Kitchen Collection (4)
- L'eggs Hanes Bali Playtex (1)
- Linen Barn (4)
- Liz Claiborne (1)
- Nike (1)
- Nine West (1)
- Oneida (4)
- OshKosh B'Gosh (1)
- Paper Factory (9)
- Perfect Look Outlet Salon (8)
- Samsonite (2)
- Totes Isotoner Sunglass World (3)
- Van Heusen (1)
- Wine Haus (9)

EATS & TREATS

- Dog Water Café (11)
- Rocky Mountain Chocolate (10)

5 TROUTDALE

5A • Columbia Gorge Premium Outlets

www.premiumoutlets.com
Address 450 NW 257th Way
Phone 503-669-8060 *Hours* Mon-Sat 10-8, Sun 10-6 *Location* Just east of Portland off I-84, exit 17.

STORES

- Adidas (1)
- Banister Shoes (1)
- Bass (1)
- Big Dog Sportswear (1)
- Book Warehouse (5)
- Brindar (1)
- Calvin Klein Jeanswear (1)
- Carter's Childrenswear (1)
- Dress Barn (1)
- Dress Barn Woman (1)
- Famous Brands Housewares (4)
- Famous Footwear (1)
- Florsheim (1)
- Fragrance Outlet (8)
- Gap Outlet (1)
- Geoffrey Beene (1)
- Great Outdoor Clothing (1)
- Harry & David (5)
- Hush Puppies & Family (1)
- Izod (1)
- Jockey (1)
- KB Toys (6)
- Kitchen Collection (4)
- Leather Loft (2)
- L'eggs Hanes Bali Playtex (1)
- Levi's Outlet by Most (1)
- London Fog (1)
- Maidenform (1)
- Mikasa (4)
- Music For A Song (5)
- Naturalizer (1)
- Norm Thompson (1)
- Olga Warner (1)
- Paper Factory (9)
- Samsonite (2)
- Totes / Sunglass World (3)
- Ultra Diamond Outlet (3)
- Van Heusen (1)
- Vans Shoes (1)
- Vitamin World (8)
- Wallet Works (2)
- Welcome Home (4)

EATS & TREATS

- Cascade Deli (11)
- Fuzziwig's Candy Factory (10)
- Rocky Mountain Chocolate (10)

6 WOODBURN

6A • Woodburn Company Stores

www.woodburncompanystores.com
Address 1001 Arney Rd *Phone* 503-981-1900 or 888-664-Shop *Hours* Mon-Sat 10-8, Sun 10-7 *Location* Thirty minutes south of Portland. Take I-5 south to exit 271, Woodburn/Hwy 214. Turn right at the first traffic light, then right on Arney Rd.

STORES

- Adidas (1)
- Banana Republic (1)
- Bass (1)
- Big Dogs (1)
- Black & Decker (4)
- Bose Factory Store (4)
- Brooks Brothers (1)
- Calvin Klein / Olga Warner's (1)
- Carter's Childrenswear (1)
- Claire's Accessories (3)
- Cole-Haan (1)
- Corning Revere (4)
- Cosmetics Company Store (8)
- Country Clutter (4)
- Dress Barn (1)
- Eddie Bauer (1)
- Factory Brand Shoes (1)
- Farberware (4)
- Gap Outlet (1)
- Great Outdoor Clothing (1)
- Harry & David (5)
- Hush Puppies & Family (1)
- Jockey (1)
- Joe Boxer (1)
- Jones New York (1)

- Jones New York Country (1)
- Kasper ASL (1)
- Kitchen Collection (4)
- Koret (1)
- Le Creuset (4)
- Leather Loft (2)
- L'eggs Hanes Bali Playtex (1)
- Lenox (4)
- Levi's / Dockers Outlet by Most (1)
- Lids (9)
- London Fog (1)
- Maidenform (1)
- Motherhood Maternity (1)
- Music For A Song (5)
- Naturalizer (1)
- Noritake (4)
- OshKosh B'Gosh (1)
- Pacific Sunwear (1)
- Piano Liquidators (5)
- Polo Ralph Lauren (1)
- Robert Scott & David Brooks (1)
- Rockport (1)
- Samsonite (2)
- Shutterbug (7)
- Stone Mountain (2)
- Sunglass Outlet (3)
- Timberland (1)
- Tommy Hilfiger (1)
- Totes / Sunglass World (3)
- Ultra Diamond Outlet (3)
- Vitamin World (8)
- Voice Stream Wireless (7)
- Watch Station (3)
- Waterford Wedgwood (4)
- WestPoint Stevens (4)
- Woodburn Book Outlet (5)

Eats & Treats

- Auntie Anne's Pretzals (10)
- Chalet Café (11)
- Coastal Creamery (10)
- Java Crew (10)
- New York Burrito (11)
- Rocky Mountain Chocolate (10)

Pennsylvania

1 • Gettysburg
2 • Grove City
3 • Hershey
4 • Lahaska
5 • Lancaster
6 • Morgantown
7 • Philadelphia
8 • Reading
9 • Somerset
10 • Tannersville

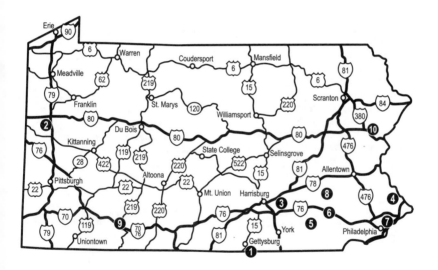

1 GETTYSBURG

1A • Gettysburg Village Factory Stores

www.gettysburgoutlets.com
Address 1863 Gettysburg Village Dr *Phone* 717-337-9705 *Hours* Jan-Mar: Mon-Thu 10-6, Fri-Sat 10-9, Sun 11-6. Apr-Dec: Mon-Sat 10-9, Sun 11-6 *Location* About 45 minutes southwest of Harrisburg. Center is located at the intersection of US 15 and Rt 97/Baltimore Pike.

STORES

- Adidas (1)
- Bass (1)
- Big & Tall Factory Store (1)
- Big Dog Sportswear (1)
- Bon Worth (1)
- Book Warehouse (5)
- Calvin Klein (1)
- Capacity (1)
- Casual Corner Annex (1)
- Casual Corner Annex Petite (1)
- Casual Corner Annex Woman (1)
- Chaps by Ralph Lauren (1)
- Christmas Tree Hill (9)
- Claire's Accessories (3)
- Corning Revere (4)
- Craftworks (4)
- Designer Deals (1)
- Dockers Outlet by Designs (1)
- Dress Barn (1)
- Dress Barn Misses (1)
- Dress Barn Woman (1)
- Eddie Bauer (1)
- Etienne Aigner (1)
- Factory Brand Shoes (1)
- Fossil (2)
- Gap Outlet (1)
- Haggar (1)
- Harry & David (5)
- Hollywood Hat & Boot (1)
- Jones New York (1)
- Jones New York Country (1)
- KB Toy Liquidators (6)
- Kitchen Collection (4)
- Kulpsville Antiques (4)
- L'eggs Hanes Bali Playtex (1)
- Levi's Outlet by Designs (1)
- Linen Barn (4)
- Music 4 Less (5)
- Naturalizer (1)
- Nautica (1)
- Nine West (1)
- Old Navy (1)
- OshKosh B'Gosh (1)
- Pacific Sunwear (1)
- Paper Factory (9)
- Pfaltzgraff (4)
- Reebok (1)
- Rue 21 (1)
- Samsonite (2)
- So Fun! Kids (1)
- Sunglass Outlet (3)
- Tools & More (9)
- Totes / Sunglass World (3)
- Van Heusen (1)
- Vitamin World (8)
- Wilson's Leather (1)
- Zales The Diamond Store (3)

EATS & TREATS

- Auntie Anne's Pretzals (10)
- Branding Iron BBQ (11)
- Corrado's Pizza (11)
- Fudgery (10)
- Fuzziwig's Candy Factory (10)
- Green Tea Chinese & Sushi Bar (11)
- Kilwin's Chocolates (10)
- Subway (11)
- TCBY & Café Cantina (11)

2 GROVE CITY

2A • Prime Outlets Grove City

www.primeoutlets.com
Address I-79 & Rt 208 *Phone* 888-545-7221 *Hours* Mon-Sat 10-9, Sun 11-6 *Location* Fifty miles north of Pittsburgh off I-79, exit 113.

STORES

- 220 Hickory by Blair (1)
- Adidas (1)
- American Outpost (1)

- Amish Oak & Country (4)
- Ann Taylor (1)
- Atlantic Luggage Co (2)
- Baby B'Gosh (1)
- Banister / Easy Spirit (1)
- Banister Shoes (1)
- Bass (1)
- Bath & Body Works (8)
- Bible Factory Outlet (5)
- Big & Tall Factory Store (1)
- Big Dogs (1)
- Black & Decker (4)
- Blowout Video (9)
- Bombay Outlet (4)
- Bon Worth (1)
- Bose Factory Store (4)
- Britches (1)
- Brooks Brothers (1)
- Calvin Klein (1)
- Carter's Childrenswear (1)
- Casual Corner (1)
- Casual Corner Woman (1)
- Chef's Outlet (4)
- Claire's Boutique (3)
- Coach (2)
- Corning Revere (4)
- Cosmetics Company Store (8)
- Country Clutter (4)
- Crabtree & Evelyn (5)
- Designer Fragrance/Cosmetics (8)
- Dress Barn/Dress Barn Woman (1)
- Eddie Bauer (1)
- Elisabeth (1)
- Esprit (1)
- Etienne Aigner (1)
- Factory Brand Shoes (1)
- Famous Brands Housewares (4)
- Farberware (4)
- Fenton Art Glass Outlet (4)
- Fossil (2)
- Gap Outlet (1)
- Geoffrey Beene (1)
- Gorant's Cards Plus (5)
- Guess? (1)
- Haggar (1)
- Harry & David (5)
- Hartstrings (1)
- Home Style (4)
- Homespun Country Store (9)
- Hometown Christmas Store (9)
- Hoover Outlet (4)
- House of Heinz (9)
- Hush Puppies & Family (1)

- Izod (1)
- J Crew (1)
- Jockey (1)
- Johnston & Murphy (1)
- Jones New York (1)
- Jos A Bank Clothiers (1)
- Journeys (1)
- Kasper ASL (1)
- KB Toys (6)
- King's Jewelry (3)
- Kitchen Collection (4)
- Koret (1)
- Leather Loft (2)
- L'eggs Hanes Bali Playtex (1)
- Levi's Outlet by Designs (1)
- Liz Claiborne (1)
- Liz Claiborne Shoes (1)
- London Fog (1)
- Maidenform (1)
- Mikasa (4)
- Motherhood Maternity (1)
- Music For A Song (5)
- Naturalizer (1)
- Nautica (1)
- Nautica Jeans (1)
- Nike (1)
- Nine West (1)
- Off 5th-Saks Fifth Avenue (1)
- Olga Warner (1)
- Oneida (4)
- OshKosh B'Gosh (1)
- PacSun (1)
- Paper Factory (9)
- Payless Shoe Source (1)
- Perfumania (8)
- Petite Sophisticate (1)
- Pfaltzgraff (4)
- Pittsburgh Steelers (1)
- Polo Jeans Co (1)
- Polo Ralph Lauren (1)
- Pro Image (1)
- Reebok (1)
- Rockport (1)
- Royal Doulton (4)
- Rue 21 (1)
- Rug Decor (4)
- S & K Menswear (1)
- Samsonite (2)
- SAS Factory Shoes (1)
- Shoebilee (1)
- Sony (4)
- Springmaid Wamsutta (4)
- Stone Mountain (2)

- Stride Rite Family Footwear (1)
- Sunglass Outlet (3)
- Timberland (1)
- Tommy Hilfiger (1)
- Totes Isotoner Sunglass World (3)
- Ultra Gold & Diamond (3)
- United Colors of Bennetton (1)
- US Post Office (9)
- Value Booksellers (5)
- Van Heusen (1)
- VF Factory Outlet (1)
- Vitamin World (8)
- Waterford Wedgwood (4)
- Welcome Home (4)
- Wendell August (9)
- Wilson's Leather (1)
- Woolrich (1)
- Zales The Diamond Store (3)

EATS & TREATS

- Arby's Roast Beef (11)
- Boardwalk Fries (11)
- Burger King (11)
- CinnaMonster (10)
- Fuzziwig's Candy Factory (10)
- Gloria Jean's Gourmet Coffee (10)
- Great Steak & Potato (11)
- Pretzel Time (10)
- Rocky Mountain Chocolate (10)
- Villa Pizza (11)
- Wok & Roll (11)

3 HERSHEY

3A • The Outlets at Hershey

www.theoutletsathershey.com

Address 46 Outlet Square *Phone* 717-520-1236 *Hours* Jan-Mar: Mon-Thu 9:30-6, Fri-Sat 9:30-9, Sun 11-5. Apr-Dec: Mon-Sat 9:30-9, Sun 11-5 *Location* From Harrisburg, follow US 322 east to State Hwy 39 (Hershey Park Dr). Follow Hershey Park Dr for 3 miles to outlet center.

STORES

- Bag & Baggage (2)
- Bass (1)
- Bella Luna (1)
- Better Deal Cellular (7)
- Big Dog Sportswear (1)
- Black & Decker (4)
- Bon Worth (1)
- Book Cellar (5)
- Bugle Boy (1)
- Capacity (1)
- Carter's Childrenswear (1)
- Casual Corner (1)
- Christmas Tree Hill (9)
- Claire's Accessories (3)
- Corning Revere (4)
- Craftworks (4)
- Dockers Outlet by Designs (1)
- Dress Barn (1)
- Easy Spirit (1)
- Factory Brand Shoes (1)
- Famous Brands Housewares (4)
- Farberware (4)
- Florsheim (1)
- Geoffrey Beene (1)
- Haggar (1)
- Hoover Outlet (4)
- Hush Puppies & Family (1)
- Izod (1)
- Jockey (1)
- Jones New York (1)
- Jones New York Country (1)
- Kasper ASL (1)
- Kitchen Collection (4)
- L'eggs Hanes Bali Playtex (1)
- Levi's Outlet by Designs (1)
- Mikasa (4)
- Music 4 Less (5)
- Naturalizer (1)
- Nautica (1)
- Nine West (1)
- Olga Warner (1)
- OshKosh B'Gosh (1)
- Paper Factory (9)
- Pfaltzgraff (4)
- Reebok (1)
- Rue 21 (1)
- Samsonite (2)
- Simpson World (9)
- So Fun! Kids (1)
- Springmaid Wamsutta (4)
- Stone Mountain (2)
- Times to Remember (9)
- Totes Isotoner Sunglass World (3)
- Toy Liquidators (6)

- Van Heusen (1)
- Vitamin World (8)
- Welcome Home (4)
- Zales The Diamond Store (3)

4 LAHASKA

4A • Penn's Purchase Factory Outlet Stores

www.pennspurchase.com
Address 5861 York Rd *Phone* 215-794-0300 *Hours* Mon-Fri 10-8, Sat 9-8, Sun 9-6 *Location* North of Philadelphia near the state line. From I-95 north take the Newtown exit. Go west on Rt 322 to Rt 413 north, follow to Buckingham. In Buckingham turn right onto Rt 263 north which merges with Rt 202 north, follow to center.

STORES

- Adidas (1)
- Bass (1)
- Bose Factory Store (4)
- Brass and Oak Gallery (4)
- Casual Corner (1)
- Coach (2)
- Craftworks (4)
- Designer Fragrance/Cosmetics (8)
- Easy Spirit (1)
- Enzo's Fine Jewelry (3)
- Etienne Aigner (1)
- Famous Footwear (1)
- Geoffrey Beene (1)
- Harry's Gifts & Collectibles (5)
- Harvey Gallery (4)
- Izod (1)
- Jones New York (1)
- Jones New York Country (1)
- Jones New York Sport (1)
- Kitchen Collection (4)
- Koret (1)
- L'eggs Hanes Bali Playtex (1)
- Linen Barn (4)
- Luggage Company (2)
- Maidenform (1)

- Nautica (1)
- Nine West (1)
- Orvis Factory Store (1)
- OshKosh B'Gosh (1)
- Petite Sophisticate (1)
- Rena Rowan (1)
- Samsonite (2)
- So Fun! Kids (1)
- Van Heusen (1)
- Vitamin World (8)
- Yeagles Collectibles (5)

EATS & TREATS

- Caffe Galleria II (11)
- Dairy Queen (11)
- La Cena Restaurant & Pizzeria (11)

5 LANCASTER

5A • Rockvale Square Outlets

www.rockvalesquareoutlets.com
Address 35 S Willowdale Dr *Phone* 717-293-9595 *Hours* Mon-Sat 9:30-9, Sun 12-6 *Location* Five miles east of Lancaster via US 30. Center is near the intersection of US 30 and Hwy 898.

STORES

- Barbizon Lingerie (1)
- Bass (1)
- Beauty Bargains (8)
- Bible Factory Outlet (5)
- Big Dog Sportswear (1)
- Black & Decker (4)
- Bon Worth (1)
- Book Warehouse (5)
- Bose Factory Store (4)
- Bruce Alan Bags (2)
- Burlington Brands (1)
- Camp Coleman (6)
- Capacity (1)
- Cape Cod Crafters (4)
- Carter's Childrenswear (1)
- Casual Corner (1)
- Casual Male Big & Tall (1)
- Catherine's (1)
- Champion Activewear / Coach (1)
- Christmas Tree Hill (9)

- Corning Revere (4)
- Craftworks (4)
- Danskin (1)
- Dress Barn (1)
- Dress Barn Woman (1)
- Easy Spirit (1)
- Enzo Angiolini (1)
- Factory Brand Shoes (1)
- Factory Linens (4)
- Farberware (4)
- Farmer's First Bank (9)
- Footfactory (1)
- Gap Clearance Store (1)
- Geoffrey Beene (1)
- Gold Toe (1)
- Haband (1)
- Haggar (1)
- Hartstrings (1)
- Izod (1)
- Jockey (1)
- Jones New York (1)
- Jones New York Sport (1)
- Kasper ASL (1)
- KB Toys (6)
- Kids Gear (1)
- Kitchen Collection (4)
- Koret (1)
- Leather Loft (2)
- Leather Outlet (2)
- L'eggs Hanes Bali Playtex (1)
- Lenox (4)
- Levi's Outlet by Designs (1)
- Liz Claiborne Shoes (1)
- London Fog (1)
- Maidenform (1)
- Music Den (5)
- Naturalizer (1)
- Nautica (1)
- Nike (1)
- Nissley Wine Shop (9)
- Noah's Landing (5)
- Oneida (4)
- Paper Factory (9)
- Payless Shoe Source (1)
- Perfumania (8)
- Perry Ellis (1)
- Pfaltzgraff (4)
- QVC Outlet (4)
- Rack Room Shoes (1)
- Reading China & Glass (4)
- Reed & Barton (4)
- Remington (4)
- Robert Scott & David Brooks (1)

- Roommakers (4)
- S & K Menswear (1)
- Samsonite (2)
- Shady Lamp Shop (4)
- Socks Galore (1)
- Sony (4)
- Spiegel Outlet (1)
- Springmaid Wamsutta (4)
- Stockroom (1)
- Stride Rite Keds Sperry (1)
- Sunglass Outlet (3)
- Tommy Hilfiger (1)
- Totes / Sunglass World (3)
- Toys & More (6)
- Van Heusen (1)
- Vitamin World (8)
- Waterford Wedgwood (4)
- Welcome Home (4)
- WestPoint Stevens (4)
- Wholesale Rug Outlet (4)
- Wicker Unlimited (4)
- Woolrich (1)
- www.Footgear (1)

EATS & TREATS

- Bob Evans (11)
- Burger King (11)
- Campbell's Soup (11)
- Country Bake Shoppe (11)
- Cracker Barrel (11)
- Food Court (11)
- Healthy Choice Deli (11)
- Herbie's Hamburgers Shakes (11)
- Jennifer's Café (11)
- Kentucky Fried Chicken (11)
- Kunzler Hot Sandwiches (11)
- Pepperidge Farm (10)
- Pizza Hut Express (11)
- TCBY (10)

5B • Tanger Outlet Center

www.tangeroutlets.com

Address 311 Stanley K Tanger Blvd *Phone* 800-408-3477 or 717-392-7260 *Hours* Jan-Feb: Mon-Thu 9-7, Fri-Sat 9-9, Sun 11-6. Mar-Dec: Mon-Sat 9-9, Sun 10-6 *Location* Northern Lancaster about 7 miles east of the junctions of US 30 and

Rt 283. Center is on the south side of US 30.

STORES

- Aerosoles (1)
- Banana Republic (1)
- Bath & Body Works (8)
- Big Dog Sportswear (1)
- Bostonian Clarks (1)
- Britches (1)
- Brooks Brothers (1)
- Calendar Club (5)
- Calvin Klein (1)
- Claire's Accessories (3)
- Coach (2)
- Columbia Sportswear (1)
- Corning Revere (4)
- Cosmetics Company Store (8)
- Country Clutter (4)
- DKNY Jeans (1)
- Donna Karan (1)
- Dress Barn (1)
- Easy Spirit (1)
- Eddie Bauer (1)
- Etienne Aigner (1)
- Florsheim (1)
- Fossil (2)
- Gap Outlet (1)
- Guess? (1)
- Harry & David (5)
- Hugo Boss (1)
- Izod (1)
- J Crew (1)
- Johnston & Murphy (1)
- KB Toys (6)
- Kenneth Cole (1)
- Le Gourmet Chef (4)
- L'eggs Hanes Bali Playtex (1)
- Liz Claiborne (1)
- Mikasa (4)
- Motherhood Maternity (1)
- Movado (2)
- Music 4 Less (5)
- Nine West (1)
- Noritake (4)
- North Face (1)
- OshKosh B'Gosh (1)
- Pacific Sunwear (1)
- Polo Jeans Co (1)
- Polo Ralph Lauren (1)
- Publishers Warehouse (5)
- Reebok (1)
- Rockport (1)
- Royal Doulton (4)
- Samsonite (2)
- SAS Factory Shoes (1)
- Skechers (1)
- So Fun! Kids (1)
- Stone Mountain (2)
- Timberland (1)
- Top of the Line Fragrances & Cosmetics (8)
- Totes / Sunglass World (3)
- Ultra Diamond Outlet (3)
- Wilson's Leather (1)
- Wilton Armetale (4)
- Zales The Diamond Store (3)

EATS & TREATS

- Rocky Mountain Chocolate (10)
- Subway (11)

6 MORGANTOWN

6A • Home Furnishings Outlet Mall

www.herby.com/home/outlets.html
Phone 800-226-8011 *Hours* Mon-Thu 10-6, Fri-Sat 10-9, Sun 12-5 *Location* South of Reading just off I-76 at exit 22 on State Hwy 10.

STORES

- Artisan's Alley (4)
- Basset For Less (4)
- Capacity (1)
- Couristan Rug (4)
- Crawford Solid Wood Furniture (4)
- Dalo Furniture (4)
- Designer Furniture (4)
- Dinette & Chair Express (4)
- Drexel Heritage (4)
- F & H Jewelry (3)
- Flexsteel Gallery (4)
- Henredon Factory Outlet (4)
- Interior Alternative (4)
- Keyboard Piano (5)
- Leather Tradition (4)
- L'eggs Hanes Bali Playtex (1)
- Natuzzi Italian Leather (4)
- Oak Gallery (4)
- Pine Gallery (4)
- Recliner Outlet (4)

- Sleeper Company (4)
- Sofamerica (4)
- Tropicraft (4)
- Tropicraft Seasons (4)
- World of Sleep Mattress (4)

7 PHILADELPHIA

7A • Franklin Mills

www.millscorp.com

Address 1455 Franklin Mills Cir *Phone* 800-336-Mall or 215-632-1500 *Hours* Mon-Fri 10-9:30, Sat 9:30-9:30, Sun 11-7 *Location* Just off I-95 and Woodhaven Road, 15 minutes north of Philadelphia city center.

STORES

- A Dollar Store (9)
- Accent On Animals (5)
- Aeropostale (1)
- Aerosoles (1)
- After Houres by Small's (1)
- Aldo Shoes (1)
- Ann Taylor (1)
- Archie Jacobson (1)
- Art Gallery Outlet (4)
- Athlete's Foot (1)
- Bally Outlet (1)
- Banana Republic (1)
- Banister Shoes (1)
- Bass (1)
- Bath & Body Works (8)
- BCBG Max Azria (1)
- Beauty Express (8)
- Bebe Outlet (1)
- Benetton (1)
- Big & Tall Factory Store (1)
- Blockbuster Video (9)
- Bombay Outlet (4)
- Boscov's (1)
- Bostonian Shoes (1)
- Briefcase Unlimited (2)
- Britches (1)
- Brooks Brothers (1)
- Burlington Coat Factory (1)
- Camera Shop (7)

- Candleman Outlet (5)
- Carter's For Kids (1)
- Charlotte Russe (1)
- Children's Place Outlet (1)
- Cingular Wireless (7)
- Claire's Accessories (3)
- Claire's Boutique (3)
- Cosmetics Company Store (8)
- CR Jewelers Outlet (3)
- Date Place Calendar (5)
- De' Village (1)
- Donna Karan (1)
- Dress Barn (1)
- Earrings World (3)
- Eddie Bauer (1)
- Electronics Boutique (4)
- Elegance (3)
- Escada Company Store (1)
- Eye Candy (1)
- Factory Brand Shoes (1)
- Flag Shop (9)
- Foot Locker (1)
- FYE - For Your Entertainment (4)
- Games & Gadgets (9)
- Games Workshop (9)
- Gap Outlet (1)
- General Cinema (9)
- Gift Gallery (5)
- Giorgio Brutini (1)
- GNC (8)
- Greg Norman (1)
- Group USA (1)
- Guess? (1)
- Hollywood Eyes (3)
- Hollywood Hat & Boot (1)
- House of Perfumes (8)
- Imposters (3)
- InJeanius (1)
- Italian Shoe Warehouse (1)
- J M Fallas (1)
- J5 Sportswear (1)
- JCPenney Outlet (1)
- Jean Outlet (1)
- Jewelry Castle (3)
- Just $1 Outlet (9)
- Kasper ASL (1)
- KB Toy Express (6)
- KB Toyworks (6)
- Kenneth Cole (1)
- Kid City (1)
- Last Call Neiman Marcus (1)
- Le Nails Boutique (8)
- Leather Limited (2)

- L'eggs Hanes Bali Playtex (1)
- LensCrafters (3)
- Levi's / Dockers (1)
- Lids (9)
- Liz Claiborne (1)
- Lollipop Boutique (1)
- Maidenform (1)
- Marshalls Megastore (1)
- MasterCuts (8)
- Maternity Works (1)
- Modell's Sporting Goods (6)
- Modern Expressions Furniture (4)
- Nailery (8)
- Nautica (1)
- News Stand of Franklin Mills (5)
- Nine West (1)
- NoName Outlet (1)
- Nordstrom Rack (1)
- Off 5th-Saks Fifth Avenue (1)
- Off Broadway Shoes (1)
- Old Navy (1)
- OshKosh B'Gosh (1)
- Pacific Sunwear (1)
- Payless Shoe Source (1)
- Perfumania (8)
- Perfume Romance (8)
- Perry Ellis (1)
- Phar-Mor (8)
- Philly Leather Outlet (1)
- Picture People (9)
- Polo Jeans Co (1)
- Polo Ralph Lauren (1)
- Publishers Outlet (5)
- Quail's Outlet Store (1)
- Radio Shack (7)
- Reebok (1)
- Remington (4)
- Ritz Camera 1 Hour Photo (7)
- Rockport (1)
- Royal Jewelers (3)
- Rue 21 (1)
- Samsonite (2)
- Sandollar Shop (5)
- Sentimental Jewelry (3)
- Skechers (1)
- Spain's Cards & Gifts (5)
- Spencer Gifts (5)
- Spirit Halloween Store (9)
- Sprint PCS Center (7)
- St John Knits (1)
- Suncoast Motion Picture Co (9)
- Sunglass Hut (3)
- SYMS (1)

- Talbots (1)
- Timeout (9)
- Tommy Hilfiger (1)
- Trade Secret Beauty Salon (8)
- Ultra Gold & Diamond (3)
- Underground Station (1)
- Urban Planet (1)
- US Post Office (9)
- Vacation Showplace (9)
- Van Heusen (1)
- Vitamin World (8)
- Watches Galore (3)
- Wilson's Leather (1)
- XOXO (1)
- Zales The Diamond Store (3)

EATS & TREATS

- Arthur Treacher's Fish & Chips (11)
- Auntie Anne's Pretzals (10)
- Bavarian Soft Pretzels (10)
- Burger King (11)
- Cajun Gourmet (11)
- China Buddha Express (11)
- China Buddha Inn (11)
- Cold Stone Creamery (10)
- Dairy Queen / Orange Julius (11)
- Deli Delicious (11)
- Espresso Station (10)
- Gloria Jean's Gourmet Coffee (10)
- Hickory Farms (10)
- Jillian's (11)
- Johnny Rockets (11)
- Keily's Cajun Grill (11)
- Lindt Chocolate (10)
- Lotus Express (11)
- McDonald's (11)
- Popeye's (11)
- Ruby Tuesday (11)
- Sbarro Italian Eatery (11)
- Subway (11)
- TJ Cinnamon's (10)
- Tropik Sun Fruit & Nut (10)

8   READING

8A • Reading Outlet Center
Address 801 N 9th St *Phone* 610-373-5495 *Hours* Jan-Mar: Mon-Fri 9:30-6, Sat 9:30-8, Sun 11-5. Apr-Dec: Mon-Wed 9:30-6, Thu-

Sat 9:30-8, Sun 11-5 *Location* Northeast of downtown Reading at the intersection of Douglas and North 9th Streets.

Stores

- $3 Store (1)
- Argentina Delights (9)
- Bass (1)
- Big & Tall Factory Store (1)
- Calvin Klein (1)
- Candie's (1)
- Carter's Childrenswear (1)
- Casual Corner (1)
- Casual Woman (1)
- Claire's Accessories (3)
- Coach (2)
- Corning Revere (4)
- Delia's (1)
- Designer Bag (2)
- Dooney & Bourke (2)
- Fila (1)
- Foot Locker (1)
- Guess? (1)
- Hartstrings (1)
- Heritage Wine (9)
- L'eggs Hanes Bali Playtex (1)
- Life Of Happiness (5)
- Maternity Works (1)
- Nautica (1)
- Nine West (1)
- Old Navy (1)
- Orvis Factory Store (1)
- Perfume Place (8)
- Petite Sophisticate (1)
- Polo Ralph Lauren (1)
- Quality Discount Apparel (1)
- Tommy Hilfiger (1)
- Van Heusen (1)
- Wilson's Leather (1)
- Yoshi Variety (1)
- Zales The Diamond Store (3)

8B • VF Outlet Village

www.vffo.com

Address 801 Hill Ave *Phone* 800-772-8336 *Hours* Mon-Thu 9-9 (Dec 25-Mar 4: 9-7), Fri 9-9, Sat 9-7 Dec 25-Jul, 9-9 Aug-Sep, 8-9

Oct-Dec 24, Sun 10-5 (Sep 24-Dec 24 10-6) *Location* West of downtown Reading and north of US 422 at 8th Ave and Hill Ave.

Stores

- Animation Gift Station (5)
- Bass (1)
- Beauty Bargains (8)
- Big Dogs (1)
- Black & Decker (4)
- Bon Worth (1)
- Book Warehouse (5)
- Bostonian Shoes (1)
- Coach (2)
- Cosmetics Company Store (8)
- Croscill (4)
- Designer Brands Accessories (2)
- Designer Fragrance/Cosmetics (8)
- Donna Karan (1)
- Dress Barn (1)
- Dress Barn Woman (1)
- Easy Spirit (1)
- Elisabeth (1)
- Etienne Aigner (1)
- Famous Brands Housewares (4)
- Fieldcrest Cannon (4)
- Geoffrey Beene (1)
- GNC (8)
- Gold Toe (1)
- Handmade Quilts (4)
- Instant Decor (4)
- Izod (1)
- Jewelry Basics (3)
- Jones New York (1)
- Kasper ASL (1)
- KB Toys (6)
- Leather Outlet (2)
- Liz Claiborne (1)
- London Fog (1)
- Mikasa (4)
- Nanny's Shoppe (9)
- New York Jewelry (3)
- Oneida (4)
- OshKosh B'Gosh (1)
- PA Lightworks (4)
- Pandora Fashion (1)
- Paper Factory (9)
- Perry Ellis (1)
- Rawlings Sporting Goods (6)
- Reading Bag & Baggage (2)
- Reading China & Glass (4)

- Reebok (1)
- Remington (4)
- Rue 21 (1)
- S & K Menswear (1)
- Samsonite (2)
- Stone Mountain (2)
- Stride Rite Keds Sperry (1)
- Sunglass World (3)
- Swank (2)
- Tommy Hilfiger (1)
- Tools & More (9)
- Totes (3)
- Van Heusen (1)
- VF Factory Outlet (1)
- Virginia Metal Crafters (4)
- Vitamin World (8)
- Woolrich (1)

EATS & TREATS
- Cappuccino Café (10)
- Food Court (11)
- Godiva Chocolatier (10)
- McDonald's (11)
- Pepperidge Farm (10)
- Pretzel Store (10)
- Rocky Mountain Chocolate (10)
- Subway (11)
- Sweet Street Desserts (10)

9 SOMERSET

9A • Factory Shops at Georgian Place
www.horizongroup.com
Address 317 Georgian Pl *Phone* 814-443-3818 *Hours* Mon-Sat 10-8, Sun 11-5 *Location* 45 minutes southeast of Pittsburgh off I-70/76, exit 10 (Rt 601 north).

STORES
- Backwoods Country Store (9)
- Banister Shoes (1)
- Bass (1)
- Bon Worth (1)
- Book Warehouse (5)
- Colonial Outdoors (9)
- Dress Barn Clearance (1)

- Dress Barn/Dress Barn Woman (1)
- Famous Footwear (1)
- Gap Clearance Store (1)
- Just for Kids (1)
- Kitchen Collection (4)
- KPD Gear (1)
- L'eggs Hanes Bali Playtex (1)
- Levi's / Dockers (1)
- Paper Factory (9)
- Somerset Dance Company (9)
- Somerset Dancewear Shop (9)
- Somerset Trust (9)
- Stone Mountain (2)
- Sweet Dreams and More (9)
- Van Heusen (1)
- Vitamin World (8)

10 TANNERSVILLE

10A • The Crossings
www.thecrossings.com
Address 285 Crossings Outlet Sq *Phone* 570-629-4650 *Hours* Mon-Sat 10-9, Sun 10-6. Winter: Sun-Wed 10-6, Thu-Sat 10-9 *Location* Between Scranton and Allentown just off I-80, exit 299.

STORES
- American Outpost (1)
- Ann Taylor (1)
- Bagmakers (2)
- Bass (1)
- Big & Tall Factory Store (1)
- Big Dog Sportswear (1)
- Bombay Outlet (4)
- Book Cellar (5)
- Bose Factory Store (4)
- Bostonian Clarks (1)
- Brooks Brothers (1)
- Burlington Brands (1)
- Camp Coleman (6)
- Candle Shoppe (5)
- Carter's Childrenswear (1)
- Casual Corner (1)
- Casual Corner Woman (1)
- Champion (1)
- Claire's Accessories (3)
- Coach (2)

- Corning Revere (4)
- Cosmetics Company Store (8)
- Craftworks (4)
- Dana Buchman (1)
- Dansk (4)
- Danskin (1)
- Designer Fragrance/Cosmetics (8)
- DKNY Jeans (1)
- Donna Karan (1)
- Easy Spirit (1)
- Enzo Angiolini (1)
- Etienne Aigner (1)
- Famous Brands Housewares (4)
- Fila (1)
- Gap Outlet (1)
- Geoffrey Beene (1)
- Greg Norman (1)
- Guess? (1)
- Harry & David (5)
- Hartstrings (1)
- Harve Benard (1)
- Home Again (4)
- Izod (1)
- J Crew (1)
- Jockey (1)
- Johnston & Murphy (1)
- Jones New York (1)
- Jones New York Country (1)
- Jones New York Sport (1)
- Jones NY Executive Suite (1)
- Kasper ASL (1)
- Kitchen Collection (4)
- Le Gourmet Chef (4)
- Leather Loft (2)
- L'eggs Hanes Bali Playtex (1)
- Levi's Outlet by Designs (1)
- Little Me (1)
- Liz Claiborne (1)
- London Fog (1)
- Maidenform (1)
- Mikasa (4)
- Movado (2)
- Music 4 Less (5)
- Nautica (1)
- Nautica Jeans (1)
- Nine West (1)
- Oneida (4)
- OshKosh B'Gosh (1)
- Perfumania (8)
- Perry Ellis (1)
- Petite Sophisticate (1)
- Pfaltzgraff (4)
- Polo Footwear (1)

- Polo Ralph Lauren (1)
- Reebok (1)
- Robert Scott & David Brooks (1)
- Rockport (1)
- Royal Doulton (4)
- Rue 21 (1)
- Samsonite (2)
- So Fun! Kids (1)
- Socks Galore (1)
- Springmaid Wamsutta (4)
- Stone Mountain (2)
- Stride Rite Keds Sperry (1)
- Sunglass Outlet (3)
- Timberland (1)
- Time Factory Watch (3)
- Tommy Hilfiger (1)
- Totes / Sunglass World (3)
- Toy Liquidators (6)
- Ultra Diamond Outlet (3)
- Van Heusen (1)
- Vans Shoes (1)
- Vitamin World (8)
- Wallet Works (2)
- Waterford Wedgwood (4)
- Westport Limited (1)
- Westport Woman (1)
- Woolrich (1)

EATS & TREATS

- American Eatery (11)
- Au Bon Pan Bakery Café (11)
- Magic Wok (11)
- Mr Deli & Just Deserts (11)
- Rocky Mountain Chocolate (10)
- Romano's Pizza (11)
- Scoops Ice Cream (10)
- Sugar Mountain Candy (10)

South Carolina

1 • Bluffton
2 • Fort Mill
3 • Gaffney
4 • Hilton Head
5 • Myrtle Beach
6 • North Myrtle Beach
7 • Santee

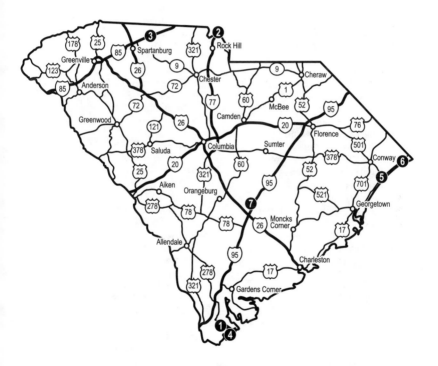

1   BLUFFTON

1A • Hilton Head Factory Stores 1 & 2

www.shophiltonhead.com

Address 1414 Fording Island Rd *Phone* 843-837-4339 or 888-Shop333 *Hours* Mon-Sat 10-9 (Jan-Feb 10-7), Sun 11-6 *Location* About 15 miles northwest of Hilton Head Island. From I-95 take exit 8 onto Hwy 278 east, follow for 13 miles. The center is about 2 miles east of the Hwy 46 and Hwy 278 junction.

STORES

- Banana Republic (1)
- Banister Shoes (1)
- Bass (1)
- Big & Tall Factory Store (1)
- Big Dog Sportswear (1)
- Book Warehouse (5)
- Brooks Brothers (1)
- Carter's Childrenswear (1)
- Casual Corner Annex (1)
- Casual Corner Annex Petite (1)
- Casual Corner Annex Woman (1)
- Claire's Accessories (3)
- Coach (2)
- Cosmetics Company Store (8)
- Cost Cutters Salon (8)
- Craftworks (4)
- Dan River (4)
- Dana Buchman (1)
- Dansk (4)
- Danskin (1)
- Dexter Shoe (1)
- Disney Catalog Outlet (5)
- Dress Barn/Dress Barn Woman (1)
- Easy Spirit (1)
- Eddie Bauer (1)
- Ellen Tracy (1)
- Enro / Damon (1)
- Escada Company Store (1)
- Etienne Aigner (1)
- Factory Brand Shoes (1)
- Gap Outlet (1)
- Geoffrey Beene Men's & Women's (1)
- Haggar (1)
- Harry & David (5)
- Hilton Head Shirt Co (1)
- J Crew (1)
- Joan Vass USA (1)
- Jockey (1)
- Johnston & Murphy (1)
- Jones New York Country (1)
- Kasper ASL (1)
- KB Toy Liquidators (6)
- Kitchen Collection (4)
- Koret (1)
- Leather Loft (2)
- L'eggs Hanes Bali Playtex (1)
- Lenox (4)
- Levi's Outlet by Designs (1)
- Lillian Vernon (9)
- Maidenform (1)
- Mikasa (4)
- Movado (2)
- Music 4 Less (5)
- Naturalizer (1)
- Nautica (1)
- Nike (1)
- Nine West (1)
- Oneida (4)
- OshKosh B'Gosh (1)
- Pacific Sunwear (1)
- Perfumania (8)
- Polo Jeans Co (1)
- Pro Golf (6)
- Rack Room Shoes (1)
- Remington (4)
- Rockport (1)
- Royal Doulton (4)
- Rue 21 (1)
- S & K Menswear (1)
- Samsonite (1)
- SAS Factory Shoes (1)
- Seiko (3)
- Strasburg Children (1)
- Stride Rite (1)
- Sunglass Hut (3)
- Sunglass World (3)
- Timberland (1)
- Tommy Hilfiger (1)
- Ultra Diamond & Gold (3)
- Van Heusen (1)
- VF Factory Outlet (1)
- Villeroy & Boch (4)
- Vitamin World (8)
- Waterford Wedgwood (4)
- Wilson's Leather (1)
- Zales The Diamond Store (3)

EATS & TREATS

- Cornerstone Grill (11)

- Good Sport Food Court (11)
- Kilwins Chocolate & Ice Cream (10)

2 FORT MILL

2A • Crossroads Mall
Address Carowinds Blvd *Phone* 803-548-5888 *Hours* Mon-Sat 10-9, Sun 1:30-6 *Location* About 10 minutes north of Rock Hill. Take I-77 to Carowinds Blvd, exit 90. Center is next to the Carowinds Amusement Park.

STORES
- Adidas (1)
- Bass (1)
- Burke's Outlet (1)
- Burlington Shoes (1)
- Capacity (1)
- Carolina Pottery (4)
- Dress Barn (1)
- Hamrick's (1)
- Lingerie Factory (1)
- Paper Factory (9)
- Sam's Factory Outlet (1)
- Sunglass Hut (3)
- Swank (2)
- Van Heusen (1)

3 GAFFNEY

3A • Prime Outlets Gaffney
www.primeoutlets.com
Address 1 Factory Shops Blvd *Phone* 864-902-9900 or 888-545-7194 *Hours* Mon-Sat 10-9, Sun 1:30-6 *Location* Twenty minutes northeast of Spartanburg off I-85, exit 90.

STORES
- Bass (1)
- Bath & Body Works (8)
- Bible Factory Outlet (5)
- Big Dogs (1)
- Blue Ridge Mountain Leather (1)
- Bombay Outlet (4)
- Book Warehouse (5)
- Bose Factory Store (4)
- Britches (1)
- Brooks Brothers (1)
- Carolina Hobbies (6)
- Carter's For Kids (1)
- Casual Corner (1)
- Casual Corner Woman (1)
- Casual Male Big & Tall (1)
- Claire's Accessories (3)
- Coach (2)
- Cost Cutters Salon (8)
- Dockers Outlet by Designs (1)
- Dress Barn/Dress Barn Woman (1)
- Etienne Aigner (1)
- Factory Brand Shoes (1)
- Famous Brands Housewares (4)
- Farberware (4)
- Fashion Outlet (1)
- Fila (1)
- Gap Outlet (1)
- Golf Manufacturer's Outlet (6)
- Haggar (1)
- Hamilton Luggage (2)
- Jockey (1)
- Jones New York (1)
- Kasper ASL (1)
- KB Toys (6)
- Kitchen Collection (4)
- L'eggs Hanes Bali Playtex (1)
- Levi's Outlet by Designs (1)
- Magic Nails (8)
- Mikasa (4)
- Music For A Song (5)
- Nautica (1)
- Nike (1)
- Nine West (1)
- OshKosh B'Gosh (1)
- Paper Factory (9)
- Perfumania (8)
- Petite Sophisticate (1)
- Pfaltzgraff (4)
- Polo Ralph Lauren (1)
- Pottery Barn Furniture (4)
- Rack Room Shoes (1)
- Rockport (1)
- Rue 21 (1)
- S & K Menswear (1)
- Sam's Factory Outlet (1)
- Samsonite/American Tourister (2)
- SAS Factory Shoes (1)
- Simply Country (9)
- Sony (4)
- Southtel Wireless (7)
- Speedway Sports (6)
- Springmaid Wamsutta (4)
- St Nick's (9)

- Strasburg Children (1)
- Stride Rite Family Footwear (1)
- Summit Jewelers (3)
- Sunglass Hut / Watch Station (3)
- Tommy Hilfiger (1)
- Totes Isotoner Sunglass World (3)
- Ultra Jewelers (3)
- Van Heusen (1)
- Vitamin World (8)
- Welcome Home (4)
- Woolrich (1)
- Zales The Diamond Store (3)

Eats & Treats

- Blimpie Subs & Salads (11)
- Cinnabon (10)
- Frank & Stein Dogs & Drafts (11)
- Great Steak & Potato (11)
- Lee's Ice Cream (10)
- Rocky Mountain Chocolate (10)
- Villa Pizza (11)
- Wok & Roll (11)

4   HILTON HEAD

4A • Shoppes on the Parkway
www.lowcountryguide.com
Address 890 William Hilton Pkwy
Phone 843-686-6233 *Hours* Mon-Sat 10-9 (Jan-Mar 15: 10-6), Sun 1-6 *Location* From I-95 exit 8 follow US 278 to Hilton Head Island. Center is near the intersection of US 278 and Queens Folley Rd.

Stores

- Anne Klein (1)
- Bogner America (1)
- Carole Little (1)
- Dansk (4)
- Designer Fragrance/Cosmetics (8)
- Dress Barn (1)
- Factory Brand Shoes (1)
- Gourmet Alligator (9)
- Harve Benard (1)
- Hilton Head Shirt Co (1)
- Islandwear (1)
- Jones New York Sport (1)
- L'eggs Hanes Bali Playtex (1)
- Lenox (4)
- Players World of Golf (6)

- Rack Room Shoes (1)
- Royal Robbins (1)
- Rue 21 (1)
- Sunglass World (3)
- Totes (3)
- Van Heusen (1)
- Vitamin World (8)

Eats & Treats

- Del Vecchio's (11)
- New York Deli (11)

5   MYRTLE BEACH

5A • Myrtle Beach Factory Stores
www.shopmyrtlebeach.com
Address 4635 Factory Stores Blvd
Phone 843-903-1614 or 888-Shop333 *Hours* Mon-Sat 9-9 (Jan-Feb 9-7), Sun 11-6 *Location* From I-95 south take exit 181 onto Hwy 38 south for 6 miles to Hwy 501 east. Follow Hwy 501 65 miles, the center will be on your left.

Stores

- Athlete's Foot (1)
- Banana Republic (1)
- Bass (1)
- Ben Silver (1)
- Big Dog Sportswear (1)
- Bose Factory Store (4)
- Britches (1)
- Brooks Brothers (1)
- Buster Brown (1)
- Camp Coleman (6)
- Carter's Childrenswear (1)
- Casual Corner Annex (1)
- Casual Corner Annex Petite (1)
- Casual Corner Annex Woman (1)
- Children's Place Outlet (1)
- Claire's Accessories (3)
- Coach (2)
- Coastal Cotton (1)
- Cole-Haan (1)
- Corning Revere (4)
- Cosmetics Company Store (8)
- Cost Cutters Salon (8)
- Crabtree & Evelyn (5)
- Craftworks (4)
- Croscill (4)
- Dalton Rug (4)

- Dansk (4)
- Danskin (1)
- Dexter Shoe (1)
- Disney Catalog Outlet (5)
- Dockers Outlet by Designs (1)
- Dress Barn (1)
- Duck Head (1)
- Easy Spirit (1)
- Eddie Bauer (1)
- Etienne Aigner (1)
- Factory Brand Shoes (1)
- Famous Brands Housewares (4)
- Fragrance Outlet (8)
- Gap Outlet (1)
- Guess? (1)
- Haggar (1)
- Harry & David (5)
- Hartstrings (1)
- Home Again (4)
- Hush Puppies & Family (1)
- Izod (1)
- J Crew (1)
- Jockey (1)
- Johnston & Murphy (1)
- Jones New York (1)
- Jones New York Country (1)
- Jones New York Sport (1)
- KB Toys (6)
- Kitchen Collection (4)
- Leather Loft (2)
- L'eggs Hanes Bali Playtex (1)
- Lenox (4)
- Levi's Outlet by Designs (1)
- Lids (9)
- Lillian Vernon (9)
- Maidenform (1)
- Movado (2)
- Music For A Song (5)
- Nautica (1)
- Nautica Jeans (1)
- New York Jewelry (3)
- Nike (1)
- Nine West (1)
- Off 5th-Saks Fifth Avenue (1)
- Olga / Warner / Calvin Klein (1)
- OshKosh B'Gosh (1)
- Pacific Sunwear (1)
- Perry Ellis (1)
- Pfaltzgraff (4)
- Polo Ralph Lauren (1)
- Rack Room Shoes (1)
- Reebok (1)
- Rockport (1)
- Royal Doulton (4)
- S & K Menswear (1)

- Samsonite (2)
- SAS Factory Shoes (1)
- Shadowline (1)
- So Fun! Kids (1)
- Stride Rite Keds Sperry (1)
- Sunglass Hut (3)
- Sunglass Outlet (3)
- T-Shirts Plus (1)
- Timberland (1)
- Tommy Hilfiger (1)
- Value Booksellers (5)
- Van Heusen (1)
- Vans Shoes (1)
- Vitamin World (8)
- Waterford Wedgwood (4)
- WestPoint Stevens (4)
- Wilson's Leather (1)

EATS & TREATS

- A & W Restaurant (11)
- American Food Court (11)
- Manchu Wok (11)
- Mrs Fields Cookies (10)
- Rocky Mountain Chocolate (10)
- Sara Lee Sandwich Shoppe (11)
- Sbarro Italian Eatery (11)
- TCBY (10)

5B • Waccamaw Factory Shoppes

www.waccamafactoryshoppes.com
Address 3200 Pottery Dr *Phone* 843-236-6152 or 800-444-Valu *Hours* Mon-Sat 9-9 (Jan-Feb 9-7), Sun 10-6 *Location* From I-95 south take exit 181 onto Hwy 38 south for 6 miles to Hwy 501 east. The center is 68 miles on the right.

STORES

- Adidas (1)
- Bible Factory Outlet (5)
- Bon Worth (1)
- Book Warehouse (5)
- Burlington Brands (1)
- Capacity (1)
- Capers (1)
- Casual Corner (1)
- Casual Male Big & Tall (1)
- Claire's Boutique (3)
- DKNY Jeans (1)
- Dollar Tree (9)

- Dress Barn (1)
- Dress Barn Petites (1)
- Dress Barn Woman (1)
- Easy Spirit (1)
- Elisabeth (1)
- Famous Footwear (1)
- Fila (1)
- Florsheim (1)
- Fossil (2)
- Full Size Fashions (1)
- Fuller Brush (8)
- Gold Outlet (3)
- Humingbird Photo (9)
- Joan Vass USA (1)
- Jody's Accessories (3)
- Kasper ASL (1)
- KB Toys (6)
- Koret (1)
- L'eggs Hanes Bali Playtex (1)
- Liz Claiborne (1)
- Mikasa (4)
- Music 4 Less (5)
- Naturalizer (1)
- Oneida (4)
- ProfessioNail (8)
- QVC Outlet (4)
- Regal Cinemas (9)
- Remington (4)
- Samsonite/American Tourister (2)
- Scent Shoppe (8)
- Sox Shoppe (1)
- Tools & More (9)
- Totes / Sunglass World (3)
- Ultra Jewelers (3)
- Umbro (1)
- Vitamin World (8)
- Wachovia Bank ATM (9)
- Welcome Home (4)

EATS & TREATS

- Corrado's Pizza (11)
- Good Shop Lollipop (10)
- Manchu Wok (11)
- O'Henry's Ice Cream (10)
- O'Henry's Too (10)

6   NORTH MYRTLE BEACH

In addition to the Barefoot Factory Stores listed below, shoppers will also find over 100 specialty and retail shops as well as waterfront restaurants.

6A • Barefoot Factory Stores

www.bflanding.com
Address 4898 Hwy 17 S *Phone* 843-272-8349 *Hours* Sun-Sat 10-9 *Location* On US 17 between Myrtle Beach and North Myrtle Beach. Center is at junction of US 17 and 48th Ave.

STORES

- Bass (1)
- Bible Factory Outlet (5)
- Dress Barn (1)
- Dress Barn Woman (1)
- Easy Spirit (1)
- Geoffrey Beene (1)
- Hawaiian Shirt Trading Co (1)
- Izod (1)
- JD Country (1)
- M R Ducks (1)
- Rack Room Shoes (1)
- S & K Menswear (1)
- Van Heusen (1)

7   SANTEE

7A • Santee Outlets

Address 1500 Village Square Blvd *Phone* 803-854-4445 *Hours* Mon-Sat 9-7, Sun 1:30-6 *Location* Fifty minutes southeast of Columbia near Lake Marion. Take exit I-95 exit 98 (Hwy 6).

STORES

- Bass (1)
- Bon Worth (1)
- Capacity (1)
- Dress Barn (1)
- Famous Footwear (1)
- Goodies & Gift Shoppe (5)
- Izod (1)
- L'eggs Hanes Bali Playtex (1)
- Paper Factory (9)
- Reader's Outlet (5)
- Rue 21 (1)
- Totes / Sunglass World (3)
- Van Heusen (1)

EATS & TREATS

- Meeting Room Café (11)

Tennessee

1 • Blountville
2 • Chattanooga
3 • Crossville
4 • Lakeland
5 • Lebanon
6 • Nashville
7 • Pigeon Forge
8 • Sevierville
9 • Union City

1 BLOUNTVILLE

1A • Factory Stores of America
www.chelseafactoryoutlets.com
Address 354 Shadowtown Rd
Phone 423-323-4281 *Hours* Mon-Sat 10-9 (Jan-Mar 10-6), Sun 12-6 *Location* North of Johnson City off I-81, exit 66.

STORES

- Bon Worth (1)
- Capacity (1)
- Carolina Pottery (4)
- Dollar General (9)
- Foozles Bookstore (5)
- L'eggs Hanes Bali Playtex (1)
- Paper Factory (9)
- Tri-Cities Cinema (9)

2 CHATTANOOGA

2A • Prime Outlets Warehouse Row
www.primeoutlets.com
Address 1110 Market St *Phone* 888-260-7620 or 423-267-1111 *Hours* Mon-Sat 10-8 (Jan-Mar 10-7), Sun 12-6 *Location* Downtown Chattanooga. From I-24 exit 179, follow US 11 north to West 11th St and turn right (east). Center is at junction of Hwy 8 (Market St) and West 11th St.

STORES

- Bass (1)
- Book Gallery (5)
- Buster Brown (1)
- Carriage Candle Factory (5)
- Coach (2)
- Corbin Menswear (1)
- Ellen Tracy (1)
- Fashions Unlimited (1)
- Geoffrey Beene (1)
- GNC (8)
- Goldsmith Shop (3)
- Joan Vass USA (1)
- Johnston & Murphy (1)
- Kasper ASL (1)
- L'eggs Hanes Bali Playtex (1)
- Nine West (1)
- OshKosh B'Gosh (1)
- Polo Ralph Lauren (1)
- Satellite Page (9)
- Strasburg Children (1)
- Tommy Hilfiger (1)
- Yves Delorme Paris / Palais Royal (4)
- Zazegnia (1)
- Zazegnia Uomo (1)

EATS & TREATS

- Blimpie Subs & Salads (11)
- Chocolate Conspiracy (10)
- Cozzoli's Pizza & Deli (11)
- Larry's Deli & Gourmet Burgers (11)
- Taiwan Express (11)

3 CROSSVILLE

3A • Factory Stores of America
www.chelseafactoryoutlets.com
Address 361 Sweeney Dr *Phone* 931-484-7165 *Hours* Mon-Thu 9-8 (Jan-Mar 9-7), Fri-Sat 9-9, Sun 12-6 *Location* Between Nashville and Knoxville off I-40, exit 320.

STORES

- Banister Shoes (1)
- Bass (1)
- Bible Factory Outlet (5)
- Bon Worth (1)
- Capacity (1)
- Claire's Boutique (3)
- Corning Revere (4)
- Dress Barn Woman (1)
- Fieldcrest Cannon (4)
- Foozles Bookstore (5)
- Kitchen Collection (4)
- Leather Factory (2)
- L'eggs Hanes Bali Playtex (1)
- Paper Factory (9)
- Rack Room Shoes (1)
- Ron Pittman Sales (9)
- Rue 21 (1)
- Silver Express (3)
- Sun Catchers (9)
- TN Orange Appeal (9)
- Totes / Isotoner (3)

- Van Heusen (1)
- VF Factory Outlet (1)
- Vitamin World (8)
- Welcome Home (4)

EATS & TREATS
- Simonton Cheese (10)
- Subway (11)

4 LAKELAND

4A • Belz Factory Outlet Mall
www.belz.com
Address 3536 Canada Rd *Phone*
901-386-3180 *Hours* Mon-Thu
10-7:30, Fri-Sat 10-9, Sun 1-6
Location Just 8 miles east of
Memphis off I-40, exit 20.

STORES
- Bass (1)
- Big Dog Sportswear (1)
- Casual Male Big & Tall (1)
- Claire's Accessories (3)
- Danskin (1)
- Dress Barn (1)
- Dress Barn Woman (1)
- Hush Puppies & Family (1)
- Latest Craze (9)
- L'eggs Hanes Bali Playtex (1)
- Lighthouse Gallery (4)
- Memorabilia (9)
- Nike (1)
- Old Time Pottery (9)
- Optical Outlet (3)
- Perfumania (8)
- Rack Room Shoes (1)
- Samsonite (2)
- Stockroom (1)
- Toy Liquidators (6)
- Van Heusen (1)
- Vitamin World (8)

EATS & TREATS
- Johnny Mac's (11)

5 LEBANON

5A • Prime Outlets Lebanon
www.primeoutlets.com

Address One Village Blvd *Phone*
615-444-0433 or 800-617-2588
Hours Mon-Sat 10-9, Sun 11-6
Location 25 miles east of Nashville
off I-40, exit 238 (Hwy 231).

STORES
- Bass (1)
- Big Dogs (1)
- Black & Decker (4)
- Book Market (5)
- Brooks Brothers (1)
- Buster Brown (1)
- Caribbean Traders (1)
- Casual Corner (1)
- Casual Corner Woman (1)
- Claire's Accessories (3)
- Coach (2)
- Cost Cutters Salon (8)
- Designer Fragrance/Cosmetics (8)
- Dress Barn/Dress Barn Woman (1)
- Duck Head (1)
- Eddie Bauer (1)
- Elisabeth (1)
- Factory Brand Shoes (1)
- Gap Outlet (1)
- Haggar (1)
- Jones New York (1)
- Jones New York Country (1)
- Kasper ASL (1)
- KB Toys (6)
- Kitchen Collection (4)
- Koret (1)
- L'eggs Hanes Bali Playtex (1)
- Lenox (4)
- Liz Claiborne (1)
- Liz Claiborne Shoes (1)
- Music 4 Less (5)
- Naturalizer (1)
- Nautica (1)
- Nike (1)
- Nine West (1)
- OshKosh B'Gosh (1)
- Paper Factory (9)
- Petite Sophisticate (1)
- Pfaltzgraff (4)
- Polo Ralph Lauren (1)
- Pure Elegance (1)
- Rack Room Shoes (1)
- Rue 21 (1)
- Samsonite (2)
- Smokey's Place (1)
- Sunglass Hut (3)

- Tommy Hilfiger (1)
- Tools & More (9)
- Totes / Sunglass World (3)
- Van Heusen (1)
- Vitamin World (8)
- WestPoint Stevens (4)
- Wilson's Leather (1)
- Zales The Diamond Store (3)

EATS & TREATS
- Frank & Stein Dogs & Drafts (11)
- Great Steak & Potato (11)
- Rocky Mountain Chocolate (10)
- Villa Pizza (11)

6 NASHVILLE

6A • 100 Oaks Mall
www.belz.com
Address 719 Thompson Ln *Phone* 615-383-6002 *Hours* Mon-Sat 10-9, Sun 12-6 *Location* In the center of Nashville at I-65 and Thompson Ln. Take exit 79 from I-65 and go right on Powell to center.

STORES
- Baby Depot (1)
- Burlington Coat Factory (1)
- Claire's Accessories (3)
- Clothing World (1)
- CompUSA (7)
- Dress Barn (1)
- Dress Barn Woman (1)
- Electronic Express (4)
- Famous Footwear (1)
- Funcoland (1)
- GNC (8)
- KB Toys (6)
- Kids in Motion (1)
- Lee Hair and Nails (8)
- Luxury Linens (4)
- Mars Music (5)
- Media Play (5)
- Michaels (9)
- Off 5th-Saks Fifth Avenue (1)
- PetsMart (9)
- Rack Room Shoes (1)
- Reebok (1)
- Regal 27 Cinemas (9)
- Rue 21 (1)

- Serendipity (3)
- TJ Maxx (1)
- Treasures (3)

EATS & TREATS
- Chao Praya (11)
- Cookie Store (10)
- Nashville Style Gyros (11)
- Sbarro's Pizza (11)
- Steak & Spud (11)
- What's the Scoop (10)

6B • Opry Mills
www.millscorp.com
Address 433 Opry Mills Dr *Phone* 877-Shop Fun *Hours* Mon-Fri 10-9:30, Sat 9:30-9:30, Sun 11-8 *Location* About 7 miles northeast of downtown Nashville between Two Rivers Pkwy and McGavock Pike, next door to the Grand Ole Opry.

STORES
- Aeropostale (1)
- Afterthoughts (3)
- Ann Taylor (1)
- Artsville (4)
- Athlete's Foot (1)
- Athlete's Foot for Her (1)
- Athlon Sports Collectibles (6)
- Banana Republic (1)
- Barnes & Noble (5)
- Bass (1)
- Bass Pro Shops Outdoor World (6)
- Bath & Body Works (8)
- Beauty Express (8)
- Bed Bath & Beyond (4)
- Bible Factory Outlet (5)
- Big Dogs (1)
- Blacklion (4)
- Boot Country (1)
- Bose Factory Store (4)
- Build-A-Bear Workshop (5)
- Carter's Childrenswear (1)
- Casual Corner Annex (1)
- Charlotte Russe (1)
- Chicago Cutlery (4)
- Children's Place Outlet (1)
- Claire's Boutique (3)
- Classic Interiors (4)

- Corning Revere (4)
- Cosmetics Company Store (8)
- Country Clutter (4)
- CR Gibson (5)
- CR Jewelers Outlet (3)
- Dexter Shoe (1)
- Dress Barn/Dress Barn Woman (1)
- Dry Ice (4)
- Earthbound Trading Co (5)
- Etienne Aigner (1)
- Eye Candy (1)
- Factory Brand Shoes (1)
- Finish Line (1)
- Flag Shop (9)
- Forget Me Not by American Greetings (5)
- Fossil (2)
- Game Stop (9)
- Games Workshop (9)
- Gap Outlet (1)
- Geoffrey Beene (1)
- Gibson Bluegrass Showcase (9)
- GNC (8)
- Golf America (6)
- Guess? (1)
- Harry & David (5)
- Hillo Hattie Store of Hawaii (1)
- Hot Topic (1)
- Hot Wax Candle (5)
- Hush Puppies & Family (1)
- Jarmen Shoe (1)
- Jewelry Box Outlet (3)
- Jockey (1)
- Journeys (1)
- Just Sports (1)
- KB Toys (6)
- Kirkland's (4)
- Le Creuset (4)
- Leather Limited (2)
- L'eggs Hanes Bali Playtex (1)
- LensCrafters (3)
- Levi's / Dockers (1)
- Lids (9)
- Limited Too (1)
- Liz Claiborne & Elisabeth (1)
- Liz Claiborne Shoes (1)
- Magnets & Logos (5)
- Maidenform (1)
- Mary Engelbreit (5)
- MasterCuts (8)
- Merlo's Cutting Edge (4)
- Mikasa (4)
- Motherhood Maternity (1)
- NASCAR Silicon Motor Speedway (6)
- Nautica (1)

- New York Cargo (1)
- Nike (1)
- Off 5th-Saks Fifth Avenue (1)
- Off Broadway Shoes (1)
- Old Navy (1)
- Oneida (4)
- Opry Nails (8)
- OshKosh B'Gosh (1)
- Pacific Sunwear (1)
- Payless Shoe Source (1)
- Perfumania (8)
- Perry Ellis (1)
- Prism Glass (4)
- Radio Shack (7)
- Reebok / Rockport (1)
- Reeds Jewelers (3)
- Regal Cinemas (9)
- Rue 21 (1)
- S & K Menswear (1)
- Samsonite Travel Expo (2)
- San Francisco Music Box (9)
- Sanrio (9)
- Select Comfort (4)
- Shaded Zebra (4)
- Shoe Carnival (1)
- Skechers (1)
- Southern Style (1)
- Spencer Gifts (5)
- Stone Mountain (2)
- Stop N Save Software (7)
- Strasburg Children (1)
- Stride Rite Keds Sperry (1)
- Sun & Ski Sports (1)
- Suncom Store (9)
- Sunglass Hut / Watch Station (3)
- Swim N Sport (1)
- T-Shirts Plus (1)
- Tennessee Sports Fan (6)
- Tommy Hilfiger (1)
- Tower Records (5)
- Ultra Diamond & Gold (3)
- Urban Planet (1)
- Van Heusen (1)
- Vans Shoes (1)
- Vitamin World (8)
- Warnaco (1)
- Watches Etc (3)
- Wilson's Leather (1)
- Zales The Diamond Store (3)

EATS & TREATS

- Alabama Grill (11)
- Apple Barn, Cider Bar & General Store (10)
- Auntie Anne's Pretzals (10)

- Burger King (11)
- Cajun Grill (11)
- Carvel Ice Cream (10)
- Chili's Too (11)
- Cinnabon (10)
- Dairy Queen / Orange Julius (11)
- Dickey's Barbecue Pit (11)
- Ghirardelli Soda Fountain (11)
- Great American Cookie (10)
- Great Steak & Potato (11)
- Jillian's (11)
- Jody Maroni's Italian Sausage (11)
- Johnny Rockets (11)
- Lotus Express (11)
- Rainforest Café (11)
- Ranch 1 (11)
- Rocky Mountain Chocolate (10)
- Sbarro Italian Eatery (11)
- Starbucks Coffee (10)
- Sweets From Heaven (10)
- TGI Fridays (11)
- Wetzel's Pretzels (10)

7 PIGEON FORGE

Pigeon Forge is located about 30 minutes southeast of Knoxville near the Great Smokey Mountains National Park. To reach the centers from I-40 exit 407, follow Hwy 66 south to US 441. Follow US 441 south into Pigeon Forge.

7A • Belz Factory Outlet World
www.belz.com
Address 2655 Teaster Ln *Phone* 865-453-7316 *Hours* Jan-Feb: Sun-Thu 10-6, Fri-Sat 10-9. Mar-Dec: Mon-Sat 9-9, Sun 10-7 *Location* Traveling south on US 441 from Sevierville, turn left on Teaster Lane and follow it around to center.

STORES
- American Tourister (2)
- Angel's Dolls & Gifts (5)
- Banister / Easy Spirit (1)
- Bass (1)
- Bible Factory Outlet (5)
- Big & Tall Factory Store (1)
- Big Dog Sportswear (1)
- Bon Worth (1)
- Burlington Brands (1)
- Buster Brown (1)
- Camp Coleman (6)
- Capacity (1)
- Capers (1)
- Caribbean Traders (1)
- Carter's Childrenswear (1)
- Casual Corner (1)
- Claire's Accessories (3)
- Cool Shades (3)
- Craftworks (4)
- Diamond Factory/Eelskin Outlet (3)
- Dickies (1)
- Dress Barn (1)
- Etienne Aigner (1)
- Famous Brands Housewares (4)
- Famous Footwear (1)
- Foozles Bookstore (5)
- Fossil (2)
- Fragrance Outlet (8)
- Full Size Fashions (1)
- Fuller Brush (8)
- Game Depot USA (9)
- General Shoe Factory (1)
- Geoffrey Beene (1)
- Hush Puppies & Family (1)
- Izod (1)
- Jaymar (1)
- Jewelry Outlet (3)
- Jockey (1)
- Koret (1)
- Leather Loft (2)
- Levi's Outlet by Designs (1)
- Mad Hatter (2)
- Maidenform (1)
- Music 4 Less (5)
- Naturalizer (1)
- Nike (1)
- Old Time Pottery (9)
- Paper Factory (9)
- Perfumania (8)
- Petite Sophisticate (1)
- Rack Room Shoes (1)
- Royal Doulton (4)
- Rue 21 (1)
- Sock World (1)
- Tools & More (9)
- Totes Isotoner Sunglass World (3)
- Toy Liquidators (6)
- Van Heusen (1)

- Vans Shoes (1)
- Vitamin World (8)
- WestPoint Stevens (4)
- Westport Limited (1)
- Westport Woman (1)
- Whoops! (1)

EATS & TREATS
- Chick'n Lick'n Broasted Chicken (11)
- Geno's Italian Eatery (11)
- Great American Cookie (10)
- New Deli (11)
- Scoops Ice Cream (10)
- Smoky Mountain Express (10)
- Smoky Mountain Fruit & Nut (10)
- Subway (11)
- Suzy Jo's Cinnamon Rolls (10)
- Sweet Shoppe (10)
- TCBY (10)

7B • Pigeon Forge Factory Outlet Mall

www.mypigeonforge.com
Address 2850 Parkway *Phone* 865-428-2828 *Hours* Jan-Mar: Sun-Thu 10-6, Fri-Sat 10-9. Apr-Dec: Mon-Sat 9-9, Sun 9-6 *Location* See introduction to Pigeon Forge.

STORES
- Arrow Shirt / Gold Toe (1)
- Aunt Marys Yarn N Needlework (9)
- Banister Shoes (1)
- Bass (1)
- Black & Decker (4)
- Book Warehouse (5)
- Boot Factory (1)
- Bugle Boy (1)
- Buxton (1)
- Capacity (1)
- Carter's Childrenswear (1)
- Chicago Cutlery (4)
- Claire's Boutique (3)
- Corning Revere (4)
- Dexter Shoe (1)
- Eagle's Eye (1)
- Eagle's Eye Kids (1)
- Fieldcrest Cannon (4)
- KB Toys (6)
- Kitchen Collection (4)
- L'eggs Hanes Bali Playtex (1)
- Mikasa (4)

- Oneida (4)
- OshKosh B'Gosh (1)
- Perfumania (8)
- Pfaltzgraff (4)
- Rack Room Shoes (1)
- Samsonite (2)
- Tools & More (9)
- Totes / Sunglass World (3)
- Van Heusen (1)
- Wallet Works (2)
- Welcome Home (4)

EATS & TREATS
- Sporty's Deli (11)

7C • RiverView Factory Outlet Mall

www.mypigeonforge.com
Address 2684 Teaster Ln *Phone* 865-429-2781 *Hours* Jan-Feb: Sun-Thu 10-6, Fri-Sat 10-9. Mar-Dec: Mon-Sat 9-9, Sun 10-7 *Location* Traveling south on US 441 from Sevierville, turn left on Teaster Lane and follow it around to center.

STORES
- Deep Discount Art & Frame (4)
- Home & Garden Factory Outlet (4)
- Hoover Outlet (4)
- Jewelry & Handbags (3)
- Parton's Candleworks (5)
- Quilt's International (4)
- Sunglass Super Store (3)
- Unique Peddler (9)
- Warehouse Golf (6)
- Workshop Tools (9)

EATS & TREATS
- Riverview Grill (11)

7D • RiverVista Factory Outlet Mall

www.mypigeonforge.com
Address Teaster Ln *Phone* 865-429-9189 *Hours* Jan-Feb: Sun-Thu 10-6, Fri-Sat 10-9. Mar-Dec: Mon-Sat

9-9, Sun 10-7 *Location* Traveling south on US 441 from Sevierville, turn left on Teaster Lane and follow it around to center.

STORES
- Angel's Dolls & Gifts (5)
- Brass Crafters (4)
- Corning Revere (4)
- Dalton Rug (4)
- Pro Shoppe (6)
- RCA Electronics (4)

7E • Tanger Outlet Center
www.tangeroutlets.com
www.mypigeonforge.com
Address 161 E Wears Valley Rd *Phone* 800-408-5775 or 865-428-7002 *Hours* Jan-Feb: Sun-Thu 10-6, Fri-Sat 10-9. Mar-Dec: Mon-Sat 9-9, Sun 10-7 *Location* Traveling south on US 441, turn left at the 2nd or 3rd traffic light in Pigeon Forge.

STORES
- Bon Worth (1)
- Coach (2)
- Easy Spirit (1)
- Eddie Bauer (1)
- Farberware (4)
- Harry & David (5)
- J Crew (1)
- Jones New York (1)
- L'eggs Hanes Bali Playtex (1)
- Liz Claiborne (1)
- Malone Outfitters (9)
- Nautica (1)
- NY, NY (1)
- OshKosh B'Gosh (1)
- Reebok (1)
- Rockport (1)
- S & K Menswear (1)
- Samsonite (2)
- Smith & Wesson (9)
- Springmaid Wamsutta (4)
- Stone Mountain (2)
- Tommy Hilfiger (1)

- Tools & More (9)
- Totes / Sunglass World (3)

EATS & TREATS
- Deli Factory (11)

7F • Z Buda Outlet Mall
www.mypigeonforge.com
Address 2850 Parkway *Phone* 865-429-3408 *Hours* Jan-Mar: Sun-Thu 10-6, Fri-Sat 10-9. Apr-Dec: Mon-Sat 9-9, Sun 9-6 *Location* See introduction to Pigeon Forge.

STORES
- A Place To Remember (9)
- Authentic Autographs (9)
- Bath & Body Boutique (8)
- Bible Warehouse (5)
- Bon Worth (1)
- Booneway Farms (9)
- Bumbershoot Books (5)
- Christmas 'N' Dolls (9)
- Fashion Tees (1)
- Fine Art & Frame (4)
- Gift Gallery (5)
- Gordon Garment Factory Outlet (1)
- Handbag Heaven (2)
- Jewelry Sample Outlet (3)
- Leather & More (2)
- Lid'l Dolly's Dresses (1)
- Manhattan Factory Stores (1)
- Moon Craft Outlet (9)
- Owen's Leather & Accessories (2)
- Peddler Gift Shop (5)
- Prestige Fragrance/Cosmetics (8)
- Shadowline (1)
- Silver & Shades (3)
- Smoky Mountain Gold & Diamond (3)
- Sock World (1)
- Sunglass World (3)
- Team Sports (6)
- Tees N Togs Etc (1)

EATS & TREATS
- Funnel Cakes (10)
- Hotdogs Etc (11)
- Maggie's Bakery & Eatery (11)
- Mountain Man Fruit & Nut (10)
- Robears Excellent Yogurt (11)
- Snack World (10)

8   SEVIERVILLE

8A • Governor's Crossing Outlet Center

Address 212 Collier Dr *Phone* 865-429-2320 or 877-429-2320 *Hours* Jan-Feb: Sun-Thu 10-6, Fri-Sat 10-9. Mar-Dec: Mon-Sat 10-9, Sun 10-7 *Location* About 25 minutes southeast of Knoxville. From I-40 exit 407, follow Hwy 66 south to US 441. The center is located between Sevierville and Pigeon Forge.

STORES
- Angel's Touch Dolls (5)
- Bon Worth (1)
- Books-A-Million (5)
- Claire's Accessories (3)
- Cost Cutters Salon (8)
- Country Clutter (4)
- Earthbound (1)
- GNC (8)
- Golf Depot (6)
- Governor's Palace Theatre (9)
- Hound Dogs (1)
- Linen Barn (4)
- Mr Gatti's (9)
- Music 4 Less (5)
- Myrick's Jewelry (3)
- Olive Branch Christian Gifts (5)
- Oneida (4)
- Perfumania (8)
- Rue 21 (1)
- Shoe Carnival (1)
- Speed Zone (6)
- Sunglass Super Store (3)
- Texas Roadhouse (9)
- Tools & More (9)
- VF Factory Outlet (1)

EATS & TREATS
- Fuddruckers (11)
- Ham 'n Goodys (11)
- NASCAR Café (11)
- Rocky River Grille (11)
- TGI Fridays (11)

8B • Tanger at Five Oaks

www.tangeroutlets.com
Address 1645 Parkway *Phone* 800-408-8377 or 865-453-1053 *Hours* Jan-Feb: Sun-Thu 10-6, Fri-Sat 10-9. Mar-Dec: Mon-Sat 9-9, Sun 10-7 *Location* About 25 minutes southeast of Knoxville. From I-40 exit 407, follow State Hwy 66 south to US 441. The center is located about 2 miles north of Pigeon Forge.

STORES
- Allen Edmonds (1)
- American Outpost (1)
- Banana Republic (1)
- Bass (1)
- Bath & Body Works (8)
- Bible Factory Outlet (5)
- Big Dog Sportswear (1)
- Black & Decker (4)
- Bombay Outlet (4)
- Bose Factory Store (4)
- Brooks Brothers (1)
- Carter's Childrenswear (1)
- Children's Place Outlet (1)
- Clothestime (1)
- Coach (2)
- Cole-Haan (1)
- Corning Revere (4)
- Cosmetics Company Store (8)
- Croscill (4)
- Dana Buchman (1)
- Dexter Shoe (1)
- Disney Catalog Outlet (5)
- Dress Barn (1)
- Dress Barn Woman (1)
- Duck Head (1)
- Eddie Bauer (1)
- Elisabeth (1)
- Fossil (2)
- Gap Outlet (1)
- Geoffrey Beene (1)
- Guess? (1)
- Haggar (1)
- Harry & David (5)
- Hartstrings (1)
- Hoover Outlet (4)
- Hush Puppies & Family (1)

- Izod (1)
- Johnston & Murphy (1)
- Kasper ASL (1)
- Kirkland's (4)
- Kitchen Collection (4)
- Koret (1)
- Le Gourmet Chef (4)
- Le Sportsac (2)
- L'eggs Hanes Bali Playtex (1)
- Lenox (4)
- Levi's Outlet by Designs (1)
- Lillian Vernon (9)
- Liz Claiborne (1)
- Liz Claiborne Shoes (1)
- Maidenform (1)
- Motherhood Maternity (1)
- Music For A Song (5)
- Nautica (1)
- Nine West (1)
- NY, NY (1)
- Old Navy (1)
- Olga Warner (1)
- OshKosh B'Gosh (1)
- Pacific Sunwear (1)
- Paper Factory (9)
- Peaches 'n Cream (1)
- Perfumania (8)
- Polo Ralph Lauren (1)
- Reebok (1)
- Reed & Barton (4)
- Rockport (1)
- SAS Factory Shoes (1)
- Socks Galore (1)
- Strasburg Children (1)
- Stride Rite (1)
- Sunglass Outlet (3)
- Timberland (1)
- Tommy Hilfiger (1)
- Tool Warehouse (9)
- Totes Isotoner Sunglass World (3)
- Ultra Diamond Outlet (3)
- Van Heusen (1)
- Villeroy & Boch (4)
- Waterford Wedgwood (4)
- Wilson's Leather (1)
- Woolrich (1)
- Zales The Diamond Store (3)

EATS & TREATS

- Country Ritz Café (11)
- Creamery (10)
- Fudgery (10)
- Mountain Edge Grill (11)
- Pepperidge Farm (10)

9 UNION CITY

9A • Factory Stores of America

www.chelseafactoryoutlets.com
Address 601 Sherwood Dr *Phone* 731-885-6465 *Hours* Mon-Thu 9-8 (Jan-May 9-7), Fri-Sat 9-9, Sun 12-6 *Location* From US 51 take the State Hwy 21 exit south to Sherwood Dr and travel west.

STORES

- Bass (1)
- Bon Worth (1)
- Capacity (1)
- Van Heusen (1)
- VF Factory Outlet (1)

Texas

1 • Allen
2 • Conroe
3 • Corsicanna
4 • Denton
5 • Fort Worth
6 • Gainesville
7 • Grapevine
8 • Hempstead
9 • Hillsboro

10 • Katy
11 • La Marque
12 • Livingston
13 • Mineral Wells
14 • New Braunfels
15 • San Marcos
16 • Sealy
17 • Sulphur Springs
18 • Terrell

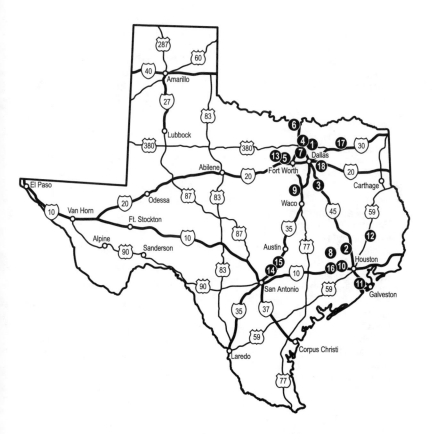

1 ALLEN

1A • Allen Premium Outlets

www.premiumoutlets.com
Address 820 W Stacy Rd *Phone* 972-678-7000 *Hours* Mon-Sat 10-9, Sun 11-6 *Location* About 20 minutes north of Dallas off US 75 north, exit 37.

STORES

- Adidas (1)
- Banana Republic (1)
- Barneys New York (1)
- Bass (1)
- BCBG Max Azria (1)
- Big Dog Sportswear (1)
- Bombay Outlet (4)
- Book Warehouse (5)
- Bostonian Clarks (1)
- Brooks Brothers (1)
- Casual Corner (1)
- Casual Corner Annex Petite (1)
- Casual Corner Woman (1)
- Claire's Accessories (3)
- Clothestime (1)
- Cole-Haan (1)
- Country Clutter (4)
- Crate & Barrel (4)
- Dansk (4)
- DKNY (1)
- Dress Barn (1)
- Dress Barn Woman (1)
- Earthbound Trading Co (5)
- Easy Spirit (1)
- Eddie Bauer (1)
- El Portal Last Stop (2)
- Etienne Aigner (1)
- Factory Brand Shoes (1)
- Fubu (1)
- Geoffrey Beene (1)
- Gold Toe (1)
- Guess? (1)
- Haggar (1)
- Izod (1)
- Jones New York Country (1)
- KB Toys (6)
- Kenneth Cole (1)
- Kitchen Collection (4)
- Le Creuset (4)
- L'eggs Hanes Bali Playtex (1)
- Lenox (4)

- Liz Claiborne (1)
- Liz Claiborne Shoes (1)
- Maidenform (1)
- Max Studio (1)
- Movado (2)
- Music For A Song (5)
- Nautica (1)
- Nine West (1)
- Off The Page Catalog Clearance (9)
- Oneida (4)
- OshKosh B'Gosh (1)
- Perry Ellis (1)
- Polo Ralph Lauren (1)
- Puma (1)
- Reebok (1)
- Samsonite (2)
- Sunglass Outlet (3)
- Timberland (1)
- Tommy Hilfiger (1)
- Ultra Diamond Outlet (3)
- Umbro (1)
- Van Heusen (1)
- Vitamin World (8)
- Waterford Wedgwood (4)
- Welcome Home (4)
- WestPoint Stevens (4)
- Wilson's Leather (1)
- Zales The Diamond Store (3)

EATS & TREATS

- China Pantry (11)
- CinnaMonster (10)
- Great Steak & Potato (11)
- Italia Express (11)

2 CONROE

2A • Prime Outlets Conroe

www.primeoutlets.com
Address 1111 League Line Rd *Phone* 936-756-0999 *Hours* Mon-Sat 10-8, Sun 10-6 *Location* North of Houston off I-45 north, exit 91.

STORES

- Bass (1)
- Bible Factory Outlet (5)
- Bon Worth (1)
- Capacity (1)
- Carter's Childrenswear (1)
- Casual Corner (1)
- Casual Male Big & Tall (1)

- Claire's Boutique (3)
- Dress Barn (1)
- Elisabeth (1)
- Etienne Aigner (1)
- Factory Brand Shoes (1)
- Farberware (4)
- GNC (8)
- Guess? (1)
- Haggar (1)
- Izod (1)
- Jockey (1)
- Kitchen Collection (4)
- Koret (1)
- L'eggs Hanes Bali Playtex (1)
- Levi's Outlet by Most (1)
- Liz Claiborne (1)
- Maidenform (1)
- Mikasa (4)
- Motherhood Maternity (1)
- N & D Nails (8)
- Naturalizer (1)
- Nike (1)
- Nine West (1)
- Oneida (4)
- OshKosh B'Gosh (1)
- Paper Factory (9)
- Perfumania (8)
- Petite Sophisticate (1)
- Pomeroy Collection (4)
- Publishers Warehouse (5)
- Royal Doulton (4)
- Rue 21 (1)
- Samsonite (2)
- SAS Factory Shoes (1)
- Socks Galore (1)
- Springmaid Wamsutta (4)
- Sterling Silver Jewelry (3)
- Sunglass Outlet (3)
- T-Shirts Plus (1)
- Tee Time Apparel (1)
- Tommy Hilfiger (1)
- Tools Etc (9)
- Toys Unlimited (6)
- Van Heusen (1)
- Vitamin World (8)
- WaWe Rugs (4)
- Wear it Out (1)
- Welcome Home (4)
- Wiggins Furniture (4)

EATS & TREATS
- Carrie's Coffee Mill (10)
- Pepperidge Farm (10)
- Pop it Up Popcorn (10)

3 CORSICANA

3A • Factory Stores of America
www.chelseafactoryoutlets.com
Address 316 Factory Outlet Dr
Phone 903-874-1503 *Hours* Mon-Thu 9-7, Fri-Sat 9-9, Sun 12-6
Location South of Dallas off I-45, exit 228.

STORES
- Banister / Easy Spirit (1)
- Bon Worth (1)
- Van Heusen (1)
- VF Factory Outlet (1)

4 DENTON

4A • Denton Factory Stores
www.dentonfactorystores.com
Address 5800 N I-35 *Phone* 940-565-5040 *Hours* Mon-Sat 10-8, Sun 11-6 *Location* About 37 miles north of Dallas/Fort Worth. Take Hwy 288 east off I-35.

STORES
- AntiqueLand (4)
- Bridal Co Outlet (9)
- Denton Cty Historical Museum (9)
- Dress Barn (1)
- Lenox (4)
- Stevens Pepperell (1)
- US Factory Outlet (9)

EATS & TREATS
- Good Eats Grill (11)

5 FORT WORTH

5A • Fort Worth Outlet Square
Address 150 Throckmorton St
Phone 817-415-3720 *Hours* Mon-Thu 10-7, Fri-Sat 10-9, Sun 12-6
Location Downtown Fort Worth at Third and Throckmorton at Tandy Center.

STORES

- Carter's For Kids (1)
- Claire's Accessories (3)
- Dress Barn Petites (1)
- Dress Barn/Dress Barn Woman (1)
- Factory Brand Shoes (1)
- Goldsmith Shop (3)
- Haggar (1)
- L'eggs Hanes Bali Playtex (1)
- Nine West (1)
- Perfumania (8)
- Publishers Warehouse (5)
- Radio Shack (7)
- Record Town (5)
- Remington (4)
- S & K Menswear (1)
- Samsonite (2)
- Spiegel Outlet (1)
- Totes / Sunglass World (3)
- Vitamin World (8)

EATS & TREATS

- Rocky Mountain Chocolate (10)

6 GAINESVILLE

6A • Prime Outlets Gainesville

www.primeoutlets.com
Address 4321 I-35 N *Phone* 888-545-7220 *Hours* Mon-Sat 10-8, Sun 11-6 *Location* 55 minutes north of Dallas/Fort Worth off I-35, exit 501.

STORES

- Baby B'Gosh (1)
- Bass (1)
- Bible Factory Outlet (5)
- Big Bears Native American (9)
- Big Dog Sportswear (1)
- Bon Worth (1)
- Brooks Brothers (1)
- Carter's Childrenswear (1)
- Casual Corner (1)
- Casual Corner Woman (1)
- Claire's Accessories (3)
- Corning Clearance (4)
- Corning Revere (4)
- Corral West Ranchwear (1)
- Dansk (4)
- Dimensions Wireless (7)
- Dress Barn/Dress Barn Woman (1)

- Factory Brand Shoes (1)
- Florsheim (1)
- Frankoma Pottery (4)
- Gap Outlet (1)
- GNC (8)
- Golden Chimes (4)
- Greg Norman (1)
- Heart of Texas (9)
- Izod (1)
- Jockey (1)
- Jones New York (1)
- Jones New York Woman (1)
- Kasper ASL (1)
- KB Toys (6)
- Kitchen Collection (4)
- Koret (1)
- Leather Loft (2)
- L'eggs Hanes Bali Playtex (1)
- Levi's Outlet by Most (1)
- Mikasa (4)
- Motherhood Maternity (1)
- Naturalizer (1)
- Nike (1)
- OshKosh B'Gosh (1)
- Paper Factory (9)
- Parkhill's Jewelry Outlet (3)
- Perfumania (8)
- Petite Sophisticate (1)
- Pomeroy Collection (4)
- Pottery Factory (4)
- Rage (1)
- Red River Art Gallery (4)
- Reebok (1)
- Rue 21 (1)
- Saguaro Leather (1)
- Samsonite (2)
- SAS Factory Shoes (1)
- Shazik's Accessories (3)
- Smart Shopper (9)
- Solar Nails (8)
- Soul Possessions (9)
- Springmaid Wamsutta (4)
- Stadium Locker Room (1)
- Sunglass Hut / Watch Station (3)
- Suzanne's (1)
- Timeless Treasures (9)
- Van Heusen (1)
- Welcome Home (4)
- Zales The Diamond Store (3)

EATS & TREATS

- Burger Grill (11)
- China Court (11)
- CinnaMonster (10)
- Corn Dog (11)

- Pretzelmania (10)
- Rocky Mountain Chocolate (10)
- Subway (11)
- Villa Pizza (11)

7 GRAPEVINE

7A • Grapevine Mills

www.millscorp.com

Address 3000 Grapevine Mills Pkwy *Phone* 972-724-4900 *Hours* Mon-Sat 10-9:30, Sun 11-7 *Location* Just 2 miles north of the Dallas/Fort Worth International Airport. From Fort Worth go north on State Hwy 121 to FM 2499, Grapevine Mills Pkwy. Turn left at the second traffic light.

STORES

- AMC 30 Theatres (9)
- Anchor Blue Clothing Co (1)
- Ann Taylor (1)
- Athlete's Foot (1)
- Avenue (1)
- Bag & Baggage (2)
- Banister Shoes (1)
- Bass Pro Shops Outdoor World (6)
- Bath & Body Works (8)
- Beauty Express (8)
- Bebe Outlet (1)
- Bed Bath & Beyond (4)
- Best Priced! Kids (1)
- Bible Factory Outlet (5)
- Big Dog Sportswear (1)
- Books-A-Million (5)
- Bose Factory Store (4)
- Brooks Brothers (1)
- Brookstone Outlet (4)
- Burlington Coat Factory (1)
- Candleman Outlet (5)
- Card America (5)
- Carter's For Kids (1)
- Casual Male Big & Tall (1)
- CCI Wireless (7)
- Charlotte Russe (1)
- Charlotte's Room (3)
- Chico's (1)
- Children's Place Outlet (1)
- Cingular Wireless (7)
- Claire's Accessories (3)

- Coach House Gifts (4)
- Coastal Cotton (1)
- Corning Revere (4)
- Country Clutter (4)
- CR Jewelers Outlet (3)
- Cutting Edge Outlet (4)
- Dallas Dancewear & Activewear (9)
- Dockers Outlet (1)
- Donna Karan (1)
- Dress Barn/Dress Barn Woman (1)
- Earthbound Trading Co (5)
- Elegant Factory Direct Jewelers (3)
- Escada Company Store (1)
- Eye Candy (1)
- Factory Brand Shoes (1)
- Fast Forward (1)
- Flag Shop (9)
- Florsheim (1)
- Foot Locker (1)
- Fragrance Depot (8)
- GameWorks (9)
- Gap Outlet (1)
- GNC (8)
- Golf America (6)
- Great Ideas Gift Outlet (5)
- Group USA (1)
- Guess? (1)
- Guitars & Cadillacs (9)
- Haggar (1)
- I Love Quilts (4)
- Icing (3)
- Izod (1)
- JCPenney Outlet (1)
- Jewelers of Las Vegas (3)
- Jewelry Box Outlet (3)
- Journeys (1)
- Just for Feet (1)
- Just Sports (1)
- KB Toys (6)
- Kenwood Factory Outlet (4)
- Kiddie Kandids (9)
- Kirkland's (4)
- Last Call Neiman Marcus (1)
- Leather Limited (2)
- Leather Loft (2)
- Lee Nails (8)
- L'eggs Hanes Bali Playtex (1)
- LensCrafters (3)
- Levi's (1)
- Lids (9)
- Liz Claiborne Shoes (1)
- MacBirdie Golf Gifts (5)
- Maidenform (1)
- Marshalls (1)
- MasterCuts (8)

- Mikasa (4)
- Motherhood Maternity (1)
- Naturalizer (1)
- Nextel (7)
- Nine West (1)
- NordicTrack (8)
- Obzeet Imported Decor (4)
- Off 5th-Saks Fifth Avenue (1)
- Off Rodeo Drive Beverly Hills (1)
- Official Dallas Cowboys Pro Shop (6)
- Old Navy (1)
- OshKosh B'Gosh (1)
- Pacific Sunwear (1)
- Payless Shoe Source (1)
- Perfumania (8)
- Perfumania Plus (8)
- Polar Ice Skating Arenas (9)
- Polo Jeans Co (1)
- Premier Fine Jewelry (3)
- Quackin' Up (1)
- Rack Room Shoes (1)
- Radio Shack (7)
- Remington (4)
- Ritz Camera 1 Hour Photo (7)
- S & K Menswear (1)
- Samsonite (2)
- Samsonite At Work (2)
- Sanrio (9)
- Scrubs & Beyond (1)
- Silver Gallery (3)
- Skechers (1)
- Spencer Gifts (5)
- Sports Authority (6)
- Stars and Legends (9)
- Stop N Save Software (7)
- Studio One Photography (7)
- Sun & Ski Sports (1)
- Sunglass Hut (3)
- Swim 'N Sport (1)
- T-Shirts Plus (1)
- Texas Basket Company (5)
- Texas Treasures (5)
- Today's News (5)
- Tommy Hilfiger (1)
- Totes / Sunglass World (3)
- TouchArtist (8)
- Two Lips Shoes (1)
- Unipaging (9)
- Urban Planet (1)
- Van Heusen (1)
- Vans Shoes (1)
- Verizon Wireless (7)
- Virgin Megastore (5)
- Vitamin World (8)
- Voice Stream Wireless (7)

- Wallet Works (2)
- Watch Station (3)
- Watches Etc (3)
- Western Warehouse (9)
- Wheels & Fitness in Motion (8)
- Wilson's Leather (1)
- Windsor Outlet (1)
- XX Me Outlet (1)
- Zales The Diamond Store (3)
- Zap Create Your Own Cap (1)

EATS & TREATS

- Auntie Anne's Pretzals (10)
- Bennigan's (11)
- Black-eyed Pea (11)
- Burger King (11)
- Candy Headquarters (10)
- Chili's Too (11)
- Cinnabon (10)
- CinnaMonster (10)
- Cold Stone Creamery (10)
- Corner Bakery Café (11)
- Cozymel's Coastal Mexican Grill (11)
- Dick Clark's American Bandstand (11)
- Dickey's Barbecue Pit (11)
- GameWorks Café (11)
- Great American Cookie (10)
- Haagen Dazs (10)
- Juice Works / TCBY (10)
- Keily's Cajun Grill (11)
- Kenny Roger's Roasters (11)
- La Salsa Fresh Mexican Grill (11)
- Nestle Tollhouse Café (11)
- Panda Express (11)
- Paradise Bakery & Café (11)
- Pretzel Time (10)
- Rainforest Café (11)
- Rocky Mountain Chocolate (10)
- Sbarro Italian Eatery (11)
- Starbucks Coffee (10)
- Steak 'n Shake (11)
- Sweet Factory (10)
- Trail Dust Steak House (11)
- Virgin Megastore Café (11)
- World Links (11)

8   HEMPSTEAD

8A • Factory Stores of America
www.chelseafactoryoutlets.com
Address 805 Factory Outlet Dr
Phone 979-826-8277 *Hours* Mon-

Thu 9-7, Fri-Sat 9-9, Sun 12-6
Location Northeast of Houston off
US 290, exit Hwy 1488.

Stores

- Banister / Easy Spirit (1)
- VF Factory Outlet (1)

9 Hillsboro

9A • Prime Outlets Hillsboro
www.primeoutlets.com
Address 104 NE I-35 *Phone* 254-
582-9205 *Hours* Mon-Sat 10-8,
Sun 11-6 *Location* Between Fort
Worth and Waco off I-35, exit
368A.

Stores

- A Cell 4 U (7)
- American Outpost (1)
- Bass (1)
- Bible Factory Outlet (5)
- Big Dogs (1)
- Black & Decker (4)
- Bombay Outlet (4)
- Carter's Childrenswear (1)
- Casual Corner (1)
- Casual Corner Woman (1)
- Casual Male Big & Tall (1)
- Claire's Accessories (3)
- Corning Revere (4)
- Decades Antiques (9)
- Dress Barn (1)
- Duck Head (1)
- Eddie Bauer (1)
- Elisabeth (1)
- Factory Brand Shoes (1)
- Famous Brands Housewares (4)
- Farberware (4)
- Fossil (2)
- Frame Gallery (4)
- Gap Outlet (1)
- Golden Chimes (4)
- Guess? (1)
- Haggar (1)
- Harold's (1)
- Harry & David (5)
- Izod (1)
- J Crew (1)
- Jockey (1)
- Jones New York (1)
- Kasper ASL (1)
- Kitchen Collection (4)
- Leather Loft (2)
- L'eggs Hanes Bali Playtex (1)
- Levi's Outlet by Most (1)
- Liz Claiborne (1)
- Maidenform (1)
- Mikasa (4)
- Motherhood Maternity (1)
- National Book Warehouse (5)
- Naturalizer (1)
- Nike (1)
- Nine West (1)
- Oneida (4)
- OshKosh B'Gosh (1)
- Paper Factory (9)
- Payless Shoe Source (1)
- Perfumania (8)
- Petite Sophisticate (1)
- Place - Day Spa (8)
- Polo Ralph Lauren (1)
- Pomeroy Collection (4)
- Pro Nails (8)
- Radio Shack (7)
- Reebok / Rockport (1)
- Rue 21 (1)
- S & K Menswear (1)
- S & S Gifts (5)
- Saguaro Leather (1)
- Samsonite (2)
- SAS Factory Shoes (1)
- Socks Galore (1)
- Springmaid Wamsutta (4)
- Stadium Locker Room (1)
- Sunglass Outlet (3)
- Totes / Sunglass World (3)
- Toys Unlimited (6)
- Ultra Fine Jewelry (3)
- Van Heusen (1)
- VF Factory Outlet (1)
- Vitamin World (8)
- Welcome Home (4)
- Wilson's Leather (1)
- Zales The Diamond Store (3)

Eats & Treats

- Café Terranella (11)
- Eats n More (11)
- Pepperidge Farm (10)
- Rocky Mountain Chocolate (10)
- Subway (11)

10 KATY

10A • Katy Mills
www.millscorp.com
Address 5000 Katy Mills Cir *Phone* 281-644-5050 *Hours* Mon-Sat 10-9:30, Sun 11-7 *Location* 25 miles west of Houston off I-10, exit 742.

STORES

- AMC 20 Theatres (9)
- Animagic (7)
- Animal Creations (9)
- Ann Taylor (1)
- As Seen On TV (5)
- Athlete's Foot (1)
- Athlete's Foot for Her (1)
- Bag & Baggage (2)
- Banana Republic (1)
- Bass (1)
- Bass Pro Shops Outdoor World (6)
- Bath & Body Works (8)
- Beauty Express (8)
- Bed Bath & Beyond (4)
- Bible Factory Outlet (5)
- Big Dogs (1)
- Black & Decker (4)
- Books-A-Million (5)
- Bose Factory Store (4)
- Brooks Brothers (1)
- Brookwood Community Store (9)
- Bugle Boy (1)
- Bui-Yah-Kah (1)
- Burlington Coat Factory (1)
- Carter's For Kids (1)
- Casual Corner Annex (1)
- Casual Corner Annex Petite (1)
- Casual Corner Annex Woman (1)
- Charlotte Russe (1)
- Children's Place Outlet (1)
- Cingular Wireless (7)
- Claire's Boutique (3)
- Cole-Haan (1)
- Corning Revere (4)
- Country Clutter (4)
- CR Jewelers Outlet (3)
- Dress Barn/Dress Barn Woman (1)
- Dresses & Beyond (1)
- Earthbound Trading Co (5)
- Express & Structure Warehouse (1)
- Eye Candy (1)
- Finish Line (1)
- Flag Shop (9)
- Forget Me Not by American Greetings (5)
- FYE - For Your Entertainment (4)
- Games Workshop (9)
- Gap Outlet (1)
- Geoffrey Beene (1)
- Global Exotics (4)
- GNC (8)
- Guess? (1)
- Guitars & Cadillacs (9)
- Haggar (1)
- Hoover Outlet (4)
- Hot Topic (1)
- House of Perfumes (8)
- Hradil Designs (4)
- Icing (3)
- Imaginations (9)
- Jewelers of Las Vegas (3)
- Jockey (1)
- Journeys (1)
- Just Sports (1)
- Kenneth Cole (1)
- Kirkland's (4)
- Kitchen Collection (4)
- Larry's Authentic Shoes (1)
- LC Nails (8)
- Leather Loft (2)
- L'eggs Hanes Bali Playtex (1)
- Lenox (4)
- Levi's / Dockers (1)
- Lids (9)
- Life Uniform (1)
- Liz Claiborne (1)
- Liz Claiborne Shoes (1)
- Marshalls (1)
- MasterCuts (8)
- Merlo's Cutting Edge (4)
- Mikasa (4)
- Motherhood Maternity (1)
- Nancy's Collection (3)
- NASCAR Silicon Motor Speedway (6)
- Naturalizer (1)
- Nautica (1)
- Off 5th-Saks Fifth Avenue (1)
- Official Dallas Cowboys Pro Shop (6)
- Old Navy (1)
- Old West Warehouse (9)
- Ornate Collection (4)
- OshKosh B'Gosh (1)
- Pacific Sunwear (1)
- Payless Shoe Source (1)

- Perfumania (8)
- Perfume Outlet (8)
- Perry Ellis (1)
- Pfaltzgraff (4)
- Polo Ralph Lauren (1)
- Pomeroy Collection (4)
- Pyramid (9)
- Rack Room Shoes (1)
- Radio Shack (7)
- Reebok (1)
- Remington (4)
- Ritz Camera 1 Hour Photo (7)
- Rue 21 (1)
- Samsonite Travel Expo (2)
- Sanrio (9)
- Select Comfort (4)
- Shoe Carnival (1)
- Skechers (1)
- Spencer Gifts (5)
- Steve and Barry's University Sportswear (1)
- Stop N Save Software (7)
- Stride Rite Keds Sperry (1)
- Sun & Ski Sports (1)
- Sunglass Hut / Watch Station (3)
- Sunglass World (3)
- Swim N Sport (1)
- T-Shirts Plus (1)
- Texas Treasures (5)
- Timberland (1)
- Tommy Hilfiger (1)
- Ultra Diamond & Gold (3)
- Urban Planet (1)
- Van Heusen (1)
- Vans Shoes (1)
- Vitamin World (8)
- Voice Stream Wireless (7)
- Walson's Jewelers (3)
- Warnaco (1)
- Watch World International (3)
- Wet Seal Outlet (1)
- Whitehall Co Jewelers (3)
- Wilson's Leather (1)
- Windsor Outlet (1)
- XOXO (1)
- Young Hui Imports (5)
- Zales The Diamond Store (3)

EATS & TREATS

- Auntie Anne's Pretzals (10)
- Burger King (11)
- Candy Headquarters (10)
- Carvel Ice Cream (10)
- Cinnabon (10)

- Dairy Queen / Orange Julius (11)
- Dickey's Barbecue Pit (11)
- Great American Cookie (10)
- Great Steak & Potato (11)
- Jillian's (11)
- Jody Maroni's Italian Sausage (11)
- Joe Mugs Coffee (10)
- Johnny Rockets (11)
- Keily's Cajun Grill (11)
- Lotus Express (11)
- Moe's Grill & Bar (11)
- Rainforest Café (11)
- Ranch 1 (11)
- Rocky Mountain Chocolate (10)
- Sbarro Italian Eatery (11)
- Starbucks Coffee (10)
- Sweet Factory (10)
- Wetzel's Pretzels / Cold Stone Creamery (10)

11 LA MARQUE

11A • Factory Stores of America
www.chelseafactoryoutlets.com
Address 11001 Delany Rd *Phone*
409-935-4882 *Hours* Mon-Sat 10-
8, Sun 12-6 *Location* 40 minutes
south of Houston off I-45, exit 13.

STORES

- American Tourister (2)
- Bass (1)
- Bon Worth (1)
- Book Warehouse (5)
- Factory Brand Shoes (1)
- Full Size Fashions (1)
- GNC (8)
- KB Toy Liquidators (6)
- Kitchen Collection (4)
- L'eggs Hanes Bali Playtex (1)
- Paper Factory (9)
- Perfumania (8)
- Pfaltzgraff (4)
- SAS Factory Shoes (1)
- Sterling Silver Jewelry (3)
- Sunglass Hut (3)
- Texas Parks & Wildlife (9)
- Tottenham's Factory Furniture (4)
- USA Theatre (9)
- Value Floor America (4)
- Van Heusen (1)
- WestPoint Stevens (4)

12 LIVINGSTON

12A • Factory Stores of America
www.chelseafactoryoutlets.com
Address 440 US 59 Loop S *Phone*
936-327-7881 *Hours* Mon-Thu 9-
7, Fri-Sat 9-9, Sun 12-6
Location One hour northeast of
Houston on Hwy 59 Loop South.

STORES
- Banister / Easy Spirit (1)
- Bon Worth (1)
- Jewelry Outlet (3)
- Van Heusen (1)
- VF Factory Outlet (1)

13 MINERAL WELLS

13A • Factory Stores of America
www.chelseafactoryoutlets.com
Address 4500 Hwy 180 E *Phone*
940-325-3318 *Hours* Mon-Thu 9-
7, Fri-Sat 9-9, Sun 12-6 *Location*
40 miles west of Fort Worth. Take
I-20 west to Hwy 180 into Mineral
Wells

STORES
- Banister / Easy Spirit (1)
- Bon Worth (1)
- Van Heusen (1)
- VF Factory Outlet (1)

14 NEW BRAUNFELS

14A • New Braunfels Marketplace
Address 651 Business Loop I-35 N
Phone 830-620-6806 or 888-
Shop333 *Hours* Mon-Sat 9-8 (Jan-
Feb 9-7), Sun 12-6 *Location* Thirty
minutes northeast of San Antonio
off I-35, exit 189 (exit 188
southbound).

STORES
- American Tourister (2)
- Bass (1)
- Bon Worth (1)
- Book Warehouse (5)
- Bugle Boy (1)
- Builder's Factory Lighting (4)
- Casual Corner (1)
- Corning Revere (4)
- Dress Barn (1)
- Dress Barn Woman (1)
- Easy Spirit (1)
- Ernesto's Jewelry (3)
- Factory Shoe Warehouse (1)
- Famous Brands Housewares (4)
- Famous Footwear (1)
- Fitz & Floyd (4)
- Full Size Fashions (1)
- Kitchen Collection (4)
- Le Creuset (4)
- Leather Loft (2)
- L'eggs Hanes Bali Playtex (1)
- Maidenform (1)
- Marsel / DLUV (9)
- Oneida (4)
- Paper Factory (9)
- Prestige Fragrance/Cosmetics (8)
- Rawlings Sporting Goods (6)
- Rue 21 (1)
- Totes / Sunglass World (3)
- Van Heusen (1)
- Wallet Works (2)
- WestPoint Pepperell (4)

15 SAN MARCOS

15A • Prime Outlets San Marcos
www.primeoutlets.com
Address 3939 I-35 S *Phone* 512-
396-2200 or 800-628-9465 *Hours*
Mon-Sat 10-9, Sun 11-6 *Location*
Midway between San Antonio and
Austin off I-35, exit 200 (exit 199
southbound).

STORES
- Ann Taylor (1)
- Anne Klein (1)
- Ashworth (1)
- Bag & Baggage (2)
- Bass (1)

- Bath & Body Works (8)
- BCBG Max Azria (1)
- Bombay Outlet (4)
- Bon Worth (1)
- Book Warehouse (5)
- Bose Factory Store (4)
- Brass World (4)
- Brooks Brothers (1)
- Bruce Alan Bags (2)
- Bugle Boy (1)
- Calvin Klein (1)
- Carter's Childrenswear (1)
- Cassona Outlet (4)
- Casual Corner (1)
- Christian Gift Outlet (5)
- Coach (2)
- Cole-Haan (1)
- Cosmetics Company Store (8)
- Country Clutter (4)
- Couristan Rug (4)
- Crabtree & Evelyn (5)
- Croscill (4)
- Dana Buchman (1)
- Danskin (1)
- Donna Karan (1)
- Dooney & Bourke (2)
- Dress Barn (1)
- Dress Barn Woman (1)
- Eddie Bauer (1)
- Ellen Tracy (1)
- Escada Company Store (1)
- Esprit (1)
- Etienne Aigner (1)
- Express Warehouse (1)
- Famous Brands Housewares (4)
- Farberware (4)
- Fila (1)
- Fragrance Outlet (8)
- Gap Outlet (1)
- Geoffrey Beene (1)
- Golf Manufacturer's Outlet (6)
- Guess? (1)
- Harold's (1)
- Harry & David (5)
- Head 2 Toe Beauty Outlet (8)
- Home Co - Fine Furniture Direct (4)
- Home Style (4)
- House of Hatten (1)
- Izod (1)
- J Crew (1)
- Jockey (1)
- Johnston & Murphy (1)
- Jones New York (1)
- Jones New York Sport (1)
- Jones NY Executive Suite (1)

- Kasper ASL (1)
- Kirkland's (4)
- Leather Loft (2)
- London Fog (1)
- Maidenform (1)
- Maternity Works (1)
- Mikasa (4)
- Movado (2)
- Napier (2)
- Naturalizer (1)
- Nike (1)
- Nine West (1)
- Off 5th-Saks Fifth Avenue (1)
- Olga Warner (1)
- OshKosh B'Gosh (1)
- Paper Factory (9)
- Perfumania (8)
- Perry Ellis (1)
- Petite Sophisticate (1)
- Polo Ralph Lauren (1)
- Pomeroy Collection (4)
- Pottery Barn Furniture (4)
- Rack Room Shoes (1)
- S & K Menswear (1)
- Samsonite (2)
- SAS Factory Shoes (1)
- SBX (1)
- Sony (4)
- Springmaid Wamsutta (4)
- Stride Rite Family Footwear (1)
- Sunglass Outfitters (3)
- Sunglass Outlet (3)
- Talbots (1)
- Tejas Lighting (4)
- Toy Liquidators (6)
- Ultra Diamond & Gold (3)
- Umbro (1)
- Unisa (1)
- Van Heusen (1)
- Vans Shoes (1)
- VF Factory Outlet (1)
- Villeroy & Boch (4)
- Vitamin World (8)
- Waterford Wedgwood (4)
- Zales The Diamond Store (3)

EATS & TREATS
- Bakery Shop (11)
- Branding Iron BBQ (11)
- Burger Works (11)
- Great Steak & Potato (11)
- Lammes Candies (10)
- Lone Star Café (11)
- Pepperidge Farm (10)
- So's Hunan (11)

- Subway (11)
- Sweet Shoppe (10)
- Villa Pizza (11)
- Vittles (11)

15B • Tanger Outlet Center

www.tangeroutlets.com
Address 4015 I-35 S *Phone* 800-408-8424 or 512-396-7446 *Hours* Mon-Sat 9-9, Sun 11-6 *Location* Midway between San Antonio and Austin off I-35, exit 200 (exit 199 southbound).

STORES

- Adidas (1)
- Aerosoles (1)
- American Outpost (1)
- Banana Republic (1)
- Bass (1)
- Bible Factory Outlet (5)
- Big Dog Sportswear (1)
- Black & Decker (4)
- Buster Brown (1)
- Camp Coleman (6)
- Candle Warehouse (5)
- Casual Male Big & Tall (1)
- Cavender's Boot City (1)
- Children's Place Outlet (1)
- Christmas Shoppe (9)
- Claiborne Menswear (1)
- Claire's Boutique (3)
- Class Perfumes & Cosmetics (8)
- Clothestime (1)
- Corning Revere (4)
- Cost Cutters Salon (8)
- Dansk (4)
- Date Place Calendar (5)
- Disney Catalog Outlet (5)
- DKNY Jeans (1)
- Dress Barn (1)
- Easy Spirit (1)
- Eddie Bauer (1)
- Elisabeth (1)
- Factory Brand Shoes (1)
- Fieldcrest Cannon (4)
- Florsheim (1)
- Fossil (2)
- Fubu (1)
- Geoffrey Beene (1)
- GNC (8)
- Golf Manufacturer's Outlet (6)
- Greg Norman (1)
- Haggar (1)
- Hamilton Beach Proctor Silex (4)
- Hartstrings (1)
- Hugo Boss (1)
- Hush Puppies & Family (1)
- Izod (1)
- Joe Boxer (1)
- Journeys (1)
- Kenneth Cole (1)
- Kitchen Collection (4)
- Koret (1)
- Laundry by Shelli Segal (1)
- Le Creuset (4)
- L'eggs Hanes Bali Playtex (1)
- Lenox (4)
- Levi's Outlet by Most (1)
- Lids (9)
- Limited Too (1)
- Linen Barn (4)
- Liz Claiborne (1)
- Metro Watch (3)
- Music For A Song (5)
- Nautica (1)
- Nautica Jeans (1)
- Noritake (4)
- Old Navy (1)
- Oneida (4)
- PacSun (1)
- Paper Factory (9)
- Perfume Studio (8)
- Pfaltzgraff (4)
- Polo Jeans Co (1)
- Quiksilver (1)
- Reebok (1)
- Remington (4)
- Rockport (1)
- Royal Doulton (4)
- Rue 21 (1)
- Rug Decor (4)
- Samsonite (2)
- Seiko (3)
- Shoe Carnival (1)
- Skechers (1)
- Spiegel Outlet (1)
- Strasburg Children (1)
- Sunglass Hut (3)
- Timberland (1)
- Tommy Hilfiger (1)
- Tools & More (9)
- Totes / Sunglass World (3)
- Understatements (1)
- Van Heusen (1)
- Welcome Home (4)
- WestPoint Stevens (4)

- Wilson's Leather (1)
- Woolrich (1)

Eats & Treats

- Bennigan's (11)
- Cracker Barrel (11)
- Fudgery (10)
- Outback Steakhouse (11)
- Pizza Inn (11)
- Rocky Mountain Chocolate (10)
- Subway (11)
- Taco Bell (11)
- TCBY (10)
- Wendy's (11)

16 Sealy

16A • Sealy Outlet Center

www.horizongroup.com
Address 3701 Outlet Center Dr
Phone 979-885-3200 **Hours** Mon-
Sat 10-8, Sun 12-6 **Location** Fifty
miles west of downtown Houston
off I-10, exit 721 (exit 720A
eastbound).

Stores

- Antique Mall I (4)
- Antique Mall II (4)
- Antique Mall III (4)
- Bass (1)
- Better Byte Computer Outlet (7)
- Clearance City (1)
- Curves For Women (1)
- Dress Barn (1)
- El Vaquero (9)
- Exit 721 (9)
- Factory Brand Shoes (1)
- Florsheim (1)
- GNC (8)
- Hradil Antiques Auction (9)
- Liz Claiborne (1)
- Mikasa (4)
- Outlet City (9)
- Razz Ma Tazz (1)
- Reebok (1)
- Rockport (1)
- Schrader's Western Wear (1)
- Spiegel Outlet (1)
- Technology Center (9)
- Van Heusen (1)

17 Sulphur Springs

17A • Factory Stores of America

Address 614 Radio Rd **Phone** 903-
885-0015 **Hours** Jan-Oct: Mon-
Thu 9-7, Fri-Sat 9-7, Sun 12-6.
Nov-Dec: Mon-Thu 9-8, Fri-Sat 9-
9, Sun 12-6 **Location** Midway
between Dallas and Texarkana.
From Dallas take the Broadway exit
off I-30, go left on Broadway then
right on Radio.

Stores

- Bass (1)
- Bon Worth (1)
- Dress Barn (1)
- Easy Spirit (1)
- Factory Brand Shoes (1)
- Factory Connection (1)
- Fieldcrest Cannon (4)
- Kitchen Collection (4)
- L'eggs Hanes Bali Playtex (1)
- Morgan Ashley (1)
- Paper Factory (9)
- Rue 21 (1)
- Van Heusen (1)
- VF Factory Outlet (1)
- World Beauty & Gift (8)

Eats & Treats

- Vittles (11)

18 Terrell

18A • Tanger Outlet Center

www.tangeroutlets.com
Address 301 Tanger Dr **Phone** 800-
409-0012 or 972-524-6034 **Hours**
Mon-Sat 9-9, Sun 11-6 **Location**
About 20 minutes east of Dallas off
I-20, exit 501.

Stores

- Bass (1)
- Bible Factory Outlet (5)
- Big Dog Sportswear (1)

- Bon Worth (1)
- Casual Corner (1)
- Claire's Accessories (3)
- Corning Revere (4)
- Dress Barn (1)
- Factory Brand Shoes (1)
- Factory Shoe Warehouse (1)
- Gap Outlet (1)
- Jockey (1)
- KB Toys (6)
- Kitchen Collection (4)
- Koret (1)
- L'eggs Hanes Bali Playtex (1)
- Levi's Outlet by Most (1)
- Liz Claiborne (1)
- Mikasa (4)
- Old Navy (1)
- OshKosh B'Gosh (1)
- Paper Factory (9)
- Perfumania (8)
- Publishers Warehouse (5)
- Reebok (1)
- Rockport (1)
- Rue 21 (1)
- Samsonite (2)
- Seiko (3)
- Totes / Sunglass World (3)
- Van Heusen (1)
- Vitamin World (8)
- Welcome Home (4)
- Wilson's Leather (1)

EATS & TREATS

- Carmona's Tex-Mex Restaurant & Cantina (11)
- Rocky Mountain Chocolate (10)

Utah

1 • Draper
2 • Park City
3 • Saint George

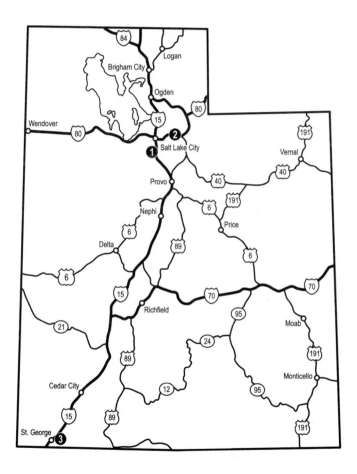

1 DRAPER

1A • Factory Stores of America
www.chelseafactoryoutlets.com
Address 12101 S Factory Outlet Dr
Phone 801-571-2933 *Hours* Mon-Sat 10-9, Sun 12-5 *Location* Twenty minutes south of Salt Lake City off I-15, exit 294.

STORES

- Adidas (1)
- Banister / Easy Spirit (1)
- Bass (1)
- Big Dog Sportswear (1)
- Bon Worth (1)
- Book Warehouse (5)
- Carter's Childrenswear (1)
- Corning Revere (4)
- Danskin (1)
- Dress Barn/Dress Barn Woman (1)
- Fads & Fashion Boutique (1)
- Famous Footwear (1)
- Healthway Imports (9)
- KB Toys (6)
- Kitchen Collection (4)
- Lee's Originals (1)
- L'eggs Hanes Bali Playtex (1)
- New Concept Vending (9)
- Omnisere Wireless (7)
- OshKosh B'Gosh (1)
- Paper Outlet (9)
- Rue 21 (1)
- S & B Amusement (9)
- Samsonite (2)
- Sugar Loaf Vending (9)
- Trolly Stop (9)
- Van Heusen (1)
- VF Factory Outlet (1)
- Vitamin World (8)
- Welcome Home (4)
- Which Watch (3)

2 PARK CITY

2A • Factory Stores at Park City
www.shopparkcity.com
Address 6699 N Landmark Dr
Phone 435-645-7078 or 888-Shop333 *Hours* Mon-Sat 10-9, Sun 11-6 *Location* About 25 minutes east of Salt Lake City off I-80, exit 145 (Rt 224/Kimball Junction). Turn right at the first traffic light onto Landmark Dr.

STORES

- Ashworth (1)
- Banana Republic (1)
- Bass (1)
- Big Dog Sportswear (1)
- Book Warehouse (5)
- Bose Factory Store (4)
- Brooks Brothers (1)
- Bruce Alan Bags (2)
- Carter's Childrenswear (1)
- Claire's Accessories (3)
- Coach (2)
- Cosmetics Company Store (8)
- Dansk (4)
- Dress Barn (1)
- Eddie Bauer (1)
- Factory Brand Shoes (1)
- Fanzz (1)
- Fossil (2)
- Gadgets & More (4)
- Gap Outlet (1)
- Geoffrey Beene (1)
- Great Outdoor Clothing (1)
- Guess? (1)
- Harry & David (5)
- Hush Puppies & Family (1)
- Jockey (1)
- Johnston & Murphy (1)
- Jones New York (1)
- KB Toys (6)
- L'eggs Hanes Bali Playtex (1)
- Levi's Outlet by Most (1)
- Liz Claiborne (1)
- Maidenform (1)
- Mikasa (4)
- Music For A Song (5)
- My Twinn (9)
- Nautica (1)
- Nike (1)
- Nine West (1)
- Old Navy (1)
- OshKosh B'Gosh (1)
- Pacific Sunwear (1)
- Paper Outlet (9)
- Pearl Izumi (1)
- Polo Ralph Lauren (1)

- Reebok (1)
- Rocky Mountain Wild Bird Station (9)
- Rue 21 (1)
- Rug Decor (4)
- Samsonite (2)
- Tommy Hilfiger (1)
- Totes / Sunglass World (3)
- Ultra Diamond & Gold (3)
- Van Heusen (1)
- Vans Shoes (1)
- Vitamin World (8)
- Welcome Home (4)
- WestPoint Stevens (4)
- Wilson's Leather (1)

3 SAINT GEORGE

3A • Zion Factory Stores
www.zionfactorystores.com
Address 245 N Red Cliffs Dr *Phone*
800-269-8687 or 435-674-9800
Hours Mon-Sat 10-9, Sun 11-6
Location Southwest corner of the
state off I-15, exit 8 (St. George
Blvd).

STORES
- Bass (1)
- Big 5 Sporting Goods (6)
- Big Dog Sportswear (1)
- Book Warehouse (5)
- Camera Corner (7)
- Canyonland Gifts (5)
- Carter's Childrenswear (1)
- Clothestime (1)
- Coach (2)
- Corning Clearance (4)
- Corning Revere (4)
- Cost Cutters Salon (8)
- Downeast Outfitters (1)
- Dress Barn (1)
- Dress Barn Woman (1)
- Eddie Bauer (1)
- Factory Brand Shoes (1)
- Fashion Ventures (1)
- Franklin Covey (5)
- KB Toys (6)
- Kitchen Collection (4)
- Little Professor Book Center (5)
- Nautica (1)
- Old Navy (1)

- OshKosh B'Gosh (1)
- Polo Ralph Lauren (1)
- Rags (1)
- Rebel Sports II (6)
- Red Dirt Shirt Co (1)
- Rue 21 (1)
- Sally's Beauty Supply (8)
- SBX (1)
- Southland Imports (5)
- St George T-Shirt Co (1)
- Standard Optical (3)
- Staples (9)
- Sunglass Hut (3)
- Van Heusen (1)
- Vitamin World (8)
- Welcome Home (4)

EATS & TREATS
- Amazonas Brazilian Grill (11)
- Café Rio (11)
- Cold Stone Creamery (10)
- European Connection (11)
- Mrs Powell's (11)
- Outback Steakhouse (11)
- Panda Express (11)
- Quizno's Classic Subs (11)
- Rocky Mountain Chocolate (10)

Vermont

1 • Brattleboro
2 • Essex
3 • Manchester

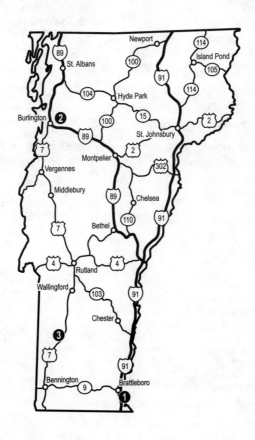

1 BRATTLEBORO

1A • Brattleboro Outlet Center
www.vermontoutlets.com
Address 580 Canal St *Phone* 800-459-4594 or 802-254-4594 *Hours* Jan-Mar: Mon-Thu 9:30-6, Fri 9:30-8, Sat 9:30-6, Sun 10-5. Apr-Jun: Mon-Thu 9:30-7, Fri 9:30-8, Sat 9:30-7, Sun 10-5. Jul-Nov 22: Mon-Sat 9:30-8, Sun 10-6. Nov 23-Dec 25: Mon-Sat 9:30-9, Sun 10-6. Dec 26-Dec 31: Mon-Thu 9:30-6, Fri 9:30-8, Sat 9:30-6, Sun 10-5 *Location* About 10 miles north of the state line in southern Vermont. The center is at exit 1, off I-91.

STORES
- Bass (1)
- Carter's Childrenswear (1)
- Dress Barn (1)
- Dress Barn Woman (1)
- Factory Handbag Store (2)
- L'eggs Hanes Bali Playtex (1)
- Mary Meyer Toy Store (6)
- Northeast Mountain Footwear (1)
- Van Heusen (1)

2 ESSEX

2A • Essex Outlet Fair
Address 21 Essex Way *Phone* 802-657-2777 *Hours* Mon-Sat 9:30-8, Sun 11-5 *Location* Fifteen minutes east of downtown Burlington. From I-89 take exit 15 (Rt 15 east), go about 2 miles to Susie Wilson Rd, turn left. Follow Susie Wilson Rd to Hwy 289 east, travel 2 miles on Hwy 289 east to exit 10, turn left on Essex Way.

STORES
- Adidas (1)
- American Tourister (2)
- Bass (1)
- Big Dog Sportswear (1)
- Bon Vivant (1)
- Book Rack (5)
- Brooks Brothers (1)
- Clay Expressions (9)
- Essex Outlets Cinema (9)
- Factory Brand Shoes (1)
- Foodee's (9)
- Jockey (1)
- Jones New York (1)
- Kinderworks (1)
- L'eggs Hanes Bali Playtex (1)
- Levi's (1)
- Magic Nails (8)
- Nine West (1)
- Northeastern Coins (9)
- Paper Factory (9)
- Polo Ralph Lauren (1)
- Rue 21 (1)
- Springmaid Wamsutta (4)
- Van Heusen (1)
- Vermont Toy & Hobby (6)
- Vitamin World (8)

EATS & TREATS
- Oriental Wok (11)

3 MANCHESTER

Nestled in the picturesque Green Mountains of Southern Vermont, is the historic towns of Manchester, Manchester Village, and Manchester Center. Shoppers here will find numerous outlets in a relaxing atmosphere. Most of the shops are within a short walk of each other, however the whole area covers a couple of miles. Located midway between Rutland and Bennington, the outlets are concentrated along the junction of Routes 11/30 & 7A.

3A • Battenkill Plaza
www.outletfind.com
Address Rt 7A *Phone* 802-362-5272 *Hours* Mon-Fri 10-6, Sat 10-7, Sun 10-5 *Location* See Manchester introduction.

STORES
- Anne Klein (1)
- Donna Karan (1)
- Ellen Tracy (1)
- Van Heusen (1)

3B • Highridge Plaza
www.outletfind.com
Address Rt 7A *Phone* 802-362-5272 *Hours* Mon-Fri 10-6, Sat 10-7, Sun 10-5 *Location* See Manchester introduction.

STORES
- Bose Factory Store (4)
- Dana Buchman (1)
- Designer Fragrance/Cosmetics (8)
- Geoffrey Beene (1)
- Home Fashions (4)
- Jockey (1)
- Liz Claiborne (1)
- Natori Outlet (1)
- Nine West (1)
- PacSun (1)
- Perfumania (8)
- Tommy Hilfiger (1)

3C • Manchester Designer Outlets
www.manchestervermont.com
Address Rts 11/30 & 7A *Phone* 800-955-Shop or 802-362-3736 *Hours* Mon-Sat 10-6, Sun 10-5 *Location* See Manchester introduction.

STORES
- Allen Edmonds (1)
- Anichini Company Store (4)

- Baccarat (9)
- Brooks Brothers (1)
- Coach (2)
- Cole-Haan (1)
- Cosmetics Company Store (8)
- Crabtree & Evelyn (5)
- Dansk (4)
- Dockers Outlet by Designs (1)
- Escada Company Store (1)
- Garnet Hill (1)
- Giorgio Armani (1)
- Hickey Freeman (1)
- J Crew (1)
- Johnston & Murphy (1)
- Jones New York (1)
- Levi's Outlet by Designs (1)
- Maidenform (1)
- Mikasa (4)
- Movado (2)
- OshKosh B'Gosh (1)
- Overland (9)
- Peruvian Connection (1)
- Polo Ralph Lauren (1)
- Seiko (3)
- Timberland (1)
- TSE (1)
- Tumi / Kipling (2)
- Versace (1)
- Yves Delorme Paris / Palais Royal (4)

EATS & TREATS
- Ben & Jerry's (10)
- Godiva Chocolatier (10)
- Lion's Share Bakery (11)

Virginia

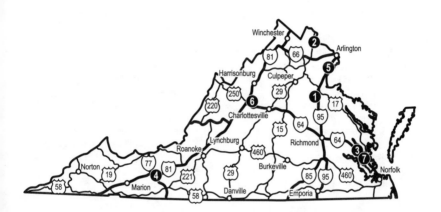

1 FREDERICKSBURG

1A • Massaponax Outlet Center
Address 904 Princess Anne St
Phone 540-898-3242 *Hours* Mon-
Thu 10-8, Fri-Sat 10-9, Sun 12-6
Location About 45 minutes north
of Richmond off I-95, exit 126.
Follow US 1 southwest to center,
which is on the left at Southpoint
Pkwy.

STORES

- Bass (1)
- Capacity (1)
- Corning Revere (4)
- Dress Barn (1)
- Dress Barn Woman (1)
- Famous Footwear (1)
- Hat Barn (1)
- Kitchen Collection (4)
- Newport News Outlet (5)
- Paper Factory (9)
- S & K Menswear (1)
- Sizes Unlimited (1)
- Springmaid Wamsutta (4)
- VA Factory Tobacco (9)
- Van Heusen (1)

2 LEESBURG

**2A • Leesburg Corner
Premium Outlets**
www.premiumoutlets.com
Address 241 Fort Evans Road NE
Phone 703-737-3071 *Hours* Mon-
Sat 10-9, Sun 11-6 *Location* About
25 minutes northwest of Arlington
at the intersection of Rt 7 and Rt
15 bypass, exit 15N off Rt 7.
Follow signs leading to Fort Evans
Rd exit (in far right lane).

STORES

- Adidas (1)
- Aerosoles (1)
- American Tourister (2)
- Banana Republic (1)
- Barneys New York (1)
- Bass (1)
- BCBG Max Azria (1)
- Bebe Outlet (1)
- Big & Tall Factory Store (1)
- Big Dog Sportswear (1)
- Book Warehouse (5)
- Bose Factory Store (4)
- Bostonian Clarks (1)
- Britches (1)
- Brooks Brothers (1)
- Burberry (1)
- Carter's Childrenswear (1)
- Chico's (1)
- Claire's Accessories (3)
- Coldwater Creek Outlet (1)
- Cole-Haan (1)
- Cosmetics Company Store (8)
- Country Clutter (4)
- Craftworks (4)
- Crate & Barrel (4)
- Dansk (4)
- Danskin (1)
- DKNY (1)
- Dockers Outlet by Designs (1)
- Dress Barn (1)
- Dress Barn Woman (1)
- Eddie Bauer (1)
- Etienne Aigner (1)
- Factory Brand Shoes (1)
- Fossil (2)
- Gap Outlet (1)
- Geoffrey Beene (1)
- Greg Norman (1)
- Harry & David (5)
- Home Elements (4)
- Hoover Outlet (4)
- Hush Puppies & Family (1)
- Izod (1)
- Jockey (1)
- Jones New York (1)
- Jones New York Country (1)
- Jos A Bank Clothiers (1)
- Kasper ASL (1)
- KB Toys (6)
- Kenneth Cole (1)
- Kitchen Collection (4)
- Le Creuset (4)
- Le Gourmet Chef (4)
- Leather Loft (2)

- L'eggs Hanes Bali Playtex (1)
- Levi's Outlet by Designs (1)
- Little Me (1)
- Liz Claiborne (1)
- Liz Claiborne Shoes (1)
- Maidenform (1)
- Mark, Fore & Strike / Boston Proper (1)
- Mikasa (4)
- Mothertime Maternity (1)
- Movado (2)
- Music For A Song (5)
- Naturalizer (1)
- Nautica (1)
- Nike (1)
- Nine West (1)
- Off 5th-Saks Fifth Avenue (1)
- Old Navy (1)
- Oneida (4)
- Oroton (2)
- OshKosh B'Gosh (1)
- PacSun (1)
- Paper Factory (9)
- Perry Ellis (1)
- Pfaltzgraff (4)
- Polo Ralph Lauren (1)
- Pottery Barn Furniture (4)
- Quiksilver (1)
- Reebok (1)
- Reed & Barton (4)
- Rockport (1)
- Samsonite (2)
- Seiko (3)
- Smithsonian (9)
- So Fun! Kids (1)
- Springmaid Wamsutta (4)
- Strasburg Children (1)
- Sunglass Outlet (3)
- Time Factory Watch (3)
- Tommy Hilfiger (1)
- Totes Isotoner Sunglass World (3)
- Ultra Diamond Outlet (3)
- Van Heusen (1)
- Vans Shoes (1)
- Vitamin World (8)
- Waterford Wedgwood (4)
- WestPoint Stevens (4)
- Williams-Sonoma Marketplace (4)
- Wilson's Leather (1)
- Zales The Diamond Store (3)

Eats & Treats
- Asian Creation (11)

- Burger King (11)
- Ranch 1 (11)
- Sbarro's Pizza (11)
- TCBY (10)

3   LIGHTFOOT

3A • Williamsburg Pottery Factory
www.williamsburgpottery.com
Address 6692 Richmond Rd *Phone* 757-564-3326 *Hours* Sun-Fri 9-6:30, Sat 8-7 *Location* From I-64 exit 234 follow Hwy 199 west to US 60. Travel north on US 60 about 2 miles to center.

Stores
- Banister Shoes (1)
- Black & Decker (4)
- Boot Hill (1)
- Fieldcrest Cannon (4)
- Glass Elite (4)
- Hanover Brass (4)
- Izod (1)
- King Neptune's Treasures (5)
- Oneida (4)
- Pens Plus (5)
- Pfaltzgraff (4)
- Prestige Fragrance/Cosmetics (8)
- Regal Ware (4)
- Rolane (1)
- Rug Gallery (4)
- S & K Menswear (1)
- Totes (3)
- Van Heusen (1)
- Wallet Works (2)
- Westport Limited (1)
- Williamsburg Pottery (4)

Eats & Treats
- Pecan Factory (10)
- Pepperidge Farm (10)

4   MAX MEADOWS

4A • Factory Merchants Fort Chiswell
www.ftchiswell.com

Address 731 Factory Outlet Dr *Phone* 540-637-6214 *Hours* Mon-Sat 9-8, Sun 12-6 *Location* Ten miles east of Wytheville in western Virginia. Take I-81 north (heading east) to exit 80.

STORES

- $9.99 Stockroom (1)
- Bass (1)
- Bible Factory Outlet (5)
- Big Dog Sportswear (1)
- Bon Worth (1)
- Book Warehouse (5)
- Capacity (1)
- Corning Revere (4)
- Dress Barn (1)
- Famous Footwear (1)
- Florsheim (1)
- GNC (8)
- Hush Puppies & Family (1)
- Kitchen Collection (4)
- L'eggs Hanes Bali Playtex (1)
- Paper Factory (9)
- Polo Ralph Lauren (1)
- Reebok (1)
- S & K Menswear (1)
- Samsonite (2)
- Tools & More (9)
- Van Heusen (1)
- Welcome Home (4)

EATS & TREATS

- Springhouse Restaurant (11)

5 PRINCE WILLIAM

5A • Potomac Mills

www.millscorp.com

Address 2700 Potomac Mills Cir *Phone* 703-643-1770 or 800-VA-Mills *Hours* Mon-Fri 10-9:30, Sat 9:30-9:30, Sun 10-7 *Location* Thirty minutes south of the D.C. area off I-95, exit 156, near Dale City. Follow Opitz Blvd west to center.

STORES

- 5-7-9 Outlet (1)
- Aeropostale (1)
- Aerosoles (1)
- AMC Theatres (9)
- Ann Taylor (1)
- Anne Klein (1)
- Art Plus (4)
- Athlete's Foot (1)
- Bally Outlet (1)
- Banana Republic (1)
- Banister Shoes (1)
- Bath & Body Works (8)
- Bebe Outlet (1)
- Benetton (1)
- Bentley's Luggage (2)
- Bible Factory Outlet (5)
- Big Dog Sportswear (1)
- Books-A-Million (5)
- Bostonian / Hanover (1)
- Britches (1)
- Brooks Brothers (1)
- Bubbles Hair Express (8)
- Burlington Coat Factory (1)
- Burlington Shoes (1)
- Calvin Klein (1)
- Cargo Outlet (4)
- Carter's Childrenswear (1)
- Casual Corner (1)
- Chesapeake Knife and Tool (9)
- Children's Place Outlet (1)
- Cingular Wireless (7)
- Claire's Boutique (3)
- Clothestime (1)
- Corning Revere (4)
- Cosmetic Center Outlet (8)
- Cosmetics Company Store (8)
- CR Jewelers Outlet (3)
- Daffy's (1)
- Disney Catalog Outlet (5)
- Donna Karan (1)
- Dress Barn (1)
- Dress Barn Woman (1)
- Easy Spirit (1)
- Eddie Bauer (1)
- Electronics Boutique (4)
- Elm Tree Cards & Gifts (5)
- Escada Company Store (1)
- Esprit (1)
- Etienne Aigner (1)
- Fadz (9)
- Famous Footwear (1)
- Fashion Time (2)

- Flag Shop (9)
- Florsheim (1)
- Foot Locker (1)
- Fossil (2)
- Fragrance Outlet (8)
- Games Workshop (9)
- Gap Outlet (1)
- Geoffrey Beene (1)
- Georgetown Leather Design (1)
- GNC (8)
- Group USA (1)
- Guess? (1)
- Hamilton Luggage (2)
- Harry & David (5)
- Home Style (4)
- Hour Eyes (3)
- Hush Puppies & Family (1)
- Ikea (4)
- JCPenney Outlet (1)
- Jockey (1)
- Jones New York (1)
- Journeys (1)
- Kasper ASL (1)
- L.L. Bean Factory Store (1)
- Laura Ashley (1)
- Le Gourmet Chef (4)
- Leather Limited (2)
- L'eggs Hanes Bali Playtex (1)
- Lego Outlet (6)
- Lenox (4)
- LensCrafters (3)
- Levi's / Dockers (1)
- Lids (9)
- Lifestyles USA (1)
- Lillian Vernon (9)
- Linen's N Things (4)
- Liz Claiborne (1)
- LJ's Fashions (1)
- LVL X Direct (1)
- Maidenform (1)
- Manhattan Diamonds (3)
- Marshalls (1)
- Mary Ellen's Country Accents (5)
- MasterCuts (8)
- Mikasa (4)
- Motherhood Maternity (1)
- Music 4 Less (5)
- Nail Trix (8)
- Nautica (1)
- Nine West (1)
- Nordstrom Rack (1)
- Off 5th-Saks Fifth Avenue (1)
- Oilily (1)

- Old Navy (1)
- Olga Warner (1)
- OshKosh B'Gosh (1)
- Pacific Sunwear (1)
- Papyrus First Class Seconds (9)
- Parade of Shoes (1)
- Payless Shoe Source (1)
- Perfumania (8)
- Perry Ellis (1)
- Petite Sophisticate (1)
- Planet Fun (9)
- Polo Ralph Lauren (1)
- Premier Jewelers (3)
- Pro Image (1)
- Rack Room Shoes (1)
- Radio Shack (7)
- Rangoni Shoes (1)
- Remington (4)
- Ritz Camera 1 Hour Photo (7)
- Royal Doulton (4)
- Rue 21 (1)
- S & K Menswear (1)
- Samsonite (2)
- San Francisco Music Box (9)
- Sanrio (9)
- Sea Dream Leather (1)
- Shade Tree (2)
- Silver Box (3)
- Small's Formal Wear (1)
- Spencer Gifts (5)
- Spiegel Outlet (1)
- Sports Authority (6)
- Sterling Super Optical (3)
- Stride Rite (1)
- Suncoast Motion Picture Co (9)
- Sunglass Hut (3)
- Swank (2)
- SYMS (1)
- Tahari (1)
- Taxco Sterling (3)
- Timberland (1)
- TJ Maxx (1)
- Tommy Hilfiger (1)
- Totes (3)
- Toy Liquidators (6)
- Ultra Jewelers (3)
- Up Against the Wall (1)
- Urban Planet (1)
- Van Heusen (1)
- Vans SkatePark (9)
- Vitamin World (8)
- Wall Music (4)
- Welcome Home (4)

- Westport Limited (1)
- World Accents (4)
- XOXO (1)
- Zales The Diamond Store (3)

EATS & TREATS

- Arby's Roast Beef (11)
- Aromi D' Italia (11)
- Auntie Anne's Pretzels (10)
- Burger King (11)
- Cajun Grill & Café (11)
- Candy World (10)
- Cinnamons (10)
- Frank & Stein and US Bistro (11)
- Freshens Yogurt (10)
- Gloria Jean's Gourmet Coffee (10)
- Haagen Dazs (10)
- Jerry's Sub Shop (11)
- Kohr Brothers / Twist Again Pretzels (10)
- Long John Silvers (11)
- Mark Moseley's Famous Fries (11)
- McDonald's (11)
- Moun Wok (11)
- Mrs Fields Cookies (10)
- Mrs Tyndall's Popcorn (10)
- Orange Julius (10)
- Piccadilly (11)
- Popeye's (11)
- Rocky Mountain Chocolate (10)
- Ruby Tuesday (11)
- Sakura Garden (11)
- Sbarro Italian Eatery (11)
- Taco Bell (11)
- Villa Pizza (11)

6 WAYNESBORO

6A • Waynesboro Village Outlets
Address 601 Shenandoah Village Dr *Phone* 540-949-5000 *Hours* Mon-Sat 10-8 (Jan-Mar 10-6), Sun 12:30-5:30. *Location* 25 minutes west of Charlottesville off I-64, exit 94 (Rt 340 south).

STORES

- Bass (1)
- Capacity (1)

- Corning Revere (4)
- Dockside Discounters (9)
- L'eggs Hanes Bali Playtex (1)
- Liz Claiborne (1)
- Newport News Outlet (5)
- Paper Factory (9)
- Virginia Metal Crafters (4)

7 WILLIAMSBURG

7A • Patriot Plaza Premium Outlets
www.premiumoutlets.com
Address 3032 Richmond Rd *Phone* 757-258-0767 *Hours* Mon-Sat 10-9, Sun 12-6 *Location* From I-64 exit 234 follow Hwy 199 west to US 60. Follow US 60 south to the center.

STORES

- Dansk (4)
- Donna Karan (1)
- Leather Loft (2)
- Lenox (4)
- Plow and Hearth (4)
- Polo Ralph Lauren (1)
- Totes Isotoner Sunglass World (3)
- Villeroy & Boch (4)
- WestPoint Stevens (4)

EATS & TREATS

- Ben & Jerry's (10)

7B • Prime Outlets Williamsburg
www.primeoutlets.com
Address 5715-62A Richmond Rd *Phone* 757-565-0702 *Hours* Jan-Feb: Sun-Thu 10-6, Fri-Sat 10-9. Mar-Dec: Mon-Sat 10-9, Sun 10-6 *Location* From I-64 exit 234 follow Hwy 199 west to US 60. Follow US 60 south to the center.

STORES

- American Outpost (1)

- Banister Shoes (1)
- Bass (1)
- Big Dogs (1)
- Bombay Outlet (4)
- Book Cellar (5)
- Bose Factory Store (4)
- Bostonian Clarks (1)
- Brass Factory (4)
- Britches (1)
- Brooks Brothers (1)
- Carter's Childrenswear (1)
- Claiborne Menswear (1)
- Coach (2)
- Cole-Haan (1)
- Collections (1)
- Cosmetics Company Store (8)
- Crabtree & Evelyn (5)
- Dana Buchman (1)
- Designer Jewelry & Fashion (3)
- Dooney & Bourke (2)
- Eddie Bauer (1)
- Elisabeth (1)
- Enzo Angiolini (1)
- Etienne Aigner (1)
- Famous Brands Housewares (4)
- Fragrance Outlet (8)
- Geoffrey Beene (1)
- Guess? (1)
- Haggar (1)
- Harold's (1)
- Harry & David (5)
- Harve Benard (1)
- Heritage Lace (4)
- Izod (1)
- J Crew (1)
- Joan Vass USA (1)
- Jockey (1)
- Jones New York (1)
- Jones New York Sport (1)
- Jos A Bank Clothiers (1)
- Kasper ASL (1)
- Kitchen Collection (4)
- Koret (1)
- La Chine Classic (1)
- Le Creuset (4)
- Le Gourmet Chef (4)
- L'eggs Hanes Bali Playtex (1)
- Lillian Vernon (9)
- Liz Claiborne (1)
- Lladro (4)
- Lucia (1)
- Maidenform (1)
- Mikasa (4)

- Motherhood Maternity (1)
- Movado (2)
- Music For A Song (5)
- Naturalizer (1)
- Nautica (1)
- Nike (1)
- Nine West (1)
- Olga Warner (1)
- Orvis Factory Store (1)
- OshKosh B'Gosh (1)
- Perfumania (8)
- Reebok (1)
- Rockport (1)
- Royal Doulton (4)
- Samsonite (2)
- Seiko (3)
- Socks Galore (1)
- Stride Rite Family Footwear (1)
- Sunglass Hut (3)
- Timberland (1)
- Tommy Hilfiger (1)
- Ultra Diamond & Gold (3)
- Van Heusen (1)
- Vans Shoes (1)
- Waterford Wedgwood (4)
- Welcome Home (4)
- Zales The Diamond Store (3)

Eats & Treats

- Ben & Jerry's (10)
- Rocky Mountain Chocolate (10)
- Sandwich Board Café (11)

7C • Williamsburg Outlet Mall

www.shopwilliamsburg.com
Address 6401 Richmond Rd *Phone* 757-565-3378 or 888-Shop333 *Hours* Jan-Feb: Mon-Thu 10-6, Fri-Sat 10-9, Sun 11-6. Mar-Dec: Mon-Sat 10-9, Sun 10-6 *Location* From I-64 exit 234 follow Hwy 199 west to US 60. The center is just north on US 60.

Stores

- Avon Beauty Center (8)
- Bass (1)
- Big & Tall Factory Store (1)

- Bon Worth (1)
- Bruce Alan Bags (2)
- Capacity (1)
- Christian Factory Outlet (5)
- Claire's Accessories (3)
- Country Antiques (4)
- Crafter's Market (4)
- Dexter Shoe (1)
- Diamonds Unlimited (3)
- Dollar Mart (9)
- Dress Barn (1)
- Dress Barn Warehouse (1)
- Dress Barn Woman (1)
- Famous Footwear (1)
- Farberware (4)
- Gold Toe (1)
- Hat & Boot (1)
- Jockey (1)
- KB Toy Liquidators (6)
- Kiddie Koncepts (9)
- L'eggs Hanes Bali Playtex (1)
- Levi's / Dockers (1)
- Linen Barn (4)
- New Concept Gifts (5)
- Newport News Outlet (5)
- Oriental Rug Outlet (4)
- Paper Factory (9)
- Rack Room Shoes (1)
- Rolane (1)
- Rue 21 (1)
- S & K Menswear (1)
- Silver Stream (3)
- Swank (2)
- Totes Isotoner Sunglass World (3)
- Tribal Trends (9)
- Vitamin World (8)
- Watch World (3)
- Zap Electronics (4)

EATS & TREATS
- All American Burgers & Dogs (11)
- Puttin'On The Dog (11)
- We "R" Nuts (10)

Washington

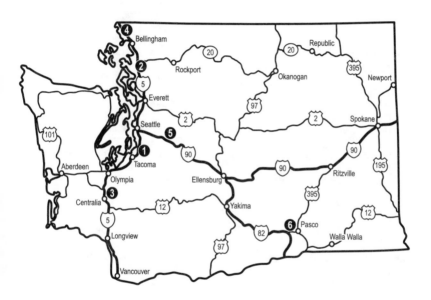

1 AUBURN

1A • SuperMall of the Great Northwest

www.supermall.com

Address Junction of Hwys 167 & 18 *Phone* 800-Say-Valu or 253-833-9500 *Hours* Mon-Sat 10-9:30, Sun 11-7 *Location* Between Seattle and Tacoma off I-5. From I-5, take exit 142A onto Hwy 18 east. Travel about 3 miles and follow the signs to SuperMall.

STORES

- Afterthoughts (3)
- America the Beautiful (4)
- Ann Taylor (1)
- As Seen On TV (5)
- Athlete's Foot (1)
- Banana Republic (1)
- Bass (1)
- Bath & Body Works (8)
- Beauty Express (8)
- Bed Bath & Beyond (4)
- Bergman Luggage (2)
- Big Dog Sportswear (1)
- Black Market Minerals (5)
- Blue Moon Jewelry (3)
- Book Warehouse (5)
- Brooks Brothers (1)
- Burlington Coat Factory (1)
- Calendar Club (5)
- Carter's Childrenswear (1)
- Casual Choice (1)
- Casual Corner Annex (1)
- Casual Corner Annex Petite (1)
- Casual Corner Annex Woman (1)
- Casual Male Big & Tall (1)
- Children's Place Outlet (1)
- Christmas Corner (9)
- Claire's Accessories (3)
- Country Clutter (4)
- Deb (1)
- DKNY (1)
- Donna Karan (1)
- Dress Barn/Dress Barn Woman (1)
- Eddie Bauer (1)
- Electronics Boutique (4)
- Elisabeth (1)
- Famous Footwear (1)
- FootAction USA (1)
- Games Workshop (9)
- Gap Outlet (1)
- Gart Sports (6)
- Giftmore (5)
- GNC (8)
- Group USA (1)
- Harry & David (5)
- In The Zone (1)
- Jewelry Outlet (3)
- Just Sports (1)
- KB Toys (6)
- Kenneth Cole (1)
- Kits Camera 1 Hour Photo (7)
- Koret (1)
- L'eggs Hanes Bali Playtex (1)
- Levi's Outlet by Most (1)
- Lids (9)
- Liz Claiborne (1)
- Maidenform (1)
- Mariposa (1)
- Marshalls (1)
- MasterCuts (8)
- Maternity Works (1)
- Men's Wearhouse (1)
- Mikasa (4)
- Naturalizer (1)
- Nordstrom Rack (1)
- Old Navy (1)
- Paper Factory (9)
- Payless Shoe Source (1)
- Perfumania (8)
- Pfaltzgraff (4)
- Piercing Pagoda (3)
- Pro Beauty Supply (8)
- Quality Rugs & Carpet (4)
- Radio Shack (7)
- Ray's Whitetail Country (9)
- Regal Cinemas (9)
- Sam Goody (5)
- Sam's Club (9)
- Sand Buds (5)
- Sarda Jewelry & Interiors (3)
- Shoe Pavilion (1)
- Spencer Gifts (5)
- Star Watch & Jewelry (3)
- Sterling Silver Jewelry (3)
- Sun Shade (9)
- TNT Jewelry (3)
- Tommy Hilfiger (1)
- Toy Works (6)
- Van Heusen (1)
- Vans Shoes (1)
- Vitamin World (8)

- Voice Stream Wireless (7)
- Wal-Mart (9)
- Walk the Dog (9)
- Waves Music (5)
- Welcome Home (4)
- Westport Ltd/Westport Woman (1)
- Wilson's Leather (1)
- Young Hui Furniture (4)
- Young Hui Imports (5)
- Zales The Diamond Store (3)
- Zumiez (1)

EATS & TREATS

- A & W Restaurant (11)
- Auntie Anne's Pretzels (10)
- Boehm's Chocolate (10)
- Burger King (11)
- Cajun Grill (11)
- Cinnabon (10)
- Dairy Queen (11)
- Great Steak & Potato (11)
- Hickory Farms (10)
- IHOP (11)
- Johnny Rockets (11)
- Karmelkorn (11)
- King Seafood (11)
- Little Tokyo (11)
- Mr Wu's Chinese (11)
- Orange Julius (10)
- Priya Indian Cuisine (11)
- Seattle's Best Coffee (10)
- Sub Express (11)
- Villa Express (11)

- Country Store (9)
- Dress Barn/Dress Barn Woman (1)
- Factory Brand Shoes (1)
- Famous Brands Housewares (4)
- Farberware (4)
- Fila (1)
- Gap Outlet (1)
- Harry & David (5)
- J Crew (1)
- Jones New York (1)
- Jones New York Country (1)
- Kitchen Collection (4)
- Leather Loft (2)
- L'eggs Hanes Bali Playtex (1)
- Liz Claiborne (1)
- Maidenform (1)
- Mikasa (4)
- Paper Factory (9)
- Reebok (1)
- Royal Doulton (4)
- Samsonite (2)
- Shoe Pavilion (1)
- Socks Galore (1)
- Tommy Hilfiger (1)
- Van Heusen (1)
- Vans Shoes (1)
- Vitamin World (8)
- Warnaco (1)
- Welcome Home (4)
- Wireless Addons (7)

EATS & TREATS

- Rascal's Coffee Bar (10)
- Rocky Mountain Chocolate (10)

2 BURLINGTON

2A • Prime Outlets Burlington
www.primeoutlets.com
Address 448 Fashion Way **Phone** 360-757-3549 **Hours** Mon-Sat 10-8, Sun 11-6 **Location** About 25 miles south of Bellingham off I-5, exit 229.

STORES

- Bass (1)
- Big Dog Sportswear (1)
- Carter's Childrenswear (1)
- Casual Corner (1)
- Coach (2)
- Corning Revere (4)

3 CENTRALIA

3A • Centralia Factory Outlets
www.centraliafactoryoutlet.com
Address 1342 Lum Rd **Phone** 360-736-3327 **Hours** Mon-Sat 9-8, Sun 10-6 **Location** Midway between Olympia and Longview off I-5, exit 82. Outlets are located on both sides of the exit.

STORES

- Banister Shoes (1)
- Bass (1)
- Big Dogs (1)

- Big Foot Outdoor (1)
- Book Warehouse (5)
- Carter's Childrenswear (1)
- Casual Corner (1)
- Cellular Connections (7)
- Christian Tree of Life Outlet (5)
- Claire's Accessories (3)
- Corning Revere (4)
- Country Clutter (4)
- Cowtown Boots (1)
- Dress Barn (1)
- Dress Barn Woman (1)
- Famous Brands Housewares (4)
- Famous Footwear (1)
- Farberware (4)
- Fieldcrest Cannon (4)
- Full Size Fashions (1)
- Helly Hansen (1)
- KB Toy Liquidators (6)
- Kitchen Collection (4)
- Lassley's Books (5)
- Leather Loft (2)
- L'eggs Hanes Bali Playtex (1)
- Levi's Outlet by Most (1)
- London Fog (1)
- Northwest Factory Co-op (1)
- Oneida (4)
- Outlet Sports NW - K2 (1)
- Paper Factory (9)
- Pfaltzgraff (4)
- Polished Apple (1)
- Quiksilver (1)
- Samsonite (2)
- Shirt Depot (1)
- Totes Isotoner Sunglass World (3)
- Van Heusen (1)
- VF Factory Outlet (1)
- Vitamin World (8)

EATS & TREATS
- TCBY (10)

4 CUSTER

4A • Peace Arch Factory Outlets
www.peacearchoutlets.com
Address 3400 Birch Bay-Lynden Rd *Phone* 360-366-3127 *Hours* Mon-Sat 10-8, Sun 11-6 *Location* Fifteen miles north of Bellingham off I-5, exit 270.

STORES
- Bass (1)
- Bugle Boy (1)
- Carter's Childrenswear (1)
- Chef's Outlet (4)
- Converse (1)
- Corning Clearance (4)
- Corning Revere (4)
- Factory Brand Shoes (1)
- Fashion Ventures (1)
- Florsheim (1)
- Helly Hansen (1)
- Izod (1)
- Kitchen Collection (4)
- L'ccessory (Claire's) (3)
- L'eggs Hanes Bali Playtex (1)
- Levi's Outlet by Most (1)
- London Fog (1)
- Mikasa (4)
- Paper Factory (9)
- Prestige Fragrance/Cosmetics (8)
- Pro Beauty Supply (8)
- Samsonite (2)
- Shoe Pavilion (1)
- Springmaid Wamsutta (4)
- Unique of Maui Cruise & Swimwear (1)
- Van Heusen (1)
- Vitamin World (8)
- Welcome Home (4)
- Woolrich (1)

EATS & TREATS
- JJ Café (11)
- Outlet Center Café (11)

5 NORTH BEND

5A • Factory Stores at North Bend
www.chelseafactoryoutlets.com
Address 461 S Fork Ave SW *Phone* 425-888-4505 *Hours* Mon-Sat 10-8 (Jan-Apr 10-7), Sun 10-6 *Location* Thirty minutes east of Seattle off I-90, exit 31.

STORES
- Adidas (1)
- Bass (1)
- Big Dog Sportswear (1)
- Black & Decker (4)

- Book Warehouse (5)
- Carter's Childrenswear (1)
- Casual Corner Woman (1)
- Claire's Accessories (3)
- Corning Revere (4)
- Dress Barn (1)
- Dress Barn Woman (1)
- Famous Brands Housewares (4)
- Famous Footwear (1)
- Farberware (4)
- Fieldcrest Cannon (4)
- Gap Outlet (1)
- Great Outdoor Clothing (1)
- Haggar (1)
- Izod (1)
- Jockey (1)
- Kitchen Collection (4)
- Leather Loft (2)
- L'eggs Hanes Bali Playtex (1)
- London Fog (1)
- Naturalizer (1)
- Nike (1)
- Northwest Gift Outlet (5)
- Olga Warner (1)
- Olympic West Outerwear (1)
- OshKosh B'Gosh (1)
- Paper Factory (9)
- Perfumania (8)
- Petite Sophisticate (1)
- Rialto Gold & Diamonds (3)
- Samsonite (2)
- Shoe Pavilion (1)
- Socks Galore (1)
- Sunglass Hut (3)
- Totes Isotoner Sunglass World (3)
- Toy Liquidators (6)
- Van Heusen (1)
- VF Factory Outlet (1)
- Vitamin World (8)
- Welcome Home (4)

EATS & TREATS
- Rocky Mountain Chocolate (10)

---

6 PASCO

6A • Broadmoor Park Outlet Mall
www.broadmooroutlet.com
Address 5238 Outlet Dr *Phone*
509-544-6168 *Hours* Mon-Sat
9:30-8 (Dec 26-Mar 31: 9:30-7),
Sun 11-6 *Location* Just east of
Richland off I-182, exit 7
(Broadmoor Blvd N), to Sandifur
Pkwy. Take a right on Sandifur
Pkwy, center is 1/2 mile on right.

STORES
- Bass (1)
- Beaux Arts (4)
- Big Dog Sportswear (1)
- Black & Decker (4)
- Centerville Western Wear (1)
- Coldwater Creek Outlet (1)
- Corning Revere (4)
- Critter's Outdoor World (9)
- Dress Barn (1)
- Dress Barn Woman (1)
- Factory Brand Shoes (1)
- Famous Brands Housewares (4)
- Full Size Fashions (1)
- GNC (8)
- Linen Barn (4)
- Mikasa (4)
- National Book Warehouse (5)
- Paper Factory (9)
- Sara Nelson Design (1)
- Sunglass Hut (3)
- Van Heusen (1)

EATS & TREATS
- Iron Rack Café (11)
- Rocky Mountain Chocolate (10)

West Virginia

1 FLATWOODS

1A • Flatwoods Factory Stores

www.flatwoodsfactorystores.com
Address I-79 exit 67 *Phone* 304-765-3300 *Hours* Mon-Sat 10-9, Sun 12-6 *Location* About 70 miles northeast of Charleston at I-79 exit 67.

STORES

- Black & Decker (4)
- Capacity (1)
- Children's Place Outlet (1)
- Corning Revere (4)
- Dress Barn (1)
- Factory Brand Shoes (1)
- Fenton Art Glass Outlet (4)
- Flatwoods Discount Liquors (9)
- Hawkins Leather (2)
- Jazce Jewelry (3)
- Lee Middleton Original Dolls (9)
- L'eggs Hanes Bali Playtex (1)
- Mossy Oak Outdoor Outlet (1)
- Nannys Country Apple (4)
- National Book Warehouse (5)
- Paper Factory (9)
- Poplar Forest (5)
- Rue 21 (1)
- Samsonite (2)
- Tommy Hilfiger (1)
- WV Pawn (9)

2 MARTINSBURG

2A • Tanger Outlet Center

www.tangeroutlets.com
Address 198 Viking Way *Phone* 800-409-0810 or 304-262-6300 *Hours* Jan-Mar 17: Mon-Wed 10-6, Thu-Sat 10-8, Sun 11-6. Mar 18-Dec: Mon-Sat 10-8, Sun 11-6 *Location* Northeast Virginia, west of Frederick, Maryland. Take I-81 to exit 13. Turn left on King St. Go over bridge and center is on your right.

STORES

- Bass (1)
- Capacity (1)
- Kitchen Collection (4)
- Liz Claiborne (1)
- Reebok (1)
- Samsonite (2)
- Van Heusen (1)

Wisconsin

1 JOHNSON CREEK

1A • Johnson Creek Outlet Center

www.outletinfo.com
Address 575 W Linmar Ln *Phone* 920-699-4111 *Hours* Jan-Feb: Mon-Thu 10-6, Fri-Sat 10-9, Sun 11-6. Mar-Dec: Mon-Sat 10-9, Sun 11-6 *Location* Midway between Milwaukee and Madison off I-94, exit 267.

STORES

- Adidas (1)
- Bass (1)
- Beauty Express (8)
- Big & Tall Factory Store (1)
- Big Dog Sportswear (1)
- Black & Decker (4)
- Bose Factory Store (4)
- Brooks Brothers (1)
- Carter's Childrenswear (1)
- Casual Corner Annex (1)
- Casual Corner Annex Petite (1)
- Casual Corner Annex Woman (1)
- Claire's Accessories (3)
- Corning Revere (4)
- Country Clutter (4)
- Dress Barn/Dress Barn Woman (1)
- Easy Spirit (1)
- Eddie Bauer (1)
- Factory Brand Shoes (1)
- Farberware (4)
- Gap Outlet (1)
- Haggar (1)
- Harry & David (5)
- Jones New York (1)
- Kasper ASL (1)
- KB Toys (6)
- Kitchen Collection (4)
- Koret (1)
- Lang Company Store (9)
- L'eggs Hanes Bali Playtex (1)
- Levi's / Dockers (1)
- Liz Claiborne (1)
- Liz Claiborne Shoes (1)
- Mikasa (4)
- Music For A Song (5)
- Nautica (1)
- Nike (1)
- Old Navy (1)
- Oneida (4)
- OshKosh B'Gosh (1)
- Paper Factory (9)
- Pfaltzgraff (4)
- Rue 21 (1)
- S & K Menswear (1)
- Samsonite (2)
- Sports Factory (6)
- Springmaid Wamsutta (4)
- Thrifty Reader (5)
- Tommy Hilfiger (1)
- Totes Isotoner Sunglass World (3)
- Ultra Diamond & Gold (3)
- Van Heusen (1)
- Vitamin World (8)
- Welcome Home (4)
- WestPoint Stevens (4)
- Wilson's Leather (1)

EATS & TREATS

- Coffee Gallery (10)
- Mel's Diner (11)
- Wurst Bros Brat Shop (11)

2 KENOSHA

2A • The Original Outlet Mall

www.kenoshaoriginaloutlet.com
Address I-94 & Hwy 50 *Phone* 262-857-7961 *Hours* Mon-Sat 10-9, Sun 11-6 *Location* About 20 minutes south of Milwaukee off I-94, exit 344 (Hwy 50 west).

STORES

- $9.99 or Less (1)
- Calendar Club (5)
- Carter's Childrenswear (1)
- Casio (4)
- Casual Male Big & Tall (1)
- Claire's Accessories (3)
- Company Store Outlet (1)
- Corning Clearance (4)
- Corning Revere (4)
- Cost Cutters Salon (8)
- CSO (1)
- Dickens Discount Books (5)

- Dress Barn (1)
- Dress Barn Woman (1)
- Eddie Bauer (1)
- Famous Footwear (1)
- Farberware (4)
- For Heaven's Sake (8)
- Fuller Brush (8)
- FYE - For Your Entertainment (4)
- GNC (8)
- Golf Shack (5)
- Hush Puppies & Family (1)
- Jewelry Castle (3)
- Jockey (1)
- KB Toy Liquidators (6)
- Keepsakes (5)
- Kids Express (1)
- Kitchen Collection (4)
- Koret (1)
- LaCrosse Footware (1)
- L'eggs Hanes Bali Playtex (1)
- Lenox (4)
- Mothertime Maternity (1)
- Natural Nails (8)
- Natural Oils & Gifts (5)
- Oneida (4)
- Panasonic "by Powerhouse" (4)
- Paper Factory (9)
- Perfect Timing (2)
- Pfaltzgraff (4)
- Plants, Etc. (4)
- Powerhouse Luggage (2)
- Rainbow Fashions (1)
- Ralph Marlin (1)
- Rue 21 (1)
- Samsonite (2)
- Santa's Corner Christmas Shop (9)
- Seventh Avenue Catalog (4)
- Socks Galore (1)
- Totes Isotoner Sunglass World (3)
- Unique Art Outlet (4)
- Van Heusen (1)
- VF Factory Outlet (1)
- WestPoint Stevens (4)
- Whitewater Outdoor (1)

EATS & TREATS

- Brownberry Bakery Outlet (11)
- Café Delights (11)
- Fifties Memories (11)
- Popcorn Train (10)
- Rocky Rococo's (11)
- Rose Subs (11)

3 MOSINEE

3A • Cedar Creek Factory Stores
www.cedarcreekmall.com
Address 10101 Market St **Phone** 715-355-0011 **Hours** Mon-Sat 10-9, Sun 11-6 **Location** About 10 minutes south of Wausau at the intersection of I-39 and Bus Hwy 51, exit 185.

STORES

- Aurora Pharmacy (8)
- Bass (1)
- Book Warehouse (5)
- Capers (1)
- Casual Male Big & Tall (1)
- Dress Barn (1)
- Dress Barn Woman (1)
- Famous Footwear (1)
- Full Size Fashions (1)
- KB Toys (6)
- Kitchen Collection (4)
- Krueger Floral 'n Gifts (5)
- Lady In Waiting (1)
- Milwaukee PC (7)
- OshKosh B'Gosh (1)
- Paper Factory (9)
- Picture Perfect (4)
- Pro Image (1)
- Shear Magic Hair & Tanning (8)
- Van Heusen (1)
- Vitamin World (8)
- Wickersham Jewelry (3)

EATS & TREATS

- Cedar Creek Café (11)
- Cedar Creek Pick n' Save Deli (11)
- Neng Lo's Buffet (11)

4 OSHKOSH

4A • Prime Outlets Oshkosh
www.primeoutlets.com
Address 3001 S Washburn St **Phone** 920-231-8911 **Hours** Mon-Sat 10-8, Sun 11-6 **Location**

Twenty miles south of Appleton off US 41, exit Hwy 44 west.

STORES

- American Girl (1)
- Athlete's Foot (1)
- Bass (1)
- Bath & Body Works (8)
- Big Dog Sportswear (1)
- Black & Decker (4)
- Book Warehouse (5)
- Carter's Childrenswear (1)
- Casual Corner (1)
- Casual Corner Woman (1)
- Claire's Accessories (3)
- Corning Revere (4)
- Dansk (4)
- Dress Barn/Dress Barn Woman (1)
- Eddie Bauer (1)
- Famous Brands Housewares (4)
- Famous Footwear (1)
- Farberware (4)
- Flame Keeper (9)
- Geoffrey Beene (1)
- Golfers Outlet (6)
- Jockey (1)
- Jones New York (1)
- KB Toys (6)
- Kitchen Collection (4)
- Lands' End Outlet (1)
- L'eggs Hanes Bali Playtex (1)
- Lenox (4)
- Levi's (1)
- Liz Claiborne (1)
- Motherhood Maternity (1)
- Nautica (1)
- Nike (1)
- OshKosh B'Gosh Super Store (1)
- Paper Factory (9)
- Perfumania (8)
- Petite Sophisticate (1)
- Pfaltzgraff (4)
- Polo Ralph Lauren (1)
- Rue 21 (1)
- Samsonite (2)
- Settler's Mill Miniature Golf (9)
- Skier's Outlet (1)
- Sports Factory (6)
- Tommy Hilfiger (1)
- Ultra Diamond & Gold (3)
- Van Heusen (1)
- Vitamin World (8)
- Wilson's Leather (1)
- Zales The Diamond Store (3)

EATS & TREATS

- Great Plains Eatery (11)
- Rocky Mountain Chocolate (10)
- Utterly Unique Cheese Co (10)

5   PLEASANT PRAIRIE

5A • Prime Outlets Pleasant Prairie
www.primeoutlets.com
Address 11211 120th Ave *Phone* 262-857-2101 *Hours* Mon-Sat 10-8, Sun 11-6 *Location* About 25 minutes south of Milwaukee off I-94, exit 347 (Hwy 165 east).

STORES

- Banana Republic (1)
- Bass (1)
- Bath & Body Works (8)
- Big Dogs (1)
- Black & Decker (4)
- Bombay Outlet (4)
- Brooks Brothers (1)
- Casual Corner (1)
- Claiborne Menswear (1)
- Columbia Sportswear (1)
- Corbin Menswear (1)
- Cosmetics Company Store (8)
- Dale of Norway (1)
- Dana Buchman (1)
- Dansk (4)
- Designer Brands Accessories (2)
- DKNY Jeans (1)
- Donna Karan (1)
- Etienne Aigner (1)
- Factory Brand Shoes (1)
- Fila (1)
- Gap Outlet (1)
- Geoffrey Beene (1)
- Geoffrey Beene Women (1)
- Haggar (1)
- Harry & David (5)
- Hoover Outlet (4)
- Izod (1)
- J Crew (1)
- Jones New York (1)

- Jones New York Country (1)
- Jones New York Woman (1)
- Liz Claiborne (1)
- Maidenform (1)
- Mikasa (4)
- Music Outlet (5)
- Naturalizer (1)
- Nike (1)
- Nine West (1)
- OshKosh B'Gosh (1)
- Pendleton (1)
- Perfumania (8)
- Polo Ralph Lauren (1)
- Rue 21 (1)
- Rug Decor (4)
- Samsonite (2)
- Seiko (3)
- Sony (4)
- Sunglass Hut (3)
- Timberland (1)
- Tommy Hilfiger (1)
- Totes Isotoner Sunglass World (3)
- Van Heusen (1)
- Versace (1)
- Vitamin World (8)
- Wilson's Leather (1)

EATS & TREATS

- Fannie May Candies (10)
- Java Dog (10)
- Pepperidge Farm (10)
- Quizno's Classic Subs (11)
- Villa Pizza (11)